WHOSE LAW?
WHAT ORDER?

a conflict approach to criminology

WHOSE LAW? WHAT ORDER?

a conflict approach to criminology

edited by

William J. Chambliss and Milton Mankoff

JOHN WILEY & SONS, INC.

New York   Santa Barbara   London   Sydney   Toronto

Library of Congress Cataloging in Publication Data:

Chambliss, William J.   comp.

Library of Congress Cataloging in Publication Data
Main entry under title:

Whose law? What order?

1. Crime and criminals—United States—Addresses,
essays, lectures.   2. Law enforcement—United States—
Addresses, essays, lectures.   I. Chambliss, William J.
II.   Mankoff, Milton.
HV6789.W48   364'.973   75-23220
ISBN 0-471-14476-2

Printed in the United States of America

10 9 8 7 6 5 4 3 2 1

DEDICATED TO
JIMMY
AND TO
FRANK TERUGGI
(1950–1973)
A VICTIM OF "LAW
AND ORDER" IN CHILE

PREFACE

The past decade has witnessed heightened public concern about criminal behavior in the United States, so much so that many political candidates have based their entire campaigns on issues pertaining to law enforcement. Every year crime rates seem to rise. The call for "law and order" grows more shrill as the nation's citizens spend untold millions of dollars on locks, burglar alarms, watch dogs, and uniformed guards, while showing more reluctance to venture into the night for fear of being assaulted. Although Americans pride themselves on having more freedom than other peoples in the world, their daily preoccupation with safety suggests precisely the opposite.

As necessity is the mother of invention, it is not surprising that public anxiety about crime has stimulated American sociologists and other social scientists to critically analyze existing theoretical perspectives utilized to comprehend criminality. A second factor in the revitalization of criminological theory has been the growing disaffection of social scientists from established institutions. The rediscovery of poverty, ghetto rebellions, and the endless nightmare of Vietnam have encouraged a distrustful attitude toward many traditional notions about American society. The challenge to criminological theory launched in the past few years has also been part and parcel of a more pervasive intellectual assault on functional sociology, consensus history, neoclassical and Keynesian economics, and behavioristic psychology. It has represented an attempt to view the relations between human beings and societies in ways that illuminate the clash of interests in the very construction and perpetuation of social institutions as well as the renewed appreciation of the complexity of human nature.

The so-called conflict criminologists, those who have been in the forefront of recent critical thinking about crime, have not been content to reanalyze and improve upon theories concerned with the question of why people become criminals. They have taken a step beyond this by going back to the history of law to learn by what criteria societies have differentiated criminal offenses from normal behavior. In this search they have recognized to a great extent that the legal system itself has "created" crime and criminals by its arbitrary categorization of certain human behaviors as illegal. Moreover, the criteria used to distinguish criminality from other forms of behavior often has reflected the interests of powerful social strata rather than manifesting a social consensus on right and wrong actions. Legal categories were frequently politically charged; and, of course, they still are. Societal elites, then, have rarely, if ever, been concerned with "law and order" in the *abstract*, but with historically specific laws and social orders which promoted their economic, political, or status interests.

In addition to the exploration of the history of legal norms, the new criminological theorists have tried to blur the popular distinction between good citizens and criminals by showing criminality is ubiquitous. Virtually all Americans have engaged in some kinds of socially disapproved activities, including those that are labeled "criminal." Nevertheless, only a small proportion of perpetrators ever come into contact with law enforcement agencies and receive formal punishment for their transgressions. Given this fact, the "criminal class" in American society is in large part an arbitrary creation of law enforcement personnel, not a reflection of the natural propensities of certain individuals to engage in criminal acts. This is not to say that no conclusions can be drawn about criminal offenders, but only that many such people cannot be radically separated from the nonoffender population on the basis of their motives and life-styles. If criminality is a normal feature of American life it is naïve to try to resolve the crime problem without a thorough examination of the social structural forces which make law violations routine.

Whose Law? What Order? is designed to present clearly the perspectives of the conflict criminologists. Although it is primarily devoted to analyzing criminality in the United States, some of the theoretical insights in the volume are applied to other societies as well. The articles selected are not the "classic" ones which seem to find their way into almost every anthology on criminology. However, each of them is addressed to central issues in the field in an original and thought-provoking manner. Part One is concerned with the development of legal norms in Western society. It discusses the economic and political context within which legal categories and specific legislation have evolved. In Part Two law enforcement is considered, with particular attention given to the sources of the discretionary behavior employed to shield some lawbreakers while exposing others. Finally Part Three examines some general theses regarding the nature of the American crime problem, focusing on the relationship between crime and the structure of the American political economy and culture.

We envision *Whose Law? What Order?* being used primarily in undergraduate and graduate courses in criminology, the sociology of deviance, and the sociology of law as a basic text or a supplement to more traditional ones. At the same time we feel that the book also has relevance in courses dealing with American society, social problems, and even introductory sociology, because its perspective illuminates fundamental concerns in all these areas of inquiry.

In regard to the division of scholarly labor, both editors are equally responsible for the overall organization of the volume and the selection of articles contained therein. While we have offered each other helpful criticism along the way, each editor has taken on specific tasks. William Chambliss is responsible for the general introductory essay, which presents a critical analysis of functional and conflict theories in criminology. Milton Mankoff wrote the introductions to each section, which serve to tie the articles to each other in a meaningful way and provide relevant supplementary material.

William Chambliss
Oslo, Norway

Milton Mankoff
New York City

February 1975

ABOUT THE AUTHORS

William J. Chambliss is an itinerant professor of sociology. He has taught on the faculties of the University of California, Santa Barbara (1967–1974) and the University of Washington (1962–1966). In addition, he has taught at Indiana University, where he received his Ph.D. in 1962, and at the University of Wisconsin, where he was a Russell Sage Resident in Sociology and Law in 1966–1967. He has been a visiting professor at the University of Ibadan, Nigeria; London School of Economics, the University of Uppsala, Sweden; and the University of Oslo, Norway, where he is presently a visiting professor in the Institute of Criminology and Criminal Law. Professor Chambliss has lectured widely in the United States and Europe, including Oxford, Cambridge, Durham, and Bristol Universities in England; the University of Belfast in Northern Ireland, and in Stockholm, Amsterdam, and East Africa. During 1973 he researched the opium and heroin traffic in Southeast Asia.

Professor Chambliss has published articles on subjects which include organized crime, juvenile gangs, criminological theory, and the sociology of law. He has edited *Crime and the Legal Process* (McGraw-Hill, 1969), *Sociological Readings in the Conflict Perspective* (Addison-Wesley, 1973), *Problems of Industrial Society* (Addison-Wesley, 1973), and *Criminal Law in Action* (Hamilton, 1975). With Robert Seidman he wrote *Law, Order and Power* (Addison-Wesley, 1971); with Harry King he wrote *Box Man: A Professional Thief's Journey* (Harper, 1972); and most recently he and Tom Ryther have published *Sociology: The Discipline and Its Direction* (McGraw-Hill, 1975).

Milton Mankoff received his Ph.D. in 1970 from the University of Wisconsin. He has taught at the University of California, Santa Barbara, and is now associate professor of sociology at Queens College and the Graduate Center, City University of New York. He is the author of numerous articles and reviews in the areas of political sociology, social stratification, social change, and the sociology of deviance. In addition, he has written and edited *The Poverty of Progress: The Political Economy of American Social Problems* (1972).

ACKNOWLEDGMENTS

Our greatest debt is to the authors whose articles appear in this book. Their research is in our opinion some of the most promising to appear in many years. We are thankful for their permission to include their work in this volume.

We are most grateful to our colleagues Peter Manning and Austin Turk who made insightful and helpful comments on earlier versions of the manuscript. Others who helped on specific articles are acknowledged in the text.

Lisa Reeve Stearns worked closely on several of the articles and the entire manuscript. As always, her imagination and encouragement were indispensable. Sharon Wiggins typed the manuscript and helped in ways which were far beyond ordinary requirements.

It is out of this collective effort that this book has resulted. We therefore express our appreciation for the help of all these generous people.

CONTENTS

CONTENTS

WHOSE LAW?
WHAT ORDER?

a conflict approach to criminology

INTRODUCTION

FUNCTIONAL AND CONFLICT THEORIES OF CRIME:

The Heritage of Emile Durkheim and Karl Marx*

William J. Chambliss

Sociology is in the throes of what Thomas Kuhn has called a period of "paradigm revolution"[1]—there is intensified criticism of the dominant theoretical paradigm and formulation of an alternative. Predictably, criminology is both a reflection of and a force behind this revolution.[2] It is too early to know the ultimate outcome, but the prevailing consensus that has characterized the past 30 years of sociological and criminological inquiry on theoretical models has been shattered. There is, at the very least, a gigantic struggle between the previously dominant, functional paradigm and the emergent conflict paradigm.

In the broader spectrum of the sociological enterprise there are many issues on which the functional and conflict perspectives part company: the importance of customs, social class, power, values, and economic structures, to mention but a few. Not surprisingly, these differences get translated into the theoretical luggage with which deviance and social control are studied.

Circumscribed by these two general paradigms are numerous theoretical traditions, at least three of which are within the conflict perspective: those that emphasize interest groups as the source of conflict within society, those which see power and its study as the starting point for sociological inquiry, and the Marxian tradition which utilizes the dialectic.

There are also several traditions within the functional paradigm, of which the most important to the study of crime and criminal law are those that stress the centrality of socialization (the learning of criminal behavior), of "life conditions" (such as being in the lower classes or in a disadvantaged position within the social structure), and of labeling and societal reactions to the etiology of criminal behavior.

A thorough discussion of all of these

*Thanks to the excellent comments of Nils Christie, Cecilie Høgård, Ivan Jankovich, Emilio Lano, Milton Mankoff, Sheldon Messinger, Richard Quinney, Tove Steng-Dahl, and Austin Turk, some errors I made in an earlier rendition of this paper have been corrected. Those that remain they could do nothing about.

1

theoretical traditions is beyond the scope of this introduction. I will discuss only the two most important current theories in the battleground of the paradigm revolution: the functionalist theories which assume value-consensus as the starting point for an understanding of crime and criminal law, and those conflict theories which are derived from the Marxian tradition with its emphasis upon historical materialism.

Durkheim's works have been the most systematic in their application of the functional paradigm to the study of crime and criminal law. Durkheim's work is also the wellspring for much contemporary functional analysis. By choosing Durkheim I am, of course, slighting many functional perspectives and therefore doing an injustice to the "richness of the paradigm." Nonetheless, a careful reading of criminological theory reveals that behind the rhetoric of disputations with other theories lies a core of assumptions which begin from the functional-consensual paradigm derived in large measure from the Durkheimian tradition.

For the example from conflict theory I will use Marxism. Unlike Durkheim, Marx never devoted himself to the systematic analysis of crime and criminal law, although in his works there are scattered references which can be very useful in constructing a Marxian theory.[3] Marxism also provides a useful starting point for a conflict approach because of the very general nature of Marx's sociological theory and the logical extension of it to crime and criminal law. As David Mandel has pointed out, Marxism is a better sociological perspective than other

conflict theories because of its greater generality:

> . . . what distinguishes Marx from "conflict theorists" such as Weber, C. W. Mills, and Dahrendorf is that Marx's concept of objective interests is part of a systematic theory of society and social change.[4]

It is also the case that sociologists of crime have either ignored Marxism completely or grossly distorted it,[5] and a more balanced interpretation of Marxism is long overdue. Moreover, the Marxian tradition offers a critical perspective which is lacking in other sociological traditions. As Quinney puts it, "Only a Marxist critique allows us to break out of the ideology and conditions of the age."[6]

The central disagreements between the functional and Marxian traditions can be broken down into four fundamental issues: the role of history in sociological analysis, the centrality of a critical analysis of the existing social conditions, the methodology apropos to social science, and the meaning attached to the normative system.[7]

From the Marxian perspective the most fundamental error of functional analysis is that it is ahistorical. This is *not* to say that it does not study history, nor that functionalists regard history as irrelevant to understanding the present. Rather, functionalists see society as a reality which is unconnected with a particular historical period and look for those social needs which all societies always have. The Marxist perspective denies that such a search will bear fruit. The Marxian analysis begins with the observation that the needs, characteristics, ideologies, and institutions of a particular society are a reflection of that society's historical condition—especially the material conditions (the mode of production) at that particular historical moment.

Secondly, the Marxian perspective differs from functionalism in that Marxism stresses the necessity for a critical analysis of the social order. Such an analysis necessitates a specification of what life could be like if the material conditions were changed. The functionalists accept as given that the social needs of a particular society must be met. The Marxist perspective specifies how the social needs of the society may contribute to the oppression of the members of that society and how the material conditions must be changed if we are to change the society's needs.

Third, the Marxian perspective sees the social scientist as necessarily engaged in bringing about the changes implied by his analysis. By implementing change (praxis) the social scientist can assess theory. The ultimate test of a theory's utility is not its logical structure or its "fit" with empirical data but its ability to create workable recipes for changing the existing set of social conditions (both material conditions and the superstructure derived therefrom).

Finally, the functional paradigm assumes some sort of value consensus in the society as the appropriate starting point for sociological analysis. With regard to crime and criminal law this leads to two fundamental principles: (1) that criminal behavior is to be understood by ascertaining why some people in the society come to adopt a set of values, norms,

and attitudes conducive to criminal behavior while most of the members of the society accept the "prevailing value system" and abide by the law and (2) that criminal law is to be understood as a body of rules which reflect the general value consensus of the society.

The Marxian paradigm does not consider value consensus an important starting point and sees whatever value consensus there is as (1) a reflection of the fact that those who control the means of production also control the production of values in the society and (2) a false consciousness since the dominant value system (if indeed there is one) will be one which oppresses subordinate classes and serves the interests of the ruling class.

MARX AND DURKHEIM ON CRIME

Marx and Durkheim both addressed the dual problem of explaining the causes and the consequences of crime and criminal law.

Durkheim postulates the presence of a set of customary beliefs which permeate "all healthy consciences"[8] in every society. Crime is best understood as behavior which occurs because one part of society (for example, the family, the schools, the division of labor, or the neighborhood) is not adequately instilling the society's agreed-upon customs into some of its members. The criminal law is explained as a reflection of the society's customary beliefs. Thus both criminal behavior and criminal law have their roots in the customs of the society.

FUNCTIONAL PARADIGM

From the functional perspective:

The law represents the value consensus of the society.

The law represents those values and perspectives which are fundamental to social order.

The law represents those values and perspectives which it is in the public interest to protect.

The state as represented in the legal system is value-neutral.

In pluralistic societies the law represents the interests of the society at large by mediating between competing interest groups.

Durkheim stated his central thesis quite clearly: for an act to be a crime that is punishable by law, it must be (1) universally offensive to the collective conscience of the people, (2) strongly opposed, and (3) a clear and precise form of behavior. In his words:

> . . . the only common characteristic of crimes is that they consist . . . in acts universally disapproved of by members of each society . . . crime shocks sentiments which, for a given social system, are found in all healthy consciences. . . .[9]

The collective sentiments to which crime corresponds must, therefore, singularize themselves from others by some distinctive property; they must have a certain average intensity. Not only are they engraven in all consciences, but they are strongly engraven.[10]

The wayward son, however, and even the most hardened egotist are not treated as criminals. It is not suffi-

cient, then, that the sentiments be strong; they must be precise.[11]

> . . . an act is criminal when it offends strong and defined states of the collective conscience.[12]

> [Those acts, to offend the common conscience, need not relate] . . . to vital interests of society nor to a minimum of justice.[13]

Durkheim argues that a single murder may have less dire social consequences than the failure of the stock market, yet the former is a crime for the reasons stated and the latter is not.

Durkheim distinguishes two types of law: restitutive and repressive. Restitutive law "is not expiatory, but consists of a simple *return to state*."[14] Repressive law is that which "in any degree whatever, invokes against its author the characteristic reaction which we term punishment."[15] Restitutive laws, or as he sometimes says, "co-operative laws with restitutive sanctions,"[16] are laws that invoke rule enforcement but (a) do not reflect the collective conscience (they reflect only the opinions of *some* of the members of society) and (b) do not reflect sentiments which are strongly felt. Therefore, these laws do *not* invoke penal sanctions but only rule enforcement. The more specialized the functions of law the less the laws represent the common conscience. As a result, they cannot then offend the common conscience since they are in fact marginal and not common to all. Thus expiatory responses are likely. "The rule which determines them cannot have the superior force, the transcendent authority which, when offended, demands expiation."[17]

For Durkheim, crime's most important function (i.e., consequence) in society was its role in establishing and preserving the moral boundaries of the community:

Crime brings together upright consciences and concentrates them. We have only to notice what happens, particularly in a small town, when some moral scandal has just been committed. They stop each other on the street. They visit each other. They seek to come together to talk of the event and to wax indignant in common. From all the similar impressions which are exchanged, for all the temper that gets itself expressed, there emerges a unique temper . . . which is everybody's without being anybody's in particular. That is the public temper.[18]

CONFLICT PARADIGM

From the perspective of the conflict paradigm, customs explain little and are only a reflection of economic realities. In capitalist societies customs may be merely "false consciousness," rather than the glue that holds society together. Crime and criminal law are not universal forms comparable between "primitive" and "civilized" societies; rather these phenomenon have unique characteristics depending on their particular historical period.

Capitalist societies are class societies within which the most fundamental division is between the class that rules (in Marx, through ownership and control of the means of production) and the classes that work for those who rule.[19] The criminal law is seen as a set of rules which come about as a result of the struggle between the ruling class and those who are ruled. The state, which is the organized reflection of the interests of the ruling class, passes laws which serve the ruling-class interests. The laws are then enforced primarily against those classes who are struggling to overthrow the ruling class.

Criminal behavior is explained by the forces of class interests and class struggle, and most fundamentally by the contradictions inherent in the social relations created by the society's particular mode of production. In capitalist societies crime and criminal law are the result of the social relations created by a system which expropriates labor for the benefit of a capitalist class.

The division of a society into a ruling class that owns the means of production and a subservient class that works for wages *inevitably* leads to conflict between the two classes. As those conflicts are manifest in rebellions and riots among the proletariat, the state, acting in the interests of the owners of the means of production (the "ruling class"), will pass laws designed to control, through the application of state-sanctioned force, those acts of the proletariat or of segments of the bourgeoisie which threaten the interests of the capitalist class.

It follows that as capitalism develops and conflicts between social classes continue or become more frequent or more violent (as result, for example, from increasing proletarianization), more acts will be defined as criminal.

There are, then, at the outset, important disagreements between the functional and conflict paradigms. The functional paradigm sees the criminal law as a reflection of those customs most strongly held in the society; criminal behavior is behavior which is in violation of those customs which are felt to be most important; criminal behavior is caused by the fact that some members of the society are not properly socialized into the customary patterns; and criminal behavior, when it occurs, reenforces the sacredness of the customs within the society.

The conflict perspective takes issue with each of these suppositions. According to it, criminal law is *not* a reflection of custom but is a set of rules laid down by the state in the interests of the ruling class and resulting from the conflicts inherent in class-structured societies; some criminal behavior is no more than the "rightful" behavior of persons exploited by the extant economic relations—what makes their behavior criminal is the coercive power of the state to enforce the will of the ruling class; criminal behavior results either from the struggle between classes wherein individuals of the subservient classes express their alienation from established social relations or from competition for control of the means of production; criminal behavior is the product of the economic and political system, and in a capitalist society some of its principal consequences are the advancement of technology, use of surplus labor, and generally the maintenance of the established relationship between the social classes. Marx says, somewhat facetiously, in response to the functionalism of bourgeois social scientists:

. . . crime takes a part of the superfluous population off the labor market and thus reduces competition among the laborers—up to a certain point preventing wages from falling below the minimum—the struggle against

crime absorbs another part of this population. Thus the criminal comes in as one of those natural "counterweights" which bring about a correct balance and open up a whole perspective of "useful" occupations. . . . The criminal . . . produces the whole of the police and of criminal justice, constables, judges, hangman, juries, etc.; and all these different lines of business, which form equally many categories of the social division of labor, develops different capacities of the human spirit, creates new needs and new ways of satisfying them. Torture alone has given rise to the most ingenious mechanical inventions, and employed many honorable craftsmen in the production of its instruments.[20]

Table 1 summarizes the major differences between functional and conflict theories with respect to the causes and consequences of crime and criminal law.

Paradigms do much more than simply supply specific causal explanations. They lead us to emphasize certain features of social reality and to ignore or at least deemphasize others.[21] The functionalist perspective emphasizes the acquisition of norms and values and the social psychological experiences of individuals that lead to this acquisition as the most important feature of social relations in understanding crime.[22] The conflict perspective emphasizes the institutional patterns—particularly the economic system—and how these patterns affect the distribution of criminality. The functionalists accept criminal law as a given—a standard reflective of the "agreed-upon values" of "the society";

the conflict perspective assumes that the criminal law is problematic and must be studied to determine how it is shaped and who gets processed as a criminal.

The accompanying propositions highlight the most important areas of disagreement between the functional and conflict paradigms of crime.[23]

Table 1

	CRIMINAL LAW		CRIMINAL BEHAVIOR	
	Cause	Consequence	Cause	Consequence
CONFLICT PARADIGM	Ruling class interests	Provide state coercive force to repress the class struggle and to legitimize the use of this force	Class divisions which lead to class struggle	Crime serves the interests of the ruling class by reducing strains inherent in the capitalist mode of production
FUNCTIONAL PARADIGM	Customary beliefs that are codified in state law	To establish procedures for controlling those who do not comply with customs	Inadequate socialization	To establish the moral boundaries of the community

ON THE CONTENT AND OPERATION OF THE CRIMINAL LAW

FUNCTIONALIST HYPOTHESES

1. Acts are defined as criminal because they offend the moral beliefs of the members of the society.

2. Those who violate the criminal law will be punished according to the prevailing customs of the society.

3. Persons are labeled criminal because their behavior goes beyond the tolerance limits of the community.

CONFLICT HYPOTHESES

Acts are defined as criminal because it is in the interests of the ruling class to so define them.

Members of the ruling class will be able to violate the laws with impunity while members of the subject classes will be punished.

Persons are labeled criminal because it is in the interests of the ruling class to so label them, whether or not the behavior would be tolerated by "the society" at large.

FUNCTIONALIST HYPOTHESES	CONFLICT HYPOTHESES
4. The lower classes are more likely to be arrested for and convicted of crime because they commit more crimes.	The lower classes are more likely to be labeled criminal because the bourgeoisie's control of the state protects themselves from such stigmatization.
5. As societies become more specialized in the division of labor, more and more laws will become restitutive rather than repressive (penal).	As capitalist societies industrialize and the gap between the bourgeoisie and the proletariat widens, penal law will expand in an effort to coerce the proletariat into submission.

ON THE CONSEQUENCES OF CRIME FOR SOCIETY

FUNCTIONALIST HYPOTHESES	CONFLICT HYPOTHESES
1. Crime establishes the limits of the community's tolerance of deviant behavior and increases moral solidarity among the members of the community.	Crime enables the ruling class to create false consciousness among the ruled by making them think their own interests and those of the ruling class are identical.
2. Crime necessitates the expenditure of energy and resources to eradicate it and is thus an economic drain on the society.	Crime reduces surplus labor by creating employment not only for the criminals but for law enforcers, locksmiths, welfare workers, professors of criminology, and other people who benefit from the existence of crime.
3. Crime offends the conscience of everyone in the community, thus creating a tighter bond among them.	Crime diverts the lower classes' attention from the exploitation they experience toward other members of their own class, rather than toward the capitalist or economic system.
4. Crime makes people aware of the interests they have in common.	Defining people as criminal permits greater control of the proletariat.
5. Crime is a real problem which all communities must cope with in order to survive.	Crime is a reality which exists only as it is created by those in the society whose interests are served by its presence.

ON THE ETIOLOGY OF CRIMINAL BEHAVIOR

FUNCTIONALIST HYPOTHESES	CONFLICT HYPOTHESES
1. Every society has a set of agreed-upon customs (rules, norms, values) which most members internalize. Criminal behavior results from the fact that some members get socialized into criminal behavior.	Criminal and noncriminal behavior stem from people acting in ways that are compatible with their class position. Crime is a reaction to the life conditions of a person's social class.
2. Criminal acts are more frequent among lower classes because the agencies of socialization (especially the family, but also the neighborhood, schools, other adult and peer groups) are less likely to work effectively, that is, in ways that lead to the internalization of noncriminal norms and behaviors.	Criminal acts are concentrated in the lower classes because the ruling class can see that only acts which grow out of lower-class life are defined as criminal.
3. The lower classes are more likely to be arrested because they commit more crimes.	The lower classes are more likely to be arrested and will then be labeled criminals because the bourgeoisie controls those who manage the law enforcement agencies.
4. Crime is a constant in societies. All societies need and produce crime.	Crime varies from society to society depending on the political and economic structures of society.
5. Socialist and capitalist societies should have the same amounts of crime if they have comparable rates of industrialization and bureaucratization.	Socialist societies should have much lower rates of crime because the less intense class struggle should reduce the forces leading to and the functions of crime.

FUNCTIONAL AND CONFLICT THEORIES OF CRIMINAL LAW

As the studies in Part One of this book show, there is little evidence to support the functionalist contention that criminal law is a body of rules which reflect strongly held moral dictates of the society. Occasionally we find a study of criminal law creation which traces legal innovations to the "moral indignation" of a particular social class or stratum.[24] It is significant, however, that the circumstances described are a far cry from the situation where laws emerge from community consensus. Rather, the research points up the role of a small minority occupying a particular class or stratum but sharing a viewpoint and a set of social experiences which brings them together as an active and effective force of social change. For example, Joseph Gusfield's astute analysis of the emergence of prohibition in the United States illustrates how these laws were brought about through the political efforts of a downwardly mobile segment of America's middle class.[25] By effort and some good luck this class was able to impose its will on the majority of the population through rather dramatic changes in the law. Svend Ranulf's more general study of *Moral Indignation and Middle Class Psychology* shows similar results, especially since the lower middle class, the emergence of which Ranulf sees as the social force behind legal efforts to legislate morality, was a decided *minority* of the population. In no reasonable way can these inquiries be taken as support for the idea that criminal laws represent *community* sentiments.

By contrast, considerable evidence shows the critically important role played by the interests of the ruling class as a major force in the creation of criminal laws. Jerome Hall's analysis of the emergence of the laws of theft and Chambliss's study of vagrancy laws both point up the salience of the economic interests of the ruling class as the fountainhead of legal changes.[26] The article by James Graham in Part One which analyzes the legislative process behind the laws attempting to control the distribution of amphetamine drugs has also shown how the owners of the means of production (in this case the large pharmaceutical companies) are involved in writing and lobbying for laws which affect their profits.

The surface appearance of legal innovations often hides the real forces behind legislation. Gabriel Kolko's studies of the creation of laws controlling the meat packing and railroad industries in the U.S. have shown how the largest corporations in these industries were actively involved in a campaign for federal control of the industries since this control would increase profits for the large manufacturers and industrialists.[27]

Research on criminal law legislation has also shown the substantial role played by state bureaucracies in the legislative process.[28] In some areas of criminal law it seems that the law enforcement agencies are almost solely responsible for the shape and content of the laws. As a matter of fact, drug laws are best understood as laws passed through efforts of law enforcement agencies which created what consensus there is.

Other inquiries point up the role of conflicting interests between organized groups of moral entrepreneurs, bureaucrats, and businessmen.[29]

In all of these studies there is substantial support for the conflict theory. The single most important force behind criminal law creation is doubtless the economic interest and political power of those social classes which either (1) own or control the resources of the society or (2) occupy positions of authority in the state bureaucracies. It is also the case that conflicts generated by the class structure of a society act as an important force for legal innovation. These conflicts may manifest themselves in an incensed group of moral entrepreneurs (such as Gusfield's lower middle class, or the efforts of groups such as the ACLU, NAACP, or Policemen's Benevolent Society) managing to persuade courts or legislatures to create new laws.[30] Or the conflict may manifest itself in open riots, rebellions, or revolutions which force new criminal law legislation.

There is, then, evidence that the conflict theory, with its emphasis on the role of the ruling classes in creating criminal laws and social class conflict as the moving force behind legal changes, is decidedly superior to the functionalist paradigm in ability to account for the creation of criminal laws.

THE CONSEQUENCES OF CRIME AND CRIMINAL LAW

MORAL BOUNDARIES OR CLASS CONFLICT?

One of the few attempts to investigate systematically the functionalist hypothesis that crime contributes to moral cohesion is Kai Erikson's imaginative study of deviance among the Puritan settlement in New England.[31] Erikson sets out to investigate the hypothesis that

. . . crime (and by extension other forms of deviation) may actually perform a needed service to society by drawing people together in a common posture of anger and indignation. The deviant individual violates rules of conduct which the rest of the community holds in high respect;

and when these people come together to express their outrage over the offense and to bear witness against the offender, they develop a tighter bond of solidarity than existed earlier.[32]

Erickson's conclusion from his study of deviance among the Puritans is that several "crime waves" were in effect created by the community in order to help establish the moral boundaries of the settlement. Yet his conclusion is hardly supported by the data he presents. During the relatively short period of some 60 odd years, this small community had three major crime waves: the Antinomian controversy of 1636, the Quaker prosecutions of the late 1650s, and the witchcraft hysteria of 1692.[33] This suggests, at the very least, that each crime wave failed miserably as a source of community consensus and cohesion; otherwise so small a group of people would certainly not have needed so many serious crime waves in so short a period of time.

More importantly, Erikson's description of the Puritan settlement and of these three "crime waves" makes it very clear that they were not precipitated by crises of morality in the community but by power struggles between those who ruled and those who were ruled. As Erikson points out:

. . . the use of the Bible as a source of law was [a problem in that] many thoughtful people in the colony soon became apprehensive because so many discretionary powers were held by the leading clique . . . "the people" themselves (which in this instance really means the enfranchised stockholders) were anxious to obtain an official code of law; and so a constitutional battle opened which had a deep impact on the political life of the Bay. On one side stood the people, soon to be represented in the General Court by elected Deputies, who felt that the Bible would supply a clearer and safer guide to law if the elders would declare at the outset how they intended to interpret its more ambiguous passages. On the other side stood the ruling cadre of the community, the ministers and magistrates, who felt that the whole enterprise would be jeopardized if they were no longer able to interpret the Word as they saw fit.[34]

Anne Hutchinson, a particularly sharp-witted and articulate woman of the community, began providing an interpretation of the Bible at odds with that of the "ruling cadre" of the community. At first her activities were seen as somewhat bizarre but of no particular consequence. In time, however, her home became a center for interpreting the Bible and began in fact to threaten the hegemony of the settlement's established authority.

Anne's talent for stirring up discussion and provoking controversy was widely respected in Boston. It must be remembered that religious activities were almost the only entertainment known in the Bay, and since the Hutchinson home always rang with the sound of religious conversation, it soon became an important community center—a kind of theological salon. As many as eighty people might gather in the parlor to talk about the sermon of the last Sabbath, and in these discussions the most

prominent voice almost always belonged to Mrs. Hutchinson herself. John Winthrop [who when he died in 1649 was the "unquestioned leader of his people and in every respect entitled to be remembered as the founder of Massachusetts"] thought her "a woman of haughty and fierce carriage, of nimble wit and active spirit, and a very voluble tongue," but visitors to her home might have added that she could debate a point of theology so compellingly that at times she seemed almost inspired. Before long, the household seminars in Mrs. Hutchinson's parlor were far more popular than the sermons of John Wilson. *Not only did most of the Boston congregation turn to her for religious counsel, but many of the ranking magistrates, including the young Governor, appeared at her meetings regularly* [emphasis added].[35]

Such appeal did not go unnoticed by the "ruling cadre" of the community and John Winthrop wrote, "It was a wonder upon what a sudden the whole church of Boston (some few excepted) were become her converts."[36] Faced with such a threat to their authority, the established church leaders responded in a time-honored fashion. They proceeded to seek and apply a label to the source of the threat that would undermine her influence. The label they chose had a long history in the church as a source of heresy and was thus very useful. Anne Hutchinson became accused of being an "antinomian." With effort the label stuck and in the end Anne Hutchinson and a few of her followers who in the beginning only "thought they were engaged in a local argument about church affairs . . . found themselves banished as criminals, disarmed as potential revolutionaries, or asked to recant crimes they had never known they were committing."[37]

The establishment was clearly threatened by Anne Hutchinson and her influence over the "young Governor from England." A power struggle ensued and in the end Anne Hutchinson and her followers lost the battle to the established authority of the church and state. As Erikson says, "Sainthood in New England had become a political responsibility as well as a spiritual condition. . . ." The case against Mrs. Hutchinson and her followers, then, was largely a political one. The arguments which emerged from the Hutchinson parlor were cloaked in the language of theology, but (to the extent that the two could be distinguished in seventeenth-century thought) the charge against them was sedition rather than heresy, *and once the leading men of the colony began to notice the effect Mrs. Hutchinson's crusade was producing among the settlers of the Bay, they moved heartily to the attack* (emphasis added).[38]

So it was not "the community" nor its search for "moral boundaries" that culminated in the labeling of Anne Hutchinson and her followers as deviants. It was rather the threat she posed to the authority, power, and economic well-being of the ruling class that was her undoing.

Some twenty years after the Antinomian crisis the Quakers entered the colony and another outbreak of criminality resulted. The situation was much the same as before:

. . . the elders of Massachusetts were confronted by an elusive group of adversaries who seldom stated their case with calm reasoning but often acted as if they possessed some special insight into the mind of God. The Antinomians spoke hazily about the "covenant of grace" and the Quakers spoke in equally vague terms about an "inner light," but both were suggesting roughly the same thing; that men should engineer their own relations with God and need not submit their religious experience to the review of any church official.[39]

The threat of the Quakers to the established power structure of Massachusetts was at first minimal. Two women arrived by boat but their arrival coincided with ". . . a worldwide reaction against the very kind of orthodoxy the settlers were trying to establish."[40] The Quaker movement, like the Hutchinsonian movement before it, gathered converts and became a threat. By the time the General Court met in October of 1658 there were ". . . perhaps two dozen foreigners traveling around the countryside in an effort to stir up dissention and a hundred or more local converts who met together for religious meetings." In early 1658 ". . . the constables raided a house in Salem and arrested nineteen inhabitants of the town who had met there with two foreign missionaries. Subsequent records of the county court indicate that this cell continued to meet in one fashion or another for many years and soon grew to a membership of over fifty people—quite a considerable number in so small a town."[41]

The courts were quick to respond to

the threat in typical Puritan fashion and passed laws which punished Quakers more severely than had heretofore been possible. There was, subsequently, a show of force against the Quakers which included the public execution of two of their members. Local constables were inspired to "prodigious feats of persecution and in the months that followed, the number of confiscations, household raids, public floggings, and the like were greatly increased."[42]

For all of the reaction against the Quakers there was little *ideological* contest to the conflict.[43] The Quakers were accused of little more than wearing hats in front of magistrates and using terms like "thee" and "thou." Yet because the movement was gaining popularity among some of the people of Massachusetts, it posed a threat to the authority of the ministers and the magistrates who controlled the colony. It was therefore defined as criminal to be a Quaker and the most severe punishments were meted out in order to stop the potential revolution.

The outbreak of witchcraft, which was the Puritan settlement's last crime wave, was somewhat different in that the response of the ruling class was not to a threat posed by those chosen as deviant (i.e., the alleged witches) but rather to more general conflicts in the community that threatened the authority and control of its leaders.

> In 1670 . . . a series of harsh arguments occurred between groups of magistrates and clergymen, threatening the alliance which had been the very cornerstone of the New England Way. In 1675 a brutal and costly war broke out with a confederacy of In-dian tribes led by a wily chief called King Phillip. In 1676 Charles II began to review the claims of other persons to lands within the jurisdiction of Massachusetts, and it became increasingly clear that the old charter might be revoked altogether. In 1679 Charles specifically ordered Massachusetts to permit the establishment of an Anglican church in Boston, and in 1684 the people of the Bay had become so pessimistic about the fate of the colony that several towns simply neglected to send Deputies to the General Court. The sense of impending doom reached its peak in 1686. To begin with, the charter which had given the colony its only legal protection for over half a century was vacated by a stroke of the royal pen, and in addition the King sent a Royal Governor to represent his interests in the Bay who was both an Anglican and a man actively hostile to the larger goals of New England.[44]

Erikson also points out that during this period there was "an even darker cloud" in the form of land disputes between landowners and personal feuds. Not being able to attack the King of England and accuse him of being a criminal (though at one point they did arrest the Royal Governor), the potential diversion of witchcraft served to give at least the appearance of a reaffirmation of authority in the hands of those who ruled. So long as the special assistants of the courts who had the power to point out witches complied with the interests of the ruling class by accusing underlings as witches and carefully avoided accusing any of the ruling elites, their word was followed and criminal sanctions were imposed. However, as will happen when functionaries are not directly answerable to the state, in time the witch-finders

> . . . were beginning to display an ambition which far exceeded their credit. It was bad enough that they should accuse the likes of John Alden and Nathaniel Cary, but when they brought up the name of Samuel Willard, who doubled as pastor of Boston's First Church and President of Harvard College, the magistrates flatly told them they were mistaken. Not long afterwards, a brazen finger was pointed directly at the executive mansion in Boston, where Lady Phips awaited her husband's return from an expedition to Canada, and one tradition even has it that Cotton Mather's mother was eventually accused.[45]

As Erikson says, under these circumstances "the leading men of the Bay began to reconsider the whole question" and decided, rather quickly in fact, that new rules of evidence should be brought to bear in witchcraft trials. In December when 52 persons were brought to trial, 49 were immediately acquitted, 3 (2 of whom were "the most senseless and ignorant creatures that could be found") were sentenced to death, and 5 others who had been condemned earlier received their death warrants. The governor eventually reprieved all eight and witchcraft trials came to an end within one year of their emergence in Salem Village.

Deviance was indeed created for the consequences it had. But the consequences were not "to establish moral boundaries"; rather, they aided those in power to maintain their position. The fact that in so short a time there were several crises that led to deviant outbreaks suggests the conflict inherent in the Puritan social structure and the inability of any one group to permanently establish "moral boundaries" that would provide a permanent harmony. Furthermore, Erikson gives no evidence that any of these crime waves actually increased social solidarity except through the elimination of alternative centers of authority or power. The branding of others as criminal, heretic, or witch served to reduce conflict with them, but this hardly qualifies as evidence that "moral boundaries" had been established.

Conflict theory proposes that acts are responded to as criminal in a capitalist society in order to serve the interests of the ruling class. Functionalists argue that crime contributes to moral solidarity in all societies and, by implication, those societies where the moral boundaries are the least well defined need the most crime. The Marxian perspective would see the amount of crime that was "needed" by a society as dependent upon the particular material conditions of that society and the resultant relationship between the social classes and the means of production. Puritan society created crime waves to help the ruling stratum maintain control of the community. There is no evidence that these crime waves increased moral solidarity, nor is there reason to conclude from this study that crime would serve the same function in another historical period. By adopting the model of functionalism, which seeks universal needs of all societies, Erikson fails to see the important role crime plays in that particular society by enabling the ruling stratum to maintain its privileged position.

RECONCILIATION OR REPRESSION

The two paradigms suggest quite different expectations for the evolution of criminal laws. According to the functional perspective, responses to deviant behavior will move increasingly toward reliance on restitution rather than repression as societies become increasingly technologized and bureaucratized. The conflict paradigm suggests almost the opposite: capitalist societies will increasingly need and use criminal laws as a tool to oppress the subject classes as class conflict deepens.

To my knowledge there has been no systematic study of the *relative* number of restitutive or repressive laws in an advanced industrial, capitalist society. It is possible that in taking *all* law into account there has been a more rapid growth in administrative, restitutive law than in penal law. On the other hand, the criminal law as such in capitalist societies has shown *no* significant trend toward reliance on restitution as a re-

placement for repressive law. Indeed, criminologists and legal scholars have noted an increasing reliance in capitalist societies on penal law to solve disputes of all kinds, including matters of personal morality.[46] This tendency in America has led to what one observer calls a "crisis in overcriminalization."[47] For example, the control of drug use, business activities, political commitments, and public expression of disagreement with state policy have fallen increasingly under penal rather than administrative or restitutive sanctions.

Perhaps more damaging to the functional hypothesis is the fact that the studies of nonindustrialized societies (Durkheim's mechanical solidarity) have consistently shown that these societies rely much more heavily on restitutive than on repressive law.[48] In fact, the opposite to Durkheim's expectations seems more tenable and has led to the suggestion that more complex, stratified societies are more likely to rely on rule enforcement than on reconciliation, whereas less stratified and less technologically complex societies will rely more on reconciliation[49] (see Table 2).

Table 2* Class, technology, and legal form

	Less Technologized, Industrialized Societies	More Technologized, Industrialized Societies
Less Stratified (Classless) Societies	Reconciliation	Mixed: Rule Enforcement- Reconciliation
More Stratified (Class) Societies	Mixed: Reconciliation- Rule Enforcement	Rule Enforcement

* Adapted from William J. Chambliss and Robert B. Seidman, *Law, Order, and Power* (Reading, Mass.: Addison-Wesley, 1971), p. 34.

Further evidence supporting the conflict view and discrediting the functional is provided by a crosscultural study of 51 societies ranging from nonindustrial to highly industrialized. The authors found that police, broadly defined, are found only in societies that have a substantive division of labor, although Durkheim's hypothesis would lead to the reverse expectation:

> Superficially at least, these findings seem directly contradictory to Durkheim's major thesis in *The Division of Labor in Society*. He hypothesized that penal law—the effort of the organized society to punish offenses against itself—occurs in societies with the simplest division of labor. As indicated, however, our data show that police are found only in association with a substantial division of labor. Even the practice of governmental punishment for wrongs against the society . . . does not appear in simpler societies. By contrast, restitutive sanctions—damages and mediation—which Durkheim believed to be associated with an increasing division of labor, are found in many societies that lack even rudimentary specialization. Thus Durkheim's hypothesis seems the reverse of the empirical situation in the range of societies studied here. [50]

FUNCTIONAL AND CONFLICT THEORIES OF THE ETIOLOGY OF CRIMINAL BEHAVIOR

It is fruitless to join the debate over whether contemporary functionalist theories of criminal etiology are adequate. The advocates of "family background," "differential association," "cultural deprivation," "Opportunity Theory," and a host of other "theories" have debated the relative merits of their explanations ad infinitum (one might even say ad nauseam). I should like, however, to present a summary of data from a study of crime and criminal law which compares selected aspects of these phenomena in Nigeria and the United States. In so doing I hope to shed some light on the points that divide functional and conflict paradigms without pretending to resolve the entire array of issues.

My data come from research in Seattle, Washington, and Ibadan, Nigeria. The research methods employed were mainly those of a participant observer. In Seattle the research spanned almost ten years (1962–1972) and in Ibadan the research took place during 1967 and 1968. In both cities the data were gathered through extensive interviewing of informants from all sides of the criminal law—criminals, professional thieves, racketeers, prostitutes, government officials, police officers, businessmen, and members of various social class levels in the community. Needless to say, the sampling was what sociologists call (with more than a slight bit of irony) "convenience samples." Any other sampling procedure is simply impossible in the almost impenetrable world of crime and law enforcement into which we embarked.

Since Nigeria and America both inherited British common law at the time of their independence, both countries have a similar foundation of statutes and common law principles. Although independence came somewhat later for

Nigeria than for America, the legal systems inherited were very similar; and the differences that do exist are not, for our purposes, of great significance.

In both Nigeria and the United States it is a crime punishable by imprisonment and fine for any public official to accept a bribe, to solicit a bribe, or to give special favors to a citizen for monetary considerations. It is also against the law in both countries to run gambling establishments, to engage in or solicit for prostitution, to sell liquor that has not been inspected and stamped by a duly appointed agency of the government, to run a taxi service without a license, etc.

And, of course, both nations share the more obvious restrictions on murder, theft, robbery, rape, and the standard array of criminal offenses. In both countries there is a striking similarity in the types of laws that do *not* get enforced and those that do.[51]

CRIME AND LAW ENFORCEMENT IN NIGERIA

In both Nigeria and the United States many laws can be and are systematically violated with impunity by those who control the political or economic resources of the society. Particularly relevant are those laws that restrict such things as bribery, racketeering (especially gambling), prostitution, drug distribution and selling, usury, and the whole range of criminal offenses committed by businessmen in the course of their business operation (white-collar crimes).

In Nigeria the acceptance of bribes by government officials is blatantly public and virtually universal. When the vice-president of a large research organization being established in Nigeria visited the head of Nigerian Customs, he was told by the Customs Director that "at the outset it is important that we both understand that the customs office is corrupt from the top to the bottom." Incoming American professors were usually asked by people they would meet at the university if they would be willing to exchange their American dollars on the black market at a better exchange rate than banks would offer. In at least one instance this request was made for the military governor of the state within which the university was located. Should the incoming American fail to meet a colleague who would wish to make an illegal transfer of funds, he would in all likelihood be approached by any number of other citizens in high places. For example, the English accountant of a leading bank near the university would often approach American professors and ask if they would like to exchange their money through him personally and thereby receive a better exchange rate than was possible if they dealt directly through the bank.

At the time of my study, tithes were paid at every level. Businessmen desiring to establish businesses found their way blocked interminably by bureaucratic red tape until the proper amount of "dash" had been given to someone with the power to effect the result desired. Citizens riding buses were asked for cigarettes and small change by army soldiers who manned check points. The soldiers, in turn, had to pay a daily or weekly tithe to superior officers in order to be kept at this preferential assignment. At the border one could bring French wine, cigarettes, and many other prohibited commodities into Nigeria, so long as prior arrangements had been made with the customs officers either in Lagos (the capital of the country) or at the check point itself. The prior arrangements included payment of a bribe.

As a result of bribes and payoffs, there flourished a large and highly profitable trade in a wide variety of vices. Prostitution was open and rampant in all of the large cities of Nigeria—it was especially well developed in those cities where commerce and industry brought large numbers of foreigners. Gambling establishments, located mainly in large European-style hotels and managed, incidentally, by Italians, catered to the moneyed set with a variety of games of chance competitive with Monte Carlo or Las Vegas. There was a large, illicit liquor trade (mostly a home-brewed, gin-like drink) and a smaller but nevertheless profitable trade in drugs that received political and legal protection through payoffs to high-level officials.

In at least Ibadan and Lagos gangs of professional thieves operated with impunity. These gangs of thieves were well organized and included the use of beggars and young children as cover for theft activities. The links to the police were sufficient to guarantee that suspects would be treated leniently—usually they were released with no charges being brought. In one instance an entire community within the city of Ibadan was threatened with total destruction by thieves. The events leading up to this are revealing. The community, which I shall call Lando, had been victimized by a gang of thieves who broke into homes and stole valuable goods. The elders of Lando hired four men to guard the community. When thieves came one

evening, the hired guards caught and killed three of them. The next day the Oba of the community was called on by two men from another part of the city. These men expressed grave concern that some of their compatriots had been killed in Lando. The Oba informed them that if any other thieves came to Lando they would be dealt with similarly. The thieves' representatives advised the Oba that if such a thing happened the thieves would burn the community to the ground. When the Oba said he would call the police, it was pointed out that the chief of police was the brother-in-law of one of the thieves. Ultimately an agreement was reached whereby the thieves agreed to stop stealing in Lando in return for the Oba's promise that the thieves could sell their stolen property in Lando on market day.

Ibadan is a very cosmopolitan city which lies in the Yoruba section of western Nigeria. Although dominated by the Yoruba, there are nonetheless large numbers of Hausa, Ibo, and other ethnic groups in the city. The Hausa—who are strongly Muslim, while the Yoruba are roughly 50 percent Christian—occupy a ghetto within Ibadan which is almost exclusively Hausa. The Hausa are an immigrant group and one might expect their crime rate to be high (see Table 3).

Table 3 Arrest rate for 1000 population, Ibadan, Nigeria, 1967

Immigrant Areas	Indigenous Area	Hausa Area
1.41	0.61	0.54

However, even though there is general belief that the Hausa are responsible for some of the more efficient and effective groups of professional thieves in the area, there are very few Hausa arrested for crime—apparently because they have a strong leadership which intervenes with payoffs and cash to government and police officials whenever a member of their community is in difficulty.

Payment of bribes to the police is usually possible whenever an arrest is likely. An incoming American who illegally photographed an airport was allowed to go (without even destroying his film) upon payment of $15 to the arresting officer. Six dollars was sufficient for the wife of an American professor to avoid arrest for reckless driving. A young son of a wealthy merchant was arrested on numerous occasions for being drunk, driving without a license, stealing, and getting into fights. On every occasion the police returned him to the custody of his parents without charges being filed when the father paid the arresting officer (or the policeman on the desk) $30 to $45.

Such practices were not atypical but were instead the usual procedure. It was said, and research bears this out, that one with money could pay to be excused from any type or amount of crime.

Who, then, did get arrested? In general, those who lacked either the money or the political influence to fix a criminal charge. The most common arrest of youth was for "street trading"—that is, selling items on the street. The second most frequent offense was "being away from home" or "sleeping out without protection." Among adults, "suspiciousness," public indecency, intoxication, and being with no visible means of support were the most common offenses. Although robbery, theft, and burglary were common offenses (in a sample of 300 residents of Ibadan, 12.7 percent reported having been the victim of burglary), arrests for these offenses were much less frequent.

Anyone who has lived or traveled in foreign countries will not be surprised by these findings. What is usually not recognized, however, is that these same kinds of things also characterize crime and criminal law enforcement in the United States (and possibly every other nation).

CRIME AND LAW ENFORCEMENT IN SEATTLE

Seattle, like Ibadan, is a city of 1 million people with its own police, government, and set of laws inherited from Great Britain. In Seattle, as in Ibadan, one can find any type of vice that suits the palate. One must travel away from the middle- and upper-class suburbs that ring the city and venture into the never-never land of skidrow derelicts, the Black ghetto, or a few other pockets of run-down hotels, cafes, and cabarets that are sprinkled along freeways and by the docks.

Here one can find prostitution, gambling, usury, drugs, pornography, bootleg liquor, bookmaking, and pinball machines.

Bookmaking, poker games, bingo parlors, off-track betting, casinos, roulette and dice games, and innumerable $2 and $5 stud-poker games are scattered liberally throughout the city.

Gambling, prostitution, drug distribution, pornography, and usury (high-interest loans) exist with the compliance, encouragement, and cooperation of the major political and law enforcement officials in the city. There is in fact a symbiotic relationship between the law enforcement-political organizations of the city and a group of *local* (as distinct from national) men who control the distribution of vices.

The payoffs and briberies in Seattle are complex. The simpler and more straightforward are those made by each gambling establishment. A restaurant or cabaret with a card room attached had to pay around $200 each month to the police and $200 to the "syndicate." In reality these were two branches of the same group of men, but the payoffs were made separately. Anyone who refused these payments was harassed by fire inspectors, health inspectors, licensing difficulties, and even physical violence from enforcers who worked for the crime cabal in the city. Similarly, places with pinball machines, pornography, bookmaking, or prostitution had to pay regularly to the "bagman," who collected a fee for the police.

Payoffs to policemen were also required of tow-truck operators, cabaret owners, and other businesses where police cooperation was necessary. Two truck drivers carried with them a matchbox with $3 in it; when asked for a light by the policeman who had called them to the scene of an accident, they gave him the matchbox with the $3 inside. Cabaret owners paid according to how large their business was. The police could extract payoffs because the laws were so worded as to make it virtually impossible to own a profitable cabaret without violating the law. For example, it was illegal to have an entertainer closer than 25 feet to the nearest customer. A cabaret, to comply with this ordinance,

would have had to have a night club the size of a large ballroom, creating an atmosphere so sterile that customers would be driven away—not to mention the fact that such large spaces are exceedingly expensive in the downtown section of the city. Thus, the police could, if they chose, close down a cabaret on a moment's notice. Payoffs were a necessary investment to assure that the police would not so choose.

The trade in licenses was notoriously corrupt. My informants generally agreed that a tow truck license required a bribe of $10,000; a cardroom license was $25,000; taxicab licenses were unavailable, as were licenses for distributing pinball machines or juke boxes. These licenses had all been issued to members of the syndicate that controlled the rackets and no outsiders were permitted in.

There were innumerable instances of payoffs to politicians and government officials for real estate deals, businesses, and stock transactions. In each case the participants were a combination of local businessmen, racketeers, local politicians, and government officials.

Interestingly, there is also a minority ghetto within Seattle where one would expect to find a high crime rate—the Japanese-American section of the city.

It is widely believed that the Japanese-Americans have a very low propensity to crime because of the family-centered orientation of the Japanese-American community. There is some evidence, however, that this perspective is largely a self-fulfilling prophecy.[52] Table 4 shows a comparison between the self-reported delinquency and actual arrest rates of Japanese-American youth for a selected year. The data suffers, of course, from problems inherent in such comparisons, but nonetheless the actual crime rate among Japanese-American youth is considerably higher than the conventional view would suggest (see Table 4).

Table 4   Comparison of arrests (for 1963) and self-reported delinquency involvement, by racial groups*

Racial Group	Percent Arrested	Percent Self-reporting High Delinquency Involvement**
White	11	53
Black	36	52
Japanese	2	36

* Based on data from Richard H. Nagasawa, "Delinquency and Non-Delinquency: A Study of Status Problems and Perceived Opportunity (M.A. thesis, University of Washington, 1965), p. 35.

** A self-reported delinquency scale was developed and the respondents were divided so that 50 percent of the sample was categorized as having high and 50 percent as having low delinquency involvement.

Thus we see that in both the Hausa area of Ibadan and the Japanese-American section of Seattle there is reason to suspect a reasonably high crime rate, but official statistics show an exceptionally low one. When discussing Hausa crime I attributed this fact to the payoffs made by Hausa leaders to the police and other government officials.

Somewhat the same sort of system prevails in Seattle, especially with regard to the rackets. Whereas prostitutes, pornography shops, gambling establishments, cabaret operators, and tow-truck operators had to pay off individually to the police and the syndicate, the Japanese-American community did so *as a community*. The tithe was collected by a local businessman and was paid to the police and the syndicate in a group sum. Individual prostitutes and vice racketeers might at times have to do special favors for a policeman or political figure, but by and large the payoffs were made collectively rather than individually.

This collective payoff was in large measure a result of the same characteristic of both the Hausa and the Japanese-American communities, namely the heterogeneous social class nature of the community. Typically, wealthy or middle-class members of the lower-class white slum or the Black ghetto moved out of these areas as rapidly as their incomes permitted. So too with Yoruba, Ibo, or other ethnic groups in Ibadan. But many, though certainly not all, upper- and middle-class Hausa in Ibadan, and Japanese-Americans in Seattle retained their residence in their respective communities. As a result the enforcement of any law became more problematic for law enforcement agencies. Arrests of any youth or adult were always accompanied by the possibility that the suspect would have a politically influential parent or friend. There was also the possibility that a payoff of some sort (including political patronage) would override the policeman's efforts. Since there was also the necessity to hide from the middle and upper class the extent to which the police closed their eyes to the rackets, it was then convenient to avoid having many police in the Hausa and Japanese-American communities. The myth of these areas as "no crime" sections of the city was thus very convenient. By contrast, since only those members of the middle and upper class who were seeking the vices would come to the skidrow area or the Black ghetto, then the presence of the police was not problematic and in fact helped to assure the "respectable" citizen that he could partake of his prurient interests without fear of being the victim of a robbery or of any violence.

As in Nigeria, all of this corruption, bribery, and blatant violation of the law was taking place while arrests were being made and people sent to jail or prison for other offenses. In Seattle over 70 percent of all arrests during the time of the study were for public drunkenness.[53] The police were actually arresting drunks on one side of a building while on the other side a vast array of other offenses was being committed.

What then are we to conclude from these data about (specifically) the etiology of criminal behavior and (more generally) the relative utility of functional and conflict paradigms?

To start, the data show the fact that criminal behavior by *any reasonable* definition of that term is *not* concentrated in the lower classes. Thus a theory of the causes of criminal behavior is suspect to the extent that it depends on the assumption that there is a higher rate of criminality in the lower classes. These data on Seattle and Ibadan link members of the ruling class, the power elite, and the racketeers in joint ventures which involve them actively and passively in criminal activities as part of their way of life.

This conclusion, ironically, is identical with that of Edwin Sutherland, only he came to this view from his study of

corporation ("white-collar") crime. However, he then proposed an explanation for criminality which was essentially social-psychological by asking why some individuals became involved in criminal behavior. My contention is that this question is meaningless. Everyone commits crime. Many, many people, whether they are poor, rich, or middling, are involved in a way of life that is criminal although no one, not even the professional thief or racketeer or corrupt politician, commits crime *all the time*. To be sure it may be politically useful to say that people become criminal through association with "criminal behavior patterns" and thereby remove the tendency to look at criminals as pathological. But such a view has little scientific value since it seeks a psychological cause of what is by its very nature a sociopolitical event. Criminality is simply *not* something that people have or don't have; crime is not something some people do and others do not. Criminal acts occur as a consequence of social relations which stem from a society's mode of production, but the label "criminal" is a matter of who can pin the label on whom. It is to Sutherland's credit that he recognized this when, in 1924, he noted that:

> An understanding of the nature of criminal law is necessary in order to secure an understanding of the nature of crime. A complete explanation of the origin and enforcement of laws would be, also, an explanation of the violation of laws.[54]

But Sutherland failed, unfortunately, to pursue the implications of his remarks. He chose instead to confront the prevailing functionalist perspective on crime with a less class-biased but nonetheless inevitably psychological explanation.

One point on which both conflict and functional theories seem quite wrong is the assumption that criminal acts, that is, acts which violate a criminal law, are more often committed by members of the lower classes. Conflict theory says this will occur as a result of the ruling class's effort to see that those acts most often committed by the lower classes are defined as crime, whereas typically "immoral" acts of the ruling classes will not be. Functional theorists see this as occurring as a result of the disorganizing features of lower-class life. In fact it seems very clear that criminal acts are widely distributed throughout the social classes in capitalist societies, that the rich, the ruling, the poor, and the working classes *all* engage in criminal activities on a regular basis. It is in the enforcement of the law that the lower classes are subject to the effects of ruling-class domination over the legal system, which results in the appearance of a concentration of criminal acts among the lower classes in the official records. In actual practice, however, the class differences do not exist. What difference there is would be a difference in the type of criminal act, not in the prevalence of criminality.

The argument that the control of the state by the ruling class would lead to a lower propensity for crime among the ruling classes fails to recognize three fundamental facts. First, the many crimes which are sometimes in the best interest of the ruling class to control (e.g., crimes of violence, bribery of public officials, and crimes of personal choice such as drug use, alcoholism, driving while intoxicated) are very likely to be as widespread among the upper classes as the lower classes, thus making it crucial that the ruling class control the law enforcement agencies in ways that provide class-structured immunity. An example would be a legal system encumbered with procedural rules which only the wealthy can afford to implement and which, if implemented, nearly guarantee immunity from prosecution. In addition, there could be more direct control through bribes, coercion, and the use of political influence.

Second, the conflict paradigm has not generally realized the extent to which laws will be passed in order to assuage the manifestation of conflict between social classes. Thus it has often been difficult to account for the emergence of laws restricting the behavior of capitalists in the course of their business—laws which have the appearance of controlling capitalists' interests in the interests of the general population. An historical analysis of such laws would show that they emerge during times of open conflict between social classes and that the real extent to which the laws interfere with capitalists' interests through enforcement, subsequent legislation, and court decisions is negligible. It is necessary to account for the emergence of such laws, but to the extent that conflict theory has stressed the ruling class's monolithic control over law making, such laws could not be accounted for.

Third, the conflict paradigm has not generally realized that the law will also reflect conflict between strata of the ruling class or between the ruling class and the "power elites" who manage the bureaucracies of the state. So, for example, laws that restrict the formation of trusts or misrepresentation in advertising or that require licenses in order to engage in business practices all generally serve to reduce competition among the ruling classes and to concentrate capital in a few hands. However, the laws apply universally and therefore could be used against monopoly capitalists as well. Thus when capitalists break these laws they are committing criminal acts. Again, the enforcement practices obviate the effectiveness of the laws and guarantee that the ruling class will rarely be implicated, but the fact of their violations must be faced.

It can also be concluded from this comparative study of Ibadan and Seattle that law enforcement systems are *not* organized to *reduce crime* or to enforce the public morality. They are organized rather to *manage* crime by cooperating with the most criminal groups and enforcing laws against those whose crimes are minimal.[55] By cooperating with criminal groups, law enforcement essentially produces more crime. Law enforcement practices of promising profit and security to those who engage in organized criminal activities from which the political, legal, and business communities profit also produce more crime by selecting and encouraging the perpetuation of criminal careers.

Thus the data from this study clearly support the conflict paradigm's assertion that criminal acts which serve the interests of the ruling class will be sanctioned while those that do not will be punished.

The data also support the conflict model's hypothesis that criminal activity is a direct reflection of class position. Thus the criminality of the lawyers, prosecuting attorneys, politicians, judges, and policemen is uniquely suited to their own class position in the society and grows out of the opportunities and strains that inhere in those positions just as surely as the drinking of the skidrow derelict, the violence of the ghetto resident, the drug use of the middle-class adolescent, and the white-collar crimes of corporation executives are suited to theirs. To argue that each of these types of criminality reflects different socializing experiences or that each type of criminality stems from social-psychological conditioning says nothing unique about crime and criminality but only posits what would have to be a general theory of human psychology—a task beyond the scope of criminology and one which has been notoriously unsuccessful.

The postulates in the paradigms which deal with expected differences between capitalist and socialist societies have not been tested by the data presented because our data come from two capitalist societies. Crime statistics which might permit a comparison are so unreliable that they are useless for the task. Even a tentative answer to this proposition must thus wait for better data.

SUMMARY AND CONCLUSION

Alvin Gouldner and Robert Friedrichs have recently pointed out that social science generally and sociology in particular are in the throes of a "paradigm revolution."[56] Predictably, criminology is both a reflection of and a force behind the revolution involved in the paradigmatic shift.

The emerging paradigm in criminology is one which emphasizes social conflict—particularly conflicts of class interests and values—as the prime characteristic of contemporary society. The paradigm which is being replaced is one within which consensus was emphasized as primary and "deviance" or "crime" was viewed as an aberration shared by some minority which had failed to be properly socialized or adequately integrated into society or, more generally, which suffered from "social disorganization." The shift in paradigm has meant more than a shift in theory —that is, more than a shift from explaining the same facts with new causal models. It has meant, at least in criminology, such a refocusing of attention that the role of the state through its legal system becomes a central focus for the study of crime. Thus the emerging paradigm shifts attention to a new set of facts: namely, away from the deviant individual onto the deviance-defining institutions of society.

Exciting as these changes are, there is a dire need to evaluate the relative merits of the competing perspectives. If the paradigmatic revolution is to be more than a mere fad we must be able to systematically show that the new paradigm is in fact superior to its forebearer. In this paper I have tried to do this first by looking at the theoretical implications of two general models of crime and criminal law and then by assessing the relative merits of these alternative interpretations with empirical data.

The general conclusion from the preceding analysis is that the conflict

paradigm raises more fundamental questions and comes closer to providing valid hypotheses than does the functional.

NOTES

[1] T. S. Kuhn, *The Structure of Scientific Revolutions*, 2nd Edition (Chicago: University of Chicago Press, 1970); Robert W. Friedrichs, *A Sociology of Sociology* (New York: The Free Press, 1970); Alvin W. Gouldner, *The Coming Crisis in Western Sociology* (New York: Basic Books, 1970).

[2] See Ian Taylor, Paul Walton, and Jock Young, *The New Criminology: For a Social Theory of Deviance* (London: Routledge and Kegan Paul, 1973); Milton Mankoff, "Societal Reaction and Career Deviance: A Critical Analysis," *The Sociological Quarterly* 12 (Spring 1971), pp. 204–218; Alex Thio, "Class Bias in the Sociology of Deviance," *American Sociologist* 8 (February 1973), pp. 1–12; Richard Quinney, *Critique of Legal Order: Crime Control in Capitalist Society* (Boston: Little, Brown, 1974).

[3] Marx's principal writings on crime and criminal law appear in the following sources: Karl Marx, *The Cologne Communist Trial* (London: Lawrence and Wishart, 1971); *The German Ideology* (London: Lawrence and Wishart, 1965), pp. 342–379; *Theories of Surplus Value* (London: Lawrence and Wishart, 1964), Vol. I, pp. 375–376; "The State and the Law" in *Karl Marx: Selected Writings in Sociology and Social Philosophy*, ed. by T. B. Bottomore and Maxmillien Rubel (New York: McGraw-Hill, 1964), pp. 215–231.

The role which Durkheim played in translating the functional paradigm into a near-theory of crime and criminal law has no counterpart within the Marxian tradition. Until recently the one serious attempt to apply the Marxian dialectic to a theory of criminal behavior was the work of the Dutch sociologist, William Bonger, *Criminality and Economic Conditions* (Boston: Little, Brown, 1916). Bonger's effort placed undue emphasis on a simplified Marxism that posits a direct line between economic privation and crime. While such a view is consistent with some of Engel's writings (see especially Frederich Engels, "The Condition of the Working Class in England," in *Karl Marx and Frederich Engels on Britain* [Moscow: Foreign Languages Publishing House, 1953], Chap. 5), it hardly does justice to the richness of the dialectical paradigm as a potentially fruitful starting point for criminological theory. Such a view also grossly distorts Marx's own view of crime (see Marx's somewhat facetious but nonetheless insightful comment on "the productivity of crime" in *Theories of Surplus Value*, Vol. 1, pp. 375–376) and it especially distorts Marx's analysis of criminal law (see above). These writings on crime and law, although scattered throughout Marx's works, nonetheless form a more imaginative application of dialectic materialism to the study of crime and criminal law than the oversimplification inherent in Marxian writings, such as the above-mentioned piece by Engels.

An illuminating recent paper by Paul Q. Hirst ("Marx and Engels on Law, Crime and Morality," *Economics and Society* 1, no. 1 [1972], pp. 28–58) argues that there can be no Marxist theory of crime or criminal law. Hirst's argument is basically that since in the dialectic paradigm criminal law is always a reflection of a society's mode of production, there is then nothing more to say. Such a view relegates all Marxian analysis to an analysis of the mode of production with no attention to "superstructure" and seems therefore to be rather more limited than is warranted by the logic of the paradigm. Furthermore, following Hirst's logic would cut us off from a fruitful source of theoretical ideas useful for an understanding of crime and criminal law, as it would also remove from the more general issue of Marxism an important source of data and theoretical refinement. Clearly Marx recognized this when he devoted so much effort to analysis of the law, as indicated by the references above.

⁴ David Mandel, "Traditions in Political Analysis and the Problem of 'What is in Men's Heads'," *The Human Factor* 11, no. 1 (Spring 1972), pp. 32–44.

⁵ For an illustration of ignoring Marxism see almost any standard introductory text in criminology or juvenile delinquency. For an example of distortion see George B. Vold, *Theoretical Criminology* (Oxford: Oxford University Press, 1958).

⁶ Richard Quinney, "Crime Control in Capitalist Societies: A Critical Philosophy of Legal Order," *Issues in Criminology* 8, no. 1 (Spring 1973), pp. 75–99. For some recent works that come generally from the conflict perspective but are not wholly within the Marxist tradition see: William J. Chambliss and Robert B. Seidman, *Law, Order, and Power* (Reading, Mass.: Addison-Wesley, 1971); Richard Quinney, *The Social Reality of Crime*, (Boston: Little, Brown, 1970); Austin Turk, *Criminality and Legal Order* (Chicago: Rand McNally, 1969); Taylor, Walton, and Young, *The New Criminology: For A Social Theory of Deviance*.

⁷ For discussion of these issues see Gerhard Lenski,

Power and Privilege (New York: McGraw-Hill, 1966); William J. Chambliss, *Sociological Readings in the Conflict Perspective*, (Reading, Mass.: Addison-Wesley, 1972); Raif Dahrendorf, "Toward a Theory of Social Conflict," *Journal of Peace and Conflict Resolution* 11 (1958), pp. 170–183; Pierre L. van den Berghe, "Dialectic and Functionalism: Toward a Theoretical Synthesis," *American Sociological Review* 28, no. 5 (October 1963), pp. 695–705; Andre Gunder Frank, *Latin America: Underdevelopment or Revolution* (New York: Monthly Review Press, 1969).

⁸ Emile Durkheim, *The Division of Labor in Society* (Glencoe: Free Press, 1949), p. 77.

⁹ Ibid., p. 73.

¹⁰ Ibid., p. 77.

¹¹ Ibid., p. 79.

¹² Ibid., p. 80.

¹³ Ibid., p. 81.

¹⁴ Ibid., p. 111.

¹⁵ Ibid., p. 70.

¹⁶ Ibid., p. 129.

¹⁷ Ibid., p. 127.

¹⁸ Ibid., p. 102.

¹⁹ The naïve view that Marx saw only two classes (the bourgeosie and the proletariat) in capitalist societies is of course fallacious. This fact does not, however, contradict the analytic usefulness of the division here proposed.

²⁰ Marx, *Theories of Surplus Value*, p. 375.

²¹ Norwood Russell Hanson, *Patterns of Discovery* (Cambridge: Cambridge University Press, 1964); Bernard Barber, "Resistance by Scientists to Scientific Discovery," *Science* 134 (1961), pp. 596–602; Kuhn, *The Structure of Scientific Revolutions*.

²² Seeing crime as resulting from being "not properly socialized" can take many forms. Most often in psychological theory it leads to explanations in terms of family relations and a breakdown of affective ties between parents and children. In social-psychological theory, improper socialization is generally attributed to coming into contact with and learning deviant behavior patterns. The Durkheimian formulation emphasized the possibility of over-socialization as well as under-socialization as important causal processes.

²³ There have been some excellent summations of differences between functional and conflict theories. One of the best is John Horton, "Order and Conflict Theories of Social Problems as Competing Ideologies," *American Journal of Sociology* 71 (May 1966), pp. 701–713. See also Lenski, *Power and Privilege*, and Chambliss, *Sociological Readings in the Conflict Perspective*.

²⁴ Svend Ranulf, *The Jealousy of the Gods*, Vols. 1

and 2 (London: Williams and Northgate, 1933; and *Moral Indignation and Middle Class Psychology* (Copenhagen: Levin & Munksgaard, 1938); Joseph Gusfield, *Symbolic Crusade: Status Politics and the American Temperance Movement* (Urbana: University of Illinois Press, 1963).

[25] Gusfield, ibid. See also Andrew Sinclair, *Era of Excess: A Social History of the Prohibition Movement* (New York: Harper & Row, 1964).

[26] Jerome Hall, *Theft, Law and Society* (Indianapolis: Bobbs-Merrill, 1952); William J. Chambliss, "A Sociological Analysis of the Law of Vagrancy," *Social Problems* 12 (Summer 1964), pp. 67–77.

[27] Gabriel Kolko, *Railroads and Regulations* (Princeton: Princeton University Press, 1965); and *The Triumph of Conservatism* (New York: Free Press of Glencoe, 1963).

[28] Alfred R. Lindesmith, *The Addict and the Law* (Bloomington: Indiana University Press, 1965); Edwin M. Lemert, *Social Action and Legal Change: Revolution within the Juvenile Court* (Chicago: Aldine, 1964); Troy Duster, *The Legislation of Morality: Law, Drugs and Moral Judgment* (New York: Free Press, 1970).

[29] Pamela A. Roby, "Politics and Criminal Law: Revision of the New York State Penal Law on Prostitution," *Social Problems* 17 (Summer 1969), pp. 83–109.

[30] Chambliss and Seidman, *Law, Order, and Power*.

[31] Kai T. Erikson, *Wayward Puritans: A Study in the Sociology of Deviance* (New York: Wiley, 1966).

[32] Ibid., p. 4.

[33] Ibid., p. 67.

[34] Ibid., p. 59.

[35] Ibid., pp. 77–78.

[36] Ibid., p. 78.

[37] Ibid., p. 71.

[38] Ibid., p. 87.

[39] Ibid., p. 108.

[40] Ibid., p. 109.

[41] Ibid., p. 118.

[42] Ibid., pp. 121–122.

[43] Ibid., pp. 126–127.

[44] Ibid., pp. 137–138.

[45] Ibid., pp. 179–180.

[46] Edwin M. Schur, *Crimes Without Victims* (Englewood Cliffs, N. J.: Prentice-Hall, 1965).

[47] Sanford Kadish, "The Crisis of Overcriminalization," *Annals of the American Academy of Political and Social Science* 374 (November 1967), pp. 157–170.

[48] Max Gluckman, *Politics, Law and Ritual in Tribal Society* (Oxford: Blackwell, 1965); Paul Bohannan, *Justice and Judgment Among the Tiv* (New York: Oxford University Press, 1957); and "The Differing Realms of Law," *American Anthropologist* 67, no. 6, part 2 (1965); Lucy Mair, *Primitive Government* (New York: Penguin Books, 1964).

[49] Chambliss and Seidman, *Law, Order, and Power*, pp. 28–37.

[50] Richard D. Schwartz and James C. Miller, "Legal Evolution and Societal Complexity," *American Journal of Sociology* 70 (September 1964), p. 166.

[51] Throughout the paper we rely on data from Ibadan and Seattle as a basis for discussing the patterns of both countries. This leap may disturb some and if so then they may consider the study as speaking only to the two cities with only a promise of more general application. From a variety of research studies and my own impressions, I am convinced that what is true of Ibadan and Seattle is true throughout both countries; but whether or not this is the case should not affect the overall conclusions of this inquiry.

[52] Richard H. Nagasawa, "Delinquency and Non-Delinquency: A Study of Status Problems and Perceived Opportunity" (M.A. thesis, University of Washington, 1965). See also William J. Chambliss and Richard H. Nagasawa, "On the Validity of Official Statistics," *Journal of Research in Crime and Delinquency* 6 (January 1969), pp. 71–77.

[53] James Q. Spradley, *You Owe Yourself a Drunk* (Boston: Little, Brown, 1970), p. 128.

[54] Edwin H. Sutherland, *Criminology* (Philadelphia: Lippincott, 1924), p. 11.

[55] I am indebted to Sheldon Messinger for suggesting the idea of "managing" crime.

[56] Alvin Gouldner, *The Coming Crisis of Western Sociology* (New York: Basic Books, 1970); Robert W. Friedrichs, *A Sociology of Sociology* (New York: Free Press, 1972).

PART ONE

THE DEVELOPMENT
OF LEGAL SANCTIONS

INTRODUCTION

Milton Mankoff

One of the essential distinctions between the functional and conflict approaches to the study of criminality is in the way each model accounts for the evolution of legal sanctions. Functionalists define acts as criminal only when they are offensive to the moral standards of the vast majority of the citizens of a community. Conflict theorists, on the other hand, consider acts criminal when they are perceived to run counter to the interests of powerful groups within a community.

The three articles which comprise this section speak to this crucial controversy. Mark Kennedy's essay, "Beyond Incrimination: Some Neglected Facets of the Theory of Punishment," argues at length that the "ethic of individual responsibility," rather than being a feature of all societies, emerged within the context of the development of the state, citizenship, and the capitalist mode of production. Prior to these developments criminality as we know it today simply did not exist. There was collective responsibility for harms visited upon persons. If one person killed another there was no possibility of arrest,

trial, conviction, and punishment. Rather, relatives and friends of the injured party had the prerogative of seeking revenge against the killer or one of his or her fellow clan members. Under these circumstances guilt or innocence had little significance because there was ordinarily no superior outside authority to which aggrieved parties could appeal for justice. The distinction between *crime* and *punishment* was blurred. Might made right. From the perspective of the victim, the killer was perpetrating a "crime"; however, the killer felt he or she was merely "punishing" an adversary.

When the modern state emerged, along with the institutions of capitalism, individual risk-taking in business required an ethic of individual responsibility for losses as well as opportunities for gain. Gradually collective responsibility became outmoded and penal law as it exists in the contemporary era was created. As Kennedy notes, however, the distinction between crime and punishment could be clearly delineated only if it were believed that the state represented a truly neutral force which made judgments in accordance with the public interest as a whole.[1] In his treatment of the bifurcation of criminal and civil law, the use of the legal system to insure the division of labor between entrepreneurs and propertyless laborers, and the functions of fines, Kennedy shows that the state in capitalist societies has represented the interests of the capitalist class as opposed to the needs of the vast majority of citizens. Yet the widespread acceptance of the role of the state and the belief that it stands as a neutral referee has meant that punishment for crime is accepted as right and proper even by relatives and friends of persons found guilty of offenses. Punishment has not served as a pretext for challenging the authority of the state and the class system which is at the base of its power. The sanctity of the state, the fact that it is "beyond incrimination," has reinforced the institutional foundations of capitalist society. Similar developments, of course, characterize other societies in which state formations have emerged.

William Chambliss' article, "The State and Criminal Law," summarizes the results of a number of studies of law creation. Specific examples, such as the use of criminal sanctions in the British colonies to force compliance with British economic interests and the emergence of vagrancy and theft laws in England, show substantial support for the general analysis of law provided by Kennedy. In examining the evolution of one of the oldest laws in the statute books, which appears to be anachronistic in modern society, Chambliss illuminates the ways in which dominant interest groups can institute and shape laws to coincide with their changing needs. One of the lessons to be drawn from the history of vagrancy

laws is that unless laws are repealed they can reemerge from a long period of disuse to provide a cloak of legitimacy for the economic and political aspirations and moral standards of those who influence and control the judicial process.

In the United States today, for example, there are laws in disuse making it possible for a president under a state of "national emergency" to authorize the police and military to incarcerate people indefinitely without having to bring specific criminal charges or show cause for the incarceration. That such laws need not be "on the books" in order for the state to take such drastic action is of course clearly demonstrated by the internment of Japanese-American citizens during World War II. However, if no such laws lie dormant, some hesitation is required to pass new ones justifying the actions of the state, which may remove its aura of legitimacy. There are numerous obscure laws which pose a threat in America today. Many of these laws deal with aspects of personal morality (particularly sexual conduct) and involve acts which may be committed routinely by vast majorities of the population (in some states it is against the law to have sexual intercourse on Sunday or in a bath tub) who are unaware that they are violating the law. An enterprising law enforcement officer could easily choose to arrest people deemed undesirable on other grounds (for example, political dissenters) by utilizing these statutes.

James Graham's essay, "Amphetamine Politics on Capitol Hill," is a timely reminder that elite control of the legal apparatus is an ongoing process that should not be identified solely with the dim past. Graham describes how the largest pharmaceutical companies intervened in the deliberations over the Comprehensive Drug Abuse and Control Act of 1970 in order to insure that considerations of public health did not hamper the pursuit of corporate profits. As a result of the exercise of corporate power and influence, amphetamines, although far more dangerous than other drugs under more severe control (for example, marijuana), escaped meaningful regulation. The Graham article does not represent an isolated case of modern-day corporate corruption of the law-making process. Corporations which systematically poison our food with toxic chemicals,[2] insure thousands of traffic deaths through faulty automotive construction and failure to institute safety features in the design of their vehicles,[3] and pollute our air[4] and water[5] are able to resist the imposition of criminal sanctions for acts that are far more menacing to the public than the depredations of burglars, drunks, prostitutes, and thieves.

NOTES

[1] For a detailed discussion on the validity and utility of seeing the state as value-neutral see William J. Chambliss and Robert B. Seidman, *Law, Order and Power* (Reading, Mass: Addison-Wesley, 1971).

[2] Daniel Zwerdling, "Death for Dinner," *The New York Review of Books*, February 21, 1974, pp. 22–24.

[3] Ralph Nader, *Unsafe at Any Speed* (New York: Essandess, 1965).

[4] John C. Esposito, *Vanishing Air: The Ralph Nader Study Group Report on Air Pollution* (New York: Grossman, 1970).

[5] James M. Fallows, *The Water Lords: Ralph Nader's Study Group Report on Industry and Environmental Crisis in Savannah, Georgia* (New York: Grossman, 1971).

BEYOND INCRIMINATION

Some Neglected Facets of the Theory of Punishment

Mark C. Kennedy

If crime and punishment are injurious to life, then each belongs to the same class of conduct and should not be viewed as two independent species of harms. Yet, what appears more certain, more part of daily experience than the assumption that "each" is independent of the other?[1] The very manner in which officious persons make dutiful their daily rounds—impersonally making decisions, soberly passing judgments, patiently accepting contrition, exacting punishments, and excusing us our misdeeds—puts us in a position to do little but accept our own conduct as culpable, theirs as beyond incrimination.

This assumption is especially difficult for professionalists to deny. What is more characteristic than treating "crime" and "punishment" as independent species —without reference either to their sameness or to how continuity of both depends on the character of dominating institutions?[2] To deny this assumption, and voice the idea that crime and penal sanctions are the same implies certain risks. But to accept it uncritically promises certain rewards which accrue from university services to commerce, and to local and federal governments. This includes sociological services to police, prison systems, corrections departments for developing programs of rehabilitation for probationers and parolees. Some may lack for desire, others perhaps wit, still others the courage either to deny the scientific value of this assumption or to discuss the institutional foundations on which it rests.

For to teach that penal sanctions are behaviorally no different from crimes might slur officialdom, offend the State, profane its sources of power, challenge the legitimacy of its monopoly over the power to pardon and punish the disobedient, jeopardize the transactions between university administrations and their off-campus supporters, and risk loss of one's own tenure and career—and this, quite apart from whether the sameness of crime and punishment is valid on scientific grounds.[3] For it is the State—as a community of ruling officials[4]—which both creates and sustains

* Source: "Beyond Incrimination: Some Neglected Facets of the Theory of Punishment," *Catalyst*, No. 5, Summer, 1970, pp. 1–37.

this dichotomy between crime and punishment. Ironically, it is the State which may also destroy it.

With penal sanction, law, and the State set over in one universe, and with crime and poverty in another, professionalists seek immediate causes of crime in ghettos, slums, broken homes, and in "multiple dwellings" where "undersocialization" is said to spawn "predelinquents" and "hard-to-reach youth." Ultimate causes are sought in impersonal conditions issuing from population density: social distance, anonymity, social isolation, social mobility—in short, social disorganization. In "the other universe" separated from this "causal" picture, are differentially enforced laws, differential justice, differential punishments and privileges—all the conditions which, though ignored, account for slums, ghettos, broken homes. Thus, when solutions are advanced, they never include major changes in criminal law, penal codes, institutional reconstruction, or any revamping of the power structure. These are assumed to be immutable "givens", and instead of changing them, some call for greater police powers and more law enforcement while others call for more work release programs (of some value to industrialists on the make for cheap labor), more psychiatric services and social workers (to "resocialize" predelinquents), more qualified probation and parole officers, and more community resources at their disposal.

What all this submerges are scientifically valid questions: (1) Are crimes and crime rates manufactured by the State? Does fixing penal sanctions to once-legal behavior accomplish this? (2) Are old crimes abolished by removal of law enforcements and penal sanctions? When a punishable act passes under civil law by removal of penal sanction, who gains and who loses? (3) What is the relation between successful political movements and revision of criminal laws? What acts, specifically described and proscribed under old criminal laws, become fully legitimate with the deposition of an old State and when it is replaced by a revolutionary regime? What effects would this have on the nature of crime and crime rates? (4) When a new State ascends and an old one collapses, do former executioners become murderers and do former murderers become executioners? At what point in revolution do punishments become crimes? (5) In countries undergoing transformation to collective ownership of instruments of production, what does private ownership mean with reference to them? If, under law, the fruits of labor are to be equally shared, what does theft mean? Under capitalism, is crime a form of entrepreneurship; under socialism, is entrepreneurship a form of crime?

Though vital to any sociology of crime and punishment, these questions are pushed aside because of the predominance of theory, research, and programs of amelioration which rest squarely upon the falsifiable assumption that crime and punishment repose in separate universes as independent species of conduct. What then is the status of this assumption? What is the nature of crime and punishment? How are they the same? What are their sustained differences?

Answers to these questions are not set forth as exhaustive or final. The problem is to explore the implications of recasting conceptions of crime and punishment into a new framework, to see what becomes explicit when these behaviors are conceived as belonging to the same class, originally separated and subsequently reified by the State as independent species. Of equal concern are implications of these sustained differences. This calls for answering two different orders of questions.

First order questions: Are we dealing with phenomena universal to all cultures, or with culturally specific phenomena limited to a period of history? If the latter, what sociocultural conditions account for such cultural and historical specificity? What institutions explain the emergence of crime and punishment as a unit class? Answers, though brief, must reveal how crime and punishment, as defined, depend for their origin and continuity upon the origin and continuity of certain institutions, and where the latter are absent, the former do not exist. Thus, it must be shown that crime comprises but one of several kinds of all norm violations, that penal sanction is but one of many kinds of reprisals against such violations. This does not mean that crime and penal sanction are behaviorally different but establishes that both emerge and continue together as manifestations of singular institutional facts.

A *second order of questions* is relevant to showing that there are no behavioral attributes intrinsic to harms of crime and punishment which warrant the assumption that they belong to behaviorally independent classes. This calls for more than establishing crime and punishment as a single class of harms, for it must be shown (1) that the criteria for separating them refer to phenomena external to actual behaviors classed by legal procedure as crime vs. punishment, (2) that even within the criminal law itself, the criteria by which crime is identified procedurally apply with equal validity to punishment. Relevant questions are:

1. What behavioral attributes common to both crime and punishment are shared, and not shared, by other classes of harms? Do these attributes justify separating these harms into different classes? If not, what criteria external to these behaviors warrant their separation into different classes?
2. Do legal criteria for identifying crime also identify punishment and/or penal sanction?

These questions will be seen to establish that the attributes by which the different legal categories of behavior (civil, criminal) are established are but criteria external to the interactions legally categorized. It will be seen that behaviors called crime and punishment not only belong to the same class but that the very differentiae of crime apply with equal validity to punishment.

THE NATURE OF CRIME
AND PUNISHMENT

Crime is here defined as a violation, by act or omission, of any criminal law. According to that law, it is also a specific conduct leading to a harm and is an act construed as a harm against a State. It follows that deviations from norms which are not criminal laws are not crimes. It also follows that in any society where such laws are absent there is no crime. Crime, then, is unique behavior. To understand this calls for some knowledge of the characteristics of criminal law as unique law.

Punishment is an intended harm imposed by one or more parties upon an individual over whom those who impose that harm have assumed or have been granted jurisdiction as a right—a right contingent upon superior coercive power or upon collectively given power to exempt an offender from any reprisal for his offense. Penal sanction is a special case of punishment, and both are special cases of intended harms generally. They differ from acts of war, for example, only insofar as reciprocal acts of war assume political equality between contenders.

CRIME AND CRIMINAL LAW
IN RELATION TO THE STATE

Under criminal law no act is crime until it violates a norm having the following characteristics: uniformity, specificity, politicality, and penal sanction. Procedurally, these characteristics become *criteria* for legal classification of any act as crime versus not crime. In legal procedure, uniformity is more an assumption than a working criterion, thus we are concerned only with the latter three characteristics. Any law failing to detail the conduct proscribed lacks specificity, and violating it is not a crime. Any law neither created nor recognized by the State as a bona fide part of its legal order and which fails to define the proscribed act as a harm against the State lacks politicality; its violation is not a crime. Any law in which a punishment is not prescribed lacks penal sanction, and its violation is not a crime.[5]

It follows that any society having no laws like this has no crime, and that crime is a unique class among all violations of conduct norms. Since politicality and penal sanction (the decisive characteristics of criminal law) presuppose a State, there can be no crime in any society which has no State.[6] The latter are still abundant in parts of the world yet untouched by Western political and economic institutions.[7]

While Stateless societies have emerged apart from Western influence, they are rare, and societies having what Weber described as "formally rational States" are either Western or have come by such political communities through Western influence. Since the formally rational State is, roughly, a post-fifteenth-century development of Western culture,[8] it follows that crime in its present character did not exist before that period and that prior to the advent of feudal States—apart from Roman law—crime as such did not exist. The same is true of penal sanction. Both are linked to the formal laws of the State and to civil institutions supported by it. Both types of law are managed by the State as a monopoly.

But while both are unique in contrast with those norm violations and punishments common to societies without States, neither seems behaviorally different from the other—in part because both crime and punishment are intended harms, and in part because both emerged historically with and are now founded upon individualism as a common ideology or value system which has as its basic premise the belief that each individual (and not social institutions) is fully responsible for his own conduct and its consequences.[9] While the era of individualism is now at an end in the West, its hold is still very evident in the State, in citizenship, in criminal law and legal procedures, and in the dominance of penal sanctions over the use of the power to pardon.

HISTORICAL CONDITIONS OF THE
ADVENT OF CRIME AND PENAL SANCTION

It is an oversimplification to say that these two classes of harms arose together in post-fifteenth-century Europe as a function of the advent of formally rational States, but what finally took place, beginning with the thirteenth century, amounts to that. What was fundamental to the birth of crime and penal sanction was fundamental to political, economic, religious, and familistic transformation generally, and essential to the transformations of these institutions was the transformation of the ethic of shared responsibility for individual conduct (the cooperative ethic) to the ethic of individual responsibility.

In part as the legacy of the collapse of feudalism and in part as a consequence of the rise of institutions of capitalism which this collapse afforded, individualism as a generalized social movement emerged from a fact of institutional chaos to a social philosophy and a normative order and transformed, as it grew, the whole of Western society and its culture. Early or late, it came eventually to find social expression in religion as Protestantism; in philosophy as empiricism and idealism, in scholastic inquiry as deductive and inductive methods of natural science, in economy as new institutions of private property, the market, entrepreneurship, rational accounting, and the redivision of labor along new social lines.

It found social expression politically with the birth of formally rational States, citizenship, the theory of social contract, and the rise and diffusion of two interlinked bodies of calculable law (civil and criminal). Just as egoism came to play the major part in the genesis of self, so did behaviorism come to play a major part in psychological inquiry. All the while, kinship was being nucleated and dispossessed, and religion was atomized and made impotent as a social control. On every side, with each new expression of individualism, the society based earlier on the ethic of shared responsibility for individual conduct vanished from the scene. When fealty was for sale, altruism was dead.[10]

The emergence of individualism, in transforming all social institutions, transformed the relation of individuals to each other, of each individual to society, and created a new relation between each person and the emergent State. In all these relations, the legal fiction that each citizen is alone responsible for his own conduct and its consequences, good or bad, became reified both at the level of self or personality and at the level of law and judicial practice. Individualism as an attitude of self is basic to guilt, and as a premise of both civil and criminal law it is elemental to the whole legal practice of incrimination. What we witness in the advent of crime and penal sanction is but one facet of the total transformation of institutional life. Remembering this, we now must look at crime and punishment in a more singular and comparative way.

FEUDAL INSTITUTIONS IN RELATION
TO HARMS AND THEIR DISPOSAL

Between the period of the last invasion of Moslems, Hungarians, and Scandinavians, and the middle of the eleventh century, Europe developed what came to be called the institutions of feudalism. This period, in Bloch's astute analysis, was the first feudal age—the second feudal age extending from the middle of that century roughly to the thirteenth.[11] In the present analysis, the first feudal age is important because its normative order and institutional systems were founded on the ethic of shared responsibility for individual conduct. Criminal law and penal sanctions had not emerged, and no territorial power had been able successfully to obtain from local social worlds the power to pardon an offender his harms; citizenship and the formally rational State were absent, and so were the institutions of capitalism. Customary law and the oral tradition prevailed and were imbedded in the religious mentality, the epic, and the folk memory.[12] Kinship and vassalage were knit by companionage—so greatly that fealty was meaningful in a double sense. Vassalage and kinship were unthinkable without friendship or companionage. Public authority had not emerged, and while vassalage meant subjection, subjection was personal and of a quasi-family character. Feudal society differed as much from those based wholly on kinship as it differs from societies dominated by the State.[13]

The second feudal age is important because in it the ethic of shared responsibility began to give way, and its normative order and institutions began to transform. A vernacular literature emerged and the oral tradition and customary law began to wane. Calculable law began to emerge, along with a host of other changes which account for the rise of citizenship, the formally rational State, and the increasing scope of the institutions of capitalism. Profound changes in economic institutions took place as the ethic of individual responsibility began to find reality in one's relation to himself, to others, and to society and State.

The thesis which will be supported historically and cross-culturally is simply that crime and penal sanction are twin products of the origin and continuity of the State and citizenship, that these institutions, founded on emergent civil and criminal law, emerged as a cluster of new institutions (entrepreneurship, private property, and the market system) all of which were originally the social manifestations of the ethic of individual responsibility for individual behavior. Thus, it follows that in absence of the State, in the absence of its laws, crime and penal sanction do not exist, and in the absence of the institutions of capitalism, their special features cannot exist.

During the first feudal age, the legal system was the rule of custom and oral tradition. It rested on the belief that whatever has been has the right to be.[14] Precedent, not innovation, ruled. It was the normative foundation of feudal society—finding its expression not in hierarchy as we know that word today but in the mutually binding obligations of mutually given oaths all the way up the feudal scale. Land, the only real capital, was tied up solidly by customary obligations and could not for that reason become a commodity for sale in any market. Labor had the same provisions. The whole notion of exclusive proprietary rights was repugnant to people generally. As Bloch put it:

> For nearly all land and a great many human beings were burdened at this time with a multiplicity of obligations differing in nature, but all apparently of equal importance. None implied that fixed proprietary exclusiveness which belonged to the conception of ownership in Roman law. The tenant who—from father to son, as a rule—ploughs the land and gathers in the crop; his immediate lord, to whom he pays dues and who, in certain circumstances, can resume possession of the land; the lord of the lord, and so on right up the feudal scale—how many persons there are who can say, each with [equal] justification . . . "That is my field!"[15]

While landed wealth was differentially though mutually shared, its usufruct did not pass from hand to hand in any important way through any market system. Just as private property was absent, so was trade—except in a marginal and irregular way. While buying and selling was not unknown, no one lived by it unless they were the few who were generally scorned as banished persons or pariahs. Even barter was peripheral, for the chief means for the distribution of goods and services—as demanded by customary law—was "aid" or tallage, and the corvée or boon work in return for protection. In such a system wages were meaningless. "The corvée furnished more laborers than hire."[16] Customary law possessed no norms which bore any similarity to civil and ciriminal laws of post-fifteenth century Europe, and certainly it possessed none having the decisive characteristics of criminal law—politicality and penal sanction. Both State and citizen were absent as continuous elements of society. These presume an ethic not present in the first feudal age—that of individual responsibility for one's conduct.

Just as the ethic of shared responsibility found institutional expression in vassalage, feudal land tenure, and the feudal system for the distribution of goods and services, so was it the basis for kinship solidarity and the restoration of peaceful relations between offenders and the wronged. What linked vassalage to the kinship system was companionage or friendship, but friendship which carried a profounder meaning by far than it carries today. People united by blood were not necessarily friends, but friendship did not exist unless people were united by blood. Moreover, friendship obligations were not weakened by the fact of differential status between friends of blood. If anything, this gave them strength. Any harm falling upon one fell upon all. Any avengement suffered by one was suffered by all members of the companionage.[17] *Treue* and fealty have their meaning here.

Even when infrequently a man was brought before a court, the ethic of shared responsibility found expression in *compurgation* or oath-helping. A collective oath was enough to clear a man accused or to confirm a complaint brought against the accused. If compurgation should result in a draw, the dispute could be settled either by trial by battle or by voluntary compensation. A defeated champion in trial by battle might be either the accused or the plaintiff, but his defeat was also the defeat of the companionage who "stood surety" for him. *Punishment was an act of war and was collective.* Those of a companionage who were not killed in battle were often hanged upon defeat. Guilt was never established until defeat was received as the verdict of God. This did not mean, however, that guilt was not felt or feared. It meant only that the "structure" of guilt was different then than now. Guilt was the fear of bringing shame upon one's kindred, not shame for having killed (for example) a member of another kindred. It had nothing to do with conscience but everything to do with honor. And the dishonor of one was the dishonor of all.[18]

Perhaps nothing better exemplifies the cooperative ethic more than the extra-judicial and quasi-judicial vendetta or *faida.* Kinship vengeance neatly balanced kinship protection of the accused from vengeance.[19] In any feud it was impossible to distinguish acts of punishment from acts of war; it was also impossible to distinguish acts of crime from acts of war. Crime and punishment were never known until after the battle was over, and when over, the guilty had already been punished. Feudal justice did not require the death of the individual who had done the killing. It did require the death of one or more of his kinsmen who protected him. Guilt was more of a projection than a feeling on the part of the killer, unless the killer had slain one of his own. In that case, punishment was self-imposed if imposed at all.

Feuds might be forestalled or terminated by arbitration and compensation, but in a social climate where "the very corpse cried out for vengeance . . . and hung withering in the house till the day when vengeance was accomplished" arbitration and compensation were ordinarily futile gestures—at least in the early stages of the feud. But a rotten corpse or even one whose bones are white may be ample inducements later on for accepting compensation. As the will for avenging the dead waned, the desire for reconciliation with indemnity heightened, and the adage "buy off the spear or feel it in your breast" had practical results.[20]

Judicial procedures, Bloch observes, were little more than "regularized vendettas" and were used only when relatives preferred that means to the feud or compensation.[21] The role of public "authority" in all matters of harms and counterharms and their settlements was negligible. No territorial authority could intervene to impose punishment on an individual without becoming, under custom, the object of a collective vendetta. Penal sanction was absent because it assumes something that did not exist—that the individual and not the kindred of the individual is responsible for the conduct of the individual. In the first feudal age, any "law" having politicality and penal sanction would have been scorned as an attempt by outsiders to profane the bonds of kinship and companionage.

But even well into the second feudal age these customs persisted as did the ethic on which they rested. In the thirteenth century, courts still recognized that any act done by one individual involved all his kindred. In Paris, Parlement still recognized the right of a man to take his vengeance on any relative of his assailant. In cases where such a victim took action in court on the grounds that he had not been involved, those grounds would not have been recognized. The assailant would have been freed.[22] The idea that each man is a citizen of the State and is alone responsible for his own conduct and its consequences was not to be found either in court procedure, in the characteristics of custom, or in judicial decisions. The State could not lodge and process complaints. That was a prerogative of the relatives alone.[23]

The power to pardon a man for any offense whatever rested not in the State or in any public authority. Forgiveness was fully a matter to be settled or granted or arranged with indemnity between disputant clans. In Flanders as in Normandy, even down to the thirteenth century, a murderer could not receive his pardon either from the King or the judges until he had first been reconciled with the kindred of the slain.[24] It is easy to pass over the significance of the power to pardon, but doing so would be a major error. For whoever has the power to pardon or to forgive also holds the power to mete out penal sanctions or to punish, and prior to the emergence of formally rational States and citizenship, the power to forgive without punishment resided among the kindreds—and punishment without forgiveness was an act of war in inter-clan disputes. It follows that neither crime nor penal sanctions can have any meaning until the power to pardon becomes the clear monopoly of the State—until the ethic of individual responsibility and citizenship become socio-cultural facts.

Rusche and Kirchheimer observe that even to the mid-sixteenth century the power to pardon still reposed with the offended party and not with the State. In cases punishable by law the offender could keep his harm out of court by compensating the offended party. Even a man sentenced to punishment by the State could avoid punishment by compensating the victim.[25] The power to pardon shifts ever so slowly to a territorial power when custom and the cooperative ethic is strong. In this connection, Weber observed that in ancient India and China, the "State" was devoted to making verses and literary masterpieces and was without power to punish or to pardon offenders, due to the deeply imbedded customs of strong peasant clans. The same applied in Europe until Roman law broke the power of similar kindreds.[26]

In the second feudal age down to 1250, repopulation and the makings of an economic revolution took shape. Given the persistence of customary law the commercial principle or what Weber called the "alien ethic"[27] grew not internally but externally and toward the East. Cloth centers emerged nearly everywhere —Flanders, Picardy, Bourges, Languedoc, Lombardy—but from the end of the eleventh century, with the creation of artisans and merchants on a vastly larger scale, in urban places, internal trade came into its own. With it came the institutionalization of private property, citizen-entrepreneurship, and the market system. Men of commerce began to compete with each other with the same unabashed ruthlessness as had characterized international trade prior to the inter-nalization of this ethic.[28] Under the market ethos, since society could not share one's risks and costs, it could not share one's opportunities and gains. Each man as an entrepreneur was responsible for himself, his conduct, and its consequences good or bad. This ethic came eventually to expression in civil and criminal law and in the rational State. But in judicial processes, especially in criminal law proce-dures, this ethic held little significance because States had not yet developed a clear monopoly over the power to pardon, and few of the ruthless practices common to the newly developing world of commerce had come to be proscribed under any legal order. Whether acts of war or of punishment and crime, the only intended harms proscribed were for the most part "blood harms" and had little to do with violations of private property, breaches of market contracts, and entitlement to allodial (private) property.[29]

Which acts of intended violence, in feuds or war or in trials by combat, are crimes and which are punishments? In the absence of any singular, dominant State capable of continually reducing feuds to crime and penal sanction, crime and penal sanction disappear, and where kinship solidarity between kindreds is strong, war disappears. Interclan marriages may have preserved solidarity in the first feudal age. Certainly no State functioned to do this. In the twelfth century, crime was held not to exist during an interregnum—not even when destruction of royal palaces was involved. In any such power vacuum, people, as usual, relied on customary means of terminating disputes. The rationale was stated simply enough: "We served our emperor while he lived; when he died, we no longer had a sovereign."[30]

Collective reprisals against feudal principalities in the second feudal period were commonplace. In 1127, for example, the Duke of Brittany confessed inability to protect his monasteries from assaults by his own vassals. Evidently the expansion of feudalism by sub-infeudation reduced certain marriages up and down the feudal scale, and with this, fealty and companionage were reduced to meaninglessness. Incentives for settling feuds by indemnity had thus vanished, and the feud along with other acts of feudal justice ceased to restore solidarity. In the absence of fealty the strength of authority collapsed and no principality could muster sufficient military force, eventually, to fill the void.[31]

Throughout both feudal ages there emerged no clear distinction between a personal leader or champion and the abstract idea of power. Not even kings were able to rise above family sentiments.[32] Against the force of custom and shared responsibility for individual conduct, States of the first feudal age were weak. With the force of custom and shared responsibility, they were strong. As bonds of fealty waned with the expansion of feudal estates—from top to bottom of the feudal scale—the ethic of shared responsibility for conduct collapsed. Feuds, wars, petty violence increased in frequency and savagery. The forms of tradition remained *as forms*, but interpersonal sentiments favoring peace gave them no meaning. What gave them meaning was the temper of violence and irreparably wounded honor. In all this, traditional authority, stripped of fealty and companionage, was powerless.

Toward the close of the second feudal age, feudalism of old had collapsed, and feudal authority in the midst of chaos was on the threshold of transformation. Under the ethic of shared responsibility, crime and penal sanction did not exist. Without it, and before the development of citizenship and the formally rational State—toward the end of feudalism—only reprisals and counterreprisals existed. In neither situation was there either criminal law or a force strong enough to impose it on each individual as an individual. Individualism without ethic and without institutions to regularize it was born of the collapse of feudal institutions.

RATIONAL INSTITUTIONS AND THEIR RELATION TO CRIME AND PENAL SANCTION

The institutional chaos of the latter middle ages—extending well into the fourteenth century—and the steady decline of the ethic of shared responsibility left feudal authority impoverished and impotent to arrest the increasing savagery of interminable feuds, wars, petty violence and brigandage. The vassalage, tied to landed interests, could no longer rely on fealty and tallage from lesser ranks for their political and economic support. Nor could perpetuity of landed wealth be relied upon from the fourteenth century on. Royal revenues and power were drying up as fealty declined, and of necessity royal authority sought revenues elsewhere, if only to raise armies to put down recalcitrants in the realm.

Not all was chaos. Petty merchants throughout Europe, once objects of scorn, had already begun to develop, with their artisans, the institutions of private property, exchange of titles to property in markets growing steadily in the second feudal age, and a labor force freed from feudal ties. Even by the thirteenth century, these merchants had become dedicated to the business of creating opportunities for continued, renewable gains—calling for stern rejection of sentiment and sympathy for any who might lose heavily in trade relations. It called for monklike pursuit of gain. Initially banished, outside the feudal city, these pariahs grew with every decline of feudal institutions, and with them grew the ethic of individual responsibility. In the midst of feudal anomie, this ethic—expressed institutionally in market contracts—finally supplanted the cooperative ethic. It did so with the eventual alliance between European monarchs and the rising merchant class.

The alliance created the formally rational State and citizenship and had direct bearing upon the advent of crime and penal sanction. Petty merchants throughout Europe gained fantastic wealth and with it power directly in consequence to the wars and feuds of the landed nobility. Such wars, in absence of fealty and tallage, had to be financed from outside the system. War loans, using land as collateral, were made to such nobles by merchants. Lands once held by nobles in perpetuity under laws of primogeniture and entail were regularly mortgaged by both parties in conflict. Every war meant that the land of one of the parties in conflict would fall to the merchant making the loan and not to the winner of the battle. Dobb observed that from the War of Roses onward, the landed wealth of Europe fell in this manner into the hands of merchants like fish into their nets.[33] As most wealth had been landed wealth held out of the market by laws of primogeniture and entail, this transfer of land to the merchant class made land a commodity for buying and selling *as private property* in the interest of profit. Any labor attached to such land under serfdom was freed from feudal ties to that land, and so were the nobles themselves. Human relations underwent profound transformation.

The plight of monarchs in raising revenues became more acute since revenues had come previously from landed nobles all the way up the feudal scale. Now in the hands of merchants, changing hands with every sale, land came to resemble mobile capital. It became clear that the destiny of monarchs was at once the prosperity of merchants. In this way the State cut its bond with family relations. The kinship aspects of the feudal State vanished. Tied to the interests of an entrepreneurial world, authority and power became abstract. In aligning itself with capital and the interests of capital, the State came to guarantee as law both the ethic and the practices which had emerged among merchants prior to the alliance.

The annuity bond arising from personal debts and war loans, the stock certificate, the bill of exchange, the commercial company, the mortgage, trust deeds, and the power of attorney—all were practices of merchants which grew with the collapse of feudal institutions and which became guaranteed in law with the alliance between monarchs and the entrepreneurial class.[34] With this alliance the remnants of shared responsibility for gains and losses were bypassed along with the social control value of customary law, kinship as a restraint upon power, and the sentiments of fealty and companionage. Local feudal worlds such as kindreds and medieval cities lost all autonomy and authority as the nation-state emerged. Everywhere cities in Europe came under the power of competing national States as a condition. Weber observed, of the perpetual struggle for power in peace and war:

> This competitive struggle created the largest opportunities for modern capitalism. The separate States had to compete for mobile capital, which dictated to them the conditions under which it would assist them to power. Out of this alliance of the State with capital, dictated by necessity, arose the national citizen class, the bourgeoisie in the modern sense of the word. Hence, it is the closed national State which afforded to capitalism its chance for development —and as long as the national State does not give place to a world empire capitalism also will endure.[35]

Just as the national State came to recognize and guarantee, as well as create, civil laws relating to market relations, private property, labor, imports, exports, and tariffs, it likewise came to have full power to create and impose criminal laws which related to the same institutions of capitalism. Under the ethic of individual responsibility, any citizen, even one forgiven by his kin or community, could be penally sanctioned as an individual by an abstract State and without much probability of reprisal against the State on the part of those who had forgiven him.

45

With the advent of the formally rational State, punishment was no longer an act of war. And any violation of criminal law—defined by the State—came to be seen as a harm against the State.

With authority behind the institutions of capitalism, and as the commercial principle became intense and diffused through the commercial and industrial revolutions, criminal law proscribed far more behaviors as crimes than had ever existed even in the second feudal age. In addition to the short list of blood harms, fornication, and adultery which had been dealt with on the shared responsibility basis, the State created new crimes and punishments directly as the institutions of capitalism advanced. Moreover, the older blood harms—including the older forms of justice—became criminal in that the State now specifically proscribed them and fixed to them penal sanctions. Thus the State obtained a monopoly over the processing of acts of violence.

Apart from the older harms criminal laws were established primarily for the protection and development of the institutions of capitalism. The reference here is not simply to penal sanctions levied against robbery, theft, burglary, or other violations of private property. It is to penal sanctions which directly controlled the manner in which social structure would develop in cities. It is to penal sanctions which had direct bearing on determining the organization of the division of labor in society and consequently upon the class structure of commercial settlements.

Criminal laws strangled the ability of lower classes (those alienated from landed feudal ties who had migrated to cities as "free labor") to possess tools or capital goods, raw materials, and also, on pain of heavy penal sanction, forbade association with guild masters.[36] In short, upward mobility became a crime unless guild masters themselves chose to elevate the status of an artisan. Thus penal sanctions guaranteed by the State guaranteed a continuous labor force (whether employed or not) and created two classes of citizens—one bound by criminal laws and penal sanctions, and another bound only by nonpunitive civil laws. The situation is hardly different today in this respect.[37] Under the formally rational State, second-class citizens are never in a position to be governed only by civil laws—they are never, therefore, beyond incrimination.

CROSS-CULTURAL PARALLELS

These historical observations have significant cross-cultural parallels. Wherever we witness a "third-world" country adopting political and economic systems roughly similar to those under the formally rational State, we find the ethic of shared responsibility for individual conduct giving way to the ethic of individual responsibility for individual conduct. Whenever we see any Western national State engaged in active warfare with any country governed by the ethic of shared responsibility, we see a State engaged in the savage business of reducing this ethic to that of individual responsibility, and in the transformation of customary institutions to "rational" institutions founded upon calculable law. This is done either directly, or indirectly through the establishment of puppet regimes on foreign soils. Submission of every individual in a territory—as an individual—to a single power reduces a war of political equals to submission of individuals as individuals and reduces a great many practices of the vanquished to the status of crimes.

The power to pardon under the formally rational State also played an increasing role in the determination of crime and penal sanction as well as a most significant role in the determination of two forms of "justice" which up to the present time measures the difference between the privileged and the nonprivileged in relation to crime and its prosecution. The State acquired the power to pardon because the power to forgive-without-punishment became meaningless in the last days of feudalism and because a few still stable forms of feudalism yielded that power to emergent States. Thus, replacing a diffused, collective act of forgiveness was the impersonal, concentrated power to pardon invested in a separated political community as an enforceable monopoly. This empowered the State to levy penal sanctions.

It was observed that the power to pardon relative to the rendering of penal sanctions is rarely used, and that penal sanctions coupled with the meaninglessness of forgiveness logically undermines the restorative power of society. The reference here was to the use of full pardon. There are, however, partial or qualitative pardons which are implicit in the reduction of corporal punishments to fines, and in some cases eventually to the abolition of fines. This amounts to the gradual abolition of punishment by means of partial pardon. It also means the abolition of crime to which penal sanction was fixed.

Just as the State can manufacture crimes by proscribing specific acts and fixing to them penal sanctions, so can the State abolish a crime by removal of these sanctions. But partial abolition of crime stems from reduction of a given penal sanction from capital or corporal punishments to fines.

As Rusche and Kirchheimer have already observed, this reduction partially legitimates the behavior to which the fine becomes attached.[38] In effect, the fine means the State's willingness to withhold punishment provided that the violator is willing and able to pay the price. It goes without saying that if the fine is a negligible amount in relation to the profit made by violating the law, under capitalism, then it will continue to be violated at no expense to the State. For those who are unable to pay such fines, the prison walls loom large indeed. It is in this sense that the State partially pardons the wealthy their harms against others in society but fails to pardon the poor for the same crimes. It is thus no mere play on words to say that crime is what poor men are in jail for.

Then what is partly legitimate for upper classes becomes totally "immoral" for lower classes. In either case the State cannot lose. Revenues from wealthy lawbreakers are more than sufficient to offset fiscal costs associated with operating and maintaining prisons—especially when one views what sink holes most prisons are. If such revenues prove inadequate, then the rest is made up by the public tax dollar. If prison maintenance comes wholly through taxes and bond issues, then revenues from fines make up a clear profit for the treasury of the State.

But there is more to this partial pardon, because of a basic ambiguity regarding how to conceive the fine. Is it actually a penal sanction? Is it, to the contrary, a tax levied for the privilege of violating criminal law? Or, is it a price charged by the State for the right or license to violate laws for which only the poor would be imprisoned? In any case, the State either becomes an entrepreneurship which exchanges the right to violate criminal law for a price called a fine—or else it becomes an agency in which the fine is standard fiscal policy very like a tax on the rich and less rich to pay for punishing the poor for having violated criminal laws the State itself created! There is a subtle mechanism here, in that the State is always in a position to proscribe as criminal only those acts which are bound to maximize revenues—if the price is right—and to maximize (or minimize) imprisonment if the price is not right or if it is beyond the ability of people to pay it.

Through manipulations such as these, the State can increase or decrease crime rates at will just as it can create whole new categories of crimes for partial legitimation when revenues are wanting. The central irony—in view of the active role of the State in the manufacture of crime—is that every civil and criminal law created by the State assumes that only the individual citizen is responsible for the act he performed and for its consequences. Through this legal fiction the State exempts itself from any responsibility for crimes and crime rates and at once exonerates itself from any guilt for having punished any man for a crime the State invented.

This ethic of individual responsibility is a legal fiction and is both socially and psychologically insupportable. It is the central myth of both citizen and State. Yet, despite the State's causal role in crime, the myth lives on as an eternal verity among most of the very people the State has punished and "rehabilitated," and among those whose lives and fortunes are governed by legally imposed conditions over which such people have little or no control. As long as consensus over the verity of this myth is high, good citizens will continue to ascribe to criminal laws a moral significance, and to this extent the position of the State is strong and secure against any serious threat of a general uprising from among those it governs.

But consensus changes. The moral value of such laws and sanctions then falls suspect. The fictional character of the theory of individual responsibility becomes clear as noonday, for the very laws thought to have had great moral significance come to be recognized not as a grass-roots manifestation of Durkheimian society but as the product of the class-bound State, bound to its narrowed interests in "peace" and war—demanding submission from second-class citizens to laws and judicial practices which serve only the interests of a few.

The illusion that the State represents the interests of all citizens then passes away, and even fools could see the vast differences between society and the political community exploiting society in the name of society and public welfare. Since fools could see it, so could most criminologists who now pander to the interests of the State in the name of science. And in the interest of saving their skins, they would "discover" and reveal what people had come to know already—that there are no scientific grounds for defining crime as an act against society and every reason to define criminal laws and penal sanctions as subdued warfare waged by one powerful segment of civil society against an individuated segment of citizens. Short of any general recognition of this, the professionalist's sinecure, begotten of service to the State and its institutions (in the name of science) is not at risk, and because of sinecure the role of the State in the manufacture of crimes is scarcely noted.

STATELESS SOCIETIES IN RELATION
TO HARMS AND THEIR DISPOSAL

The Nuer, the Bantu of Kavirondo, and the Tallensi are without States in that no one of them possesses a separated, continuous political community having any judicial, lawmaking, or executive capacity either to govern the members of society as citizens or to be solely in charge of relations with outside tribes in peace or war.[39] Calculable law as it has come to exist in the West—in either of its civil or criminal forms—is absent. Thus, in these societies there are no norms characterized by politicality and penal sanction. Citizenship and entrepreneurship as these appear in formally and substantively rational States are absent. And the only occasion in which a person may come under the ethic of individual responsibility for his conduct is the rare instance when collective punishment is levied in the forms of physical pain, death, and banishment. Even here, where the punished is regarded as a victim of evil spirits and is believed to be practicing witchcraft, it cannot be certain whether it is the individual or the spirit assumed to possess him who is believed to be the victim of punishment. This means that the idea of individual responsibility does not exist as an ethic. All that is known is that magical ceremonies repeatedly failed to terminate harms.

In none of these societies do crime and penal sanction exist. What is observable are harms and counterharms, their settlement by arbitration and compensation (between clans), as well as harms within clans and their settlement magically. Only as a last resort is anything like punishment rendered. It must be emphasized here that punishment is not necessarily a penal sanction. While penal sanction is a punishment, not all punishments are penal sanctions.

Penal sanction is a State-specified punishment *fixed* in law to a conduct *specifically* proscribed by any law which has *politicality*, and crime is the specific conduct to which a penal sanction is fixed. Both imply a State. While punishments may take place in absence of a State, no punishment is a penal sanction unless a State is present. While crime does not exist where penal sanctions are absent, no intended harm can be a crime unless penal sanctions are present. Punishment alone does not signify a crime has taken place, but penal sanction does. In absence of penal sanction, a punishment signifies only that either an intended or unintended harm took place or was believed to have taken place. Punishment without penal sanction is a rule of custom. Penal sanction is a rule of State law.

In further clarification, civil law, as it emerged in Western culture, also implies a State—as well as citizenship and the ethic of individual responsibility for conduct. While it has politicality, it lacks penal sanction. Violations of it, when pressed by an injured party, require only that the party be compensated for his loss. Nothing is paid to the State by way of fine or other punishment. But compensation without punishment is not what determines whether a law is a civil one. This is a common error. What makes a law a civil one is the fact that it has *politicality* without penal sanction and is guaranteed by the State—since failure to comply with a civil court order becomes a violation of criminal law and subject to penal sanction. Thus, civil law, either created or recognized by the State as part of its legal order, is calculable and is the epitome of formally rational law.

Some students of culture neglect this point and often violate their own rules of method in doing so by assuming that what is the product of Western culture must apply to all other cultures. Thus Wagner, for example, observed how impossible it is to distinguish criminal from civil law among the Bantu of Kavirondo—as if there were a distinction to be made.[40] That society, without a State, has neither. Custom lacks politicality, guaranteed law, as well as penal sanction. This point is respected, however, by Evans-Pritchard who observed that among the Nuer (a Stateless society also) there is no law in the strict sense because there is no one among the Nuer with legislative or judicial functions.[41]

Without any significant distortion of the situations which we find in these three societies, the following applies. One who kills another from a different clan receives the protection of his own clan since each is jointly responsible for the conduct of any one member. Feuds following such an incident may be avoided by ceremony and mediation conducted by elders or diviners who arrange satisfactory settlement by agreed-upon compensation which the clan of the killer pays. Punishment does not take place. Feuds may be terminated either by this same method or by the death of any member of the clan of the killer. It is not essential that the killer be the one to die by avengement. In this situation neither crime nor punishment take place. Killings take place and they are acts of warfare. Each clan engaged in a feud operates on the principle of collective responsibility. Even in cases where a killing takes place within a clan, individual responsibility does not appear except in extreme cases of often repeated harms. Among the Bantu of Kavirondo, clan solidarity is so strong that when one kills another the immediate recourse is to sacrifice an animal to propitiate the spirits and to hold purification ceremonies to make it safe for the killer's kinsmen to resume relations with him.[42]

When punishment occurs in these Stateless societies, the most serious forms are banishment and death. Either may take place—but only for intraclan harms—after ceremonies have repeatedly failed to make the offender stop his offenses. Ceremonies of restoration and punishment are collective. Restorations amount to collective forgiveness without punishment and are quite different from formal pardons conducted by a State. Moreover, formal pardons take place most infrequently and penal sanctions are commonplace in societies having States, whereas in Stateless society forgiveness without punishment is commonplace while punishments are rare.

Perhaps the most threatening form of punishment is banishment, and the implications of banishment are both interesting and significant. Only when a man is banished does the principle of individual responsibility apply to him. Only then, out from under the protection of the ethic of shared responsibility for his conduct, does he experience the full meaning of being fully responsible for his livelihood, and for any encounters he may have with others. Deprived of everything which once had meaning for him, he may be set upon by anyone either in his own or from another clan for any reason whatever. The responsibility for the consequences of any act he may perform is his alone to bear.

Like the citizen the banished man is removed from the protection of his kindred and the sentiment attached thereto. Unlike the citizen the banished has no institutional life outside kinship bonds short of migration, perhaps, to cities dominated by Western institutions. Pariahlike, between two worlds, at anyone's mercy, his fate is only his own to ponder. There are no market relations to be established with others like himself, no State to guarantee them under civil laws or to bring market behavior and private property under control of criminal law and penal sanctions. But neither the banished nor the citizen may find either protection or restoration to good standing through traditional institutions of kinship and religion as founded on the ethic of shared responsibility. Therein is their sameness.

While the above historical and cross-cultural observations support answers to first order questions posed initially, and while they support the thesis of this work, drawing them together is reserved until the presentation of the second part of this study which deals with the sameness of crime and penal sanctions. It is sufficient here only to note that crimes and penal sanctions are not universal but are unique forms of intended harms limited to specific countries and to a definite period of Western history. They emerged, roughly, as a post-fifteenth-century phenomenon and as an integral part of a cluster of new institutions expressing individualism as an ethic—*viz.*, formally rational States, citizenship, the institutions of capitalism, and calculable laws composed of two related legal orders (guaranteed civil or commercial laws, and criminal codes which both comprise the legal basis of the citizen role). While general features of crime (blood harms, feuds) are determined by the State and citizenship, special features are determined by the emergence and development of the institutions of capitalism in which innovated criminal laws were instrumental in the creation and early solidification of the division of labor of capitalism, in expropriation of both the tools and materials of work from artisans, and in creating a permanent split between occupational types (entrepreneurs-laborers). Thus these laws solidified for masters only, the role and class of citizen-entrepreneur. With power fully behind this class, any act could become criminal simply by fixing a penal sanction to it and processing it through a growing judicial machinery. When the ethic of shared responsibility collapsed, and when anomie created the ethic and the institutions of individualism, no penal sanction could then be interpreted as an act of war subject to collective reprisal. Then, the formally rational State could stand immune to intended harms lodged against it from outraged clans, for kinship based on the traditional ethic was utterly smashed. Henceforth, any violence by the State against any family member was given and accepted as penal sanctioning of a citizen. Forgiveness without punishment was meaningless, and many forms of communal punishments had become crimes.

CRIME AND PENAL SANCTION
AS A SINGLE BEHAVIORAL CLASS

Establishing crime and penal sanction as a single class involves more than observing that each is injurious, for innumerable acts of chance daily result in injury to others. Such acts are neither crimes nor punishments. Moreover, even though crimes and punishments are both intended, the fact of intent does not by itself establish that crimes and penal sanctions are the only harms which intent subsumes. Since there are other intended harms outside the crime-penal sanction complex, crime and penal sanction comprise but one part of the total behavioral class of intended harms.[43]

Even so, it is valid to state that no harm can be either crime or penal sanction without intent, when "intent" is a deliberate functioning to reach a goal. It was established in the first part of this work that feuds, wars, trials by combat, and communally given punishments have, when rational States appear, become crimes and that crimes do not exist prior to the advent of such States. Thus, these acts fall outside the crime-penal sanction complex. Even communally given punishments do not fall within the State-given class of punishments called penal sanctions. Thus, formal punishment in the modern political sense refers only to penal sanctions.

Apart from these "pre-State" harms which do not fall under the crime-penal sanction complex, there are other intended harms which, under modern States, fall outside this complex but are condoned by such States as noncriminal harms. Yet, any one of them can be made a crime by the State, first by defining it as a harm against the State, and second by attaching to it a penal sanction. This method of creating crime—or of abolishing it by removal of penal sanctions—is as characteristic today in the treatment of psychotic and civil harms as it was when, historically, traditional forms of justice (collective reprisals, feuds, trials by combat, and communal punishments) were outlawed as crimes. What then are the other intended harms which fall today outside the crime and penal sanction complex; what attributes characterize them which do not characterize crime and penal sanction? The following may be observed:

1. Harms not proscribed as crime which fall under civil or guaranteed law:[44] violations of civil contract agreements, disputed claims involving legal interpretation of liabilities and obligations under contractual agreements, inability to meet contracted obligations, losses due to another's profit, losses

in recovery of bad debts, bankruptcy losses, and innumerable other harms in commercial transactions covered by civil laws and regulated by civil courts and commissions.

2. Harms against the general public by private commercial corporations: fraud, deceptive packaging, mislabeling, distribution of toxic foods, drugs, and cosmetics.[45]

3. Harms "excusable" upon legal proof of nonresponsibility of the offender at the time of his proscribed performance: juvenile harms in certain States, cases of "legal insanity"—as governed by statute, judicial procedure or both.

4. Excused harms involving direct violation of criminal laws but which are formally ignored at law enforcement level, or which are handled extralegally in civil courts or within private professional associations such as the American Medical Association: medical malpractices, fee splitting among doctors, violations of a variety of criminal laws by corporation executives, violations of rights of minorities by police and military personnel, violations of blue laws. (Interestingly, long unenforced laws come daily to be used by police in violating civil rights of minorities—arresting a man for violating old "syndicalist laws" would fall here.)

Harms listed above share with crimes and penal sanctions the attribute of intent, and they tell us something indirectly about crime and penal sanction as a single behavioral class. A few observations may be made in this connection:

1. With one exception, the above harms are either not punishable or are excusable. Intended harms falling under civil law call only for restitution, not repression.[46]

2. There is nothing intrinsic to any of the above harms, nothing to be observed in behaviors themselves, which could warrant their being outside the crime-penal sanction class of harms. Depending upon whether the State proscribes and penally sanctions any of these harms, any of them could fall under the classification of crime—just as any crime could become a civil harm with the removal of its penal sanction and its definition as a harm against the State. Indeed, this has been much of the history of the making and the abolition of crimes by the State. Debt ceased being a crime in this manner and became a civil matter. Early, traditional actions based upon customs—as seen —became crimes by State manipulation of penal sanctions and politicality. Examples are so numerous as to observe an integral relation, an interflow through time, between civil and criminal acts. *Either can become the other.*

3. The only criteria which determine whether any behavior is civil or criminal are not behavioral criteria (as many psychologists, ministers, philosophers, and "sociologists" suppose) but are external criteria applied by the State— chiefly, politicality and penal sanction.

4. Whatever determines the civil or criminal status of any specific conduct are the purely external manipulations of law, law enforcement, and penal sanc-

tions; and any group, whatever its value system, upon achieving control of political machinery can make anything criminal (at least for a while) and can prevent condemnation of anything insofar as it can maintain itself securely against collective reprisal.

5. Punishability of an act is determined by the power of the State. Ultimately this power rests upon the intensity and spread of the myth that each individual is responsible for his own conduct and that the State is not. At the same time, this power is determined by who holds command over the means of political violence—the instruments of penal sanction.

What may be inferred from these observations of civil and other harms which bears upon the singular character of crime and penal sanction?

All intended harms of the crime-penal sanction complex are punishable. That is, if crime and penal sanction are essentially the same things, then as a class they *both* must differ from the above-listed harms in being punishable and not excusable. Certainly anything the State defines as criminal is punishable and is not excusable except as the State exercises its power of pardon. Interestingly, in civil harms where the power to pardon rests not with the State but with citizen associations, the State has no power to punish. Only until this power to pardon civil harms is usurped by the State does the State have the power to punish. In any such instance, the usurpation is accomplished by statute proscribing a civil harm as criminal and pardonable, and fixing to it a penal sanction in lieu of pardon by the State.

THE PUNISHABILITY OF PENAL SANCTIONS AND THE REBIRTH OF CRIME

Anything legally proscribed as criminal is punishable, but is penal sanction itself punishable? If crime and penal sanction are both punishable, then by these external criteria they belong to the same class, and it is only by these external criteria that they differ fundamentally from all other intended harms. Indeed it is vain to look for any State-supported rationale under which penal sanctions performed by the State are punishable as crimes. But one need not search far back in history, or look in vain cross-culturally for cases where punishments have transmuted into crimes through social movements and revolutions which transform the institutional structure of society. It is exactly in such transformations where the true relation between crimes and penal sanctions is most clearly seen.

With the decay of consensus over the legitimacy of dominating social institutions and laws supporting them, further penal sanctions imposed by the State for violations of such laws have come to be viewed collectively as themselves criminal (in the nontechnical sense). But the technical fact of criminality is not established until the threat of collective reprisal against the State is made good by the deposition of the State, or else is terminated by the collapse of the movement against the State. In the latter case few changes take place in the criminal law and the characteristics of crime remain relatively unchanged. But where political movements succeed, where State-supported institutions are transformed, many of the old proscriptions under criminal law disappear—giving place to new proscriptions subject to pardon and penal sanction. Crime is thus reborn but with a different face.

With the rise of a new political community to full power and with full or partial transformation of once dominant institutions, what once was criminal becomes legal, immune to reprisal by the State. If economic institutions are transformed, a host of activities covered only by civil laws and guaranteed restitutions are proscribed as criminal and penally sanctioned. Just as the new State makes legal much of what once was criminal, so it also makes criminal much of what once was legal, as both civil and criminal laws are transformed. Moreover, what once were meted out as punishments by the old State are punished as crimes by the new one.

THE REDUCTION OF CRIMES AND
PENAL SANCTIONS TO REPRISALS

On the eve of successful revolutionary movements, when one State totters and a new one ascends, the dichotomy between crime and penal sanction blurs and vanishes with the decline of the power of the descending State to keep this dichotomy alive and credible in the minds of citizens now risen in open revolt. Citizenship, as a role defined in civil and criminal law, itself disappears as hour by hour the descending State loses ability to secure itself against those reprisals which blindly it insists are crimes. Crime and penal sanctions then reduce merely to intended harms and counter harms—to reprisals and counter reprisals between two separate, warring States.

Until the issue of power is settled in this trial by combat, no harm is either crime or penal sanction, simply because neither the ascending nor the descending State can create and apply to the other any laws having politicality and penal sanction. In this power vacuum, penal sanctions become acts of war; crimes are the same. The object of each State is to transmute the other's harms to the status of crimes, and to force acceptance of its own harms as penal sanctions. This is the primary objective in all warfare involving States locked in a power struggle with other States; it makes no difference whether one State emerged from among those governed by an older State or whether two nation-States are at war. The objective is the same. Wars differ sharply from feuds in this regard. In feuds, political submission is not an objective; avengement is. When feuds end, each party goes back home with its equality intact. When wars end, equality of the parties at war is unthinkable. The vanquished are never at home.

Until this objective is reached, neither the ascending nor the descending State has the power to pardon the other, and forgiveness is impossible. Murders and executions are indistinguishable—having become killings, the casualties of war, they have little meaning until long buried and come to be remembered as heroic sacrifices in the struggle for justice and law. They then become part of the State's community of memories, officially approved by "educated" men. But in the struggle, what is moral and what is not are totally inaccessible to reason, because reason, like God, is anyone's slave until the issue of power is settled. Whatever becomes moral in the long run depends upon how the war is terminated and upon whose values become institutionalized in everyday society as meaningful law, not merely as enforceable statutes.

The above inference that all harms in the crime-penal sanction complex are punishable is supported by every case of institutional transformation in the history of any society undergoing one. Except in social upheaval, penal sanctions are not *immediately* punishable as crimes, but because institutional transformations may be expected to take place at any future time, the following principle is valid:

> Any harm punishable by the State as crime stands ultimately in the same status as any harm imposed by that State as punishment.

Penal sanctions are punishable as crimes whenever institutional transformations take place, and the illusion that crime and penal sanction comprise two independent species of behavior is sustained as if factual only when a given State and its institutions are either supported by consensus or else when (by coercion) that State can otherwise keep itself immune to successful reprisals from any source.

THE EXCUSABILITY OF INTENDED HARMS IN RELATION TO CRIME AND PENAL SANCTION

In the list of intended harms outside the crime-penal sanction complex, it was seen that such harms were either excused or were excusable—that they were not immediately punishable by the State. Neither excusability nor punishability have anything to do with the nature of the actual conduct which is excused or punished. Thus there is nothing intrinsic to behavior itself which determines either its punishability or its excusability. Moreover, any harm in the civil category can —either by revolution or by the State's manipulation of law—become punishable or subject to penal sanction. Also, any harm in the criminal category can become a wholly civil matter by removal of penal sanction. It is the State, therefore, which determines at any given time what specific acts are excusable or punishable.

Even within the crime category, certain harms are excusable or at least are condoned or ignored by the State, inasmuch as scores of violations of various criminal laws, applicable only to professions and executives, are processed as if merely civil matters in courts where no penal sanctions can be meted out. Thus, the more command one has of central institutions, the greater his immunity to punishment, the less his probability of arrest and incrimination in criminal court. This observation means only that differential excusability and punishability is a social fact of differential proximity to political power. It is scarcely headline material—except for sociologists whose slum theory of crime is still prevalent in the classroom. By and large, just as civil laws applied only to the old guild masters, and criminal laws only to artisans, so does the same situation prevail today. The closer one is to power, the less the risk of incrimination, and the more "civil" are one's harms against others.

Nonpunishability of civil harms today attests only to the positive interest of the State to maintain certain institutions such as semiprivate national and multinational corporations, national and transnational markets, and militarism as part of this complex. Differential excusability will continue to exist insofar as this interest is continuous. The important fact is not that these institutions are "economic" but that business is a system of power,[47] and that these institutions are the means of international power politics and are part of the total arsenal for making war at home and abroad—of reducing behaviors globally to the status of crimes.

VICTIMIZATION AS A COMMON FEATURE
OF CRIME AND PENAL SANCTION

There being no behavioral attributes among civil harms to warrant the separation of civil harms from those of the crime penal sanction complex, it is necessary to see if distinguishing attributes might be found among crimes and penal sanctions which are not common to civil harms. Here, victimization appears as such an attribute, but again under control of the State as will be seen.

Both crime and penal sanction presuppose a victim, i.e., a personal or abstract object upon whom an intended harm is imposed. In both, the victim is clear-cut. For crime, the victim is by definition the State, the political community which defines crime as an intended harm against itself. For penal sanction, the victim is a citizen reduced to the status of convict. Intended harms of civil law jurisdiction presuppose no clear-cut victim, and if the term "victim" has any meaning in market relations, its meaning refers only to nonpunishable torts, unless a clear violation of criminal law is involved and is prosecuted as such. In market relations, if victimization exists without violation of criminal law, the "victim" is indefinite, usually not known personally to the injuring party. "Victims" are diffuse.

Who is the victim when a man deliberately, under capitalism, initiates bankruptcy procedures? Who is the victim in contracts where one man who agreed to hold the other harmless against certain losses incurred those losses even when the second party caused them? Who is the victim when California orange growers corner the market and cause Florida growers heavy losses? Unambiguous answers to such questions are impossible. In most cases, the intent was to make profit by any legal means, not to make victims. Nothing about victimization here is as clear-cut as when a man murders another or when an executioner electrocutes him for having done it. But civil harms do pass under the jurisdiction of criminal law and become crimes. It is just here where the meaning of victim and victimization becomes clear.

When a civil harm passes under criminal law, the absence of a clear-cut victim continues to hold. But since that act is now defined as a harm against the State, the "victim" becomes the State. There are at least three types of "crimes" in which this is seen: (1) acts involving personal indulgence either for pleasure or for inflicting injury or death on oneself, (2) acts involving personal and collective protest, and (3) acts which are outlawed forms of entrepreneurship, or illegal enterprises of capitalism.

The first type includes, for example, "pot smoking," taking LSD, shooting hard narcotics. While other people may be harmed in these acts of self-indulgence, the idea of intended victim is unclear—except by definition when the State intervened to declare itself the victim. *The second type* includes, for example, certain peaceful demonstrations, "sedition," obstructing "justice," alleged treason, failures to comply with draft requirements, active aid to persons to avoid the draft, public speeches against the draft which encourage resistance to the draft or to other State-supported policies. *The third type* includes, for example, prostitution, shilling, buying and selling hard narcotics, certain forms of gambling, making and selling bootleg whiskey, operating a wire service, playing the numbers game, and a host of other enterprises outlawed by the State as harmful to itself.

The only clear-cut "victim" in any of the above cases is the political community which defined these acts as harms against itself. Nothing seems more clear than that crime, legally construed, refers not to any person as victim but only to the State. When civil harms pass under criminal law, whether a real, personal victim was intended or not is not really an important question in deciding the criminality of the act.

Like civil harms, direct victims are not clearly visible in the above actions. Penal sanctions are fixed to these actions not because they may be harmful to others, for that is incidental, but because the State has proscribed them as harmful to its own interests. In short, crime has nothing to do with the fact that one person may intentionally harm another but everything to do with the manipulation of law, with the application of criteria *external* to the acts of harm themselves. Victimization stands with excusability and punishability as externally imposed characteristics which all too often are regarded as intrinsic to the behavior in question. One of the principal ironies of this is the great lengths that are taken in criminal court procedures to prove that "intent" was present in the act—as if "intent," even if subject to proof, were actually important.

There are indeed other harms proscribed by the State in which a direct victim is clearly visible: theft, burglary, robbery, sexual assault, fraud, embezzlement, confidence games, fee splitting in medicine, industrial espionage, price rigging among a multitude of corporation executives in bidding for government contracts, kidnapping. These intended harms cut across the whole scale of social classes. But here an important question arises: *are these harms crimes because the offender had in mind an intended victim, or are they crimes because in each case the State had defined itself as victim?* If there were no difference between the interests of the State and the welfare of all people it governs, then any offense by one person against another would at once be a harm against the State. But the State takes only token action in high crimes, and presses hard on low ones. Apparently, the State is less a victim of high crimes than of low ones like rape, robbery, and embezzlement. In each of the above cases, the fact that an offender may have had in mind an intended victim as object of harm is incidental. A crime, by State definition, is a harm against the State. On few occasions do murderers have the State in mind as the intended victim; yet it is the State-as-victim for which the man is punished. This must be true, unless the State is willing to say that crime is not a harm against the State.

As in all previous cases, attributes of behavior are not responsible for any legal class of behavior. What is responsible for civil harms and what is responsible for those deemed criminal are criteria external to the social behavior in question. By manipulation of proscription, politicality, and the power to punish and pardon, the State can make itself the symbolic victim of any act whatever—whether actually harmful or not—by defining it as such and by prosecution on the assumption that it is true.

The whole process from arrest through imprisonment to post confinement adjustment is a process of victimization not of the State but of the person who was judged to have made the State a victim. This process holds the full meaning of incrimination. It constitutes a life-long stigmatization of the "criminal"—a source of wealth for psychiatrists, ministers, police, judges, lawyers, clerks, politicians, social workers, and writers of novels. It is a State-created opportunity for continued renewable gains by a whole hierarchy of occupational types whose life-style is utterly dependent upon the continuation, not the termination, of this process. Nothing would harm the State more than to have no crime at all. It is this process which involves identification of the whole person by one act, and ultimately either making that person accept that narrowed self or to accept "rehabilitation" as based on the assumption that the narrowed self was the whole self. Is it not strange that when tried executives serve suspended sentences, they are denied the "benefits" of rehabilitation?

In legal procedure the personal victim of crime, though incidental, is often hard to identify, but the victim of punishment never is. Arrested, mugged, fingerprinted, numbered, tried, punished, released to officials, his identity is externally never uncertain. Punishment is an unambiguous consequence of a symbolic harm, but is only one part of the total process of victimization or incrimination, and unless the incriminated come to see themselves as criminals (either with pride or guilt), there are no behavioral characteristics by which the person of a criminal and the person of a punitive agent are separable as distinctly different species. The attributes which separate crime from penal sanction are external criteria—external to the social interaction to which these criteria are applied. Thus far it has only been shown that crime and penal sanction do not belong to behaviorally independent classes. What remains is to show that they are essentially the same. This recalls the question: do legal criteria for identifying crime also identify punishments meted out by the State?

THE SAMENESS OF CRIME AND PENAL SANCTION

Establishing that crime and penal sanction are the same may proceed by taking the criteria which the State uses for determining whether an act is criminal, and then testing to see if these same criteria apply with equal validity to penal sanctions. If they do, then even within the criminal law there is no way to differentiate crime from penal sanction on behavioral grounds, because the State's differentiae would establish merely that any penal sanction may also be regarded as criminal.

The differentiae of crime in relation to penal sanction derive from the characteristics of criminal law (uniformity, politicality, specificity, and penal sanction), and of these only specificity refers to the actual conduct in question or on trial. These characteristics are construed legally as criteria by which to determine whether a given performance is a crime, not whether the performer is criminal. Thus, proof of a crime is not itself taken as proof of criminality. Yet, the differentiae of crime, *derived* from the characteristics of criminal law, are used procedurally in court to determine criminality.

The present objective is not to test the scientific value of using these criteria as proofs but to see if they apply also to formal punishment. To demonstrate this, the same procedure used by Sutherland and Cressey will be followed, but with one difference. Instead of providing a case involving a crime to demonstrate the applicability of a given criterion, a case involving a penal sanction will be used (as in the table below). This is sufficient to the kind of proof required here, because if these differentiae are only the differentiae of *crime*, then no one of them could possibly be illustrated with a case of penal sanction—unless, of course, there *is* a real difference behaviorally between crime and penal sanction.[48]

BEHAVIORAL DIFFERENTIAE OF BOTH CRIME AND PENAL SANCTION

RULE	CASE AND RESULT
1. There must be an external consequence or harm. Mere intention without harm is insufficient.	A man is dead, having been executed by the State.
2. There must be a conduct leading to the harm.	In line of command, an authorized person closed the switch and caused a man, condemned in court, to die by electrocution.
3. Intent or *mens rea* (a deliberate functioning to reach a goal) must have been present.	Upon conviction in criminal court, after deliberated verdict of guilty, a man was sentenced to die by electrocution at an appointed time and place. In custody, that man was electrocuted as specified at that time and place.

RULE	CASE AND RESULT
4. Fusion or concurrence between intent and conduct must have existed.	*Case where fusion is absent:* a prison warden caused the wrong man to be electrocuted but deliberately (in error) acted to execute the condemned one. Penal sanction did not take place.
5. A "causal relation" between the harmful conduct and the harm must have been present.	*Case showing absence of causal relation:* While executing a condemned man, the latter died from food poisoning contracted earlier from the kitchen. This took full effect an instant before the switch was thrown. Penal sanction did not occur because causal relation was absent.

In the above five differentiae, what identifies crime and criminality also identifies penal sanction and punitive agents. In fact, it is far less complicated a task to identify penal sanction by the differentiae of crime than it is to identify crime—owing to the fact that proofs of existence of conduct, external harm, intent, fusion, and causal relation are all authentically recorded in State offices.

The above differentiae refer to behavior and its related attributes having to do with interaction, intent and causal relations involved with social interaction. They apply as well to penal sanction as to crime. The remaining two differentiae, presented below, are external to actual conduct and its attributes. And they are the only differentiae by which any possible distinction can be made between crime and penal sanction.

External Differentiae of Crime

A. The harm must be legally forbidden, i.e., proscribed in penal law, (Politicality)

B. There must be a legally prescribed punishment. (Penal Sanction)

It is quite obvious that these two differentiae of crime cannot be also the differentiae of punishment by the State. It follows that these externally applied measures are the only measures by which the State not only identifies crime, but they are at once the measures by which the State can manufacture crime at will. There is nothing in the first five differentiae to prevent them from applying with equal validity to penal sanctions. In terms of these few criteria, crime and formal punishment are one and the same forms of conduct. What the last two differentiae above reveal is that the only criteria by which these intended harms are made into distinct and independent classes reduce in the last analysis to power and who holds it. It is power alone which creates and sustains the illusion that crime and punishment are independent, mutually exclusive species of conduct. This illusion is basic to nearly all teachings of modern criminologists, armchair philosophers, psychiatrists and psychologists —all of whom claim validity for their positions on purely scientific grounds. Ironically, however, no position is less certain than theirs because this dichotomy, created and reified by the State and founded upon the fiction that only the governed are responsible—each for his own harms—is justifiable only on political and ideological grounds. To accept that only individuals *as individuals* are responsible for crime is at once to accept that the State is in no way a determinative factor in its advent and continuation—and this in the face of the fact that by manipulation of these external criteria whole categories of crime, either gradually or by revolutionary means, can be and have been abolished and replaced with others.

SUMMARY

Within the initial definitions, first and second order questions may now be answered on the basis of historical, cross-cultural and legalistic observations made in the foregoing sections. Crime and penal sanction in being limited to specific countries and to a period of Western history are not universal but are a function of the emergence of formally rational States, of citizenship under such states, and of the transfer of the power of pardon from communities based upon the ethic of shared responsibility to a political or territorial community founded upon the fiction of individual responsibility. With these institutions developed two related legal orders: State-guaranteed commercial and/or civil codes, and criminal laws—both of which define the general role expectations of citizenship at any given point in the history of formally rational States and the institutions supporting them.

While general characteristics of crime are determined by the emergence and continuation of the State and citizenship, special characteristics—with reference to what specific acts are proscribed—are determined by the kinds of institutions —socialist, capitalist, etc.—which the State supports. In the present study, these special features are determined by the emergence of the institutions of capitalism and by guaranteed commercial codes corresponding to emergent criminal laws which are meaningful only within a context where the market system, private property, and private laws of contract predominate.

The chief business of the State is to reduce the institutions founded upon the ethic of shared responsibility for individual conduct to those founded upon the fiction of individual responsibility while at the same time avoiding the probability of successful reprisals against itself. Obtaining a clear monopoly over the power to pardon is fundamental to this end. Any weakening of the solidarity of kinship and religious institutions, any weakening of social movements of citizens bent upon reconstruction of institutions supported by the State is instrumental to this end. The power of the State is enhanced accordingly. This principle holds regardless of whether one State, through war, reduces the acts of another to the status of crimes or whether a new State emerges within the corpus of society ruled by the State which is challenged.

With the power to pardon solidified, politicality and penal sanction as chief characteristics of the criminal law uncontestably emerge. It is only then that crime—as defined by the State itself—becomes possible. It is only then that the continuity of crime in some form becomes fundamental to the very existence of the State. And this form is determined by what the State chooses to sanction penally.

That the dichotomy between crime and penal sanction is sustained only by those who command the sources of political power is attested to whenever full or partial institutional transformations take place within societies already governed by a State. With the emergence of strong political movements, this dichotomy disappears as an enforceable entity, as all intended harms by either the ascendent or the descendent State reduce to counting the wounded and the dead—to reprisals and counterreprisals—in short, to war. And until the issue of power is settled in this trial by combat, crime and penal sanction are meaningless except as war. When the issue of power is settled, the dichotomy is again reified, and if later consensus stands behind it, crime and penal sanction will again be seen, erroneously, as mutually exclusive species of human conduct. The "morality" of the victorious will have become imposed; murders and executions will have risen again from their status of mere killings, and crimes and penal sanctions will have been reborn. The most crucial condition in keeping this dichotomy credible among the governed is the ability of the State to secure itself against collective reprisal from any source whatever.

Under the characteristics of the criminal law, and under the differentiae of crime, there are no criteria intrinsic to the behaviors called crime which can warrant separating crime and punishment as two mutually exclusive classes of conduct. Any harm punishable by the State as crime stands ultimately in the same status as any harm imposed by that State as a penal sanction. Moreover, of all the differentiae said to identify crime and criminality, the bulk of them apply with equal validity to penal sanctions. The two which clearly distinguish crime from penal sanctions are, again, the external criteria of politicality and penal sanction. And these are the chief measures by which the State can manufacture or abolish crime according to its own interests, and until the advent of institutional transformation, can remain beyond recrimination.

NOTES

[1] This assumption is reified daily by mass media's hue and cry about "the crime problem," "crime waves," the "need for more law and order," "more law enforcement" in "society's war on crime," more (but reformed) prisons, more rehabilitation (for the poor), more psychiatry and social services for "multi-problem families," more urban renewal.

[2] Textbooks typically discuss "crime" under Part I, and "punishment" under Part II, without discussing their common features or how punishments become crimes and vice versa. They agree that crime is relative but fail to state that the same is so of punishment. Even Georg Rusche and Otto Kirchheimer see punishment in a separate orbit—transforming its methods only when mutations occur in the economic system. See *Punishment and Social Structure* (New York: Columbia University Press, 1939), *passim*.

[3] These risks and rewards for professional services to off-campus supporters probably mean that any science of crime and punishment will not take place in academia.

[4] Max Weber, *On Law in Economy and Society*, trans. by E. Shils and M. Rheinstein (New York: Simon and Schuster, 1967), pp. 48, 162, 338 ff. The term "State" is used here in the sense of a coercive political community as defined by Weber. It may be seen as an ascendent political movement or "community of destiny" in Weber's terms.

[5] E. H. Sutherland and D. R. Cressey, *Principles of Criminology*, Seventh Edition (New York: Lippincott, 1966), pp. 10–13.

[6] This point was first made by C. R. Jeffery in his Ph.D. dissertation, *An Institutional Approach to a Theory of Crime* (Indiana University, 1954), Ch. I.

[7] E. E. Evans-Pritchard and M. Fortes, *African Political Systems* (London: Oxford University Press, 1958). See Introduction and last three chapters.

[8] Max Weber, *General Economic History*, trans. by Frank Knight (New York: Collier, 1961), pp. 232–258. "Roughly" is used here because the foundations of Weber's formally rational state appeared incipiently in the 12th century but did not appear in full until the time Weber specified.

[9] *Ibid.* p. 232. See references to "citizenship" and to the internalization of the "alien ethic" or commercial principle into each European country—as sharply contrasting with cooperative values —making each individual citizen, apart from his clan, responsible for his own conduct in market behavior.

[10] Marc Bloch, *Feudal Society*, trans. by L. A. Manyon, (Chicago: University of Chicago Press, 1964), Vol. I, pp. 208–210.

[11] *Ibid.*, Vol. I, Parts I and II, *passim*.

[12] *Ibid.*, pp. 72–103.

[13] *Ibid.*, Vol. II, pp. 443–444.

[14] *Ibid.*, Vol. I, pp. 109–116 ff.

[15] *Ibid.*, p. 116.

[16] *Ibid.*, p. 67.

[17] *Ibid.*, pp. 123–125.

[18] *Ibid.*, p. 125.

[19] *Ibid.*, p. 126. See Bloch's distinction between active and passive solidarity.

[20] *Ibid.*, p. 129.

[21] *Ibid.*, p. 128.

[22] *Ibid.*, pp. 128–129.

[23] *Ibid.*

[24] *Ibid.*, p. 129.

[25] Rusche and Kirchheimer, *op. cit.*, see note 26, p. 213.

[26] Weber, *General Economic History*, *op. cit.*, pp. 250 ff.

[27] *Ibid.*, p. 232.

[28] *Ibid.*

[29] Bloch, *op. cit.*, Vol. II, pp. 365 ff.

[30] *Ibid.*, p. 409 ff. Acts like this were regular in this period, because principalities were weak—no longer holding consensus and strong military forces. Under weak principalities "crime" meant only the clash of armies. Upholding custom in feuds led inadvertently (with other causes) to individuation of society through loss of fealty, meaningful epics, and the obsoleteness of the folk memory.

[31] *Ibid.*, Chapter XXX, pp. 408–421.

[32] *Ibid.*, p. 10 ff.

[33] Maurice Dobb, *Studies in the Development of Capitalism, Revised Edition* (New York: International Publishers, 1963), Ch. V, especially pp. 186–198.

[34] Weber, *General Economic History*, *op. cit.*, pp. 247–253 ff.

[35] *Ibid.*, p. 249.

[36] Rusche and Kirchheimer, *op. cit.*, Chapter II. See reference made to R. H. Tawney and to the latter's support of the above statement (note 19) where the State is described as a class State whose criminal laws protected only the interests of large capitalistic guild masters and held labor captive.

[37] E. H. Sutherland, *White Collar Crime* (New York: Holt, Rinehart & Winston, 1949).

[38] Rusche and Kirchheimer, *op. cit.*

[39] Evans-Pritchard and Fortes, *op. cit.*, *passim*. These observations also applied to other Bantu offshoots—Kikuyu, Meru, Embu—prior to imposition of British rule on these societies. See, D. H. Rawcliffe, *Struggle for Kenya* (London: Victor Gollancz, Ltd., 1954), *passim*, and Jomo Kenyatta's treatment of Kikuyu political institutions in *Facing Mount Kenya* (London: Secker and Warburg, 1938), *passim*.

[40] Gunter Wagner, "The Political Organization of the Bantu of Kavirondo," in Evans-Pritchard and Fortes, *op. cit.*, pp. 217–218.

[41] E. E. Evans-Pritchard, "The Nuer of the Southern Sudan," in Evans-Pritchard and Fortes, *op. cit.*, pp. 293–294.

[42] Wagner, *op. cit.*, p. 202 ff.

[43] Sutherland and Cressey, *op. cit.*, pp. 12–13. Jerome Hall's differentiae of crime are reduced by these men to seven criteria. Both Hall and these men fail to indicate that their differentiae of crime apply with equal force to penal sanction. See Hall's *Principles of Criminal Law*, Second Edition (Indianapolis: Bobbs-Merrill, 1960), pp. 14–26. See definition of intent as differing from motive.

[44] Weber, *On Law in Economy and Society*, *op. cit.*, pp. 12, 49–59; for discussion of State versus extra-State law, see pp. 16–17.

[45] Fred Cook, "The Corrupt Society," *The Nation*, June 1–8, 1963 Special Issue, *passim*.

[46] Emile Durkheim, *The Division of Labor in Society* (Glencoe, Ill.: Free Press, 1960), pp. 70–133, discussion of repressive and restitutive sanctions.

[47] Robert Brady, *Business as a System of Power* (New York: Columbia University Press, 1943).

[48] Sutherland and Cressey, *op. cit.*, pp. 12–13.

THE STATE AND CRIMINAL LAW*

William J. Chambliss

The creation of laws that define behavior as criminal or delinquent begins with enactment of legislation or a court decision that stipulates penal sanctions for the commission or omission of an act. The specific details of the process vary from country to country but the broad outlines are the same: some constituted body of officials declares some acts to be punishable by penal sanctions administered by the state. The state acts as a presumably independent agent enforcing the presumed morality of the people. There are of course places where this presumption is blatantly absurd and is not defended even by the law enforcers themselves: South Africa and Rhodesia, for example, where those who control the state are admittedly a tiny minority whose legislative acts are openly designed to support a system in which a few whites benefit from the oppression of many Africans.

Such extreme examples as South Africa can hardly be said to provide adequate evidence, however, for the view that the criminal law is a mere reflection of the interests of a few. There are in fact a number of theories of law creation and a substantial body of research evidence available to help us decide what social forces determine the content of criminal law.

MODELS OF RULE CREATION

Theories of the origin of criminal law parallel rather closely general theories of society. The chief division is between those who see the state as being controlled by

* Some of the materials in this article (the sections on the emergence of the adversary process and the discussion of "public interest") were written by Robert Seidman for our book *Law, Order and Power* (Reading, Mass.: Addison-Wesley, 1971). I am grateful to him for these materials as well as his imaginative and generous help in preparing this paper. An earlier version of this paper appeared as "The State, the Law and the Definition of Behavior as Criminal or Delinquent" in *Handbook of Criminology*, ed. by Daniel Glaser (Chicago: Rand McNally, 1974), pp. 7–43.

Source: "The State, the Law, and the Definition of Behavior as Criminal or Delinquent," in Glaser, *Handbook of Criminology*, © 1974 by Rand McNally College Publishing Company, Chicago, pp. 8–18, 21–43.

and reflecting the interests of particular social classes and those who see the state as responding to the views of the general public. The Marxian view that "in every era the ruling ideas are the ideas of the ruling class" anchors one end of this theoretical debate and the natural-law view that the state is merely the reflection and translation of the *volksgeist* anchors the other. In between are a host of lower-level (i.e., less general) theories that see the criminal law as reflecting the organized efforts of "moral entrepreneurs" (Becker, 1963), bureaucratic interests (Chambliss, 1969; Hetzler, 1971), and downwardly mobile social classes (Gusfield, 1963) on the one hand, or that see the law as reflecting "perceived social needs" (Hall, 1952), the "public interest" (Auerbach et al., 1961) and "moral indignation" (Ranulf, 1933) on the other. We shall look at each of these theoretical models and see the degree to which extant empirical data on the creation of criminal law is compatible with the models.

In the end, we will conclude that none of the more prominent theories can account for the creation of all criminal law. It is, nevertheless, clear from the research evidence that some models come closer to providing a general explanation than do others. The paradigm that is most compatible with the facts is one that recognizes the critical role played by social conflict in the generation of criminal law. The conflicts may be manifested in violent confrontations between social classes or more genteelly in the form of institutionalized dispute-settling procedures. Regardless of the form the conflict takes, in the end it is the existence of the structurally induced conflicts between groups in the society that determines the form and content of the criminal law. Of course, not all groups or social classes are equally potent and those which control the economic resources of the society will influence the shape of the law more profoundly and more permanently than will any other group or class. Nonetheless, there are limits to the power of a "ruling class" or "ruling elite" to determine the law's content. These limits are set in the course of history as the society moves through those struggles which result from its particular organizational structure.

THE CREATION OF CRIMINAL LAW AND ECONOMIC ELITES

Research into the origins of criminal laws substantiates quite clearly the important role played in their creation by those classes that control the economic resources of the society. Whether looked at in terms of *consequences*—that is, the effect the laws have after passage—or the *dynamics* of the law-making process, the results are very much the same: those social classes who control the resources of the society are more likely to have their interests represented by the state through the criminal law than are any and all other social groups. First, we shall look at those instances where the definition of behavior as criminal or delinquent has arisen as a result of *direct involvement* on the part of economic elites in the rule-creation process.

A number of historical, cross-cultural, and contemporary studies of criminal law creation have shown how criminal laws are consciously and explicitly enacted to serve the interests of those who control the economic resources. Nowhere is this more clearly illustrated than in laws used to coerce an otherwise unwilling labor force into providing that labor which is the basis for the economic structure of the society. England's colonial policies in Africa are illustrative.

THE CREATION OF CRIMINAL LAW AND ECONOMIC INTERESTS

When England began colonizing Africa one of the first and last problems faced was to establish procedures by which the colonies could be made economically profitable. Being a nation of laws, it was not surprising to find legal institutions at the forefront of the struggle. The history of colonial law, which is only now being written, is replete with the open involvement of white elites in the creation of criminal laws designed to serve their economic interests. Indeed, it is not off the mark to say that the entire history of colonial criminal law legislation is that of a dominant social class defining as criminal those acts which it served their economic interests to so define. The corollary of this is that colonial law did *not* usually define as criminal those acts which, although offensive to the Englishman's "notions of justice, equity and good conscience," were not offensive to his economic interests.[1]

The East African "poll tax" and "registration" laws are instructive in this regard. East Africa had a settler economy. Whites moved in and established large plantations for raising tea, coffee, and sisal for export and sale abroad. Such an economic system depended upon the ready availability of masses of cheap labor. There were, however, few incentives for the Africans to leave their villages and work arduously on the white man's farms. Criminal laws were created which guaranteed the settlers a constant source of cheap labor (Seidman, 1971). Sir Harry Johnston noted:

> Given abundance of cheap labour, the financial security of the Protectorate is established. . . . All that needs to be done is for the Administration to act as friends of both sides, and introduce the native labourer to the European capitalist. A gentle insistence that the native should contribute his fair share to the revenue of the country by paying his tax is all that is necessary on our part to ensure his taking a share in life's labour which no human being should avoid (Johnston, 1895:96).

A similar view is also expressed by the governor of Kenya:

> We consider that taxation is the only possible method of compelling the native to leave his Reserve for the purpose of seeking work . . . it is on this (taxation) that the supply of labour and the price of labour depends. To raise the rate of wages would not increase but would diminish the supply of labour. A rise in the rate of wages would enable the hut or poll tax of a family, sub-tribe, or

tribe to be earned by fewer external workers (Sir Percy Girovard, as quoted in Lees, 1924:186).

To effect the Africans' compliance with this system of forced labor, criminal law sanctions of fines, imprisonment, and corporal punishment were imposed on people who failed to pay their taxes.

Even with this incentive to ensure that the African take "a share of life's labour which no human being should avoid," the settler's labor problems were not solved, for:

> Labourers who deserted as soon as they had earned enough to pay their taxes were no use to the settlers. To meet their (the settlers') demands, the government in 1919 put into effect a native registration ordinance which compelled all Africans over the age of sixteen to register by giving a set of fingerprint impressions, which were then forwarded to a central fingerprint bureau. By this method, nearly all deserters could be traced and returned to their employers if they broke a contract. Fines (up to $75.00) and imprisonment (up to 90 days) were imposed for a host of minor labour offenses. Another form of compulsion took shape in vagrancy laws which operated against Africans who left the reserves without becoming wage earners (Aaronovitch & Aaronovitch, 1947:99–100).[2]

The colonial setting was, of course, a unique one but the general character of the criminal law and the definition of behavior as deviant that it illustrates is not at all atypical. The development of vagrancy laws in England and the United States is also a history of defining certain acts as criminal in order to serve the interests of the ruling class. Again we find this explicitly articulated in the statutes themselves. In 1274 a prevagrancy statute was passed whose primary goal was to protect the church, which was at this time a mainstay of the ruling class, from the impoverished seeking shelter:

> Because that abbies and houses of religion have been overcharged and sore grieved, by the report of great men and other, so that their goods have not been sufficient for themselves, whereby they have been greatly hindered and impoverished, that they cannot maintain themselves, nor such charity as they have been accustomed to do; it is provided, that none shall come to eat or lodge in any house of religion, or any other's foundation than of his own, at the costs of the house, unless he be required by the governor of the home before his coming hither (3 Ed. 1 c. 1).

Even more to the point was the history of the vagrancy statutes from 1349 onward, a history of legislative enactment and innovation designed to provide labor for the established economic elites of the society. Of considerable importance in the analysis that follows is to note that as the economic resources of the society change (from feudal agrarianism to commerce and trade), the content and focus of the criminal law changes.

In 1349 the first vagrancy statute was passed and the wording of this statute made its intention quite clear:

Because that many valiant beggars, as long as they may live of begging, do refuse to labour, giving themselves to idleness and vice, and sometimes to theft and other abominations; it is ordained, that none upon pain of imprisonment shall, under the colour of pity or alms, give any thing to such which may labour, or presume to favour them towards their desires; so that thereby they may be compelled to labour for their necessary living.

It was further provided by this statute that:

every man and woman, of what condition he be, free or bond, able in body, and within the age of threescore years, not living in merchandise nor exercising any craft, nor having of his own whereon to live, nor proper land whereon to occupy himself, and not serving any other, if he in convenient service (his estate considered) be required to serve, shall be bounded to serve him which shall him require. . . . And if any refuse, he shall on conviction by two true men, . . . be committed to gaol till he find surety to serve.

And if any workman or servant, of what estate or condition he be, retained in any man's service, do depart from the said service without reasonable cause or license, before the term agreed on, he shall have pain of imprisonment (23 Ed. 3).

There was also in this statute the stipulation that the workers should receive a standard wage. In 1351 this statute was strengthened by the stipulation:

And none shall go out of the town where he dwelled in winter, to serve the summer, if he may serve in the same town [25 Ed. 3 (1351)].

By statute [34 Ed. 3 (1360)] the punishment for these acts became imprisonment for 15 days and if they "do not justify themselves by the end of that time, to be sent to gaol till they do."

The prime mover for the creation of these laws was the Black Death, which struck England about 1348. Among the many disastrous consequences of the plague on the social structure was the fact that it decimated the labor force. It is estimated that by the time the pestilence had run its course at least 50 percent of the population of England had died from the plague. This decimation of the labor force would necessitate rather drastic innovations in any society but its impact was heightened in England where, at this time, the economy was highly dependent upon a ready supply of cheap labor.

Even before the pestilence, the availability of an adequate supply of cheap labor was becoming a problem for the feudal landowners. The Crusades and various wars had made money necessary to the lords and, as a result, the lords frequently agreed to sell the serfs their freedom in order to obtain the needed funds. The serfs, for their part, sought to escape from serfdom (by "fair means" or "foul") because the larger towns, which were becoming commercial and trade centers during this period, could offer the serf greater personal freedom as well as a higher standard of living.

> By the middle of the 14th century the outward uniformity of the manorial system had become in practice considerably varied . . . for the peasant had begun to drift to the towns and it was unlikely that the old village life in its unpleasant aspects should not be resented. Moreover the constant wars against France and Scotland were fought mainly with mercenaries after Henry III's time and most villages contributed to the new armies. The bolder serfs either joined the armies or fled to the towns, and even in the villages the free men who held by villein tenure were as eager to commute their services as the serfs were to escape. Only the amount of "free" labor available enabled the lord to work his demesne in many places (Bradshaw, 1915:54).

And he says regarding the effect of the Black Death:

> in 1348 the Black Death reached England and the vast mortality that ensued destroyed that reserve of labour which alone had made the manorial system even nominally possible (p. 54).

The immediate result of these events was, of course, no surprise: wages for the "free" man rose considerably and this increased, on the one hand, the landowner's problems and, on the other hand, the plight of the unfree tenant. For although wages increased for the personally free laborers, it, of course, did not necessarily add to the standard of living of the serf; if anything it made his position worse because the landowner would be hard pressed to pay for the personally free labor which he needed and would thus find it more and more difficult to maintain the standard of living for the serf which he had heretofore supplied. Thus the serf had no alternative but flight if he chose to better his position. Furthermore, flight generally meant both freedom and better conditions, since the possibility of work in the new weaving industry was great and the chance of being caught small (Bradshaw, 1915:57).

It was under these conditions that we find the first vagrancy statutes emerging. There is little question but that these statutes were designed for one express purpose: to force laborers (whether personally free or unfree) to accept employment at a low wage in order to insure the landowner an adequate supply of labor at a price he could afford to pay. Caleb Foote concurs with this interpretation when he notes that the antimigratory policy behind vagrancy legislation began

> as an essential complement of the wage stabilization legislation which accompanied the breakup of feudalism and the depopulation caused by the Black Death. By the Statutes of Labourers in 1349–1351, every able-bodied person without other means of support was required to work for wages fixed at the level preceding the Black Death; it was unlawful to accept more, or to refuse an offer to work, or to flee from one county to another to avoid offers of work or to

seek higher wages, or to give alms to able-bodied beggars who refused to work (Foote, 1956:615).

In short, as Foote says in another place, this was an "attempt to make the vagrancy statutes a substitute for serfdom" (p. 615). This same conclusion is equally apparent from the wording of the statute, where it is stated:

> Because great part of the people, and especially of workmen and servants, late died in pestilence; many seeing the necessity of masters, and great scarcity of servants, will not serve without excessive wages, and some rather willing to beg in idleness than by labour to get their living: it is ordained, that every man and woman, of what condition he be, free or bond, able in body and within the age of three-score years, not living in merchandise, (etc.) be required to serve. . . .

The innovation in the law was a direct result of the aforementioned changes in the social setting. The law was clearly and consciously designed to serve the interests of the ruling class of feudal landlords at the expense of the serfs or working classes. The vagrancy laws were designed to alleviate a condition defined by the lawmakers as undesirable. The solution was to attempt to force a reversal, as it were, of a social process which was well under way; that is, to curtail mobility of laborers in such a way that labor would not become a commodity for which the landowners would have to compete.

A SHIFT IN FOCAL CONCERN

Following the squelching of the Peasants' Revolt in 1381, the services of the serfs to the lord "tended to become less and less exacted, although in certain forms they lingered on till the seventeenth century. . . . By the sixteenth century few knew that there were any bondmen in England . . . and in 1575 Queen Elizabeth listened to the prayers of almost the last serfs in England . . . and granted them manumission" (Bradshaw, 1915: 61).

In view of this change we would expect corresponding changes in the vagrancy laws. Beginning with the lessening of punishment in the statute of 1503, we find these changes. However, instead of remaining dormant (or becoming more so) or being negated altogether, the vagrancy statutes experienced a shift in focal concern. With this shift the statutes served a new and equally important function for the ruling class of England. The first statute that indicates this change was adopted in 1530 [22 H. 8. c. 12 (1530)]. It stated:

> If any person, being whole and mighty in body, and able to labour, be taken in begging, or be vagrant and can give no reckoning how he lawfully gets his living . . . and all other idle persons going about, some of them using divers and subtil crafty and unlawful games and plays, and some of them feigning themselves to have knowledge of . . . crafty sciences . . . shall be punished as provided.

What is most significant about this statute is the shift from an earlier concern with laborers to a concern with *criminal* activities. To be sure, the stipulation of persons "being whole and mighty in body, and able to labour, be taken in begging, or be vagrant" sounds very much like the concerns of the earlier statutes. Some important differences are apparent, however, when the rest of the statute includes those who "can give no reckoning how he lawfully gets his living"; "some of them using divers and subtil crafty and unlawful games and plays." This is the first statute which specifically focuses upon these kinds of criteria for adjudging someone a vagrant.

It is significant that in this statute the severity of punishment is increased so as to be greater not only than that provided by the 1503 statute but the punishment is more severe than that which had been provided by *any* of the pre-1503 statutes as well. For someone who is merely idle and gives no reckoning of how he makes his living the offender shall be:

> had to the next market town, or other place where they [the constables] shall think most convenient, and there to be tied to the end of a cart naked, and to be beaten with whips throughout the same market town or other place, till his body be bloody by reason of such whipping [22 H. 8. c. 12 (1530)].

But, for those who use "divers and subtil crafty and unlawful games and plays," etc., the punishment is "whipping at two days together in manner aforesaid." For the second offense, such persons are:

> scourged two days, and the third day to be put upon the pillory from nine of the clock till eleven before noon of the same day and to have one of his ears cut off [22 H. 8. c. 12 (1530)].

And if he offend the third time "to have like punishment with whipping, standing on the pillory and to have his other ear cut off."

This statute (1) makes a distinction between types of offenders and applies the more severe punishment to those who are clearly engaged in "criminal" activities, (2) mentions a specific concern with categories of "unlawful" behavior, and (3) applies a type of punishment (cutting off the ear) which is generally reserved for offenders who are defined as likely to be fairly serious criminals.

Only five years later we find for the first time that the punishment of death is applied to the crime of vagrancy. We also note a change in terminology in the statute:

> . . . and if any ruffians . . . after having been once apprehended . . . shall wander, loiter, or idle use themselves and play the vagabonds . . . shall be eftsoons not only whipped again, but shall have the gristle of his right ear clean cut off. And if he shall again offend, he shall be committed to gaol till the next sessions; and being there convicted upon indictment, he shall have judgment to suffer pains and execution of death, as a felon, as an enemy of the commonwealth [27 H. 8. c. 25 (1535)].

It is significant that the statute now makes persons who repeat the crime of vagrancy felons. During this period then, the focal concern of the vagrancy statutes becomes a concern for the control of felons and is no longer primarily concerned with the movement of laborers.

These statutory changes were a direct response to changes taking place in England's social structure during this period. We have already pointed out that feudalism was decaying rapidly. Concomitant with the breakup of feudalism was an increased emphasis upon commerce and trade. The commercial emphasis in England at the turn of the sixteenth century is of particular importance in the development of vagrancy laws. With commercialism came considerable traffic bearing valuable goods. Where there were 169 important merchants in the middle of the fourteenth century, there were 3,000 merchants engaged in foreign trade alone at the beginning of the sixteenth century (Hall, 1952:21). England became highly dependent upon commerce for its economic surplus. Italians conducted a great deal of the commerce of England during this early period and were held in low repute by the populace. They were subject to attacks by citizens and, more important, were frequently robbed of their goods while transporting them. "The general insecurity of the times made any transportation hazardous. The special risks to which the alien merchant was subjected gave rise to the royal practice of issuing formally executed covenants of safe conduct through the realm" (Hall, 1952:23).

Such a situation not only called for the enforcement of existing laws but also called for the creation of new laws which would facilitate the control of persons preying upon merchants transporting goods. The vagrancy statutes were revived in order to fulfill just such a purpose. Persons who had committed no serious felony but who were suspected of being capable of doing so could be apprehended and incapacitated through the application of vagrancy laws once these laws were refocused so as to include "any ruffians . . . [who] shall wander, loiter, or idle use themselves and play the vagabonds" [27 H. 8. c. 25 (1535)].

The new focal concern is continued in 1 Ed. 6. c. 3 (1547) and in fact is made more general so as to include:

> Whoever man or woman, being not lame, impotent, or so aged or diseased that he or she cannot work, not having whereon to live, shall be lurking in any house, or loitering or idle wandering by the highway side, or in streets, cities, towns, or villages, not applying themselves to some honest labour, and so continuing for three days; or running away from their work; every such person shall be taken for a vagabond. And . . . upon conviction of two witnesses . . . the same loiterer [shall] be marked with a hot iron in the breast with the letter V, and adjudged him to the person bringing him, to be his slave for two years.

Should the vagabond run away, upon conviction, he was to be branded by a hot iron with the letter S on the forehead and be thenceforth declared a slave forever. And in 1571 there is modification of the punishment to be inflicted, whereby the offender is to be "branded on the chest with the letter V" (for vagabond). And, if he is convicted the second time, the brand is to be made on the forehead. It is worth noting here that this method of punishment, which first appeared in 1530 and is repeated here with somewhat more force, is also an indication of a change in the type of person to whom the law is intended to apply. For it is likely that nothing so permanent as branding would be applied to someone who was wandering but looking for work, or at worst merely idle and not particularly dangerous per se. On the other hand, it could well be applied to someone who was likely to be engaged in other criminal activities in connection with being "vagrant."

By 1571 in the statute of 14 E. 1. c. 5 the shift in focal concern is fully developed:

All rogues, vagabonds, and sturdy beggars shall . . . be committed to the common gaol . . . he shall be grievously whipped, and burnt thro the gristle of the right ear with a hot iron of the compass of an inch about. . . . And for the second offense, he shall be adjudged a felon, unless some person will take him for two years in to his service. And for the third offense, he shall be adjudged guilty of felony without benefit of clergy.

And there is included a long list of persons who fall within the statute:

proctors, procurators, idle persons going about using subtil, crafty and unlawful games or plays; and some of them feigning themselves to have knowledge of . . . absurd sciences . . . and all fencers, bearwards, common players in interludes, and minstrels . . . all jugglers, pedlars, tinkers, petty chapmen . . . and all counterfeiters of licenses, passports and users of the same.

The major significance of this statute is that it includes all the previously defined offenders and adds some more. Significantly, those added are more clearly criminal types, counterfeiters, for example. It is also significant that there is the following qualification of this statute: "Provided also, that this act shall not extend to cookers, or harvest folks, that travel for harvest work, corn or hay."

The emphasis upon the criminalistic aspect of vagrants continues in chapter 17 of the same statute:

Whereas divers *licentious* persons wander up and down in all parts of the realm, to countenance their *wicked behavior*; and do continually assemble themselves armed in the highways, and elsewhere in troops, *to the great terror* of her majesty's true subjects, the *impeachment of her laws*, and the disturbance of the peace and tranquility of the realm; and whereas many outrages are daily committed by these dissolute persons, and more are likely to ensue if speedy remedy be not provided (italics added).

With minor variations (e.g., offering a reward for the capture of a vagrant) the statutes remain essentially of this nature until 1743. In 1743 there was once more an expansion of the types of persons included such that

all persons going about as patent gatherers, or gatherers of alms, under pretense of loss by fire or other casualty; or going about as collectors for prisons, gaols, or hospitals; all persons playing or betting at any unlawful games; and all persons who run away and leave their wives or children . . . all persons wandering abroad, and lodging in alehouses, barns, out-houses, or in the open air, not giving good account of themselves,

were types of offenders added to those already included.

In sum, the foregoing analysis of the vagrancy laws demonstrates that these laws were a legislative innovation which reflected the socially perceived necessity of providing an abundance of cheap labor to England's ruling class of landowners during a period when serfdom was breaking down and when the pool of available labor was depleted. With the eventual breakup of feudalism the need for such laws disappeared and the increased dependence of the economy upon commerce and trade rendered the former use of the vagrancy statutes irrelevant. As a result, for a substantial period the vagrancy statutes were dormant, undergoing only minor changes and, presumably, being applied infrequently. Finally, the vagrancy laws were subjected to considerable alteration through a shift in the focal concern of the statutes. Whereas in their inception the laws focused upon the "idle" and "those refusing to labor," after the turn of the sixteenth century the emphasis came to be upon "rogues," "vagabonds," and others who were suspected of being engaged in criminal activities. During this period the focus was particularly upon "roadmen" who preyed upon citizens who transported goods from one place to another. The increased importance of commerce to England during this period brought forth laws to protect persons engaged in this enterprise and the vagrancy statutes provided one source for such protection by refocusing the acts to be included under these statutes.

The more recent history of the vagrancy statutes has continued to repeat the same basic process. During times of harvest in states where agriculture is big business, vagrancy statutes are enforced as a means of providing cheap labor (Spradley, 1970). Conversely, during periods of recession when there is an over-abundance of cheap labor, these same statutes are used to restrict the mobility of the unemployed [*Edwards* v. *California*, 314 U.S. 160 (1941)].

These historical data are essential if we are to comprehend the rule-creation process but they cannot tell us what the process is today. Presumably the role of the ruling class in the creation of criminal laws could have changed substantially in recent years. The available evidence suggests that this has not happened. Indeed, what evidence there is suggests that *even those laws that appear to be contrary to the interests of those who control the economic resources were in fact created to help them increase their profits.*

Since the 1900s there has been a heady growth in America of criminal laws ostensibly designed to curb the excesses of private enterprise. The Sherman antitrust laws, pure food and drug laws, restrictions on the use of "unfair competition," and the like have emerged as a whole new area of criminal law. On the surface it would appear that these laws represent strong evidence that under certain circumstances criminal laws are passed that are purposely and explicitly contrary to the interests of the most powerful economic sectors of the society. Closer examination reveals, however, that even laws that are, on the surface, inimical to the interests of those who control the resources of the society, are laws that, in fact, were promoted and shaped by those very same groups as a means of enhancing and improving their control over the means of production.

Gabriel Kolko has provided historical analysis of the emergence of laws regulating the railroad and meat-packing industries that demonstrates quite clearly that in these areas the laws were, in fact, promoted and shaped by the largest companies in these fields in an effort to control competition from smaller companies and to insure better markets for the large companies' products (Kolko, 1963, 1965).

In the latter part of the nineteenth century the railroad industry was in a state of chaos created by intense competition and national economic crises. In June 1877 a general strike of railroad workers surprised and incapacitated the industry. One consequence of the strike was to establish the role that the state would have in conflicts between workers and industry:

> Out of the crisis came a working view of the role of the state in industrial society which was consistently applied during the next three decades: if for some reason the power of various key business interests was endangered, even for causes of their own making, the state was to intervene to preserve their dominant position (Kolko, 1965:12).

The fact that this principle emerged from the strike was doubtless no surprise to the railroad owners. They had, after all, become established and powerful largely through the cooperation of the state in the early years of their development (Hurst, 1950, 1956). The strike, however, underlined for them the value to be had from stronger cooperation with the federal bureaucracy.

Thus began a movement within the railroad industry itself to seek federal regulation. Previous efforts at pooling by competitive railroads had been largely a failure and the industry had remained intensely competitive.

Profits were low for many companies and bankruptcies not uncommon. Eventually the major railroad companies came to realize that federal regulation which would establish uniform prices at a level guaranteeing profits to the industry was an acceptable and desirable solution. It was, in effect, the use of criminal law legislation to benefit the larger, established railroads to the disadvantage of the smaller ones. Price and policy regulation by the federal government reduced competition and thus eliminated the possibility that a small company might take business away from a larger one. Although widely touted as antimonopoly legislation, the establishment of the Interstate Commerce Commission and enactment of the statutes controlling railroad activities were essentially moves to encourage monopolies within the railroad industry.

The history of criminal law legislation geared ostensibly to regulate the unsanitary practices of the meat-packing industry shows the same underlying motivation. The large meat-packing firms were suffering financially in competition with smaller firms which were able to undersell them. The entire industry engaged in incredibly unsanitary processing practices that resulted in widespread illness. The larger firms were also being hurt by the fact that the often unhealthy meat sold abroad was reducing the demand in Europe for American meat products. A solution to both problems for the large corporations was legislation creating government inspection of meat processing. This would, of course, raise the cost of producing the meat but for the large firms the increased cost would be minimal as it could be spread over a large output. For the small firms, however, the increased cost would destroy their competitive advantage. Simultaneously, meat-inspection laws would improve the health qualities and thereby enable American manufacturers to compete favorably for European markets. Realizing this led the large meat-packers to lobby for federal regulations to control the industry. The government responded to these pressures by passing laws making it a crime to produce meat under unsanitary conditions. The legislation thus aided the large meat-packers in their competition with smaller firms. Upton Sinclair, who inadvertently popularized the unsanitary conditions in the meat-packing industry (he was mainly concerned with working conditions when he wrote in 1904 but it was sanitation that became the issue), accurately described both the reason for passing and the effects of the meat-packing regulations:

> The Federal inspection of meat was, historically, established at the packers' request; . . . it is maintained and paid for by the people of the United States for the benefit of the packers; . . . men wearing the blue uniforms and brass buttons of the United States service are employed for the purpose of certifying to the nations of the civilized world that all the diseased and tainted meat which happens to come into existence in the United States of America is carefully sifted out and consumed by the American people (Sinclair, 1906:3).

During the legislative debates establishing federal inspection of meat, the large meat-packers were consulted and helped draw up the bills. Samuel H. Cowan, the lawyer for the National Livestock Association, was asked to write a bill acceptable to the packers, which he did. When President Roosevelt criticized the bill, Senator Wadsworth responded: "I told you on Wednesday night when I submitted the bill to you, that the packers insisted before our committee on having a rigid inspection law passed. Their life depends on it. They placed no obstacle in our way" (Kolko, 1963: 106).

When the bill was finally passed and the head of the Department of Agriculture announced to a gathering of the large meat-packers his department's intention to enforce the new laws strictly and rigidly, he was greeted with a round of applause from the industry. For the new laws would, as George Perkins wrote to J. P. Morgan, "be of very great advantage . . . as it will practically give [the meat-packers] a government certificate for their goods" (Kolko, 1963:106).

The active involvement by the ruling classes in criminal law legislation is certainly not limited to managing legislation directly affecting their economic interests and capital profits. It also includes actively sponsoring and supporting legislation that will help achieve political stability within which ongoing economic relations can be sustained. Anthony Platt has traced the development of juvenile justice laws in the United States. He argues that:

The Child Saving movement tried to do for the criminal justice system what industrialists and corporate leaders were trying to do for the economy—that is, achieve order, stability and control while preserving the existing class system and distribution of wealth (Platt, 1972:15).

Similarly, Jeremy Felt has argued that the abolition of child labor (laws making it a criminal offense to employ children under a specified age in certain branches of manufacture) was *not*, as is popularly believed, the result of a commitment to humane labor practices on the part of legislators but rather:

The abolition of child labor would be viewed as a means of driving out marginal manufacturers and tenement operators, hence increasing the consolidation and efficiency of business (Felt, 1965:45 as quoted in Platt, ibid.:39).

The credibility of Felt's argument is supported by the fact that in 1974 there still remained industries in which child labor was exploited mercilessly—particularly agriculture, where large corporations as well as small farmers rely upon children of all ages to pick potatoes, strawberries and other agricultural products during the harvest season. The fact that it would be humane to abolish these practices has apparently fallen on deaf ears where the use of child labor remains profitable for large and small producer alike.

Economic interests also become involved in criminal law legislation in order to protect themselves against laws that would interfere with their profits. Lobbyists at the state and national level are expected to advise their respective employers (for example, the drug industry, the American Medical Association, the National Association of Manufacturers) if any laws are pending in the legislature which might affect them. The study by James Graham, "Amphetamine Politics on Capitol Hill," shows how the drug industry actually participated in the writing of legislation which was ostensibly designed to curb drug industry practices deemed harmful to the public (Graham, 1971). The Comprehensive Drug Abuse Prevention and Control Act of 1970, which was strongly supported by President Nixon and Attorney General Mitchell as an important piece of ammunition in the arsenal against crime, was, in effect, an important piece of ammunition in the arsenal of the drug industry to reduce competition from unorganized entrepreneurs.

THE MOBILIZATION OF BIAS

Thus far we have dealt only with laws where there was a conscious effort by lawmakers (legislatures and appellate courts) to protect the interests of the economic elites of the society. Important as this is as a source of definition of behavior as criminal or delinquent, it leaves out a whole world of criminal law formation which reflects the interests of economic elites *not* consciously but nonetheless effectively. The key to understanding this aspect of criminal law creation is Schattschneider's concept, "the mobilization of bias."[3]

All forms of political organization have a bias in favor of the exploitation of some kinds of conflict and the suppression of others because organization is the mobilization of bias (Schattschneider, 1960:71).

The criminal law creation process organizes into it the views of those classes who control the economic resources as a result of the entire matrix of recruitment, socialization, and situational pressures upon those who create the laws. Legislatures, appellate court judges, and committee members are drawn largely from upper-class members of society; legal advice comes disproportionately from law firms whose principal clients are the major industrial and financial corporations of the country; interest groups are organized to define problems and influence lawmakers in the interests of those who have the resources to finance and support the existence of specialists in the rule-creation process.

Furthermore, "some issues are organized into politics while others are organized out" (Schattschneider, 1960:71). The mobilization of bias also includes the fact that much of what takes place in the creation of rules is "non-decision-making." For example, neither legislature nor appellate court in the United States would consider the question of whether it is criminal for a motion picture magnate to spend $20,000 on a birthday party for his daughter while people are starving a few blocks from the night club he rented for the occasion, or whether it should be a crime for the wife of the Attorney General of the United States to have 200 pairs of shoes while people in the Appalachian Mountains cannot afford shoes to send their children to school. It is simply assumed as part of the prevailing definition of reality that such an issue is "beyond the pale" of lawmaking institutions.

In the end, the mobilization of bias accounts for the emergence and focus of much of the criminal law in ways that are compatible with the dominant economic interests of the society. Even the structure of the criminal law process is influenced by the structural bias inherent in the operation and functioning of the law in a class-structured society. Take, for example, the emergence of the adversary process—one of the cornerstones of Anglo-American law frequently viewed as a fundamental feature insuring that the criminal law process will be unbiased and provide equal treatment to all regardless of their social or economic position. In fact, this process emerged and was maintained precisely because it provided a means of perpetuating the inequality that was so fundamental to the society in which it emerged.

The principle of the adversary process as a key part of criminal procedure emerged in England during the period from 1300 to 1600.[4] Among the early tribal groups of England, criminal disputes were handled by kinship groups; "trial" was a matter of accomplishing some reconciliation between the offending parties. "Guilt" was not at issue: only the maintenance of group harmony was of consequence (Chambliss & Seidman, 1971:28–36).

Before the fourteenth century, criminals were apprehended primarily by devices rooted in the *gemeinschaft* character of English rural life. The arrest of persons not yet indicted was a responsibility of the community. In the thirteenth century, for example, a *vill*—the smallest administrative "governmental" unit of the country—might be liable for failure to arrest those who had committed homicide; or, if the vill could not pay, the *hundred*—the next larger unit—was liable. As these older institutions decayed between the fourteenth and early sixteenth centuries, the law came to rely on the individual action of the citizen:

> Just as in the older law, all these rules [of pleading and of trial] must be put in motion and strictly obeyed by the parties at their own risk so now the parties must put in motion the machinery (Holdsworth, 1924a:598).

The modern state gradually took shape in England between the twelfth and sixteenth centuries. It was constructed on the ashes of feudalism and resulted from the bloody conflicts that raged between the Crown and barons, led by the Tudor monarchs, Henry VII, Henry VIII, and Elizabeth I. The Crown was supported by the ruling oligarchies of the towns and especially by the ruling elite of London. The victory of the Crown was thus a victory for the London elites.

Following the emergence of the state in this period there was a long period of instability and constant danger to its existence. There was no standing army and no police force. That the state through its control of the legal system supported the progressive weighting of the scales of justice in favor of the prosecution was not surprising.

The list of limitations on the ability of the accused to protect himself during the period between the sixteenth and mid-eighteenth centuries makes long and—to our values—painful reading. To insure that the jurors felt the weight of the evidence, witnesses were allowed to be called by the Crown, but not by the defense; the defendant, unsworn, had to reply to the evidence against him as best he could from memory. In *Throckmorton's* case [1 St. Tr. 869 (1554)], a trial for high treason, for example, a witness referred to some statements made by a man called Arnold. Throckmorton, seeing a friend, Fitz Williams, in the audience, called upon him to be sworn as a witness to rebut the testimony. One of the commissioners trying the case said: "Go your ways, Fitz Williams, the court hath nothing to do with you. Peradventure you would not be so ready in a good cause" [1 St. Tr. 885 (1554)]. Statutes were enacted in 1589 and 1607 allowing witnesses for the defense, but, illogically enough, prohibiting their being sworn.

Statutes were passed making it more difficult for accused persons to get bail. In the absence of bail, an accused person remained incarcerated before trial, making it more difficult for him to prepare his case [31 Eliz. c. 4 (1588)]. Inquisitorial proceedings against suspects were permitted by justices of the peace, the Privy Council, or the judges [4 James 1 c. 1 sec. 6 (1606)].

> The magistrates interpreted their power widely. They actively got up the case against the prisoner, not only by questioning him and the witnesses against him, but also by searching for evidence against him. . . . These examinations were conducted secretly, and the evidence was communicated to the prosecutor and the judge, but not to the prisoner (Holdsworth, 1924b:91).

In addition, the Council used torture and incarceration to extract confessions, and in important cases simply disregarded what procedural rules there were.

Even that hallowed palladium of English liberty, the jury, did not remain immune from tampering. After Throckmorton had defended himself so brilliantly that the jury acquitted him, they were committed to prison for their verdict. Four submitted and apologized, but eight were haled before the Star Chamber some six months and more after the trial. They were discharged only after payment of £250 in fines (three, who were not worth so much, were fined £60). The foreman forfeited £2,000. This rigor was fatal to Sir John Throckmorton, who was found guilty and therefore was executed upon the same evidence on which his brother had been acquitted.

In charges of felony and treason the defendant was at first not allowed to have counsel. Indeed, he was not even permitted a copy of the statute under which he was being tried. Slowly, counsel were admitted to argue points of law for the accused. Not until the latter part of the eighteenth century was defense counsel permitted to cross-examine witnesses, and it was 1836 before defense counsel was permitted to address the jury (Williams, 1963:7–8).

The judges did not regard themselves as impartial arbiters between the individual and the state; their commitment to their royal masters was, more frequently than not, made quite clear. In the *Elwes* case [2 St. Tr. 936 (1554)], for example, Lord Coke, the presiding judge, cross-examined the accused closely, and finally produced against him a statement made by a man named Franklin. The statement had been made privately and not even upon oath before Coke himself, at five o'clock in the morning, before the court sat (Stephen, 1883:332).

The conduct of prosecutors was similarly open in its bias. The great Lord Coke himself, acting as prosecutor of Sir Walter Raleigh, abused the latter unmercifully before the jury:

Lord Coke:	Thou art the most vile and execrable traitor that ever lived.
Raleigh:	You speak indiscreetly, barbarously and uncivilly.
Lord Coke:	I want words sufficient to express thy viperous treasons.
Raleigh:	I think you want words, indeed, for you have spoken one thing half a dozen times.
Lord Coke:	Thou are an odious fellow. Thy name is hateful to all the realm of England for thy pride.
Raleigh:	It will go hard to prove a measuring case between you and me, Mr. Attorney.
Lord Coke:	Well, I will now make it appear that there never lived a viler viper upon the face of the earth than thou (Stephen, 1883:333).

The judges' feeling that they were part of the governing arm is perhaps nowhere made clearer than in Raleigh's case. The accused insisted on the right to call as witness, Cobham, who had confessed to treason implicating Raleigh, but who had retracted his confession. Justice Warburton said:

I marvel, Sir Walter, that you, being of such experience and wit, should stand on this point: for so many horse stealers may escape, if they may not be condemned without witnesses (Stephen, 1883:334–35).

The unflagging support which the towns had given the Tudors withered shortly after the defeat of the Spanish Armada, and so did the feudal landowner's last hope for power in England. Almost immediately, the townsmen began to oppose the new Tudor aristocracy, an opposition that broke into open rebellion under Cromwell. The weighted scales in criminal trials did not reach a better balance during this period, but remained largely as before.

Following the "Glorious Revolution" in 1688, however, a relatively long period of tranquility in British government ensued, which was the century and a half during which the aristocratic constitution held sway. Active threat of revolution disappeared. The aristocracy were firmly in control of the government without significant challenge. The machinery of justice in the countryside centered around the justice of the peace, almost invariably a member of the landed gentry, who acted both as local administrator and as magistrate. The initiation of criminal prosecutions, in this relatively calm epoch, fell more and more on private persons. The notion of the independence of the judiciary, first clearly identified as a significant political fact in 1688, was more easily entrenched as political stability became less closely entwined with the criminal process.

Then the introduction of commerce and trade brought into existence the new entrepreneurial class which ultimately was to force the aristocrats to share the reins of power. The emerging class of merchants and financiers was greatly helped by the intellectual revolution that was taking place all over Europe. In criminal law, the most important consequence of this revolution was the developing notion of *nullum crimen sine lege* and *nulla poena sine lege*—no crime without a law and no punishment without a law. The concept of *nulla poena* embodied the emerging capitalist classes' need for clarity, on which their entire economic enterprise rested. The law was a means of limiting the powers of the aristocratic government, which excluded them and used its powers indiscriminately through the courts to put down their organizations.

The adversary system was, for the capitalists, a device by which rational and sensible decisions in the legal order could be made, in which the prosecutor's suspicions could be challenged, and in which the state could be compelled to submit suspicions to verification. The individualistic nature of the adversary process was conducive to these ends; and it was congenial with the new capitalist class just as in the economic realm they relied on individual enterprise: "Every man must fend for himself."

The result of the mobilization of bias in favor of the emerging elite was a system of litigation in which formal differentiation on the basis of birth, wealth, or position was abolished. The rhetoric was that all men were equal before the law. In an old saw, the law was magnificently impartial: both rich and poor would be arrested for sleeping under bridges. In fact, the adversary system provided only a paper equality.

Without affirmative aid to the poor or ignorant, the protections of the adversary system were limited to protection of the emergent capitalist class from discriminatory treatment by the old aristocracy. In a non-decision-making mobilization of bias, the new laws conveniently failed to provide real access to the benefits of the adversary process for the workers or the poor.

The private prosecution of offenses was one of the advantages of the criminal law system for the new ruling groups in England. The costs of prosecution were, at first, borne by the private prosecutor entirely. By 1861, however, as a result of almost a century of piecemeal legislation, the private prosecutor obtained the right to recover, after conviction, the costs of the prosecution, which in England included not merely relatively trivial court costs, but counsel fees as well. Conversely, in case of an acquittal, the prosecutor had to pay the costs incurred by the accused. Even as amended in 1861, the law still obviously favored the wealthy for they could better take the risk of losing the prosecution than could the working class or the poor.

Private prosecution, moreover, met the needs of the new industrial elites another way. By making the enforcement of criminal law, like the enforcement of the civil law, a matter of litigation between private parties, the state as represented by the judge became a mere arbiter between private interests. The state was made to appear as providing a neutral framework within which conflict and struggle could take place according to rules, thus ensuring that private initiative would be allowed the fullest play. As James Fitzjames Stephen, L.J., said in his spirited defense of nineteenth-century English criminal procedure:

> No stronger or more effectual guarantee can be provided for the due observance of the law of the land, by all persons under all circumstances, than is given by the power, conceded by the English system, of testing the legality of any conduct of which he disapproves, either on private or public grounds, by a criminal prosecution. Many such prosecutions, both in our days and in earlier times, have given legal vent to feelings in every way entitled to respect, and have decided peaceably, and in an authentic manner, many questions of great constitutional importance (Stephen, 1883:496).

These reforms in criminal procedure were not easily won. The statute of 1836, which finally gave the accused person full right to the counsel, for example, was strongly opposed by 12 of the 15 judges; Justice Park even threatened to resign if the bill were passed. (He reconsidered after the enactment [Williams, 1963:8].) But in time the elements of what in this country we call due process became entrenched in English law.

The adversary system was thus an ideal arrangement which met the demands of the new masters of industry and commerce. They demanded and, in time, achieved a system of litigation that at once gave them a defense against the old aristocratic government and guaranteed their advantage over all lower classes.

In the United States, the Bill of Rights was framed while this great sea of change was under way in English criminal procedure. The Founding Fathers, having just rebelled against precisely the same aristocratic government against which the new English industrialist class was still struggling, demanded legal-rational legitimacy. They wrote into the new Constitution most of the significant reforms that were still being incubated in England: due process of law, the independence of the judiciary, the right to a jury, *habeas corpus*, the right to counsel, the right to summon witnesses in defense, the right to bail, indictment by grand jury, the privilege against self-incrimination. In short, due process ensured the institution of the adversary system and resolved a major conflict between competing elites without redistributing power or privilege to the lower classes. Significantly, all this came about in England and the United States through the mobilization of bias in the criminal law-making process as the perspective and needs of those who control societies' economic resources get translated into law.

THE LAW OF THEFT AND
THE MOBILIZATION OF BIAS

The heart of a capitalist economic system is the protection of private property, which is, by definition, the cornerstone upon which capitalist economies function.[5] It is not surprising, then, to find that the criminal law reflects this basic concern. Of particular interest to understanding the creation of legal rules is that during feudal times, when landowners were the undisputed masters of the economic resources of the society, laws concerning theft were largely unsophisticated, unsubtle, and narrowly defined. It was only with the advent of commerce and trade in Europe that the laws of theft that hold sway in contemporary capitalistic societies took their present form. Only as the feudal landowners lost control over the resources of the society and, therefore, over the law-making machinery did laws of theft emerge to protect the interests of the developing economic elites. This process took place largely through mobilization of bias and was effected through a series of decisions rendered by the appellate courts in England.

A turning point in the law of theft came in the *Carrier* case, which was decided in England in 1473:

> The facts are simple enough: the defendant was hired to carry certain bales to Southampton. Instead of fulfilling his obligation, he carried the goods to another place, broke open the bales and took the contents. He was apprehended and charged with felony (Hall, 1952:4).

At the time that the defendant was arrested and tried with a felony there was no law in England that made it a crime for anyone to convert to their own use goods which they came by legally. There had been an earlier rule applicable to servants but this had subsequently been disallowed prior to the *Carrier* case. Yet despite this lack of prevailing common law or legislative enactment a tribunal of the most learned judges in England decided against the defendant and found him guilty of larceny. By so doing they essentially established a new law and one which was central to the well-being of the emergent class of capitalist traders and industrialists.

There was, of course, great debate at the time of the decision, first among the judges making the decisions, then among legal scholars. There was no possibility that the new law could be justified logically but it was possible for the judges to create legal fictions that justified the decision. In this way the interests of the new upper class were protected, not through their direct involvement in law creation but through the "perceived need" of the judges sitting on the highest courts of the time. The "perceived need," of course, represented the mobilization of a bias which favored the interests of the dominant economic class.

Following the *Carrier* case in 1473, the law of theft expanded and developed throughout the sixteenth, seventeenth, and eighteenth centuries with the decisions in the eighteenth century playing the major role. "Larceny by servant" became established in the sixteenth century and over time the courts continuously interpreted cases so as to expand at every turn the legal definition of "possession of the master" to include even instances where the master had never seen the goods, so long as the servant placed goods received by him in a receptacle of his master. The courts also broadened the interpretation of "servant" to include cashiers, clerks, and persons hired to transport goods from place to place.

The law was, however, not always construed in ways consistent with the interests of the now dominant business class. In 1799, in the case of *King* v. *Joseph Bazeley*, the court found a bank clerk who had taken a hundred pounds and pocketed the money without putting it into the possession of the bank, even so far as placing it in a drawer and later withdrawing it, "not guilty." The former stretching of the law of theft had apparently reached its limit and would have required too great an innovation even in an area of law where innovation by judges had been the characteristic trend for the preceding 300 years. Shortly after the *Bazeley* case, in the same year, the first embezzlement statute [39 Geo. III c. 85 (1799)] was passed thus absolving the appellate courts of the necessity for creating embezzlement laws.

In time, through legislative enactment and appellate court decisions, the law of theft was extended to include protection for the property owners against "larceny by trick," as well as all forms of converting property of others to personal use without the express consent and legal agreement of the original owner. It also became a crime for a third party to receive stolen property, thus adding one more thread to the ever-tightening web of protection for property owners. In 1692 it was enacted that:

> And forasmuch as thieves and robbers are much encouraged to commit such offenses, because a great number of persons make it their trade and business to deal in the buying of stolen goods; be it therefore enacted by the authority aforesaid, that if any person or persons shall buy or receive any goods or chattel that shall be feloniously taken or stolen from any other person, knowing the same to be stolen, he or they shall be taken and deemed an accessary or accessaries to such felony after the fact, and shall incur the same punishment, as

an accessary or accessaries to the felony after the felony committed (3 and 4 W. and M. c. 9, IV).

BUREAUCRACIES AS A SOURCE OF CRIMINAL LAW

The argument and the data presented thus far have all been to the effect that those classes that control a society's economic resources also determine the content and form of the criminal law: the definition of what is criminal or delinquent. That this is so can scarcely be denied but it is not the whole story. First, there are groups other than economic elites capable of influencing and determining criminal laws. Second, conflicts which inhere in the structure of society also bring about changes in the prevailing definitions of crime.

Among nonelite groups that are a source of definitions of behavior as criminal or delinquent, none is more important in modern society than the bureaucracies that carry out the work of the state. Government bureaucracies may, in the last analysis, be controlled by those who influence the society's economic resources (see Chambliss, 1971), but they also have a life and a force of their own which increasingly influence what is defined as criminal or delinquent. The power of established bureaucracies to influence society's definition of behavior as deviant has been superbly documented in Foucault's study of *Madness and Civilization* (1965).

Prior to the fifteenth and sixteenth centuries there had been established in Europe, mostly in France and England, many leprosariums—as many as 200 in France alone. In the late fifteenth and early sixteenth centuries these leprosariums became emptied, probably due to the end of the Crusades, which apparently fostered the spread of leprosy. These hospitals and their administrative machinery stood unused or were in danger of becoming unused. By various royal decrees, obviously affected by the economic conditions of the times (the unemployed group swelled with returning Crusaders), these institutions began to house a whole host of misfits—beggars, criminals, insane and diseased persons—who were not needed or could not be used in the labor force. What is significant is the tendency of the bureaucracies that formerly dealt with lepers to be perpetuated by becoming institutions for housing the criminal, sick, insane, and vagrant.

During the Middle Ages madness was considered a touch of the divinity. One might be odd behaviorally but he was viewed as existing on some other plane of being. The madman was more the fool, the jester, perhaps the genius. Fools were sometimes put on ships, left to drift from port to port, only to be pushed out to sea again after a certain town had looked and been reminded of foolishness. Hence the name "Ship of Fools." In the literature one finds madness as a voyage—another country. There is no element of depravity. And from a voyage of exile one may return "home."

The sense of moral degeneracy or depravity in the individual does not attach itself to the concept of madness until *after* the emergence from confinement. It seems very clear that the institution itself shaped the concept of madness. The confinement was a brutalizing experience. Boredom and abominable conditions led to illness and pain. Even those who did not become sick physically became less than coherent after years of chains and damp walls. Madness was not seen as a medical problem, rather the insane were viewed as beasts, forfeiting their humanity by their behavior. But again the "touch of the divine" hung on from the Middle Ages, except now it was not a touch of genius, of eccentric inspiration, but the touch of doom, of "falling from grace," of falling from humanity into bestiality—a God-given, inscrutable weakness in character.

The point of interest here is that for economic reasons, but in no small measure solely for the purpose of using an established bureaucratic structure, a whole host of "social problems" were created by the state. The bureaucracy thus created the laws and the law created the public view of the act.

Since the precedent was established in Europe, the role of bureaucracies in the creation of criminal laws has steadily increased in influence. Today the most important bureaucratic sources of new law are the law-enforcement bureaucracies themselves.

The fact that law-enforcement bureaucracies have become an important source of criminal law creation is quite ironic. It is akin to relying on General Motors as the prime source of laws setting automotive safety standards. Often, the treatment of representatives of law-enforcement bureaucracies by legislatures and judges assumes that by virtue of the bureaucracies' special role in society they necessarily possess a special expertise. A host of evidence suggests just the opposite: that by virtue of their special role, they have an especially biased view that would make objective testimony impossible. In general, law-enforcement agencies' concern with criminal law creation (either in legislatures or courts) leads to the emergence of laws which contribute to the smooth functioning of the law-enforcement bureaucracy irrespective of whether or not the laws are in the interest of society at large. Take, for example, the history of drug laws in the United States.

In no area of criminal law legislation have the law-enforcement agencies been more active than in the area of drug control. In the earlier discussions of the Comprehensive Drug Abuse Prevention and Control Act of 1970 I pointed out how the Department of Justice and the Bureau of Narcotics and Dangerous Drugs participated in drafting this legislation and then in guiding it through the committees and houses of Congress. The influence of law-enforcement bureaucracies was apparent in both what they did and did not do. On the one hand, they were instrumental in defining the drug problem as primarily a problem of "freaks" and "criminal types," thus clearly focusing the scope of the law on the lower class and the youth groups taking drugs. The information which these agencies had on the relationship between the legal manufacture of drugs and the illegal drug market was only produced when demanded by congressmen. The law-enforcement agencies, in short, acted in the interests of the drug manufacturers both in the content of the proposed legislation and in the information supplied to the lawmakers. Such a stance was good bureaucratic strategy in that it reduced the likelihood of opposition to the bill from a powerful lobby. Furthermore, it did *not* make the law enforcers responsible for enforcing laws against the will of strong economic interests. At the same time the bill did provide greater license for law enforcers to arrest and prosecute those classes and groups who could be processed with relative freedom from bureaucratic strain (Chambliss, 1969). The 1970 drug law is not unique: indeed, it is no exaggeration to say that the entire set of rules governing the enforcement of antidrug laws has derived more from regulations of the law-enforcement bureaucracies than from legislators or appellate-court decisions (Lindesmith, 1965).

It was largely due to the efforts of the Federal Narcotics Bureau (later renamed the Bureau of Narcotics and Dangerous Drugs) that in 1937 the Marihuana Tax Act was passed:

> Prior to 1937 Mr. Anslinger (then the director of the Federal Bureau of Narcotics) and the Bureau of Narcotics had spearheaded a propaganda campaign against marihuana on the grounds that it produced an immense amount of violent crime such as rape, mayhem, and murder, and that many traffic accidents could be attributed to it (Lindesmith, 1965:230).

The campaign and the propaganda were spearheaded by and paid for with funds from the Bureau that would have the responsibility for the enforcement of the law. The bill was passed with little discussion in Congress. The congressmen apparently assumed that the Bureau of Narcotics was the ultimate authority on such matters and did not see it as necessary or wise to call for outside testimony. This was a classic case of an organization being in a position to expand its domain vastly and to legitimize its need for greater resources by controlling the information available to the lawmakers.

The Narcotics Bureau had also created public support for antimarijuana legislation by feeding magazines and newspapers stories on the dangers of marijuana. Becker's comparison (1963) of the number of articles dealing with marijuana for the years preceding and following the 1937 Congress reveals the emergence of media interest in a previously dormant issue. That this media interest was fanned by the Narcotics Bureau is evidenced by the fact that the articles contained cases supplied by the Bureau as well as "data" distributed by Bureau personnel (Becker, 1963).

The lawmaking function of the bureaucracy was extended as well to the state level. Through the production and distribution of information and through personal influence the Bureau of Narcotics activated state and municipal law-enforcement agencies and obtained passage of antimarijuana laws duplicating the federal laws in most of the states.

The laws governing the use of opiates in the United States show a similar pattern. In the U.S. prior to 1914 addicts could and did readily obtain drugs from pharmacies, physicians, and even mail-order houses. In 1914 the Harrison Act was passed as a revenue measure, and was designed "to make the entire process of drug distribution within the country a matter of record" (Lindesmith, 1965). The act did not make it a crime to be an addict or to take drugs. However, the administrative orders of the Federal Narcotics Bureau and the Bureau's careful selection of court cases in effect translated the Harrison Act into a law that punished drug addicts for their addiction (Lindesmith, 1965). The Federal Narcotics Bureau also through administrative practices—even in the face of laws contradicting these practices—pursued a policy of arresting and prosecuting selected medical doctors who provided drugs for addicts. These practices were effective in creating a law by administrative practice which was never created by legislature or appellate court (Lindesmith, 1965). In the end, the policies and propaganda of the Narcotics Bureau also created public support for its policies where none existed originally (Becker, 1963; Duster, 1970).

An analysis of juvenile-court legislation in California has also shown the power of law-enforcement bureaucracies in creating law (Lemert, 1970). Lemert's analysis of the emergence and functioning of the California Youth Authority makes clear how bureaucratic needs may determine the shape of law:

> the pressing need for a budget to support the C.Y.A.'s Division of Institutions has meant that where the choice has had to be made between upgrading juvenile court operation through new legislation and maintaining dominant organizational interests, the latter has prevailed. . . . The need to support and administer existing institutions, as well as construct new ones, soon established budgetary priority for the Division of Institutions, and came to occupy the largest share of time, energies, and attention of administrators and staff. Recruitment practices, in-training programs, and job assignments tended to preserve a custodial pattern of action within the Division of Institutions, despite the California Youth Authority's informal dedication and official allegiance to the purposes of individualized treatment (Lemert, 1970:56, 52).

It is likely that these cases do little more than expose the more visible examples of bureaucratic involvement in the creation of laws. The general rule of law creation that emerges is that bureaucracies will use their resources, power, and influence to obtain passage and suppression of laws that represent the interests of the bureaucracies themselves. The "public interest" or the long-range goals of law are largely irrelevant or at least are only secondary to the interests of the bureaucracies in running and expanding trouble-free organizations.

PUBLIC INDIGNATION

Part of the mythology that surrounds the law is the view that new laws are created as a result of a change in the values of "the people." This perspective, which is often espoused by social scientists as well as lawyers, sees an assumed "value-consensus" of the community as the root of all law. As we have seen from the data presented, such a view scarcely does justice to the realities of legislation. There is, nevertheless, a substantial body of data which indicates that public views on morality *do* affect legislation, especially those views of segments of the public which get representation by groups of moral entrepreneurs: that is, groups organized to influence lawmaking and enforcement according to their view of morality.

Some of the earliest systematic work on the issue of public indignation and criminal law legislation was done by the Danish sociologist Svend Ranulf in the two classical studies, *The Jealousy of the Gods* (1933) and *Moral Indignation and Middle Class Psychology* (1938). Ranulf shows by careful historical analysis that in both Greece and Europe the "disinterested tendency to punish" for moral breaches emerges with the development of a lower-middle class. Ranulf's explanation for this phenomenon is that moral indignation stems from a basic tendency of the lower-middle class to envy the position of the more affluent classes. This psychological interpretation is not particularly enlightening but, as Ranulf notes, accepting the historical sequence of events does not necessitate the acceptance of his explanation.

More recently Troy Duster (1970) and Joseph Gusfield (1963) have contributed to the study of the role of public indignation with their studies of drug laws and prohibition, respectively.

Duster's study is largely devoted to a refutation of the cliché that we "cannot legislate morality"; or in the words of William Graham Sumner, stateways cannot make folkways. Duster shows quite clearly how the passage of the antidrug law in 1914 (the Harrison Act), combined with the propagandizing and bureaucratic efforts of federal law-enforcement agencies, led eventually to widespread acceptance among the middle classes of the idea that drug use was immoral, sinful, and dangerous.

Further evidence of the role of moral entrepreneurs as a force creating changes in the criminal law is provided by Joseph Gusfield's study (1963) of the emergence of prohibition laws. Gusfield argues persuasively that the moving force behind the emergence of prohibition laws was an organized effort by those segments of the middle class who saw their economic and social position being threatened by changing economic forces. It was essentially the decline of the importance of small-town society with its middle-class, rural background that created a constituency desirous of asserting its importance through law. This threatened, downwardly mobile class managed to bring sufficient political pressure that laws were passed to placate them (Sinclair, 1964).

The effects of public indignation on the emergence and shape of the criminal law are also provided by an examination of the role of groups organized to protect the "public interest." In the United States much of the law governing criminal procedure has been written and rewritten by groups of moral entrepreneurs, especially the American Civil Liberties Union and the National Association for the Advancement of Colored People (Chambliss & Seidman, 1971). The ACLU has been particularly active in criminal law cases where their concern has been with police procedures. In a series of landmark decisions of the U.S. Supreme Court, the ACLU provided funds and legal counsel which virtually rewrote the laws governing police behavior. These moral entrepreneurs, although protecting the rights of the lower classes, are themselves composed of middle-class members of the community and are supported by financial contributions from that same middle class.

It is not the case, however, that the moral indignation of the middle classes is any guarantee that criminal laws will be passed. In general it appears that middle-class indignation is most likely to culminate in the creation of new law when the indignation coalesces into a working organization with specific roles and financial backing.

Middle-class organizations are, for the most part, unable to combat or counteract the forces of the classes who control the economic resources of the society. As we saw earlier in the history of criminal law legislation, the economic elites' interests are protected by their ability to directly influence legislation and by their mobilization of bias which flows from their position in the society. During the discussion of the Drug Abuse Prevention and Control Act of 1970, for example, the interests of the law-enforcement bureaucracies and the drug industry were so fully represented that the moral indignation of the middle class, which was ostensibly the basis for the passage of the law, was simply an excuse used to legitimize a law which was first and foremost a reflection of the wishes of more powerful interests.

The groups of moral entrepreneurs who represent the indignation of at least some segment of the middle class fare best when they engage less potent forces than the economic elites. In particular, their effect on criminal law legislation is likely to be most noticeable where they engage the law-enforcement bureaucracies or only small businesses.

Such was the case in a recent debate in New York over revision of the laws concerning prostitution (Roby, 1969). The issue arose over Article 230 (one of approximately 520 sections) of the 1965 New York State Penal Law. Sections 230.00, 230.05, and 230.10 of the code provide:

§ 230.00   Prostitution

A person is guilty of prostitution when such person engages or agrees or offers to engage in sexual conduct with another person in return for a fee.

Prostitution is a violation. L. 1965, c. 1030, eff. Sept. 1, 1967.

§ 230.05   Patronizing a prostitute

A person is guilty of patronizing a prostitute when:

1. Pursuant to a prior understanding, he pays a fee to another person as compensation for such person or a third person having engaged in sexual conduct with him; or

2. He pays or agrees to pay a fee to another person pursuant to an understanding that in return therefor such person or a third person will engage in sexual conduct with him; or

3. He solicits or requests another person to engage in sexual conduct with him in return for a fee.

Patronizing a prostitute is a violation. L. 1965, c. 1030, eff. Sept. 1, 1967.

§ 230.10   Prostitution and patronizing a prostitute; no defense

In any prosecution for prostitution or patronizing a prostitute, the sex of the two parties or prospective parties to the sexual conduct engaged in, contemplated, or solicited is immaterial, and it is no defense that:

1. Such persons were of the same sex; or
2. The person who received, agreed to receive or solicited a fee was a male and the person who paid or agreed or offered to pay such fee was a female. L. 1965, c. 1030, eff. Sept. 1, 1967.

At the time this revised code was proposed prostitution was subject to a penalty of up to three years in a reformatory or a year in jail. Further, prostitution was, until 1960, defined by court decisions as an act committable only by a female. In 1960, by court decision, homosexuality was incorporated under the umbrella of the statute (Roby, 1969:87).

The new code on prostitution made two significant changes: first, it included as a violation patronizing a prostitute and, second, it greatly reduced the penalty for prostitution by making the act a "violation" rather than a crime. The maximum sentence for a violation is fifteen days rather than a year in jail.

In 1961 the governor of New York appointed a commission to recommend needed revisions of the Penal Law and the Code of Criminal Procedure. The commission staff relied heavily on the advice of Chief Justice John M. Murtagh, a judge nationally known for his concern with criminal procedures in dealing with prostitution. The commission members also relied on Great Britain's *Wolfenden Report* (1963), the model penal codes of the American Bar Association, and procedures in other states.

After four years of work the commission held "public hearings" on the proposed penal code revision. "The public" was probably unaware of the event but some special interest groups were not. Of the 520 articles only the one dealing with prostitution was revised as a result of these hearings. The major change wrought was the addition of "patronizing a prostitute" as a violation, something which was *not* included in the commission's original proposed code. The major proponent for including "patronizing" was the American Social Health Association, which argued that the only way to control the spread of disease effectively was by punishing the patron. The Association's view was buttressed by arguments from Dorris Clarke, attorney and retired chief probation officer of the New York City Magistrates Court. Further support came from testimony of an independent doctor who argued that since both customer and prostitute were guilty, both should be punished.

Combating this position were Judge Murtagh and a few spokesmen for the police who argued that the police needed to have the confidence of customers in order to get testimony against prostitutes.

The opposition was, at this point, no match in number or organization and thus the patron clause was written into the law.

On the eve of the new law becoming effective the police relaxed their enforcement policies. Subsequently a rumor circulated that there was an influx of prostitutes into the city. The source of the rumor is not clear but:

New York politicians, businessmen, and the police may have begun to talk about an influx of prostitutes and the need for a "cleanup" because they were dissatisfied with the law becoming "soft" on prostitutes (Roby, 1969:94).

During this time police department representatives began telling newsmen of increases in prostitution.

The commission that had drafted the new law denied these allegations. In any event, in August 1967 midtown businessmen and the New York Hotel Association, along with politicians and government officials, pressured the police to get rid of the prostitutes in the area of Times Square.

Approximately two weeks before the new law was to become effective the police made a series of raids around Times Square and arrested suspected prostitutes by the score! On August 20 alone 121 were arrested on Times Square. Between August and September 23, 1,300 arrests were made. Most of those that *followed* the date when the new law became effective (September 1) were for loitering or disorderly conduct.

The New York Civil Liberties Union, the Legal Aid Society, and a New York judge all made vociferous protests over the mass arrest of persons for disorderly conduct and loitering when it was obvious, even to the police, that these charges would not stand up in court. The NYCLU reported on September 22, 1967:

> In a press release, the New York Civil Liberties Union protested police practices in the "Times Square cleanup campaign." The NYCLU reported, "Literally hundreds of women have been arrested and charged with disorderly conduct during the summer months, and the situation still continues." ". . . There is a conspiracy on the part of the police to deprive these women of their civil rights by arresting them on insubstantial charges." ". . . Women are being arrested in a dragnet and charged with disorderly conduct and loitering in order to raise the number of arrests." ". . . Many innocent girls are undoubtedly being caught in the net and the entire practice is an outrageous perversion of the judicial process. Furthermore, women who refuse to submit to the unlawful practices of the police have been manhandled."
>
> The Union reported Judge Basel saying, "I don't doubt that most of them are prostitutes, but it is a violation of the civil liberties of these girls. Even streetwalkers are entitled to their constitutional rights. The District Attorney moved in all these cases to have the charges thrown out, but in every case the girls were arrested after it was too late for night court, so they were kept over night with no substantial charges pending against them" (Roby, 1969:95).

The police roundup continued. From September 23 to September 30 another 1,100 arrests were made. These arrests brought the total from August 20 to September 30 to 2,400; this total was only 200 less arrests in six weeks than had been reported during the preceding six months. Significantly, only 61 percent of the arrests for violation of the prostitution ordinance involved the arrest of patrons despite the fact that the only legal basis for arresting prostitutes was for a policeman to observe a patron offering and a prostitute accepting a fee.

Thus began a campaign by the police department, in cooperation with the hotel association and businessmen in the area, to change those parts of the new penal code that liberalized the prostitution laws. In September 1967 the police department prefiled amendments to be considered by the 1968 legislature. These amendments, in effect, would have given the police almost complete discretion in the arrest of suspected prostitutes; they would have returned prostitution to the status of a crime, thus increasing the penalties, and these amendments would have effectively enabled the police to avoid the application of the law to patrons without formally changing this part of the penal code.

The mayor of New York City created a committee to look into the new law and the problem of prostitution. The committee in the end recommended that prostitution be reclassified a crime instead of its present status as a "violation" (thereby the penalty would have increased from fifteen days to one year in jail). But the committee did *not* recommend adopting any of the other changes advocated by the police and the hotel association. When this proposal was presented before the state legislature, it went to a Senate committee which voted *against* sending the bill back to the Senate: thus the law was kept as passed in 1967 for another year. In the end, the welfare, civil liberties, and bar association interests dominated over the interests of the police and the businessmen with respect to the severity of the sanctions and the criteria for making an arrest. The police and businessmen held sway over enforcement policies but this did *not* culminate in any immediate change in the law.

The New York Bar Association, NYCLU, and Legal Aid Society, along with some prominent public figures, proved to be more potent forces in shaping the formal law than did the police and the hotel owners association.

The analysis of the New York controversy over prostitution makes this point. For the most part the controversy over the new law was limited to different groups of moral entrepreneurs from the middle class: civil liberties and welfare groups on the one side, police and small businessmen on the other. The issue was largely irrelevant to the economic elites of the state or even to the bulk of the city population, and as a result, they were apathetic. To the extent that the upper classes were represented at all in the debate, the new legislation was tacitly supported, judging from the support given by the bar associations and commissions in their suggested revisions. This case also illustrates how police, prosecutorial, and judicial discretion can subvert the law. The 1965 revision made patrons, who doubtless represented the entire spectrum of social classes, equally culpable. The police, however, through selective enforcement, rendered this aspect of the law virtually meaningless and forced reconsideration by the lawmakers.

MODELS OF LAW CREATION

Until recently the prevailing view in modern social thought—both legal and social science—has centered on one or more of the following propositions:

1. The law represents the value-consensus of the society.
2. The law represents those values and perspectives which are fundamental to social order.
3. The law represents those values and perspectives which it is in the public interest to protect.
4. The state as represented in the legal system is value-neutral.
5. In pluralistic societies the law represents the interests of the society at large by mediating between competing interest groups.

Among sociologists the work of Emile Durkheim is the outstanding example of the systematic analysis of law from this perspective. It is, therefore, worth spending some time appraising Durkheim's thesis as put forth in *The Division of Labor in Society* (1893). My concern here will not be to point out contradictions, inconsistencies, or tautologies in Durkheim's work but only to explore how closely Durkheim's thesis fits with extant empirical data.

Durkheim stated his central thesis quite clearly: for an act to be a crime that is punishable by law, it must be (1) universally offensive to the collective conscience of the people, (2) strongly opposed, and (3) a clear and precise form of behavior. In his words:

> the only common characteristic of crimes is that they consist . . . in acts universally disapproved of by members of each society . . . crime shocks sentiments which, for a given social system, are found in all healthy consciences (1893:73).

> The collective sentiments to which crime corresponds must, therefore, singularize themselves from others by some distinctive property; they must have a certain average intensity. Not only are they engraven in all consciences, but they are strongly engraven (p. 77).

> The wayward son, however, and even the most hardened egotist are not treated as criminals. It is not sufficient, then, that the sentiments be strong; they must be precise (p. 79).

> An act is criminal when it offends strong and defined states of the collective conscience (p. 80).

Those acts, to offend the common conscience, need not relate ". . . to vital interests of society nor to a minimum of justice" (1893:81). Durkheim argues that a single murder may have less dire social consequences than the failure of the stock market, yet the former is a crime for the reasons stated and the latter is not.

Durkheim distinguishes two types of law: Restitutive and Repressive. Restitutive law "is not expiatory, but consists of a simple *return to state*" (1893:111). Repressive law is one which "in any degree whatever, invokes against its author the characteristic reaction which we term punishment" (p. 70). Restitutive laws, or as he sometimes says, "co-operative laws with restitutive sanctions" (p. 129), are laws that invoke rule enforcement but which (a) do not reflect the collective conscience (they reflect only the opinions of *some* of the members of society), and (b) do not reflect sentiments that are strongly felt. Therefore, these laws do *not* invoke penal sanctions but only rule enforcement. The more specialized the functions of law, the less the laws represent the common conscience. As a result, they cannot then offend the common conscience since they are in fact marginal and not common to all. Thus expiatory responses are likely. "The rules which determine them cannot have the superior force, the transcendent authority which, when offended, demands expiation" (1893:127).

There is very little evidence in the studies of the process by which laws are created that would support Durkheim's thesis. It is obvious that, contrary to Durkheim's expectations, industrial societies have tended to pass more and more repressive laws (Kadish, 1967) and that these laws have reflected special interests to a greater extent than they reflect the feelings of "all healthy consciences." Indeed, the reverse is closer to the mark: the collective conscience is largely irrelevant to the creation of laws. What relationship there is tends to be a consequence rather than a cause of new laws.

A view closely related to Durkheim's has also held considerable influence. This is the often-expressed belief that criminal law represents an attempt to control acts which it is in the "public interest" to control. Auerbach et al. attempted a listing of minimal elements of "the public interest":

(a) It is in the "public interest" that our nation be free from outside dictation in determining its destiny; that it have the power of self-determination. . . .

(b) It is in the public interest to preserve the legitimated institutions through which conflicts in our society are adjusted and peaceful change effected, no matter how distasteful particular decisions reached by these institutions may be to particular groups in our society. In other words, the preservation of democracy—government with the freely given consent of the governed—is in the public interest.

(c) It is in the public interest that no group in our society should become so powerful that it can submerge the claims of all other groups.

(d) It is in the public interest that all claims made by individuals and groups in our society should at least be heard and considered by the law-making authorities. This proposition, which calls for recognition of the freedom to speak and to associate with others in pursuit of group interests, is a fundamental assumption of the democratic order.

(e) It is in the public interest that every individual enjoy a minimum decent life and that the degree of inequality in the opportunities open to individuals be lessened (1961:661).

A variety of arguments suggest that this statement of a national public interest is invalid. Even assuming that there were a value-consensus on these propositions, the range of questions that come before law-making agencies and the state is largely outside their scope. Such a view is not a very useful or interesting guide to the study of lawmaking, for very few questions coming before lawmakers actually touch on any of these generalized objectives. Rather, they tend to be much narrower: What should the penalty be for prostitution? Should the patron be punished? Does the law of theft include "breaking bale and carrying away"? Are amphetamines to be included as dangerous drugs? Should students engaged in disruption in state universities automatically be expelled upon conviction? The usual questions coming before law-making authorities only rarely touch on the large questions suggested by any list of supposed "public interests."

Second, even if one were to accept these statements of "the public interest," the actual questions coming before lawmakers that even touch on these objectives are never very simple. Whether or not the United States ought to simply turn itself over to a foreign power, for example, is a question that has never come and doubtless never will come before any legislature. Rather, the question is always partial and problematic: Is joining the United Nations, and the surrender of sovereignty *pro tanto*, for example, too serious an invasion of the "public interest" in independence? If "freedom to speak" is "a fundamental assumption of the democratic order," then it can be argued that no private individual or corporation ought to control newspapers, television, or other institutions of the mass media, which instead should be equally available to all without regard to their financial resources. That would require government control of the mass media, which might well be regarded as the negation of free speech. While, no doubt, it is in the public interest that every individual should enjoy the minimum essentials of a decent life, exactly how much is a "minimum"? Is it in the public interest to reduce the size of "big business" in order to keep that group from attaining too much power, even if it can be shown that large economic units are more efficient than smaller ones? And if one decides to reduce the size of "big business," what is to be the standard of acceptable maximum size?

Third, is it true that even this list of "the minimal elements of the public interest" would be unanimously accepted? It is notable for omitting any reference to minimum protection for property. Many members of the propertied classes, at least in the American society, would insist that such a guarantee is an essential component of the "public interest." The list omits any statement that equality of treatment before the law regardless of race or color is a necessary ingredient of "the public interest"; white racists would hardly complain of this omission but others surely would.

Fourth, what a majority conceives of as "the public interest" at any period in history is not a constant. Not so long ago a majority of the lawmakers believed that it was in the public interest to prevent any citizen from buying alcoholic beverages. Not very long before that, in the long view of history, no doubt a majority believed that it was in the public interest to burn wretched old women at the stake as witches. How can one be sure that today's perception of "the public interest" is not merely an evanescent reflection of the value-sets of the majority?

Finally, consider the second of the propositions put forward, the broadest and most overarching of all: "It is in the public interest to preserve the legitimated institutions through which conflicts in society are adjusted and peaceful change effected." So long as real poverty exists, it seems clear that the fifth assertion of "the public interest," i.e., "that every individual enjoy a minimum decent life," is sharply in conflict with the second. Which of these interests is to be overriding? The repeated phenomenon of urban rioting in the ghettos of America suggests that there is no value-consensus on the relative weight to be given to any of these propositions which purport to define "the public interest."

The reason why this or any other set of claimed "public interest" elements, a commonly held *summum bonum*, can never adequately describe the actual state of affairs can be explained philosophically as well as empirically. John Dewey (1938) has argued that a distinction must be made between *that which is prized* and the *process of valuation*. No doubt we all have general, culturally acquired objectives, i.e., things which are prized. In any specific instance, however, how we define these generalized goals depends on a complex process of considering objective constraints, relative costs and benefits, and the valuation of alternative means. In this process of valuation, our generalized objectives are necessarily modified and changed as they become concrete and definite—i.e., in Dewey's language, as they become ends-in-view. Whatever the relative cultural agreement on general, broad prizings, there is never any complete agreement on any specific end in view.

The particular norms prescribed by law always are specific. They always command the role-occupant to act in specific ways. It is always a statement, not of generalized prizings, but of a specific end in view. It is the result of a process of valuation. On that valuation there is never complete agreement, for there is no complete agreement on the relative weightings to be given the various prizings held in different strata of the society, nor on the relative valuation to be given to different means.

In short, every assertion that a specific law should have a certain content must necessarily reflect the process of valuation of its proponents, and by the same token, it will be opposed to the processes of valuation of its opponents. The nature of law as a normative system, commanding what ought to be done, necessitates that it will favor one group as against another. The proof, whatever academic model-builders may say, lies in the fact that there is some opposition to *every* proposed new rule, whether or not the lawmakers themselves are unanimous. Even a declaration of war in the face of armed attack is never supported by the *entire* population.

That the law necessarily advances the values of some groups in society and opposes others reflects the fact that in any complex, modern society there is no value-consensus that is relevant to the law. That is so because of the very nature of the different "webs of life" that exist. It is a function of society itself.

For many of the same reasons, the view that the state is a value-neutral agent which weighs competing interests and distributes the available resources equitably is equally untenable. There are, indeed, competing interests but the competitors enter the arena with vastly different resources and, therefore, much different chances of success (Reich, 1964; Domhoff, 1970). The state, rather than being value-neutral, is, in fact, an agent of the side which controls the production and distribution of the society's available resources. The criminal law is then first and foremost a reflection of the interests and ideologies of the governing class—whether that class is private industry or state bureaucracy. Only secondarily, and even then only in minor ways, does the criminal law reflect the value-consensus, the public interest, or the sifting and weighing of competing interests.

A model more consistent with the realities of legal change must take into account differences in power which stem largely from differences in control over the economic resources of the society. More importantly, an adequate model to account for the definition of behavior as criminal or delinquent must recognize that in societies with social class divisions there is inevitably conflict between social classes and it is this class conflict which is the moving force for legal changes. Actions of the ruling class or representatives thereof as well as the machinations of moral entrepreneurs and the mobilization of bias all reflect attempts by various social classes to have their own interests and ideologies implemented by the state through the legal system.[6] It is, of course, true that the conflicts that are the basis of legal changes are not fought by equals. Thus those who control the economic and political resources of the society will inevitably see their interests and ideologies more often represented in the law than will others.

There are, of course, issues that are of only minor consequence to the established economic and political relations in the society. Such issues may be described by the pluralist perspective that sees different interest groups of more or less equal power arguing in the value-neutral arena of state bureaucracies. It seems clear that such instances are rare, and, in fact, even when the issue is the wording of prostitution laws or the changes in juvenile court laws there are differences in power between groups and these differences will usually determine the outcome of the struggle.

SUMMARY AND CONCLUSION

From the Black Death in feudal England where the vagrancy laws emerged and were shaped, through the Star Chamber in the fifteenth century where judges defined the law of theft in order to protect the interests of the ruling classes, to the legislatures of New York and California and the appellate courts of the United States lies a vast array of criminal laws that have been created, contradicted, reformulated, and allowed to die. Constructing a general theory that can account for such a wide range of events is no simple task. It is not surprising that such efforts often fall short of their goal.

Looking only at the two most general models of rule creation, the "value-consensus" and the "ruling class" models, and pitting them against the extant empirical data leave little doubt but that both fall short of the mark. The value-consensus model which suggests that community consensus is the moving force behind the definition of behavior as criminal and delinquent finds little support in the systematic study of the development of criminal law. The ruling class model falls short as an adequate explanation to the extent that it posits a monolithic ruling class which sits in jurisdiction over a passive mass of people and passes laws reflecting only the interests of those who rule.

On the other hand, the importance of the ruling class in determining the shape of the criminal law cannot be gainsaid—whether that influence is through direct involvement in the law-creating process or merely through the mobilization of bias. Nor, for that matter, can the influence of "public opinion" (especially as this is organized around moral entrepreneurs) be ignored as a source of criminal law. Thus both general models contain some valuable truths to which must be added the important role played by bureaucracies, vested interest groups, and even individuals acting virtually alone (Lewis, 1966).

An alternative model compatible with the data is best described as a conflict theory of legal change. The starting point for this theory is the recognition that modern, industrialized society is composed of numerous social classes and interest groups who compete for the favors of the state. The stratification of society into social classes where there are substantial (and at times vast) differences in wealth, power, and prestige inevitably leads to conflict between the extant classes. It is in the course of working through and living with these inherent conflicts that the law takes its particular content and form. It is out of the conflicts generated by social class divisions that the definition of some acts as criminal or delinquent emerges.

So long as class conflicts are latent, those who sit at the top of the political and economic structure of the society can manipulate the criminal laws to suit their own purposes. But when class conflict breaks into open rebellion, as it often does in such societies (Rubenstein, 1970), then the state must enact legislation and the courts reinterpret laws in ways that are perceived as solutions to the conflict. During times of manifest class conflict, legislatures and courts will simultaneously create criminal laws that provide greater control over those groups who are engaged in acts disruptive to the status quo and laws which appear to alleviate the conditions which are seen as giving rise to the social conflicts.

In between crises or perhaps as an adjunct to the legislative-judicial innovations taking place because of them, bureaucracies can mobilize and moral entrepreneurs organize to plead their case before the law-making bodies. Without the changes in economic structure that accompanied England's transition from feudalism to capitalism the laws of theft and vagrancy (to mention only two) would not have taken the form they did, just as the Supreme Court decisions and legislative enactments of the 1960s that effectively refocused substantial areas of the criminal law would not have taken place without the riots, rebellions, and overt social conflicts which characterized that historical period in America.

Crime is a political phenomenon. What gets defined as criminal or delinquent behavior is the result of a political process within which rules are formed which prohibit or require people to behave in certain ways. It is this process which must be understood as it bears on the definition of behavior as criminal if we are to proceed to the study of criminal *behavior*. Thus to ask "why is it that some acts get defined as criminal while others do not" is the starting point for all systematic study of crime and criminal behavior. Nothing is inherently criminal, it is only the response that makes it so. If we are to explain crime, we must first explain the social forces that cause some acts to be defined as criminal while other acts are not.

NOTES

[1] Note, for example, the toleration of a complete lack of due process within tribes as long as the tribe worked and contributed to the colonial regime; see Clairmonte (1969) and Seidman (1971).

[2] For a discussion of a similar use of criminal law in Guatemala, see Appelbaum (1966).

[3] This concept was first suggested by Schattschneider (1960). See also Bachrach and Baratz (1962, 1970).

[4] I am indebted to Robert Seidman for this analysis, which appeared in Chambliss and Seidman (1971).

[5] This section draws heavily upon Hall (1952), but does not come to the same theoretical conclusion he does.

[6] Most broadly conceived, each of these sources of law may be summarized under the concept of "interest groups" (Quinney, 1970). But such a general concept does little more than provide an umbrella under which to put these various social processes. Further, the notion of "interest groups" often leads to the erroneous implication that competition for control of or influence over the state is a battle between equals where social class differences are largely irrelevant. It seems analytically wiser to deal with all the sources of criminal law creation and to see them as stemming from basic conflicts within the society.

REFERENCES

Aaronovitch, S., and K. Aaronovitch.
    1947   Crisis in Kenya. London: Lawrence & Withorp.

Appelbaum, Richard P.
    1966   "Seasonal migration in San Ildefonso: its causes and its consequences." Public and International Affairs 4 (Spring):117–159.

Auerbach, D., K. Garrison, W. Hurst, and S. Mermin.
    1961   The Legal Process: An Introduction to Decision-Making by Judicial, Legislative, Executive, and Administrative Agencies. San Francisco: Chandler.

Bachrach, Peter, and Morton Baratz.
    1962   "Two faces of power," American Political Science Review 51 (December): 947–952.

    1970   Power and Poverty: Theory and Practice. New York: Oxford University Press.

Becker, Howard.
    1963   Outsiders: Studies in the Sociology of Deviance. New York: Free Press of Glencoe.

Bradshaw, F.
    1915   A Social History of England. London: University of London Press.

Carson, W. G. O.
    1971   "The sociology of crime and the emergence of criminal laws." Paper presented at the British Sociological Association, London, April.

Chambliss, William J.
    1964   "A sociological analysis of the law of vagrancy." Social Problems 12 (Summer):67–77.

1967   "Types of deviance and the effectiveness of legal sanction." Wisconsin Law Review 1967 (Summer):703–723.

1969   Crime and the Legal Process. New York: McGraw-Hill.

1971   "Vice, corruption, bureaucracy and power." Wisconsin Law Review 1971 (Winter):1150–1173.

Chambliss, William J., and Robert B. Seidman.
1971   Law, Order and Power. Reading, Mass.: Addison-Wesley.

Clairmonte, Paul.
1969   "Nigeria under colonial rule." Ibadan, Nigeria: Behavioral Science Research Institute, University of Ibadan (mimeographed).

Cloward, Richard A., and Lloyd E. Ohlin.
1960   Delinquency and Opportunity: A Theory of Delinquent Gangs. Glencoe, Ill.: Free Press.

Cohen, Albert K.
1955   Delinquent Boys. Glencoe, Ill.: Free Press.

Cressey, Donald R.
1968   "Culture conflict, differential association, and normative conflict." Pp. 43–54 in Marvin Wolfgang (ed.), Crime and Culture: Essays in Honor of Thorsten Sellin. New York: Wiley.

Deutscher, Irwin.
1955   "The petty offender." Federal Probation 19 (June):609–617.

Dewey, John.
1938   Logic: The Theory of Inquiry. New York: Holt.

Domhoff, G. William.
1970   The Higher Circles. New York: Random House.

Durkheim, Emile.
1893   The Division of Labor in Society. Translation by George Simpson. Glencoe, Ill.: Free Press (1947 edition).

Duster, Troy.
1970   The Legislation of Morality: Law, Drugs and Moral Judgment. New York: Free Press.

Foote, Caleb.
1956   "Vagrancy-type law and its administration." University of Pennsylvania Law Review 104:603–650.

Foucault, Michael.
1965   Madness and Civilization: A History of Insanity in the Age of Reason. New York: Pantheon Books.

Friedman, Lawrence, and Stewart Macaulay.
1969   Law and the Behavioral Sciences. Indianapolis: Bobbs-Merrill.

Glaser, Daniel.
1971   "Criminology and public policy." American Sociologist 6:30–37.

Graham, James M.
1971   Profits At All Costs: Amphetamine Politics on Capitol Hill. Ann Arbor: University of Michigan (mimeographed).

Gusfield, Joseph R.
   1963   Symbolic Crusade: Status Politics and the American Temperance Movement.
           Urbana: University of Illinois Press.
Halisbury, Earl of.
   1912   The Laws of England. Bell Yard, Temple Bar, London: Butterworth & Co.
Hall, Jerome.
   1952   Theft, Law, and Society. Revised Edition. Indianapolis: Bobbs-Merrill.
Hetzler, Antoinette.
   1971   "The law: a study of administrators as mediators of legal change." Ph.D.
           dissertation, University of California at Santa Barbara.
Holdsworth, Sir William.
   1924a   A History of English Law, vol. 3. Boston: Little, Brown.
   1924b   A History of English Law, vol. 5. Boston: Little, Brown.
Hurst, J. Willard.
   1950   The Growth of American Law: The Law Makers. Boston: Little, Brown.
   1956   Law and Conditions of Freedom. Madison: University of Wisconsin Press.
Jeffery, C. Ray.
   1957   "The development of crime in early English society." Journal of Criminal Law,
           Criminology and Police Science 47 (March–April):647–666.
Johnston, Sir Harry.
   1895   Trade and General Conditions Report. Nyasaland.
Kadish, Sanford H.
   1967   "The crisis of overcriminalization." Annals of the American Academy of Political
           and Social Science 374 (November):157–170.
Kolko, Gabriel.
   1963   The Triumph of Conservatism. New York: Free Press of Glencoe.
   1965   Railroads and Regulations. Princeton: Princeton University Press.
Lees, Norman.
   1924   Kenya. London: Leonard & Virginia Woolf.
Lemert, Edwin M.
   1967a   Human Deviance, Social Problems and Social Control. Englewood Cliffs, N.J.:
           Prentice-Hall.
   1967b   "Legislating change in the juvenile court." Wisconsin Law Review 1967
           (Spring):421–448.
   1970   Social Action and Legal Change: Revolution within the Juvenile Court.
           Chicago: Aldine.
Lenski, Gerhard.
   1966   Power and Privilege. New York: McGraw-Hill.
Lewis, Anthony.
   1966   Gideon's Trumpet. New York: Vintage Books.
Lindesmith, Alfred R.
   1965   The Addict and the Law. Bloomington: Indiana University Press.
   1968   Addiction and Opiates. Chicago: Aldine.

Merton, Robert K.
    1957   "Social structure and anomie." Chap. 4 in Robert K. Merton, Social Theory and Social Structure. Glencoe, Ill.: Free Press.

Miller, Walter B.
    1958   "Lower class culture as a generating milieu of gang delinquency." Journal of Social Issues 14(3):5–19.

Platt, Anthony.
    1972   "The Triumph of Benevolence: The Origins of the Juvenile Justice Systems in the United States." Berkeley: University of California (mimeographed).
    1969   The Child Savers: The Invention of Delinquency. Chicago: University of Chicago Press.

Quinney, Richard.
    1970   The Social Reality of Crime. Boston: Little, Brown.

Ranulf, Svend.
    1933   The Jealousy of the Gods, vols. 1, 2. London: Williams & Northgate Ltd.
    1938   Moral Indignation and Middle Class Psychology, Copenhagen: Levin & Munks-gaard.

Reich, Charles A.
    1964   "The new property." Yale Law Journal 73 (April):733–787.

Roby, Pamela A.
    1969   "Politics and criminal law: revision of the New York state penal law on prostitution." Social Problems 17 (Summer):83–109.

Rubenstein, Richard E.
    1970   Rebels in Eden. Boston: Little, Brown.

Schattschneider, E. E.
    1960   The Semi-Sovereign People: A Realist's View of Democracy in America. New York: Holt, Rinehart & Winston.

Schwartz, Richard, and Jerome Skolnick.
    1971   Society and the Legal Order. New York: Basic Books.

Seidman, Robert B.
    1971   "Law and Development." Madison: University of Wisconsin (mimeographed).

Sellin, Thorsten.
    1938   Culture Conflict and Crime. New York: Social Science Research Council Bulletin 41.

Sinclair, Andrew.
    1964   Era of Excess: A Social History of the Prohibition Movement. New York: Harper & Row.

Sinclair, Upton.
    1906   The Jungle. Cambridge, Mass.: Bentley Roberts, Inc.

Spradley, James P.
    1970   You Owe Yourself a Drunk. Boston: Little, Brown.

Steng-Dahl, Tove.
    1974   "The Emergence of the Norwegian Child Welfare Law." Scandinavian Studies in Criminology 5:83–97.

Stephen, J. F.
   1883   A History of the Criminal Law of England, vol. 1. London: Macmillan.
Sutherland, Edwin H.
   1924   Criminology. Philadelphia: Lippincott.
Sutherland, Edwin H., and Donald R. Cressey.
   1970   Criminology. Eighth Edition. Philadelphia: Lippincott.
Tannenbaum, Frank.
   1938   Crime and the Community. New York: Columbia University Press.
Walker, Nigel.
   1968   Crime and Insanity in England. 2 volumes. Edinburgh: Edinburgh University
           Press.
Williams, Glanville L.
   1963   The Proof of Guilt: A Study of English Criminal Trial. London: Stevens.
Wolfenden Report.
   1963   Report of the Committee on Homosexual Offenses and Prostitution. New York:
           Stein & Day.

AMPHETAMINE POLITICS
ON CAPITOL HILL

James M. Graham

The American pharmaceutical industry annually manufactures enough amphetamines to provide a month's supply to every man, woman and child in the country. Eight, perhaps ten, billion pills are lawfully produced, packaged, retailed and consumed each year. Precise figures are unavailable. We must be content with estimates because until 1970, no law required an exact accounting of total amphetamine production.

Amphetamines are the drug of the white American with money to spend. Street use, contrary to the popular myths, accounts for a small percentage of the total consumption. Most of the pills are eaten by housewives, businessmen, students, physicians, truck drivers and athletes. Those who inject large doses of "speed" intravenously are but a tiny fragment of the total. Aside from the needle and the dose, the "speed freak" is distinguishable because his use has been branded as illegal. A doctor's signature supplies the ordinary user with lawful pills.

All regular amphetamine users expose themselves to varying degrees of potential harm. Speed doesn't kill, but high sustained dosages can and do result in serious mental and physical injury, depending on how the drug is taken. The weight-conscious housewife, misled by the opinion-makers into believing that amphetamines can control weight, eventually may rely on the drug to alter her mood in order to face her monotonous tasks. Too frequently an amphetamine prescription amounts to a synthetic substitute for attention to emotional and institutional problems.

Despite their differences, all amphetamine users, whether on the street or in the kitchen, share one important thing in common—the initial source of supply. For both, it is largely the American pharmaceutical industry. That industry has skillfully managed to convert a chemical, with meager medical justification and considerable potential for harm, into multihundred-million-dollar profits in less than 40 years. High profits, reaped from such vulnerable products, require exten-

Source: "Amphetamine Politics on Capitol Hill," *Society*, Vol. 9, No. 3, January, 1972, pp. 14–23.

sive, sustained political efforts for their continued existence. The lawmakers who have declared that possession of marijuana is a serious crime have simultaneously defended and protected the profits of the amphetamine pill-makers. The Comprehensive Drug Abuse Prevention and Control Act of 1970 in its final form constitutes a victory for that alliance over compelling, contrary evidence on the issue of amphetamines. The victory could not have been secured without the firm support of the Nixon Administration. The end result is a national policy which declares an all-out war on drugs which are *not* a source of corporate income. Meanwhile, under the protection of the law, billions of amphetamines are overproduced without medical justification.

HEARINGS IN THE SENATE

The Senate was the first house to hold hearings on the administration's bill to curb drug abuse, The Controlled Dangerous Substances Act (S.3246). Beginning on September 15, 1969, and consuming most of that month, the hearings before Senator Thomas Dodd's Subcommittee to Investigate Juvenile Delinquency of the Committee on the Judiciary would finally conclude on October 20, 1969.

The first witness was John Mitchell, attorney general of the United States, who recalled President Nixon's ten-point program to combat drug abuse announced on July 14, 1969. Although that program advocated tighter controls on imports and exports of dangerous drugs and promised new efforts to encourage foreign governments to crack down on production of illicit drugs, there was not a single reference to the control of domestic manufacture of dangerous drugs. The president's bill when it first reached the Senate placed the entire "amphetamine family" in Schedule III, where they were exempt from any quotas and had the benefit of lesser penalties and controls. Hoffman-LaRoche, Inc. had already been at work; their depressants, Librium and Valium, were completely exempt from any control whatsoever.

In his opening statement, Attorney General Mitchell set the tone of administrative policy related to amphetamines. Certainly, these drugs were "subject to increasing abuse"; however, they have "widespread medical uses" and therefore are appropriately classed under the administration guidelines in Schedule III. Tightmouthed John Ingersoll, director of the Bureau of Narcotics and Dangerous Drugs (BNDD), reaffirmed the policy, even though a Bureau study over the last year (which showed that 92 percent of the amphetamines and barbiturates in the illicit market were legitimately manufactured) led him to conclude that drug companies have "lax security and recordkeeping."

Senator Dodd was no novice at dealing with the pharmaceutical interests. In 1965 he had steered a drug abuse bill through the Senate with the drug industry fighting every step of the way. Early in the hearings he recalled that the industry "vigorously opposed the passage of (the 1965) act. I know very well because I lived with it, and they gave me fits and they gave all of us fits in trying to get it through."

The medical position on amphetamine use was first presented by the National Institute of Mental Health's Dr. Sidney Cohen, a widely recognized authority on drug use and abuse. He advised the subcommittee that 50 percent of the lawfully manufactured pep pills were diverted at some point to illicit channels. Some of the pills, though, were the result of unlawful manufacture as evidenced by the fact that 33 clandestine laboratories had been seized in the last 18 months.

Dr. Cohen recognized three categories of amphetamine abuse, all of which deserved the attention of the government. First was their "infrequent ingestion" by students, businessmen, truck drivers and athletes. Second were those people who swallowed 50-75 milligrams daily without medical supervision. Finally, there were the speed freaks who injected the drug intravenously over long periods of time. Physical addiction truly occurs, said Dr. Cohen, when there is prolonged use in high doses. Such use, he continued, may result in malnutrition, prolonged psychotic states, heart irregularities, convulsions, hepatitis and with an even chance of sustained brain damage.

As the hearings progressed, the first two classes of abusers described by Dr. Cohen would receive less and less attention, while the third category—the speed freaks—would receive increasing emphasis. The amphetamine industry was not at all unhappy with this emphasis. In fact, they would encourage it.

Ingersoll had already said that BNDD statistics indicated that only 8 percent of illicit speed was illegally manufactured. Thomas Lynch, attorney general of California, testified that his agents had in 1967 successfully negotiated a deal for one-half million amphetamine tablets with a "Tijuana cafe man." Actual delivery was taken from a California warehouse. All of the tablets seized originated with a Chicago company which had not bothered to question the authenticity of the retailer or the pharmacy. Prior to the 1965 hearings, the Food and Drug Administration completed a ten-year study involving 1,658 criminal cases for the illegal sale of amphetamines and barbiturates. Seventy-eight percent of all convictions involved pharmacists, and of these convictions 60 percent were for illicit traffic in amphetamines.

The pharmacists were not the source of illicit diversion, according to the National Association of Retail Druggists (NARD) and the National Association of Chain Drug Stores. Indeed, NARD had conducted an extensive educational program combating drug abuse for years, and, as proof of it, introduced its booklet, "Never Abuse—Respect Drugs," into the record. Annual inventories were acceptable for Schedule I and II drugs, NARD continued, but were unwarranted for the remaining two schedules which coincidentally included most of their wares —unwarranted because diversion resulted from forged prescriptions, theft and placebo (false) inventories.

The amphetamine wholesalers were not questioned in any detail about diversion. Brief statements by the National Wholesale Druggists Association and McKesson Robbins Drug Co. opposed separate inventories for dangerous drugs because they were currently commingled with other drugs. Finally, the massive volume of the drugs involved—primarily in Schedule III—was just too great for records to be filed with the attorney general.

DODGING THE DIVERSION ISSUE

The representative of the prescription drug developers was also not pressed on the question of illicit diversion. Instead, the Pharmaceutical Manufacturers' Association requested clarifications on the definitional sections, argued for formal administrative hearings on control decisions and on any action revoking or suspending registration, and endorsed a complete exemption for over-the-counter nonnarcotic drugs.

With some misgivings, Carter-Wallace Inc. endorsed the administration bill providing, of course, the Senate would accept the president's recommendation that meprobamate not be subjected to any control pending a decision of the Fourth Circuit as to whether the drug had a dangerously depressant effect on the central nervous system. On a similar special mission, Hoffman-LaRoche Inc. sent two of its vice-presidents to urge the committee to agree with the president's recommendation that their "minor tranquilizers" (Librium and Valium) remain uncontrolled. Senator Dodd was convinced that both required inclusion in one of the schedules. The Senator referred to a BNDD investigation which had shown that from January 1968 to February 1969, three drug stores were on the average over 30,000 dosage units short. In addition, five inspected New York City pharmacies had unexplained shortages ranging from 12 to 50 percent of their total stock in Librium and Valium. Not only were the drugs being diverted, but Bureau of Narcotics information revealed that Librium and Valium, alone or in combination with other drugs, were involved in 36 suicides and 750 attempted suicides.

The drug company representatives persisted in dodging or contradicting Dodd's inquiries. Angry and impatient, Senator Dodd squarely asked the vice-presidents, "Why do you worry about putting this drug under control?" The response was as evasive as the question was direct: there are hearings pending in HEW, and Congress should await the outcome when the two drugs might be placed in Schedule III. (The hearings had begun in 1966; no final administrative decision had been reached and Hoffman-LaRoche had yet to exercise its right to judicial review.)

In the middle of the hearings, BNDD Director Ingersoll returned to the subcommittee to discuss issues raised chiefly by drug industry spokesmen. He provided the industry with several comforting administrative interpretations. The fact that he did not even mention amphetamines is indicative of the low level of controversy that the hearings had aroused on the issue. Ingersoll did frankly admit that his staff had met informally with industry representatives in the interim. Of course, this had been true from the very beginning.

The president of the American Pharmaceutical Association, the professional society for pharmacists, confirmed this fact: his staff participated in "several" Justice Department conferences when the bill was being drafted. (Subsequent testimony in the House would reveal that industry participation was extensive and widespread.) All the same, the inventory, registration and inspection (primarily "no-knock") provisions were still "unreasonable, unnecessary and costly administrative burden(s)" which would result in an even greater "paper work explosion."

For the most part, however, the administration bill had industry support. It was acceptable for the simple reason that, to an unknown degree, the "administration bill" was a "drug company bill" and was doubtless the final product of considerable compromise. Illustrative of that give-and-take process is the comparative absence of industry opposition to the transfer of drug-classification decision and research from HEW to Justice. The industry had already swallowed this and other provisions in exchange for the many things the bill could have but did not cover. Moreover, the subsequent windy opposition of the pill-makers allowed the administration to boast of a bill the companies objected to.

When the bill was reported out of the Committee on the Judiciary, the amphetamine family, some 6,000 strong, remained in Schedule III. Senator Dodd apparently had done some strong convincing because Librium, Valium and meprobamate were now controlled in Schedule III. A commission on marijuana and a declining penalty structure (based on what schedule the drug is in and whether or not the offense concerned trafficking or possession) were added.

DEBATE IN THE SENATE—ROUND I

The Senate began consideration of the bill on January 23, 1970. This time around, the amphetamine issue would inspire neither debate or amendment. The energies of the Senate liberals were consumed instead by unsuccessful attempts to alter the declared law enforcement nature of the administration bill.

Senator Dodd's opening remarks, however, were squarely directed at the prescription pill industry. Dodd declared that the present federal laws had failed to control the illicit diversion of lawfully manufactured dangerous drugs. The senator also recognized the ways in which all Americans had become increasingly involved in drug use and that the people's fascination with pills was by no means an "accidental development": "Multihundred-million-dollar advertising budgets, frequently the most costly ingredient in the price of a pill, have, pill by pill, led, coaxed and seduced post-World War II generations into the 'freaked-out' drug culture. . . . Detail men employed by drug companies propagandize harried and harassed doctors into pushing their special brand of palliative. Free samples in the doctor's office are as common nowadays as inflated fees." In the version adopted by the Senate, Valium, Librium and meprobamate joined the amphetamines in Schedule III.

HEARINGS IN THE HOUSE

On February 3, 1970, within a week of the Senate's passage of S.3246, the House began its hearings. The testimony would continue for a month. Although the Senate would prove in the end to be less vulnerable to the drug lobby, the issue of amphetamines—their danger and medical justification—would be aired primarily in the hearings of the Subcommittee on Public Health of the Committee on Interstate and Foreign Commerce. The administration bill (H.R. 13743), introduced by the chairman of the parent committee, made no mention of Librium or Valium and classified amphetamines in Schedule III.

As in the Senate, the attorney general was scheduled to be the first witness, but instead John Ingersoll of the BNDD was the administration's representative. On the question of amphetamine diversion, Ingersoll gave the administration's response: "Registration is . . . the most effective and least cumbersome way" to prevent the unlawful traffic. This coupled with biennial inventories of all stocks of controlled dangerous drugs and the attorney general's authority to suspend, revoke or deny registration would go a long way in solving the problem. In addition, the administration was proposing stronger controls on imports and exports. For Schedules I and II, but not III or IV, a permit from the attorney general would be required for exportation. Quotas for Schedules I and II, but not III or IV, would "maximize" government control. For Schedules III and IV, no approval is required, but a supplier must send an advance notice on triple invoice to the attorney general in order to export drugs such as amphetamines. A prescription could be filled only five times in a six-month period and thereafter a new prescription would be required, whereas previously such prescriptions could be refilled as long as a pharmacist would honor them.

The deputy chief counsel for the BNDD, Michael R. Sonnenreich, was asked on what basis the attorney general would decide to control a particular drug. Sonnenreich replied that the bill provides one of two ways: either the attorney general "finds *actual street abuse* or an interested party (such as HEW) feels that a drug should be controlled." (Speed-freaks out on the street are the trigger, according to Sonnenreich; lawful abuse is not an apparent criterion.)

The registration fee schedule would be reasonable ($10.00—physician or pharmacist; $25.00—wholesalers; $50.00—manufacturers). However, the administration did not want a formal administrative hearing on questions of registration and classification, and a less formal rule-making procedure was provided for in the bill.

Returning to the matter of diversion, Sonnenreich disclosed that from July 1, 1968 to June 30, 1969, the BNDD had conducted full-scale compliance investigations of 908 "establishments." Of this total, 329 (or about 36 percent) required further action, which included surrender of order forms (162), admonition letters (38), seizures (36) and hearings (31). In addition to these full-scale investigations, the Bureau made 930 "visits." (It later came to light that when the BNDD had information that a large supply of drugs was unlawfully being sold, the Bureau's policy was to warn those involved and "90 percent of them do take care of this matter.") Furthermore, 574 robberies involving dangerous drugs had been reported to the Bureau.

Eight billion amphetamine tablets are produced annually, according to Dr.

Stanley Yolles, director of the National Institute of Mental Health, and although the worst abuse is by intravenous injection, an NIMH study found that 21 percent of all college students had taken amphetamines with the family medicine cabinet acting as the primary source—not surprising in light of the estimate that 1.1 billion prescriptions were issued in 1967 at a consumer cost of $3.9 billion. Of this total, 178 million prescriptions for amphetamines were filled at a retail cost of $692 million. No one knew the statistics better than the drug industry.

Representing the prescription-writers, the American Medical Association also recognized that amphetamines were among those drugs "used daily in practically every physician's armamentarium." This casual admission of massive lawful distribution was immediately followed by a flat denial that physicians were the source of "any significant diversion."

The next witness was Donald Fletcher, manager of distribution protection, Smith Kline & French Laboratories, one of the leading producers of amphetamines. Fletcher, who was formerly with the Texas state police, said his company favored "comprehensive controls" to fight diversion and stressed the company's "educational effort." Smith Kline & French favored federal registration and tigher controls over exports (by licensing the exporter, *not* the shipment). However, no change in present record-keeping requirements on distribution, production or inventory should be made, and full hearings on the decisions by the attorney general should be guaranteed.

The committee did not ask the leading producer of amphetamines a single question about illicit diversion. Upon conclusion of the testimony, Subcommittee Chairman John Jarman of Oklahoma commented, "Certainly, Smith Kline & French is to be commended for the constructive and vigorous and hard-hitting role that you have played in the fight against drug abuse."

Dr. William Apple, executive director of the American Pharmaceutical Association (APhA), was the subject of lengthy questioning and his responses were largely typical. Like the entire industry, the APhA was engaged in a massive public education program. Apple opposed the inventory provisions, warning that the cost would be ultimately passed to the consumer. He was worried about the attorney general's power to revoke registrations ("without advance notice") because it could result in cutting off necessary drugs to patients.

Apple admitted organizational involvement "in the draft stage of the bill" but all the same, the APhA had a "very good and constructive working relationship" with HEW. Apple argued that if the functions are transferred to Justice, "We have a whole new ball game in terms of people. While some of the experienced people were transferred from HEW to Justice, there are many new people, and they are law-enforcement oriented. We are health-care oriented." Surely the entire industry shared this sentiment, but few opposed the transfer as strongly as did the APhA.

Apple reasoned that since the pharmacists were not the source of diversion, why should they be "penalized by costly overburdensome administrative requirements." The source of the drugs, Apple said, were either clandestine laboratories or burglaries. The 1965 Act, which required only those "records maintained in the ordinary course of business" be kept, was sufficient. Anyway, diversion at the pharmacy level was the responsibility of the pharmacists—a responsibility which the APhA takes "seriously and (is) going to do a better job (with) in the future."

Congress should instead ban the 60 mail-order houses which are not presently included in the bill. (One subcommittee member said this was a "loophole big enough to drive a truck through.") The corner druggist simply was not involved in "large-scale diversionary efforts."

The Pharmaceutical Manufacturers' Association (PMA) was questioned a bit more carefully in the House than in the Senate. PMA talked at length about its "long and honorable history" in fighting drug abuse. Its representative echoed the concern of the membership over the lack of formal hearings and requested that a representative of the manufacturing interests be appointed to the Scientific Advisory Committee. Significantly, the PMA declined to take a position on the issue of transfer from HEW to Justice. The PMA endorsed the administration bill. PMA Vice-President Brennan was asked whether the federal government should initiate a campaign, similar to the one against cigarettes, "to warn people that perhaps they should be careful not to use drugs excessively." Brennan's response to this cautious suggestion is worth quoting in full:

> I think this is probably not warranted because it would have the additional effect of giving concern to people over very useful commodities. . . . There is a very useful side to any medicant and to give people pause as to whether or not they should take that medication, particularly those we are talking about which are only given by prescription, I think the negative effect would outweigh any sociological benefit on keeping people from using drugs.

"LIMITED MEDICAL USE"

There was universal agreement that amphetamines are medically justified for the treatment of two very rare diseases, hyperkinesis and narcolepsy. Dr. John D. Griffith of the Vanderbilt University School of Medicine testified that amphetamine production should be limited to the needs created by those conditions: "A few thousand tablets (of amphetamines) would supply the whole medical needs of the country. In fact, it would be possible for the government to make and distribute the tablets at very little cost. This way there would be no outside commercial interests involved." Like a previous suggestion that Congress impose a one cent per tablet tax on drugs subject to abuse, no action was taken on the proposal.

The very next day, Dr. John Jennings, acting director of the Food and Drug Administration (FDA), testified that amphetamines had a "limited medical use" and their usefulness in control of obesity was of "doubtful value." Dr. Dorothy Dobbs, director of the Marketed Drug Division of the FDA, further stated that there was now no warning on the prescriptions to patients, but that the FDA was proposing that amphetamines be labeled indicating among other things that a user subjects himself to "extreme psychological dependence" and the possibility of "extreme personality changes . . . (and) the most severe manifestation of amphetamine intoxication is a psychosis." Dr. Dobbs thought that psychological dependence even under a physician's prescription was "quite possible."

Congressman Claude Pepper of Florida, who from this point on would be the recognized leader of the antiamphetamine forces, testified concerning a series of hearings which his Select Committee on Crime had held in the fall of 1969 on the question of stimulant use.

Pepper's committee had surveyed medical deans and health organizations on the medical use of amphetamines. Of 53 responses, only one suggested that the drug was useful "for *early* stages of a diet program." (Dr. Sidney Cohen of NIMH estimated that 99 percent of the total legal prescriptions for amphetamines were ostensibly for dietary control.) Pepper's investigation also confirmed a high degree of laxness by the drug companies. A special agent for the BNDD testified that by impersonating a physician, he was able to get large quantities of amphetamines from two mail-order houses in New York. One company, upon receiving an order for 25,000 units, asked for further verification of medical practice. Two days after the agent declined to reply, the units arrived. Before Pepper's committee, Dr. Cohen of NIMH testified that amphetamines were a factor in trucking accidents due to their hallucinatory effects.

Dr. John D. Griffith from Vanderbilt Medical School, in his carefully documented statement on the toxicity of amphetamines, concluded "amphetamine addiction is more widespread, more incapacitating, more dangerous and socially disrupting than narcotic addiction." Considering that 8 percent of all prescriptions are for amphetamines and that the drug companies make only one-tenth of one cent a tablet, Dr. Griffith was not surprised that there was so little scrutiny by manufacturers. Only a large output would produce a large profit.

Treatment for stimulant abuse was no easier than for heroin addiction and was limited to mild tranquilization, total abstinence and psychiatric therapy. But, heroin has not been the subject of years of positive public "education" programs nor has it been widely prescribed by physicians or lawfully produced. A health specialist from the University of Utah pointed out that the industry's propaganda had made amphetamines "one of the major ironies of the whole field of drug abuse. We continue to insist that they are good drugs when used under medical supervision, but their greatest use turns out to be frivolous, illegal and highly destructive to the user. People who are working in the field of drug abuse are finding it most difficult to control the problem, partly because they have the reputation of being legal and good drugs."

The thrust of Pepper's presentation was not obvious from the questioning that followed, because the subcommittee discussion skirted the issue. Pepper's impact could be felt in the subsequent testimony of the executive director of the National Association of Boards of Pharmacy. The NABP objected to the use of the word "dangerous" in the bill's title because it "does little to enhance the legal acts of the physician and pharmacist in diagnosing and dispensing this type of medication." (The Controlled Dangerous Substances Act would later become the Comprehensive Drug Abuse Prevention and Control Act of 1970.)

As in the Senate hearings, Ingersoll of the BNDD returned for a second appearance and, this time, he was the last witness. Ingersoll stated that he wished "to place . . . in their proper perspective" some "of the apparent controversies" which arose in the course of testimony. A substantial controversy had arisen over amphetamines, but there was not a single word on that subject in Ingersoll's prepared statement. Later, he did admit that there was an "overproduction" of amphetamines and estimated that 75 percent to 90 percent of the amphetamines found in illicit traffic came from the American drug companies.

Several drug companies chose to append written statements rather than testifying.

Abbott Laboratories stated that it "basically" supported the administration bills and argued that because fat people had higher mortality rates than others, amphetamines were important to the public welfare, ignoring the charge that amphetamines were not useful in controlling weight. Abbott then argued that because their products were in a sustained-release tablet, they were "of little interest to abusers," suggesting that "meth" tablets per se cannot be abused and ignoring the fact that they can be easily diluted.

Eli Lilly & Co. also endorsed "many of the concepts" in the president's proposals. They as well had "participated in a number of conferences sponsored by the (BNDD) and . . . joined in both formal and informal discussions with the Bureau personnel regarding" the bill. Hoffman-LaRoche had surely watched, with alarm, the Senate's inclusion of Librium and Valium in Schedule III. They were now willing to accept all the controls applying to Schedule III drugs, including the requirements of recordkeeping, inventory, prescription limits and registration as long as their "minor tranquilizers" were not grouped with amphetamines. Perhaps, the company suggested, a separate schedule between III and IV was the answer. The crucial point was that they did not want the negative association with speed and they quoted a physician to clarify this: "If in the minds of my patients a drug which I prescribe for them has been listed or branded by the government in the same category as 'goofballs' and 'pep pills' it would interfere with my ability to prescribe . . . and could create a mental obstacle to their . . . taking the drug at all."

When the bill was reported out of committee to the House, the amphetamine family was in Schedule III, and Hoffman-LaRoche's "minor tranquilizers" remained free from control.

DEBATE IN THE HOUSE—ROUND I

On September 23, 1970, the House moved into Committee of the Whole for opening speeches on the administration bill now known as H.R. 18583. The following day, the antiamphetamine forces led by Congressman Pepper carried their arguments onto the floor of the House by way of an amendment transferring the amphetamine family from Schedule III into Schedule II. If successful, amphetamines would be subject to stricter import and export controls, higher penalties for illegal sale and possession and the possibility that the attorney general could impose quotas on production and distribution. (In Schedule III, amphetamines were exempt from quotas entirely.) Also, if placed in Schedule II, the prescriptions could be filled only once. Pepper was convinced from previous experience that until quotas were established by law the drug industry would not voluntarily restrict production.

Now the lines were clearly drawn. The House hearings had provided considerable testimony to the effect that massive amphetamine production coupled with illegal diversion posed a major threat to the public health. No congressman would argue that this was not the case. The House would instead divide between those who faithfully served the administration and the drug industry and those who argued that Congress must act or no action could be expected. The industry representatives dodged the merits of the opposition's arguments, contending that a floor amendment was inappropriate for such "far-reaching" decisions.

"Legislating on the floor . . . concerning very technical and scientific matters," said subcommittee member Tim Lee Carter of Kentucky, "can cause a great deal of trouble. It can open a Pandora's Box" and the amendment which affected 6,100 drugs "would be disastrous to many companies throughout the land."

Paul G. Rogers of Florida (another subcommittee member) stated that the bill's provisions were based on expert scientific and law enforcement advice, and that the "whole process of manufacture and distribution had been tightened up." Robert McClory of Illinois, though not a member of the subcommittee, revealed the source of his opposition to the amendment:

> Frankly . . . there are large pharmaceutical manufacturing interests centered in my congressional district. . . . I am proud to say that the well-known firms of Abbott Laboratories and Baxter Laboratories have large plants in my (district). It is my expectation that C. D. Searl & Co. may soon establish a large part of its organization (there). Last Saturday, the American Hospital Supply Co. dedicated its new building complex in Lake County . . . where its principal research and related operations will be conducted.

Control of drug abuse, continued McClory, should not be accomplished at the cost of imposing "undue burdens or (by taking) punitive or economically unfair steps adversely affecting the highly successful and extremely valuable pharmaceutical industries which contribute so much to the health and welfare of mankind."

Not everyone was as honest as McClory. A parent committee member, William L. Springer of Illinois, thought the dispute was basically between Pepper's special committee on crime and the subcommittee on health and medicine chaired by John Jarman of Oklahoma. Thus phrased, the latter was simply more credible than the former. "There is no problem here of economics having to do with any drug industry."

But economics had everything to do with the issue according to Representative Jerome R. Waldie of California: "(T)he only opposition to this amendment that has come across my desk has come from the manufacturers of amphetamines." He reasoned that since the House was always ready to combat crime in the streets, a "crime that involved a corporation and its profits" logically merits equal attention. Waldie concluded that the administration's decision "to favor the profits (of the industry) over the children is a cruel decision, the consequences of which will be suffered by thousands of our young people." Pepper and his supporters had compiled and introduced considerable evidence on scientific and medical opinions on the use and abuse of amphetamines. It was now fully apparent that the evidence would be ignored because of purely economic and political considerations. In the closing minutes of debate, Congressman Robert Giaimo of Connecticut, who sat on neither committee, recognized the real issue: "Why should we allow the legitimate drug manufacturers to indirectly supply the (sic) organized crime and pushers by producing more drugs than are necessary? When profits are made while people suffer, what difference does it make where the profits go?"

Pepper's amendment was then defeated by a voice vote. The bill passed by a vote of 341 to 6. The amphetamine industry had won in the House. In two days of debate, Librium and Valium went unmentioned and remained uncontrolled.

DEBATE IN THE SENATE—ROUND II

Two weeks after the House passed H.R. 18583, the Senate began consideration of the House bill. (The Senate bill, passed eight months before, continued to languish in a House committee.) On October 7, 1970, Senator Thomas Eagleton of Missouri moved to amend H.R. 18583 to place amphetamines in Schedule II. Although he reiterated the arguments used by Pepper in the House, Eagleton stated that his interest in the amendment was not solely motivated by the abuse by speed freaks. If the amendment carried, it would "also cut back on abuse by the weight-conscious housewife, the weary long-haul truck driver and the young student trying to study all night for his exams."

The industry strategy from the beginning was to center congressional outrage on the small minority of persons who injected large doses of diluted amphetamines into their veins. By encouraging this emphasis, the drug companies had to face questioning about illicit diversion to the "speed community," but they were able to successfully avoid any rigorous scrutiny of the much larger problem of lawful abuse. The effort had its success. Senator Thomas J. McIntyre of New Hampshire, while noting the general abuse of the drugs, stated that the real abuse resulted from large doses either being swallowed, snorted or injected.

Senator Roman Hruska of Nebraska was, not surprisingly, the administration and industry spokesman. He echoed the arguments that had been used successfully in the House: The amendment seeks to transfer between 4,000 and 6,000 products of the amphetamine family; "some of them are very dangerous" but the bill provides a mechanism for administrative reclassification; administration and "HEW experts" support the present classification and oppose the amendment; and, finally, the Senate should defer to the executive where a complete study is promised.

It would take three to five years to move a drug into Schedule II by administrative action, responded Eagleton. Meanwhile amphetamines would continue to be "sold with reckless abandon to the public detriment." Rather than placing the burden on the government, Eagleton argued that amphetamines should be classed in Schedule II and those who "are making money out of the misery of many individuals" should carry the burden to downgrade the classification.

Following Eagleton's statement, an unexpected endorsement came from the man who had steered two drug control bills through the Senate in five years. Senator Dodd stated that Eagleton had made "a good case for the amendment." Senator John Pastore was sufficiently astonished to ask Dodd pointedly whether he favored the amendment. Dodd unequivocally affirmed his support. Dodd's endorsement was clearly a turning point in the Senate debate. Hruska's plea that the Senate should defer to the "superior knowledge" of the attorney general, HEW and BNDD was met with Dodd's response that, if amphetamines were found not to be harmful, the attorney general could easily move them back into Schedule III. In Schedule II, Dodd continued, "only the big powerful manufacturers of these pills may find a reduction in their profits. The people will not be harmed." With that, the debate was over and the amendment carried by a vote of 40 in favor, 16 against and 44 not voting.

Dodd may have been roused by the House's failure, without debate, to subject Librium and Valium to controls which he had supported from the beginning. Prior to Eagleton's amendment, Dodd had moved to place these depressants in Schedule IV. In that dispute, Dodd knew that economics was the source of the opposition: "It is clearly evident . . . that (the industry) objections to the inclusion of Librium and Valium are not so much based on sound medical practice as they are on the slippery surface of unethical profits." Hoffman-LaRoche annually reaped $40 million in profits—"a tidy sum which (they have) done a great deal to protect." Senator Dodd went on to say that Hoffman-LaRoche reportedly paid a Washington law firm three times the annual budget of the Senate subcommittee staff to assure that their drugs would remain uncontrolled. "No wonder," exclaimed Dodd, "that the Senate first, and then the House, was overrun by Hoffman-LaRoche lobbyists," despite convincing evidence that their drugs were connected with suicides and attempted suicides and were diverted in large amounts into illicit channels.

By voice vote Hoffman-LaRoche's "minor tranquilizers" were brought within the control provisions of Schedule IV. Even Senator Hruska stated that he did not oppose this amendment, and that it was "very appropriate" that it be adopted so that a "discussion of it and decision upon it (be) made in the conference."

The fate of the minor tranquilizers and the amphetamine family would now be decided by the conferees of the two houses.

IN CONFERENCE

The conferees from the Senate were fairly equally divided on the issue of amphetamine classification. Of the eleven Senate managers, at least six were in favor of the transfer to Schedule II. The remaining five supported the administration position. Although Eagleton was not appointed, Dodd and Harold Hughes would represent his position. Hruska and Strom Thurmond, both of whom had spoken against the amendment, would act as administration spokesmen.

On October 8, 1970, before the House appointed its conferees, Pepper rose to remind his colleagues that the Senate had reclassified amphetamines. Although he stated that he favored an instruction to the conferees to support the amendment, he inexplicably declined to so move. Instead, Pepper asked the conferees "to view this matter as sympathetically as they think the facts and the evidence they have before them will permit." Congressman Rogers, an outspoken opponent of the Pepper amendment, promised "sympathetic understanding" for the position of the minority.

Indeed, the minority would have to be content with that and little else. All seven House managers were members of the parent committee, and four were members of the originating subcommittee. Of the seven, only one would match support with "sympathetic understanding." The other six were not only against Schedule II classification, but they had led the opposition to it in floor debate: Jarman, Rogers, Carter, Harley Staggers and Ancher Nelsen. Congressman Springer, who had declared in debate that economics had nothing to do with this issue, completed the House representation. Not a single member of Pepper's Select Committee on Crime was appointed as a conferee. On the question of reclassification, the pharmaceutical industry would be well represented.

Hoffman-LaRoche, as well, was undoubtedly comforted by the presence of the four House subcommittee conferees: the subcommittee had never made any attempt to include Valium and Librium in the bill. On that question, it is fair to say that the Senate managers were divided. The administration continued to support no controls for these depressants.

At dispute were six substantive Senate amendments to the House bill: three concerned amphetamines, Librium and Valium; one required an annual report to Congress on advisory councils; the fifth lessened the penalty for persons who gratuitously distributed a small amount of marijuana; and the sixth, introduced by Senator Hughes, altered the thrust of the bill and placed greater emphasis on drug education, research, rehabilitation and training. To support these new programs, the Senate had appropriated $26 million more than the House.

The House, officially, opposed all of the Senate amendments.

From the final compromises, it is apparent that the Senate liberals expended much of their energy on behalf of the Hughes amendment. Although the Senate's proposed educational effort was largely gutted in favor of the original House version, an additional $25 million was appropriated. The bill would also now require the inclusion in state public health plans of "comprehensive programs" to combat drug abuse and the scope of grants for addicts and drug-dependent persons was increased. The House then accepted the amendments on annual reports and the possession charge for gratuitous marijuana distributors.

The administration and industry representative gave but an inch on the amphetamine amendment: only the liquid injectible methamphetamines, speed, would be transferred to Schedule II. All the pills would remain in Schedule III. In the end, amphetamine abuse was restricted to the mainlining speed freak. The conference report reiterated the notion that further administrative action on amphetamines by the attorney general would be initiated. Finally, Librium and Valium would not be included in the bill. The report noted that "final administrative action" (begun in 1966) was expected "in a matter of weeks." Congress was contented to await the outcome of those proceedings.

ADOPTION OF THE CONFERENCE REPORT

Pepper and his supporters were on their feet when the agreement on amphetamines was reported to the House on October 14, 1970. Conferee Springer, faithful to the industry's tactical line, declared that the compromise is a good one because it "singles out the worst of these substances, which are the liquid, injectible methamphetamines and puts them in Schedule II." If amphetamine injection warranted such attention, why, asked Congressman Charles Wiggins, were the easily diluted amphetamine and methamphetamine pills left in Schedule III? Springer responded that there had been "much discussion," yes and "some argument" over that issue, but the conferees felt it was best to leave the rest of the amphetamine family to administrative action.

Few could have been fooled by the conference agreement. The managers claimed to have taken the most dangerous and abused member of the family and subjected it to more rigorous controls. In fact, as the minority pointed out, the compromise affected the least abused amphetamine: lawfully manufactured "liquid meth" was sold strictly to hospitals, not in the streets, and there was no evidence of any illicit diversion. More importantly, from the perspective of the drug manufacturers, only 5 of the 6,000-member amphetamine family fell into this category. Indeed, liquid meth was but an insignificant part of the total methamphetamine, not to mention amphetamine, production. Pepper characterized the new provision as "virtually meaningless." It was an easy pill for the industry to swallow. The Senate accepted the report on the same day as the House.

Only Eagleton, the sponsor of the successful Senate reclassification amendment, would address the amphetamine issue. To him, the new amendment "accomplish(ed) next to nothing." The reason for the timid, limpid compromise was also obvious to Eagleton: "When the chips were down, the power of the drug companies was simply more compelling" than any appeal to the public welfare.

A week before, when Dodd had successfully classified Librium and Valium in the bill, he had remarked (in reference to the House's inaction): "Hoffman-

LaRoche, at least for the moment, have reason to celebrate a singular triumph, the triumph of money over conscience. It is a triumph . . . which I hope will be shortlived."

THE BILL BECOMES LAW

Richard Nixon appropriately chose the Bureau of Narcotics and Dangerous Drugs offices for the signing of the bill on November 2, 1970. Flanked by Mitchell and Ingersoll, the president had before him substantially the same measure that had been introduced 15 months earlier. Nixon declared that America faced a major crisis of drug abuse, reaching even into the junior high schools, which constituted a "major cause of street crime." To combat this alarming rise, the president now had 300 new agents. Also, the federal government's jurisdiction was expanded: "The jurisdiction of the attorney general will go far beyond, for example, heroin. It will cover the new types of drugs, the barbiturates and amphetamines that have become so common *and are even more dangerous because of their use*" (author emphasis).

The president recognized amphetamines were "even more dangerous" than heroin, although he carefully attached the qualifier that this was a result "of their use." The implication is clear: the president viewed only the large dosage user of amphetamines as an abuser. The fact that his full statement refers only to abuse by "young people" (and not physicians, truck drivers, housewives or businessmen) affirms the implication. The president's remarks contained no mention of the pharmaceutical industry, nor did they refer to any future review of amphetamine classification. After a final reference to the destruction that drug abuse was causing, the president signed the bill into law.

PART TWO

THE POLITICAL ECONOMY
OF LAW ENFORCEMENT

INTRODUCTION

Milton Mankoff

The previous section has suggested that the conflict approach, rather than the functional perspective, more accurately depicts the origin and development of legal sanctions in Western capitalist societies. However, the mere existence of legal sanctions, be they the product of conflict or consensus, does not exhaust the concerns of criminologists and sociologists of law. Laws attain their social power and mold societies chiefly through their enforcement. Unenforced laws have little deterrent value. If laws that derive from the consensus of community members are rarely or inequitably enforced, and laws which arise out of severe social conflict and represent the imposition of the wishes of one social group over others are enforced with great rigor, social life will differ significantly from that in a setting where only consensually based laws are enforced.

Taking this into consideration, how is one to characterize law enforcement in the United States? The three articles in this section suggest that police practices are highly inconsistent in dealing with different offenses and offenders. Evelyn

Parks's essay, "From Constabulary to Police Society," traces the development of the police force from its inception, when it involved all adult male members of a community on a rotating part-time basis and acted only upon the complaints of citizens, to its contemporary status as a full-time occupation charged with the prevention of crime regardless of whether there is a complainant. In the course of this transformation the American police gradually came to serve the wealthy and powerful rather than the "community." The creation and selective enforcement of vice laws are singled out by Parks as a vehicle by which the elites attempted to control the behavior of the lower classes.

William Chambliss's observation of two youth gangs from opposite sides of the tracks buttresses Parks's contention that there are different law enforcement systems for different classes of people. Middle-class gang members are much more likely to have their illegal acts defined as *pranks* than their working- and lower-class counterparts, whose antisocial behaviors are often considered to be *crimes*. Moreover, Chambliss suggests that the labeling of certain persons as *criminals* and others as *pranksters* has profound implications for their future careers. The stigmatization which typically accompanies having a criminal record and being punished by the legal system makes it difficult for persons so labeled to become reintegrated into the community. Employers are reluctant to hire people with criminal records.[1] Political rights such as voting are often lost and social ostracization may also occur. Given societal rejection, it is not surprising for many youths who have acquired criminal records to resume antisocial behavior patterns since attempts to conform with community norms have not been rewarded with the possibility of economic and social opportunities.

If Parks and Chambliss are correct in their assessment of law enforcement practices in the United States, it would not be too much of an exaggeration to say that crime itself is defined in the social world as illegal activities engaged in by the powerless. There are exceptions, of course, and an aroused citizenry can occasionally force legal authorities to prosecute and punish the privileged. This, however, is the exception rather than the rule. Studies of self-reported criminality indicate that virtually all Americans have committed illegal acts punishable by prison terms.[2] Nevertheless, the overwhelming majority of prisoners in the nation's jails are from the ranks of the economically and socially disadvantaged.

One of the crucial questions pertaining to law enforcement, and one which is not dealt with very adequately in the scholarly literature, is how policemen define their roles in such a manner that differential enforcement occurs.[3] The vast majority of policemen come from working-class backgrounds rather than from the ranks of the upper and middle classes. One might reasonably expect that the police would therefore sympathize more readily with the lower than the upper classes. A recent study of police attitudes in Vienna, Austria, is pertinent to answering these questions. A systematic study of the attitudes of Vienna policemen by a team of sociologists and criminologists revealed that for the most part the police do identify more readily with the working class than they do with the upper classes.[4] Furthermore, the police in Vienna certainly do not see themselves as serving as the bulwark of the "ruling class." On the contrary, they believe that their principal tasks are to prevent acts of violence, thefts and burglaries, find and arrest criminals, and help in emergencies. On the other hand, the policemen did not see it as an important part of their job to prevent illegal demonstrations or maintain order in business life. More surprising to those who would see the policeman as a willing and *conscious* representative of ruling-class interests is the fact that when asked, "Who deserves better treatment and who gets it if the police intervene?" the policemen reported consistently that it is "the little guy" who deserves and gets better treatment: the pedestrian rather than the car driver, the juvenile rather than the adult, the customer rather than the shopkeeper, and the worker rather than the employer.

It is difficult to know how to interpret such data. Perhaps Viennese police differ in social and psychological characteristics and in social attitudes from their

American counterparts. Another possibility is that the role of the Viennese police, in its historical and contemporary manifestation, varies from the American model. Also, there is, of course, the possibility that the police officers gave researchers "socially acceptable" responses, or that they are not aware of their actual behaviors on the street. The fact remains that policing as an organized enterprise typically ends up serving the interests of businessmen rather than customers, of drug importers rather than drug users, of employers rather than workers. In times of mass labor strife or demonstrations the police often attack demonstrators with a vengeance; in the enforcement of laws it is the drunks and ghetto residents who fill the jails while the businessmen's crimes against consumers go unobserved and unpunished.[5] It is the transgressions of lower-class youth that occupy the attention of the police while the equally or perhaps even more serious offenses of the middle class go unnoticed.

It is likely that differential law enforcement is something that is learned from other policemen on the beat and from superiors in police departments with career rewards and punishments being dispersed according to the degree to which one conforms to the prevailing rules of the game. This still begs the question of how the rules became established in the first place. In any case, scholars need to explore more thoroughly the linkages between societal elites and police.

If it is difficult to understand the tolerance of working-class police for the illegal actions of the well-to-do and powerful in general, William Cham-

bliss's discovery of the interrelationships among racketeers, economic and political elites, bureaucrats and law enforcement people in a major American city helps us recognize some of the sources of the cooptation of the police in the organization and distribution of vice. The unwillingness to interfere in the rackets is a direct result of the fact that those who control the police (the economic elites and the political office holders) benefit personally and as a class from the organization of vice into a profitable corporation in which key members of different groups share the profits.

The studies that follow are admittedly only a small sampling of the inquiries that have been and need to be done if we are to fully understand the role of law enforcement agencies. They are a beginning, however, in that they point to the necessity of analyzing law enforcement as a system of relationships which are inherently in conflict and operating under the constraints of political and economic forces beyond the control of the individuals who occupy roles and positions in the system.

NOTES

[1] Richard D. Schwartz and Jerome Skolnick, "Two Studies of Legal Stigma," *Social Problems* 10 (Fall 1962), pp. 133–142.
[2] Richard Quinney, *The Problem of Crime* (New York: Dodd, Mead, 1974), pp. 116–118.
[3] Studies that bear on this issue include: Michael Banton, *The Policeman in the Community* (London: Tavistock, 1964); Donald J. Black, "Police Control of Juveniles," *American Sociological Review* 35 (August 1970), pp. 733–748; Donald J. Black, "The Social Organization of Arrest," *Stanford Law Review* 23 (June 1971), pp. 1007–1111; John P. Clark and Richard E. Sykes, "Some Determinants of Police Organization and

Practice in a Modern Industrial Democracy" in *Handbook of Criminology*, ed. by Daniel Glaser (Chicago: Rand McNally, 1974), pp. 455–494; Arthur Niederhoffer, *Behind the Shield: The Police in Urban Society* (Garden City, N.Y.: Doubleday, 1967); Albert J. Reiss, Jr., *The Police and the Public* (New Haven: Yale University Press, 1971); Jerome Skolnick, *Justice Without Trial: Law Enforcement in Democratic Society* (New York: Wiley, 1967); and James Q. Wilson,

Varieties of Police Behavior (Cambridge: Harvard University Press, 1968).

[4] Marina Fischer-Kowalski, Fritz Leitner and Heins Steinert, "Status Management and Interactional Conflict of the Police in Vienna," mimeographed (Vienna, 1974), pp. 1–8.

[5] James Q. Spradley, *You Owe Yourself a Drunk* (Boston: Little, Brown, 1969); William J. Chambliss, ed., *Criminal Law in Action* (Santa Barbara: Hamilton, 1975).

FROM CONSTABULARY TO POLICE SOCIETY:

Implications for Social Control

Evelyn L. Parks

The history of social control in the United States is the history of transition from "constabulary" to "police society" in which the proliferation of criminal laws, enforcement officials, criminal courts and prisons was not essentially for the protection of the "general welfare" of society but was for the protection of the interests and life-styles of but one segment of society—those holding positions of wealth, "respectability," and power.

The establishment of a police society in the United States made possible a new conception of law and order in which more effective control of the population was feasible. Central to this conception were laws governing the private behavior of citizens where no self-defined victims are involved—the vice laws. Thus, the growth of the police was necessary for the growth of both law and crime.

TRANSITION FROM A
CONSTABULARY TO A POLICE SOCIETY

The first official responsible for the enforcement of law and order in the New World was the constable. The law as written was oppressive—outlawing swearing, lying, sabbath breaking, and night walking—and gave to the constable almost totalitarian powers to enforce the laws.[1] However, the constable did not use his power to discover and punish deviation from the established laws. Rather, he assisted complaining citizens if and when they sought his help. This reflected the conception of law during colonial times: the written law was regarded as an ideal, rather than as prescriptions actually to be enforced.

Initially, the constableship was a collective responsibility which all able-bodied men were expected to assume. It was not a specialized occupation or an income-producing job, but a service to the community. The constableship was so thankless

---

Source: "From Constabulary to Police Society," *Catalyst*, No. 5, Summer, 1970, pp. 76–97. By permission of the author and publisher.

a task, however, that as early as 1653, fines were sometimes levied against anyone refusing to serve.[2]

The constable served only during the day. At night, the towns formed a citizens' watch or night watch. Supposedly, each adult male took his turn, but as with the constable those who could hired substitutes. In contrast to our present police the concerns of the night watch were more closely related to the general welfare. They included looking out for fires, reporting the time, and describing the weather.

Thus, there was no *one* specialized agency responsible for social control. Not only was the power divided between the constable and the night watch, but initially, both were volunteer services rotated among the citizens. This lack of specialization of enforcement of law and order extended to a comparative lack of specialization in the punishment of offenders. Although prisons were constructed as early as 1637, they were almost never kept in good enough condition to prevent jailbreaks. The financial costs of jails were considered prohibitive; corporal punishments, such as whippings, were preferred.[3] Thus, there was no specialized penal system, staffed and available.

EARLY POLICE

The constabulary was not able to survive the growth of urban society and the concomitant economic specialization. Charles Reith writes that voluntary observance of the laws

> can be seen to have never survived in effective form the advent of community prosperity, as this brings into being, inevitably, differences in wealth and social status, and creates, on this basis, classes and parties and factions with or without wealth and power and privileges. In the presence of these divisions, community unanimity in voluntary law observance disappears and some other means of securing law observance and the maintenance of authority and order must be found.[4]

By 1800 in the larger cities the constabulary had changed from a voluntary position to a quasi-professional one, being either appointed or elected and providing an income. Some people resisted this step, claiming that such police were threats to civil liberty, and that they performed duties each citizen should perform himself. However, in the 1840s and 1850s, the night watch was gradually incorporated into an increasingly professionalized police, establishing twenty-four-hour responsibility and in other ways beginning to institute the type of law enforcement that we have today.[5]

In the 1850s, cities began to employ detectives. The earliest detectives represented an attempt to apply the conception of the constableship to urban society. That is, the duties of the detective were to assist in recovering stolen property, not to prevent crime. However, this application of the constableship to the emerging urban society proved ineffective. For one thing, to recover stolen property effectively, familiarity with criminals was a necessary qualification and quite naturally ex-criminals were often hired. For another, detectives became corrupted through taking advantage of a system known as compromises. Under this system, it was legal for a thief to negotiate with the robbed owner and agree to return part of the stolen goods, if the thief could remain free. Detectives, however, would often supplement their salaries by accepting thieves' offers of a portion of the stolen goods in exchange for their immunity.[6]

Understandably, detectives were reluctant to devote their time to anything other than large-scale robbery. Murder, an amateur crime at this time, went uninvestigated. Detectives essentially served the private interests of big business at the expense of the general public.

By 1880, the detective force as such had acquired such adverse publicity that in most places they were formally abolished. Their functions and services however were incorporated into the regular police. Compromises were no longer legally acceptable.

HISTORICAL SOURCES OF THE CHANGE
FROM CONSTABULARY TO POLICE

Central to the development of the professional police is the development of economic inequality. Seldon Bacon in his study of the development of the municipal police sees the increasing economic specialization and the resulting "class stratification" as the primary cause for the development of police.[7] He argues that specialists could exploit the increasing dependence of the populace on their services. Cities responded by creating specialized offices of independent inspectors who attempted to prevent exploitation or cheating of the populace. For example, the necessity in New Amsterdam to rely on specialized suppliers of firewood led as early as 1658 to the employment of firewood inspectors. Regulation of butchers, bakers, and hack drivers showed the same consequences of the inability of the citizen to rely on his own resources in a period of increasing specialization.[8]

By the time of the emergence of the professional police, the list of regulatory or inspectorial officials had grown quite long. Bacon describes the development of "the night police, the market police, street police, animal police, liquor police, the vagabond and stranger police, vehicle police, fire police, election police, Sunday police and so on."[9] Gradually, many of these special police or inspectors were removed from the professional police to other municipal agencies. "Only slowly did regulation for the public good and the maintenance of order become themselves specializations and the full-time career police develop."[10]

The other central element in the development of the professional police was rioting, which is closely related to economic inequality. Usually, riots are an attempt by the have-nots to seek a redress of grievances from those with power and wealth. The solid citizens, on the other hand, wanted to prevent riots, to stop the disturbances in the streets. An official history of the Buffalo police states that in March of 1834 complaints of riot and disorder continued to pour in upon the Mayor. "Rowdies paraded the streets at night, unmolested, and taxpayers became alarmed regarding both life and property."[11] Roger Lane writes of Boston that "The problem of mob violence . . . soon compelled the municipality to take a more significant step, to create a new class of permanent professional officers with new standards of performance."[12]

David Bordua and Albert Reiss write:

> The paramilitary form of early police bureaucracy was a response not only, or even primarily, to crime *per se*, but to the possibility of riotous disorder. Not crime and danger but the "criminal" and "dangerous classes" as part of the urban social structure led to the formation of uniformed and military organized police. Such organizations intervened between the propertied elites and the propertyless masses who were regarded as politically dangerous as a class.[13]

Riots became so frequent that the traditional method of controlling them by use of military forces became less and less effective. Military forces were unable to arrive at the scene of trouble before rioting had already reached uncontrollable proportions. This illustrates how the military may be able temporarily to enforce laws but are ineffective for sustained law enforcement.[14] The police, not the military, represent the continued presence of the central political authority.

Furthermore, in a riot situation, the direct use of social and economic superiors as the agents of suppression increases class violence.

> If the power structure armed itself and fought a riot or a rebellious people, this created more trouble and tension than the original problem. But, if one can have an independent police which fights the mob, then antagonism is directed toward police, not the power structure. A paid professional police seems to separate "constitutional" authority from social and economic dominance.[15]

These trends toward the establishment of a paramilitary police were given further impetus by the Civil War. It was the glory of the Army uniform that helped the public accept a uniformed police. Previously, the police themselves, as well as the public, had objected to uniforms as implying a police state with the men as agents of a king or ruler. A uniformed police was seen as contradictory to the ideals of the American Revolution, to a republic of free men.[16] But after 1860 the police began to carry guns, although at first unofficially. Within twenty years, however, most cities were furnishing guns along with badges.

THE PROFESSIONAL POLICE
AND THE NEW CONCEPT OF LAW

As the cities changed from a constabulary to a professional police, so was there a change in the conception of law. Whereas the constable had only investigated crimes in which a citizen had complained, the new professional police were expected to *prevent* crime. A preventive conception of law requires that the police take the initiative and seek out those engaged in violating the law—those engaged in specific behaviors that are designated as illegal. Once an individual has been arrested for breaking a law, he is then identified, labeled and treated as a criminal. The whole person then becomes a criminal—not just an individual who has broken a law. Since now too, professional police were responsible for maintaining public order—seen as preventing crime—they came to respond to individuals who committed unlawful acts as criminal persons—as wholly illegitimate.

Processing people through this machinery stigmatizes people—i.e., publicly identifies the whole person in terms of only certain of his behavior patterns. At the same time, this often leads to acceptance by such persons of that identity. In this and other ways the transition to police society *created* the underworld. A professional police creates a professional underworld.[17]

The "yellow press" which had emerged by the middle of the nineteenth century focused on crime and violence. This helped confirm the new definition and stigmatization of the criminal person. Reporters obtained their stories by attending police courts. Police court reportage became so popular that even the conservative press eventually came to adopt it. And the police became guides to the newly discovered underworld.[18]

The establishment of a professional police concerned with prevention increases the power of the state. Roger Lane writes:

> Before the 1830s the law in many matters was regarded as the expression of an ideal. The creation of a strong police raised the exciting possibility that the ideal might be realized, that morality could be enforced and the state made an instrument of social regeneration.[19]

With the idea of prevention, then, law loses its status as only an ideal and becomes a real prescription actually to be enforced.

Those involved in the reform movements of the 1830s were quick to demand the services of the new police. Although they had originally objected to hiring paid, daytime police, they soon began to welcome the police as part of the reform movement, seeing the police as "moral missionaries" eventually eliminating crime and vice.[20] As Howard Becker writes, "The final outcome of a moral crusade is a police force."[21]

During the first half of the nineteenth century, the professional police increasingly took over and expanded the duties of the constableship. This led to the police themselves becoming specialists in the maintenance of public order, which involved a transition to emphasizing the prevention of crime, and the role of law as ideal became an attempt to enforce laws as real prescriptions governing conduct. In this way the police, as an agency of the state, took over the function of social control from the members of the local community. The historical sources of the change were economic inequality and increasing riots. Thus, the police became an agency of those with wealth and power for suppressing the attempts by the have-nots to redistribute the wealth and power.

Thus, the professional police gave the upper classes an extremely useful and powerful mechanism for maintaining the unequal distribution of wealth and power:

law, which is proclaimed to be for the general welfare, is in fact an instrument in class warfare. This is most clearly demonstrated by looking at the history of the vice laws. Social control is at its greatest when the state has the power to govern the private behavior of citizens—when the state can declare illegal and punish acts in which all parties are willing participants.

THE VICE LAWS AS SOCIAL CONTROL: THE CASE OF ALCOHOL

The most celebrated vice problem in America is the use of alcohol. The use of alcohol dates back to early colonial times, during which nearly everybody drank: men, women, and children—it was an indispensable part of living. Drinking was usually family-centered and family-controlled, or part of community events. [22]

In early colonial times, mostly wine and beer were imbibed, with hard liquor (distilled spirits) in third place. However, hard liquor was much easier to transport as well as less subject to spoilage than wine and beer or the grains from which they were derived. As the colonies developed a market economy, this pushed the manufacturing and selling of hard liquors rather than beer and wine. The manufacturing and selling of hard liquor became an important part of the developing colonial commerce. "During the years immediately preceding the Revolution, more than 600,000 gallons were shipped abroad annually." [23]

As the manufacturing changed from wine and beer to hard liquor, so did the drinking habits of the colonists. By the end of the eighteenth century about 90 percent of the alcohol consumed in this country was in the form of hard liquor. "By 1807, it is recorded that Boston had one distillery for every forty inhabitants—but only two breweries." [24]

Just as the drinking began to change from beer and wine to hard liquor, so also, around 1750, the context began to change from a family activity to an individual one. Men, especially young, unattached men, and other "peripheral segments" of society, began to do most of the drinking. [25] Saloons and taverns, instead of the home, became the place to drink.

These changes brought about a great increase in the amount and frequency of intoxication. Spirits are more intoxicating than either wine or beer, and the context of the saloon places no restrictions on consumption. The thirty years preceding and the fifty years following the American Revolution was an era of extremely heavy drinking. [26]

THE TEMPERANCE & PROHIBITION MOVEMENT

As the amount and frequency of drunkenness increased so did social concern about drinking. Drunkenness was often accompanied by destructive behavior. Intoxication came to be seen "as a threat to the personal well-being and property of peaceful citizens." [27] In this way, the call to moderation was an attempt to control those who were seen as a threat by the "solid" citizens. And so the Temperance movement began in the last half of the eighteenth century.

In the 1830s the Temperance movement altered its goal from moderation to abstinence. Why did abstinence, rather than moderation, become the symbol of respectability? Joseph R. Gusfield, who has interpreted the Temperance/Prohibition movement in terms of its symbolic meanings and status conflicts, considers the Temperance movement and ultimately Prohibition as a quest for honor and power. Gusfield argues that coercive reform, or the change from temperance to abstinence, became necessary with the decline of the pre-civil war Federalist aristocracy and the rise to social and political importance of the "common man," that which is symbolized by Andrew Jackson's election to the presidency.[28]

> To make the new common man respond to the moral ideals of the old order, was both a way of maintaining the prestige of the old aristocracy and an attempt to control the character of the political electorate.[29]

Lyman Beecher, a leading Temperance leader, puts it more forcefully.

> When the laboring classes are contaminated, the right to sufferage becomes the engine of destruction . . . As intemperance increases, the power of taxation will come more and more into the hands of men of intemperate habits and desperate fortunes; of course, the laws will gradually become subservient to the debtor and less efficacious in protecting the rights of property.[30]

The insistence on total abstinence came just when the country's drinking habits were becoming more moderate and changing from hard liquors back again to wine and beer. In 1800, when most drinking was of hard liquor, 90 percent of the white population was from Britain. By 1840, the immigration of ethnic groups from southern, central, and eastern Europe (where drinking habits were of wine and beer) acted as a moderating influence on the drinking habits of the nation.[31] Only total abstinence, then, would be a symbol of power and respectability—moderation was not enough to indicate superiority.

The change from moderation to abstinence was reflected in the laws of Massachusetts. In 1835, a Massachusetts statute revision made single incidences of drunkenness a punishable offense. Prior to this only the habitually drunk were usually arrested. In Boston, the number of drunk arrests jumped from the few hundred annually during the 1830s to several thousand in the 1840s and 1850s. Even before the middle of the century, Theodore Parker believed that "the 'rude tuition' of courts and constables was improving the drinking habits of the Irish immigrants."[32] In 1841, the Boston Society for the Suppression of Intoxication petitioned for a doubling of the police force.[33]

Thus, the Temperance/Prohibition movement was an effort to control the "dangerous classes," to make them conform to middle-class standards of respectability. As is so often the case, the stated goals of improving society or helping the unfortunates muted the fact that this "help" came in the form of control—the police power of the state. Not only did alcohol use come to be universally defined as a social problem, but criminal law and police enforcement was commonly seen as the solution to the problem.

The thought and research of seemingly all fields could be used to support the claims of the prohibitionists. Based on research done in the last half of the nineteenth century, scientists began to describe the negative effects alcohol has on the human body, and for the first time, claimed that even moderate drinking might cause liver, kidney, and heart diseases.[34]

In 1914, psychiatrists and neurologists meeting in Chicago adopted a resolution concluding that the availability of alcoholic beverages caused a large amount of mental, moral, and physical degeneracy and urged the medical profession "to take the lead in securing prohibitory legislation."[35]

Temperance groups were even able to utilize mortality studies done by insurance companies. A study drawing on the experience of two million policy holders between 1885 and 1908 concluded that those who drank the equivalent of only two glasses of beer each day showed a mortality rate of 18 percent higher than average. Furthermore, those who drank two ounces or more of alcohol each day were found to have a mortality rate of 86 percent higher than insured lives in general.[36]

Social workers, lawyers and judges began to claim that alcohol played an important role in crime. On the basis of a study of 13,402 convicts in 12 different states, the community leaders of one city concluded that "intemperance had been the sole cause of crime in 16 percent of the cases, the primary cause in 31 percent, and one of the causes in nearly 50 percent."[37] Alcohol was also claimed to be an important factor in prostitution and venereal disease. (One physician reported that 70 percent of all venereal infection in men under 25 was contracted while under the influence of alcohol.)[38]

In addition, prohibitionists claimed the use of alcoholic beverages was an important factor in domestic unhappiness and broken homes. "According to a study by the U.S. Bureau of the Census, for the years 1887–1906, nearly 20 percent of all divorces were granted for reasons of intemperance."[39]

Even notable academicians argued that alcohol was one of the chief factors creating crime and that the state ought to abolish it.[40] A noted sociologist felt that instituting national prohibition would reduce crime and poverty, improve the position of women and children, benefit the home, purify politics, and elevate the status of the wage earner.[41]

THE VOLSTEAD ACT AND ENFORCEMENT

The prohibitionists were successful and in 1918, the Volstead Act was passed. As is well known, the attempt to enforce the Volstead Act resulted in corruption unparalleled in American history. Stories of dry agents and other governmental personnel responsible for enforcement conniving with smugglers or accepting bribes appeared in the newspapers day after day. For example, in Philadelphia, a grand jury investigation in 1928 showed that one police "inspector had $193,533.22 in his bank account, another had $102,829.45, and a third had $40,412.75. One police captain had accumulated a nest egg of $133,845.86, and nine had bank accounts ranging from $14,607.44 to $68,905.89."[42]

By the fall of 1923 in Philadelphia, things were so bad that the mayor requested President Harding to lend the city the services of Brigadier General Smedley D. Butler of the Marine Corps, a famous soldier of World War I. General Butler arrived and began a whirlwind round of raids and arrests. At first it appeared he would succeed in enforcing the Volstead Act, but then: places were found empty when raids were attempted (they had been warned); the courts would dismiss cases brought before them. General Butler stuck it out for two years before returning to the Marine Corps, declaring the job had been a waste of time: "Trying to enforce the law in Philadelphia," he said, "was worse than any battle I was ever in."[43]

When the Volstead Act was passed, the justice department made no special preparation to handle extra violators. The result is that within a few months federal courts throughout the country were overwhelmed by the number of dry cases, and Emory R. Buckner, United States Attorney from New York, told a congressional committee in 1926 that

> . . . violators of the Volstead Act were being brought into the Federal Building in New York City at the rate of about fifty thousand a year, and the United States Attorney's office was five months behind in the preliminary steps of preparing cases.[44]

The volume of law-breakers was so tremendous that those who could pay the fines and/or bribe the officials went free. A jury trial was impossible.[45]

And so goes the story of the attempt to enforce Prohibition. It is generally thought of as such a fiasco, such an aberration of American justice that those who study it feel a need for an explanation of its existence. This need for explanation, however, usually does not extend to our other vice laws, such as drug laws, which are still seen as supporting democracy and justice for all.

THE VICE LAWS AS SOCIAL CONTROL: THE CASE OF NARCOTIC DRUGS

The scientific condemnation of the dangers involved in the use of alcohol did not extend even to warnings about the dangers in the use of opium and its derivatives. Indeed, the use of such drugs was systematically encouraged in the nineteenth century. Opium constituted the main therapeutic agent of medical men for more than 2000 years—through the nineteenth century. A physician writes:

> Even in the last half of the nineteenth century, there was little recognition of and less attention paid to overindulgence in or abuse of opium. It was a panacea for all ills. When a person became dependent upon it so that abstinence

symptoms developed if a dose or two were missed, more was taken for the aches and pains and other discomforts of abstinence, just as it was taken for similar symptoms from any other cause.[46]

In 1804 a German chemist isolated morphine. In this country, morphine began to be applied hypodermically in the 1850s. At first, it was declared that administration through the skin, as opposed to through the mouth, was *not* habit forming. Although there were soon isolated warnings that the hypodermic habit was even harder to break than the oral habit, the great majority of textbooks on the practice of medicine failed to issue any warning of the dangers of the hypodermic use of morphine until 1900.[47]

In 1898 heroin was isolated. Heroin is approximately three times as powerful as morphine and morphine is more potent than opium. Opium is generally smoked while its derivatives are taken orally or with hypodermic needles.[48] At first it was also claimed that heroin was free from addiction-forming properties, possessing many of the virtues and none of the dangers of morphine and codeine. Heroin was even recommended as a treatment for those addicted to morphine and codeine. For the next few years, doctors continued to report in medical journals on the curative and therapeutic value of heroin, either omitting any reference to addiction, or assuming any addiction to be very mild and much less bothersome than morphine addiction. It was 1910 before the medical profession began to warn of the addictive dangers of heroin.[49]

Throughout the nineteenth century, if overindulgence was necessary, many preferred addiction to narcotics than alcohol. In 1889 a doctor observed:

> The only grounds on which opium in lieu of alcohol can be claimed as reformatory are that it is less inimical to healthy life than alcohol, that it calms in place of exciting the baser passions, and hence is less productive of acts of violence and crime; in short, that as a whole the use of morphine in place of alcohol is but a choice of evils, and by far the lesser. . . .
> I might, had I time and space, enlarge by statistics to prove the law-abiding qualities of opium-eating peoples, but of this anyone can perceive somewhat for himself, if he carefully watches and reflects on the quiet, introspective gaze of the morphine habitue and compares it with the riotous devil-may-care leer of the drunkard.[50]

During the nineteenth century it was primarily the respectable rather than the criminal classes who used the drug. It has been suggested that part of the reason the use of opium became so popular at this time was that the respectable people "crave the effect of a stimulant but will not risk their reputation for temperance by taking alcoholic beverages."[51]

Drugs could be purchased openly and cheaply from the drugstores. Not only could the narcotics themselves be bought, but many kinds of opiate-containing patent medicines were advertised. Anyone interested could buy paregoric, laudanum, tincture of opium, morphine, Womslow's Soothing Syrup, Godfrey's Cordial, McMumn's Elixir of Opium, or others.[52] "The more you drink," one tonic advertised, "the more you want." Mothers fed their babies 750,000 bottles of opium-laced syrup a year.[53]

Whereas white Americans previously had used opium in all other derivative forms, the smoking of opium was introduced by Chinese immigrants in California, and was outlawed in San Francisco in 1875.[54] This is the first time opium or any of its derivatives was outlawed in the United States. It appears that the legislation outlawing opium was an attempt to control the Chinese immigrants, to make them conform to the "American Way of Life," much as the drinking laws in Boston in the 1830s and 1840s were used to control the Irish immigrants.

THE HARRISON ACT AND ENFORCEMENT

In 1914 Congress passed the Harrison Act. While with the Volstead Act it is clear that total abstinence was the goal and intent of the law, it is unclear as to the actual intentions of Congress when the Harrison Act was passed. Some authors contend that the Harrison Act was intended only as a revenue measure, attempting to tax drugs. The desire was to regulate the use of drugs, not to impose abstinence. The careful wording of the Harrison Act which allows for medical doctors to treat or prescribe drugs for addict-patients is referred to as evidence. Whatever the original intentions of Congress, through a series of Supreme Court rulings, by 1922 the Harrison Act came to mean total abstinence for all.[55]

As with the Volstead Act, legislation of the Harrison Act was easier than enforcement. It is difficult to enforce laws preventing activities in which all parties are willing participants. This is especially true when the contraband object is very small in size. In this way, the existence of laws prohibiting crimes without victims increases the power of the police as it necessitates and legitimates a close surveillance of the population.

In order to enforce laws preventing activities in which there is no citizen-complainant, police must develop an information system and much of police energy is devoted to finding lawbreakers.[56] "The informer system has become such an intrinsic component of police work that the abilities of a professional detective have come to be defined in terms of his capacity to utilize this system."[57] Or as Westley puts it: "A detective is as good as his stool pigeon." Westley adds further that the solutions to crimes are largely the result of bargains detectives make with underworld figures.[58]

The relation of detective to informer is illustrated by the following newspaper report on the retirement of Mr. Dean J. Gavin, Detective Sgt. of the Buffalo police, after 34 years of police work, 17 of them as a member of the Narcotics Squad.

> His contacts in the underworld are legion. And when he sends out a message seeking information on anything from a burglary to a narcotics delivery, the tenants in crime's jungle make certain that Dean Gavin gets the answers.

The criminals who maintain the information-gathering network for Detective Sgt. Gavin have a universal contempt for the police . . . but they respect him.[59]

Police, then, need informers to enforce the vice laws. The existence of vice laws assures the police of a sizeable group who are in need of the favors and generosity of the police, and thus are willing to serve as informers for those favors. Police can reward the cooperative informer by reduced sentences or failure to prosecute. The stiffer and more severe the penalty, the greater the amount of bargaining power or discretion in the hands of the police—the greater the penalty, the greater the power of the police.

The police-informer system rests on the ability of the police to withhold prosecution if they desire. This means the cooperation of the District Attorney and even the courts is necessary. An informer system assumes the absence of an injured party, and of a citizen-complainant.

The difficulty of enforcing laws without a complainant is clearly shown in the enforcement of the narcotic laws. The addict-informer becomes the chief source of information for violation of the narcotic laws. Police attempt to arrest the big-time operator through the addict-informer. "The Bureau of Narcotics is authorized to pay the 'operating expenses' of informants whose information leads to seizure of drugs in illicit traffic."[60] Narcotic agents will supply informants with drugs, money to purchase drugs, or allow them to steal for money to purchase drugs. Thus, the law permits narcotic agents to do precisely what it forbids the doctor—supply the addicted with drugs.

Some lawyers have been disturbed at the Federal Bureau's dependence on informers. In a 1960 decision, Judge David Bazelon of the U.S. Court of Appeals for the District of Columbia Circuit criticized the Narcotic bureau:

It is notorious that the narcotics informer is often himself involved in the narcotics traffic and is often paid for his information in cash, narcotics, immunity from prosecution, or lenient punishment . . . Under such stipulation it is to be expected that the informer will not infrequently reach for shadowy leads, or even seek to incriminate the innocent.[61]

In March 1969, in New York, a district judge acquitted a defendant who had been enticed into addiction by an informer for the Bureau of Narcotics. The judge said the defendant's participation in the crime "was a creation of the productivity of law-enforcement officers."[62]

Once an individual is labeled an addict by the police, there is no restraint on their power. Police can break into a known addict's residence. If they find narcotics in his possession or marks on his arm, they can demand that he "rat" on his source or spend ninety days in jail and face the "cold turkey" treatment. Once an individual has had "narcotic" dealings with the police, he can expect further dealings. If he should object to strong-arm methods or lack of "due process," the police can threaten to punish him with the full force of the laws.

It appears then, that the enforcement of laws against activities in which there is no citizen-complainant does not occur along legal lines. Establishing laws which proscribe such activities and establishing a police force to discover and prosecute persons who engage in such activities maximizes the possibilities of social control, in that it necessitates and legitimates a close surveillance of the population.

SELECTIVE ENFORCEMENT OF THE VICE LAWS: THE IMMUNITY OF THE POWERFUL

It has been argued that the police and the legal system serve the interests of the powerful. This has been shown previously in that the powerful are able to get their own moral values passed as laws of the land—this is part of the definition of power. Also, however, they appear to be immune from the application or enforcement of the law. This can be substantiated by looking at the mechanics of enforcement. The police tend to divide the populace into two groups—the criminal and the noncriminal—and treat each accordingly. In police academies the recruits are told: "There are two kinds of people you arrest: those who pay the fine and those who don't."[63]

William Westley asked the policemen in his study to describe the section of the general public that likes the police. Replies included:

> The law-abiding element likes the police. Well the people that are settled down are polite to policemen, but the floaters—people who move around—are entirely different. They think we are after them.[64]

Westley concludes that "the better class of people," those from better residential neighborhoods and skilled workers, are treated with politeness and friendliness, because "that is the way to make them like you." In the policeman's relation to the middle class, "The commission of a crime by an individual is not enough to classify him a criminal."[65]

> He sees these people [middle class] as within the law, that is, as being within the protection of the law, and as a group he has to observe the letter of the law in his treatment of them. Their power forces him to do so. No distinction is gained from the apprehension of such a person. Essentially, they do not fall into the category of potential criminals.[66]

Whereas, for people in the slums, the patrolman feels that roughness is necessary, both to make them respect the policeman and to maintain order and conformity. Patrolmen are aware that it is slum dwellers' lack of power which enables him to use roughness and ignore "due process."

Skolnick writes that the police wish that "civil liberties people" would recognize the differences that police follow in applying search and seizure laws to respectable citizens and to criminals.[67]

The immunity of those with power and wealth to having the law apply to them is so traditional that the police in one city were able to apply the normally withheld law enforcement to political officials as a measure of collective bargaining. The report of the activities of the Police Locust Club (police union), of Rochester, New York, on the front page of the local newspaper is remarkable.

The first move was to ticket cars owned by public officials for violations of the state Motor Vehicle Law.

According to the club president, Ralph Boryszewski, other steps will include:

Refusal to "comply with requests from politicians for favors for themselves and their friends . . ."

Cracking down on after-hours spots and gambling establishments "which have been protected through the silent consent of public officials."

"These evils have existed as long as the police department has, and the public should know what's going on," Boryszewski said today. The slowdown is "really a speedup in enforcement of the law," he said. "The public won't be hurt, we're after the men who think they're above the law."[68]

A Vermont urologist was charged with failure to file an income tax return for the years 1962, 1963, and 1964. However, he entered a plea of nolo on the 1964 charge only. "The judge said he accepted the lesser plea solely because it might jeopardize the doctor's standing in the medical profession."[69]

Drug users who fail to fit the "dope fiend" image, that is, drug users who are from the "respectable" or upper classes, are not regarded as narcotic criminals and do not become part of the official reports. When the addict is a well-to-do professional man, such as a physician or lawyer, and is well spoken and well educated, then prosecutors, policemen, and judges alike seem to agree that "the harsh penalties of the law . . . were surely not intended for a person like this, and, by an unspoken agreement, arrangements are quietly made to exempt him from such penalties."[70] The justification usually offered for not arresting addicted doctors and nurses is that they do not resort to crime to obtain drugs and are productive members of the community. "The only reason that users in the medical profession do not commit the crimes against property which other addicts do, is, of course, that drugs are available to them from medical sources."[71]

The more laws a nation passes, the greater the possible size of the criminal population. In 1912, Roscoe Pound pointed out "of one hundred thousand persons arrested in Chicago in 1912, more than one-half were held for violations of legal precepts which did not exist twenty-five years before."[72] Ten years ago, it was established that "the number of crimes for which one may be prosecuted has at least doubled since the turn of the century."[73]

The increase has been in misdemeanors, not felonies. Sutherland and Gehlke, studying trends from 1900–1930, found little increase in laws dealing with murder or robbery. "The increase came in areas where there was no general agreement: public morals, business ethics, and standards of health and safety."[74]

The prevention of felonies, and the protection of the community from acts of violence, is usually given as the *raison d'etre* of criminal law and the justification for a police system and penal sanctions. Yet, most police activity is concerned with misdemeanors, not felonies. Seldon Bacon writes

> What are the crimes which hurt society so often and so intensely that the society must react to such disorder and must react in an effective way (i.e. with organization, equipment, and specialization)? The answer of the modern criminologist to this question is felonies. The case studies however, clearly indicate that society does not react in these ways to felonies nearly as much as to misdemeanors. Indeed, the adjustment to felonious activity is a secondary if not a tertiary sphere of action. Moreover, judicial studies of the present day point to the same findings, misdemeanor cases outnumber felony cases 100 to 1. Yet the criminologists without exception have labored almost exclusively in the sphere of felonies.[75]

One writer noted that "in the three years from 1954 through 1956 arrests for drunkenness in Los Angeles constituted between 43 and 46 percent of all arrest bookings."[76] The importance of this is not in the prevalence of drunkenness as much as it is in the easy rationale afforded the police for maintaining order and conformity, for "keeping the peace."[77] Now that marijuana smoking is apparently so widespread, laws preventing its use give police an excuse to arrest anyone they see as a threat to "order."

Becker writes, "In America, only about six out of every hundred major crimes known to police result in jail sentences."[78] In addition, only about 20 percent of original reports find their way into criminal statistics.[79] It appears then, that the police have considerable discretion in deciding which violators to punish, or in deciding when an individual has committed a violation.

The greater the number of punitive laws, and the stiffer the penalties, the easier it is to attempt enforcement of any *one* law. Police threaten prostitutes with arrest, using the threat to get a lead on narcotic arrests; if the prostitute informs, then there is no arrest or reduced charges.[80] Liquor laws can be used to regulate or control "homosexual" bars.[81] Burglary informants as well as narcotic informants are usually addicts. Skolnick writes, "In general, burglary detectives permit informants to commit narcotic offenses, while narcotic detectives allow informants to steal."[82]

As early as 1906, Professor Ernst Freund commented upon the range of criminal legislation. "Living under free institutions we submit to public regulation and control in ways that appear inconceivable to the spirit of oriental despotism."[83]

As the laws increase in range and number, the population is criminalized, especially the population from low economic background, minority racial groups, or nonconformists in other ways. John I. Kitsuse writes about those labeled as deviant.

> For in modern society, the socially significant differentation of deviants from the non-deviant population is increasingly contingent upon circumstances of

situation, place, social and personal biography, and the bureaucratically organized activities of agencies of control.[84]

CONCLUSION

The attempt to enforce vice laws, as laws prohibiting activities in which there is no self-defined victim, is frequently referred to as the attempt to enforce "conventional morality." The implication is that other laws, like laws proscribing murder, have something like a metaphysical transcultural base. Today, however, many conventional sociologists and criminologists have come to the conclusion that *all* activities of police and criminal courts, not just those concerned with vice laws, enforce the moral order—enforce conformity—rather than enforce the law. Bordua and Reiss write, "Police above all link daily life to central authority; moral consensus is extended through the police as an instrument of legitimate coercion."[85] Alan Silver sees the extension of moral consensus and the development of the professional police as aspects of the same historical development—the "police are official representatives of the moral order."[86]

This appears to be an apparent conclusion when one realizes that "nothing is a crime which the law does not so regard and punish."[87] As Durkheim suggests, yesterday's bad taste is today's criminal law.[88] Or, as Becker writes, "Deviance is not a quality of the act the person commits, but rather a consequence of the application by others of rules and sanctions to an 'offender'."[89] F. L. Wines writes:

> Crime is not a character which attaches to an act . . .
> It is a complex relation which the law created between itself and the law breaker. The law creates crime. It therefore creates the criminal, because crime cannot be said to exist apart from the criminal.[90]

As Saint Paul said, "Without the law, sin is dead."

Instituting prohibitive laws against any activity establishes the "language of punishment." The existence of "the autocratic criminal law . . . compels and accustoms men to control their fellows without their consent and against their wills. It conveys to them the idea that such must be and is inevitable."[91]

For purposes of social control, then, the effects of laws prohibiting murder and beer drinking are the same. The enforcement of both serves to maintain the unequal distribution of power and wealth.

It appears, therefore, that there are no substantive distinctions among the ideas of enforcing the moral order, enforcing conventional morality, enforcing conformity, enforcing the law, and maintaining the unequal distribution of power. Crimes are violations of those moral values that the nation-state enforces through punitive law. The morality enforced is always the morality of those in power and it is primarily enforced upon those without power. That a group's morality and value system is enforced is part of the definition of its having power. To put it thus, the

unequal distribution of power and wealth is maintained in part by police enforcement of the morality and value system of those with power and wealth.

The vast number of our laws provides the means for selective enforcement, and
selective enforcement means the immunity of the rich and powerful. The greater
the number of laws, the easier it is to control those without power and wealth. The
content of the laws is not crucial for purposes of social control. What is crucial is
the power to establish the "language of punishment" (or conversely, "the language
of legitimacy"), the power to institute both the enforcers of law—the police—and
the violators of law—the criminals.

NOTES

[1] Carl Bridenbaugh, *Cities in the Wilderness: The First Century of Urban Life in America* 2nd ed. (New York: A. A. Knopf, 1955 [first published 1938]), p. 64.

[2] *Ibid.*, p. 65.

[3] Carl Bridenbaugh, *Cities in Revolt: Urban Life in America* 1743–1776 (New York: A. A. Knopf, 1955), p. 119.

[4] Charles Reith, *The Blind Eye of History: A Study of the Origins of the Present Police Era* (London: Farber and Farber, 1952), p. 210.

[5] David Bordua and Albert Reiss, Jr., "Law Enforcement," in Paul F. Lazarsfeld and others, *The Uses of Sociology* (New York: Basic Books, 1967), p. 276.

[6] Edward Crapsey, *The Nether Side of New York* (New York: Sheldon and Co., 1872), pp. 15–16. Today, "compromises" sometimes occur in civil rather than criminal court cases, or as "out of court" settlements, available only in white-collar criminality. See Edwin H. Sutherland, "White Collar Criminality" in *Radical Perspectives on Social Problems*, ed. by Frank Lindenfeld (New York: Macmillan Co., 1968), pp. 149–159.

[7] Seldon Bacon, *The Early Development of American Municipal Police*, (unpublished Ph.D. dissertation, Yale University, 1939), Vol. I and II.

[8] Bacon, *op. cit.*, Vol. I, cited in Bordua and Reiss, *op. cit.*, p. 277.

[9] *Ibid.*, pp. 279–80.

[10] Bordua and Reiss, *op. cit.*, p. 280.

[11] Mark S. Hubbell, *Our Police and Our City: A Study of the Official History of the Buffalo Police Department* (Buffalo: Bensler and Wesley, 1893), pp. 57–58.

[12] Roger Lane, *Policing the City—Boston* 1822–1885 (Cambridge: Harvard University Press, 1967), p. 26.

[13] Bordua and Reiss, *op. cit.*, p. 282.

[14] Reith, *op. cit.*, p. 19.

[15] Alan Silver, "The Demand for Order in Civil Society: A Review of Some Themes in the History of Urban Crime, Police, and Riot," ed. by David J. Bordua, *The Police: Six Sociological Essays* (New York: Wiley, 1967), pp. 11–12.

[16] Raymond Fosdick, *American Police Systems* (New York: The Century Co., 1921), p. 70.

[17] See Lane, *op. cit.*, p. 54.

[18] *Ibid.*, p. 50.

[19] *Ibid.*, p. 222.

[20] *Ibid.*, p. 49.

[21] Howard S. Becker, *Outsiders: Studies in the Sociology of Deviance* (New York: Free Press of Glencoe, 1963), p. 156.

[22] Robert Straus, "Alcohol," in *Contemporary Social Problems*, Second Edition, ed. by Robert K. Merton and Robert A. Nisbet (New York: Harcourt, Brace, and World, 1966), p. 244.

[23] Herbert Asbury, *The Great Illusion: An Informal History of Prohibition* (Garden City, N.Y.: Doubleday, 1950), p. 7.

[24] Straus, *op. cit.*, p. 245.

[25] Asbury, *op. cit.*, pp. 13–14, Straus, *op. cit.*, p. 246.

[26] Asbury, *op. cit.*, p. 13.

[27] Straus, *op. cit.*, p. 246.

[28] Joseph R. Gusfield, *Symbolic Crusade: Status Politics and The American Temperance Movement* (Urbana: University of Illinois Press, 1966).

[29] *Ibid.*, p. 21.

[30] Lyman Beecher, *Six Sermons on Intemperance* (New York: American Trust Society, 1843), pp. 57–58, quoted in Gusfield, *ibid.*, p. 43.

[31] Straus, *op. cit.*, p. 249.

[32] Lane, *op. cit.*, p. 49.

[33] *Ibid.*

[34] J. H. Timberlake, *Prohibition and the Progressive Movement* 1900–1920 (Cambridge: Harvard University Press, 1963), p. 41.

[35] *Anti-Saloon League, Proceedings*, 1919, pp. 45–46, quoted in *Ibid.*, p. 47.

[36] Edward B. Phelps, "The Mortality from Alcohol in the United States—the Results of a Recent Investigation of the Contributory Relation with Each of the Assigned Causes of Adult Mortality," International Congress of Hygiene and Demography, *Transactions*, 1912 (6 vols., Washington, 1913), Vol. I, pp. 813–822, quoted in Timberlake, *op. cit.*, pp. 54–55.

[37] John Koren, *Economic Aspects of the Liquor Problem* (Boston, 1899) p. 30, quoted in Timberlake, *op. cit.*, p. 57.

[38] John B. Huber "The Effects of Alcohol," *Collier's Weekly*, Vol. 57, June 3, 1916, p. 32, quoted in Timberlake, *op. cit.*, p. 58.

[39] George Elliot Howard, "Alcohol and Crime: A Study in Social Causation," *The American Journal of Sociology*, Vol. 24, July 1918, p. 79, quoted in Timberlake, *op. cit.*, p. 58.

[40] Howard, *op. cit.*, pp. 61–64, 80, quoted in Timberlake, *op. cit.*, p. 60.

[41] Edward A. Ross, "Prohibition as a Sociologist Sees It," *Harper's Monthly Magazine*, Vol. 142, January, 1921, p. 188; this article was reprinted in Ross' *The Social Trend* (New York, 1922), pp. 137–160, and quoted in Timberlake, *op. cit.*, pp. 60–61.

[42] Asbury, *op. cit.*, p. 185.

[43] *Ibid.*, p. 186.

[44] *Ibid.*, p. 169.

[45] *Ibid.*, pp. 169–170.

[46] Nathan E. Eddy, "The History of the Development of Narcotics," *Law and Contemporary Problems*, Vol. 22, Winter 1957, p. 3.

[47] Charles E. Terry and Mildred Pellens, *The Opium Problem* (New York: Haddon Craftsmen, 1928), p. 72.

[48] Alfred R. Lindesmith, *Addiction and Opiates* (Chicago: Aldine, 1968 ed. [first published 1947]), p. 208.

[49] Terry and Pellens, *op. cit.*, pp. 78–85.

[50] J. R. Black, "Advantages for Substituting the Morphia Habit for the Incurably Alcoholic," *Cincinnati Lancet-Clinic*, vol. 22, 1889, pp. 537–541, quoted in Lindesmith, *op. cit.*, pp. 211–212.

[51] Rufus King, "Narcotic Drug Laws and Enforcement Policies," *Law and Contemporary Problems*, Vol. 22, Winter 1957, p. 113.

[52] Lindesmith, *op. cit.*, p. 210.

[53] Stanley Meisler, "Federal Narcotics Czar," *The Nation*, February 20, 1960, p. 159.

[54] Terry and Pellens, *op. cit.*, p. 73.

[55] See Lindesmith, *op. cit.*, p. 6. and King, *op. cit.*, p. 121.

[56] See Jerome Skolnick and J. Richard Woodworth, "Bureaucracy, Information and Social Control: A Study of Morals Detail," in Bordua, *The Police: Six Sociological Essays*, *op. cit.*, pp. 99–136.

[57] Jerome H. Skolnick, *Justice Without Trial: Law Enforcement in Democratic Society* (New York: Wiley, 1967), p. 238.

[58] William A. Westley, *The Police: A Sociological Study of Law, Custom, and Morality* (unpublished Ph.D. dissertation, University of Chicago, 1951), pp. 70–71.

[59] Ray Hill, "Even the Crooks He Pursues Respect Gavin," *Buffalo Evening News*, February 3, 1968, Sunday edition.

[60] Edwin M. Schur, *Crime Without Victims: Deviant Behavior and Public Policy* (Englewood Cliffs, N.J.: Prentice-Hall, Inc., 1965), p. 135.

61 Meisler, *op. cit.*, p. 160.
62 *Ibid.*
63 Wesley, *op. cit.*, p. 95.
64 *Ibid.*, p. 161.
65 *Ibid.*, p. 166.
66 *Ibid.*, p. 167.
67 Skolnick, *Justice Without Trial, op. cit.*, p. 147.
68 Everson Moran, "Officials' Cars Tagged in Police 'Slowdown,' " *The Times Union*, Greater Rochester Edition, July 2, 1968, p. 1.
69 *Rutland Daily Herald*, April 19, 1969, p. 7.
70 Alfred R. Lindesmith, *The Addict and the Law* (Bloomington: University of Indiana Press, 1965), p. 90.
71 *Ibid.*
72 Quoted in Frances A. Allen, "The Borderland of Criminal Law: Problems of 'Socializing' Justice," *The Social Service Review*, Vol. 32, June 1958, p. 108.
73 *Ibid.*
74 Cited in Richard C. Fuller, "Morals and the Criminal Law," *Journal of Criminal Law, Criminology, and Police Science*, Vol. 32, March–April 1942, pp. 625–626.
75 Bacon, Vol. II, *op. cit.*, p. 784.
76 Allen, *op. cit.*, p. 111.
77 Egon Bittner notes that "patrolmen do not really enforce the law, even when they do invoke it, but merely use it as a resource to solve certain pressing problems in keeping the peace." Egon Bittner, "The Police on Skid Row: A Study of Peace Keeping," *The American Sociological Review*, Vol. 32, October 1967, p. 710.
78 Becker, *op. cit.*, p. 171.
79 Skolnick, *Justice Without Trial, op. cit.*, p. 173.
80 *Ibid.*, p. 125.
81 Schur, *op. cit.*, p. 81.
82 Skolnick, *Justice Without Trial, op. cit.*, p. 129.
83 Quoted in Allen, *op. cit.*, p. 108.
84 John I. Kitsuse, "Societal Reaction to Deviant Behavior: Problems of Theory and Method," *Social Problems*, Vol. 9, Winter 1962, p. 256.
85 Bordua and Reiss, *op. cit.*, p. 282.
86 Silver, *op. cit.*, in Bordua, *The Police: Six Sociological Essays, op. cit.*, p. 14.
87 F. H. Wines, *Punishment and Reformation: An Historical Sketch of the Rise of the Penitentiary Systems* (New York: Crowell and Co., 1895), p. 13.
88 Emile Durkheim, *The Rules of Sociological Method*, Eighth Edition (New York: Free Press, 1966).
89 Becker, *op. cit.*, p. 9.
90 Wines, *op. cit.*, p. 24.
91 Paul Reiwald, *Society and Its Criminals*, tran. by T. E. James (London: William Heineman, 1949), p. 302.

THE SAINTS AND THE ROUGHNECKS

William J. Chambliss

Eight promising young men—children of good, stable, white upper-middle-class families, active in school affairs, good pre-college students—were some of the most delinquent boys at Hanibal High School. While community residents and parents knew that these boys occasionally sowed a few wild oats, they were totally unaware that sowing wild oats completely occupied the daily routine of these young men. The Saints were constantly occupied with truancy, drinking, wild driving, petty theft and vandalism. Yet not one was officially arrested for any misdeed during the two years I observed them.

This record was particularly surprising in light of my observations during the same two years of another gang of Hanibal High School students, six lower-class white boys known as the Roughnecks. The Roughnecks were constantly in trouble with police and community even though their rate of delinquency was about equal with that of the Saints. What was the cause of this disparity? the result? The following consideration of the activities, social class and community perceptions of both gangs may provide some answers.

THE SAINTS FROM MONDAY TO FRIDAY

The Saints' principal daily concern was with getting out of school as early as possible. The boys managed to get out of school with minimum danger that they would be accused of playing hookey through an elaborate procedure for obtaining "legitimate" release from class. The most common procedure was for one boy to obtain the release of another by fabricating a meeting of some committee, program or recognized club. Charles might raise his hand in his 9:00 chemistry class and asked to be excused—a euphemism for going to the bathroom. Charles would go to Ed's math class and inform the teacher that Ed was needed for a 9:30 rehearsal of

Source: "The Saints and the Roughnecks," *Society*, Vol. 11, No. 11, November-December, 1973, pp. 24–31. By permission of the author and publisher. This paper has been revised slightly for this volume.

the drama club play. The math teacher would recognize Ed and Charles as "good students" involved in numerous school activities and would permit Ed to leave at 9:30. Charles would return to his class, and Ed would go to Tom's English class to obtain his release. Tom would engineer Charles' escape. The strategy would continue until as many of the Saints as possible were freed. After a stealthy trip to the car (which had been parked in a strategic spot), the boys were off for a day of fun.

Over the two years I observed the Saints, this pattern was repeated nearly every day. There were variations on the theme, but in one form or another, the boys used this procedure for getting out of class and then off the school grounds. Rarely did all eight of the Saints manage to leave school at the same time. The average number avoiding school on the days I observed them was five.

Having escaped from the concrete corridors the boys usually went either to a pool hall on the other (lower-class) side of town or to a cafe in the suburbs. Both places were out of the way of people the boys were likely to know (family or school officials), and both provided a source of entertainment. The pool hall entertainment was the generally rough atmosphere, the occasional hustler, the sometimes drunk proprietor and, of course, the game of pool. The cafe's entertainment was provided by the owner. The boys would "accidentally" knock a glass on the floor or spill cola on the counter—not all the time, but enough to be sporting. They would also bend spoons, put salt in sugar bowls and generally tease whoever was working in the cafe. The owner had opened the cafe recently and was dependent on the boys' business which was, in fact, substantial since between the horsing around and the teasing they bought food and drinks.

THE SAINTS ON WEEKENDS

On weekends the automobile was even more critical than during the week, for on weekends the Saints went to Big Town—a large city with a population of over a million 25 miles from Hanibal. Every Friday and Saturday night most of the Saints would meet between 8:00 and 8:30 and would go into Big Town. Big Town activities included drinking heavily in taverns or nightclubs, driving drunkenly through the streets, and committing acts of vandalism and playing pranks.

By midnight on Fridays and Saturdays the Saints were usually thoroughly high, and one or two of them were often so drunk they had to be carried to the cars. Then the boys drove around town, calling obscenities to women and girls; occasionally trying (unsuccessfully so far as I could tell) to pick girls up; and driving recklessly through red lights and at high speeds with their lights out. Occasionally they played "chicken." One boy would climb out the back window of the car and across the roof to the driver's side of the car while the car was moving at high speed (between 40 and 50 miles an hour); then the driver would move over and the boy who had just crawled across the car roof would take the driver's seat.

Searching for "fair game" for a prank was the boys' principal activity after they left the tavern. The boys would drive alongside a foot patrolman and ask directions to some street. If the policeman leaned on the car in the course of answering the question, the driver would speed away, causing him to lose his balance. The Saints were careful to play this prank only in an area where they were not going to spend much time and where they could quickly disappear around a corner to avoid having their license plate number taken.

Construction sites and road repair areas were the special province of the Saints' mischief. A soon-to-be-repaired hole in the road inevitably invited the Saints to remove lanterns and wooden barricades and put them in the car, leaving the hole unprotected. The boys would find a safe vantage point and wait for an unsuspecting motorist to drive into the hole. Often, though not always, the boys would go up to the motorist and commiserate with him about the dreadful way the city protected its citizenry.

Leaving the scene of the open hole and the motorist, the boys would then go searching for an appropriate place to erect the stolen barricade. An "appropriate place" was often a spot on a highway near a curve in the road where the barricade would not be seen by an oncoming motorist. The boys would wait to watch an unsuspecting motorist attempt to stop and (usually) crash into the wooden barricade. With saintly bearing the boys might offer help and understanding.

A stolen lantern might well find its way onto the back of a police car or hang from a street lamp. Once a lantern served as a prop for a reenactment of the "midnight ride of Paul Revere" until the "play," which was taking place at 2:00 AM in the center of a main street of Big Town, was interrupted by a police car several blocks away. The boys ran, leaving the lantern on the street, and managed to avoid being apprehended.

Abandoned houses, especially if they were located in out-of-the-way places, were fair game for destruction and spontaneous vandalism. The boys would break windows, remove furniture to the yard and tear it apart, urinate on the walls and scrawl obscenities inside.

Through all the pranks, drinking and reckless driving the boys managed miraculously to avoid being stopped by police. Only twice in two years was I aware that they had been stopped by a Big City policeman. Once was for speeding (which they did every time they drove whether they were drunk or sober), and the driver managed to convince the policeman that it was simply an error. The second time they were stopped they had just left a nightclub and were walking through an alley. Aaron stopped to urinate and the boys began making obscene remarks. A foot patrolman came into the alley, lectured the boys and sent them home. Before the boys got to the car one began talking in a loud voice again. The policeman, who had followed them down the alley, arrested this boy for disturbing the peace and took him to the police station where the other Saints gathered. After paying a $5.00 fine, and with the assurance that there would be no permanent record of the arrest, the boy was released.

The boys had a spirit of frivolity and fun about their escapades. They did not view what they were engaged in as "delinquency," though it surely was by any reasonable definition of that word. They simply viewed themselves as having a little fun and who, they would ask, was really hurt by it? The answer had to be no one, although this fact remains one of the most difficult things to explain about the gang's behavior. Unlikely though it seems, in two years of drinking, driving, carousing and vandalism no one was seriously injured as a result of the Saints' activities.

THE SAINTS IN SCHOOL

The Saints were highly successful in school. The average grade for the group was "B," with two of the boys having close to a straight "A" average. Almost all of the boys were popular and many of them held offices in the school. One of the boys was vice-president of the student body one year. Six of the boys played on athletic teams.

At the end of their senior year, the student body selected ten seniors for special recognition as the "school wheels"; four of the ten were Saints. Teachers and school officials saw no problem with any of these boys and anticipated that they would all "make something of themselves."

How the boys managed to maintain this impression is surprising in view of their actual behavior while in school. Their technique for covering truancy was so successful that teachers did not even realize that the boys were absent from school much of the time. Occasionally, of course, the system would backfire and then the boy was on his own. A boy who was caught would be most contrite, would plead guilty and ask for mercy. He inevitably got the mercy he sought.

Cheating on examinations was rampant, even to the point of orally communicating answers to exams as well as looking at one another's papers. Since none of the group studied, and since they were primarily dependent on one another for help, it is surprising that grades were so high. Teachers contributed to the deception in their admitted inclination to give these boys (and presumably others like them) the benefit of the doubt. When asked how the boys did in school, and when pressed on specific examinations, teachers might admit that they were disappointed in John's performance, but would quickly add that they "knew that he was capable of doing better," so John was given a higher grade than he had actually earned. How often this happened is impossible to know. During the time that I observed the group, I never saw any of the boys take homework home. Teachers may have been "understanding" very regularly.

One exception to the gang's generally good performance was Jerry, who had a "C" average in his junior year, experienced disaster the next year and failed to graduate. Jerry had always been a little more nonchalant than the others about the liberties he took in school. Rather than wait for someone to come get him from class, he would offer his own excuse and leave. Although he probably did not miss any more classes than most of the others in the group, he did not take the requisite pains to cover his absences. Jerry was the only Saint whom I ever heard talk back to a teacher. Although teachers often called him a "cut up" or a "smart kid," they never referred to him as a troublemaker or as a kid headed for trouble. It seems likely, then, that Jerry's failure his senior year and his mediocre performance his junior year were consequences of his not playing the game the proper way (possibly because he was disturbed by his parents' divorce). His teachers regarded him as "immature" and not quite ready to get out of high school.

THE POLICE AND THE SAINTS

The local police saw the Saints as good boys who were among the leaders of the youth in the community. Rarely, the boys might be stopped in town for speeding or for running a stop sign. When this happened the boys were always polite and contrite and pled for mercy. As in school, they received the mercy they asked for. None ever received a ticket or was taken into the precinct by the local police.

The situation in Big City, where the boys engaged in most of their delinquency, was only slightly different. The police there did not know the boys at all, although occasionally the boys were stopped by a patrolman. Once they were caught taking a lantern from a construction site. Another time they were stopped for running a stop sign, and on several occasions they were stopped for speeding. Their behavior was as before: contrite, polite and penitent. The urban police, like the local police, accepted their demeanor as sincere. More important, the urban police were convinced that these were good boys just out for a lark.

THE ROUGHNECKS

Hanibal townspeople never perceived the Saints' high level of delinquency. The Saints were good boys who just went in for an occasional prank. After all, they were well dressed, well mannered and had nice cars. The Roughnecks were a different story. Although the two gangs of boys were the same age, and both groups engaged in an equal amount of wild-oat sowing, everyone agreed that the not-so-well-dressed, not-so-well-mannered, not-so-rich boys were heading for trouble. Townspeople would say, "You can see the gang members at the drugstore, night after night, leaning against the storefront (sometimes drunk) or slouching around inside buying cokes, reading magazines, and probably stealing old Mr. Wall blind. When they are outside and girls walk by, even respectable girls, these boys make suggestive remarks. Sometimes their remarks are downright lewd."

From the community's viewpoint, the real indication that these kids were in for trouble was that they were constantly involved with the police. Some of them had been picked up for stealing, mostly small stuff, of course, "but still it's stealing small stuff that leads to big-time crimes." "Too bad," people said. "Too bad that these boys couldn't behave like the other kids in town; stay out of trouble, be polite to adults, and look to their future."

The community's impression of the degree to which this group of six boys (ranging in age from 16 to 19) engaged in delinquency was somewhat distorted. In some ways the gang was more delinquent than the community thought; in other ways they were less.

The fighting activities of the group were fairly readily and accurately perceived by almost everyone. At least once a month, the boys would get into some sort of fight, although most fights were scraps between members of the group or involved only one member of the group and some peripheral hanger-on. Only three times in the period of observation did the group fight together: once against a gang from across town, once against two blacks and once against a group of boys from another school. For the first two fights the group went out "looking for trouble"—and they found it both times. The third fight followed a football game and began spontaneously with an argument on the football field between one of the Roughnecks and a member of the opposition's football team.

Jack had a particular propensity for fighting and was involved in most of the brawls. He was a prime mover of the escalation of arguments into fights.

More serious than fighting, had the community been aware of it, was theft. Although almost everyone was aware that the boys occasionally stole things, they did not realize the extent of the activity. Petty stealing was a frequent event for the Roughnecks. Sometimes they stole as a group and coordinated their efforts; other times they stole in pairs. Rarely did they steal alone.

The thefts ranged from very small things like paperback books, comics and ballpoint pens to expensive items like watches. The nature of the thefts varied from time to time. The gang would go through a period of systematically stealing items from automobiles or school lockers. Types of thievery varied with the whim of the gang. Some forms of thievery were more profitable than others, but all thefts were for profit, not just thrills.

Roughnecks siphoned gasoline from cars as often as they had access to an automobile, which was not very often. Unlike the Saints, who owned their own cars, the Roughnecks would have to borrow their parents' cars, an event which occurred only eight or nine times a year. The boys claimed to have stolen cars for joy rides from time to time.

Ron committed the most serious of the group's offenses. With an unidentified associate the boy attempted to burglarize a gasoline station. Although this station had been robbed twice previously in the same month, Ron denied any involvement in either of the other thefts. When Ron and his accomplice approached the station, the owner was hiding in the bushes beside the station. He fired both barrels of a double-barreled shotgun at the boys. Ron was severely injured; the other boy ran away and was never caught. Though he remained in critical condition for several months, Ron finally recovered and served six months of the following year in reform school. Upon release from reform school, Ron was put back a grade in school, and began running around with a different gang of boys. The Roughnecks considered the new gang less delinquent than themselves, and during the following year Ron had no more trouble with the police.

The Roughnecks, then, engaged mainly in three types of delinquency: theft, drinking and fighting. Although community members perceived that this gang of kids was delinquent, they mistakenly believed that their illegal activities were primarily drinking, fighting and being a nuisance to passersby. Drinking was limited among the gang members, although it did occur, and theft was much more prevalent than anyone realized.

Drinking would doubtless have been more prevalent had the boys had ready access to liquor. Since they rarely had automobiles at their disposal, they could not travel very far, and the bars in town would not serve them. Most of the boys had little money, and this, too, inhibited their purchase of alcohol. Their major source of liquor was a local drunk who would buy them a fifth if they would give him enough extra to buy himself a pint of whiskey or a bottle of wine.

The community's perception of drinking as prevalent stemmed from the fact that it was the most obvious delinquency the boys engaged in. When one of the boys had been drinking, even a casual observer seeing him on the corner would suspect that he was high.

There was a high level of mutual distrust and dislike between the Roughnecks and the police. The boys felt very strongly that the police were unfair and corrupt. Some evidence existed that the boys were correct in their perception.

The main source of the boys' dislike for the police undoubtedly stemmed from the fact that the police would sporadically harass the group. From the standpoint of the boys, these acts of occasional enforcement of the law were whimsical and uncalled for. It made no sense to them, for example, that the police would come to the corner occasionally and threaten them with arrest for loitering when the night before the boys had been out siphoning gasoline from cars and the police had been nowhere in sight. To the boys, the police were stupid on the one hand, for not being where they should have been and catching the boys in a serious offense, and unfair on the other hand, for trumping up "loitering" charges against them.

From the viewpoint of the police, the situation was quite different. They knew, with all the confidence necessary to be a policeman, that these boys were engaged in criminal activities. They knew this partly from occasionally catching them, mostly from circumstantial evidence ("the boys were around when those tires were slashed"), and partly because the police shared the view of the community in general that this was a bad bunch of boys. The best the police could hope to do was to be sensitive to the fact that these boys were engaged in illegal acts and arrest them whenever there was some evidence that they had been involved. Whether or not the boys had in fact committed a particular act in a particular way was not especially important. The police had a broader view: their job was to stamp out these kids' crimes; the tactics were not as important as the end result.

Over the period that the group was under observation, each member was arrested at least once. Several of the boys were arrested a number of times and spent at least one night in jail. While most were never taken to court, two of the boys were sentenced to six months' incarceration in boys' schools.

THE ROUGHNECKS IN SCHOOL

The Roughnecks' behavior in school was not particularly disruptive. During school hours they did not all hang around together, but tended instead to spend most of their time with one or two other members of the gang who were their special buddies. Although every member of the gang attempted to avoid school as much as possible, they were not particularly successful and most of them attended school with surprising regularity. They considered school a burden—something to be gotten through with a minimum of conflict. If they were "bugged" by a particular teacher, it could lead to trouble. One of the boys, Al, once threatened to beat up a teacher and, according to the other boys, the teacher hid under a desk to escape him.

Teachers saw the boys the way the general community did, as heading for trouble, as being uninterested in making something of themselves. Some were also seen as being incapable of meeting the academic standards of the school. Most of the teachers expressed concern for this group of boys and were willing to pass them despite poor performance, in the belief that failing them would only aggravate the problem.

The group of boys had a grade point average just slightly above "C." No one in the group failed either grade, and no one had better than a "C" average. They were very consistent in their achievement or, at least, the teachers were consistent in their perception of the boys' achievement.

Two of the boys were good football players. Herb was acknowledged to be the best player in the school and Jack was almost as good. Both boys were criticized for their failure to abide by training rules, for refusing to come to practice as often as they should, and for not playing their best during practice. What they lacked in sportsmanship they made up for in skill, apparently, and played every game no matter how poorly they had performed in practice or how many practice sessions they had missed.

TWO QUESTIONS

Why did the community, the school and the police react to the Saints as though they were good, upstanding, nondelinquent youths with bright futures but to the Roughnecks as though they were tough, young criminals who were headed for trouble? Why did the Roughnecks and the Saints in fact have quite different careers after high school—careers which, by and large, lived up to the expectations of the community?

The most obvious explanation for the differences in the community's and law enforcement agencies' reactions to the two gangs is that one group of boys was "more delinquent" than the other. Which group *was* more delinquent? The answer to this question will determine in part how we explain the differential responses to these groups by the members of the community and, particularly, by law enforcement and school officials.

155

In sheer number of illegal acts, the Saints were the more delinquent. They were truant from school for at least part of the day almost every day of the week. In addition, their drinking and vandalism occurred with surprising regularity. The Roughnecks, in contrast, engaged sporadically in delinquent episodes. While these episodes were frequent, they certainly did not occur on a daily or even a weekly basis.

The difference in frequency of offenses was probably caused by the Roughnecks' inability to obtain liquor and to manipulate legitimate excuses from school. Since the Roughnecks had less money than the Saints, and teachers carefully supervised their school activities, the Roughnecks' hearts may have been as black as the Saints', but their misdeeds were not nearly as frequent.

There are really no clear-cut criteria by which to measure qualitative differences in antisocial behavior. The most important dimension of the difference is generally referred to as the "seriousness" of the offenses.

If seriousness encompasses the relative economic costs of delinquent acts, then some assessment can be made. The Roughnecks probably stole an average of about $5 worth of goods a week. Some weeks the figure was considerably higher, but these times must be balanced against long periods when almost nothing was stolen.

The Saints were more continuously engaged in delinquency but their acts were not for the most part costly to property. Only their vandalism and occasional theft of gasoline would so qualify. Perhaps once or twice a month they would siphon a tankful of gas. The other costly items were street signs, construction lanterns and the like. All of these acts combined probably did not quite average $5 a week, partly because much of the stolen equipment was abandoned and presumably could be recovered. The difference in cost of stolen property between the two groups was trivial, but the Roughnecks probably had a slightly more expensive set of activities than did the Saints.

Another meaning of seriousness is the potential threat of physical harm to members of the community and to the boys themselves. The Roughnecks were more prone to physical violence; they not only welcomed an opportunity to fight, they went seeking it. In addition, they fought among themselves frequently. Although the fighting never included deadly weapons, it was still a menace, however minor, to the physical safety of those involved.

The Saints never fought. They avoided physical conflict both inside and outside the group. At the same time, though, the Saints frequently endangered their own and other people's lives. They did so almost every time they drove a car, especially if they had been drinking. Sober, their driving was risky; under the influence of alcohol it was horrendous. In addition, the Saints endangered the lives of others with their pranks. Street excavations left unmarked were a very serious hazard.

Evaluating the relative seriousness of the two gangs' activities is difficult. The community reacted as though the behavior of the Roughnecks was a problem, and they reacted as though the behavior of the Saints was not. But the members of the community were ignorant of the array of delinquent acts that characterized the

Saints' behavior. Although concerned citizens were unaware of much of the Roughnecks' behavior as well, they were much better informed about the Roughnecks' involvement in delinquency than they were about the Saints'.

VISIBILITY

Differential treatment of the two gangs resulted in part because one gang was infinitely more visible than the other. This differential visibility was a direct function of the economic standing of the families. The Saints had access to automobiles and were able to remove themselves from the sight of the community. In as routine a decision as to where to go to have a milkshake after school, the Saints stayed away from the mainstream of community life. Lacking transportation, the Roughnecks could not make it to the edge of town. The center of town was the only practical place for them to meet since their homes were scattered throughout the town and any noncentral meeting place put an undue hardship on some members. Through necessity the Roughnecks congregated in a crowded area where everyone in the community passed frequently, including teachers and law enforcement officers. They could easily see the Roughnecks hanging around the drugstore.

The Roughnecks, of course, made themselves even more visible by making remarks to passersby and by occasionally getting into fights on the corner. Meanwhile, just as regularly, the Saints were either at the cafe on one edge of town or in the pool hall at the other edge of town. Without any particular realization that they were making themselves inconspicuous, the Saints were able to hide their time-wasting. Not only were they removed from the mainstream of traffic, but they were almost always inside a building.

On their escapades the Saints were also relatively invisible, since they left Hanibal and traveled to Big City. Here, too, they were mobile, roaming the city, rarely going to the same area twice.

DEMEANOR

To the notion of visibility must be added the difference in the responses of group members to outside intervention with their activities. If one of the Saints was confronted with an accusing policeman, even if he felt he was truly innocent of a wrongdoing, his demeanor was apologetic and penitent. A Roughneck's attitude was almost the polar opposite. When confronted with a threatening adult authority, even one who tried to be pleasant, the Roughneck's hostility and disdain were clearly observable. Sometimes he might attempt to put up a veneer of respect, but it was thin and was not accepted as sincere by the authority.

School was no different from the community at large. The Saints could manipulate the system by feigning compliance with the school norms. The availability of cars at school meant that once free from the immediate sight of the teacher, the boys could disappear rapidly. And this escape was well enough planned that no administrator or teacher was nearby when the boys left. A Roughneck who wished to escape for a few hours was in a bind. If it were possible to get free from class, downtown was still a mile away, and even if he arrived there, he was still very visible. Truancy for the Roughnecks meant almost certain detection, while the Saints enjoyed almost complete immunity from sanctions.

BIAS

Community members were not aware of the transgressions of the Saints. Even if the Saints had been less discreet, their favorite delinquencies would have been perceived as less serious than those of the Roughnecks.

In the eyes of the police and school officials, a boy who drinks in an alley and stands intoxicated on the street corner is committing a more serious offense than is a boy who drinks to inebriation in a nightclub or a tavern and drives around afterwards in a car. Similarly, a boy who steals a wallet from a store will be viewed as having committed a more serious offense than a boy who steals a lantern from a construction site.

Perceptual bias also operates with respect to the demeanor of the boys in the two groups when they are confronted by adults. It is not simply that adults dislike the posture affected by boys of the Roughneck ilk; more important is the conviction that the posture adopted by the Roughnecks is an indication of their devotion and commitment to deviance as a way of life. The posture becomes a cue, just as the type of the offense is a cue, to the degree to which the known transgressions are indicators of the youths' potential for other problems.

Visibility, demeanor and bias are surface variables which explain the day-to-day operations of the police. Why do these surface variables operate as they do? Why did the police choose to disregard the Saints' delinquencies while breathing down the backs of the Roughnecks?

The answer lies in the class structure of American society and the control of legal institutions by those at the top of the class structure. Obviously, no representative of the upper class drew up the operational chart for the police which led them to look in the ghettos and on streetcorners—which led them to see the demeanor of lower-class youth as troublesome and that of upper-middle-class youth as tolerable. Rather, the procedures simply developed from experience—experience with irate and influential upper-middle-class parents insisting that their son's vandalism was simply a prank and his drunkenness only a momentary "sowing of wild oats" —experience with cooperative or indifferent, powerless, lower-class parents who acquiesced to the laws' definition of their son's behavior.

ADULT CAREERS OF THE SAINTS
AND THE ROUGHNECKS

The community's confidence in the potential of the Saints and the Roughnecks apparently was justified. If anything, the community members underestimated the degree to which these youngsters would turn out "good" or "bad."

Seven of the eight members of the Saints went on to college immediately after high school. Five of the boys graduated from college in four years. The sixth one finished college after two years in the army, and the seventh spent four years in the air force before returning to college and receiving a B.A. degree. Of these seven college graduates, three went on for advanced degrees. One finished law school and is now active in state politics, one finished medical school and is practicing near Hanibal, and one boy is now working for a Ph.D. The other four college graduates entered submanagerial, managerial or executive training positions with larger firms.

The only Saint who did not complete college was Jerry. Jerry had failed to graduate from high school with the other Saints. During his second senior year, after the other Saints had gone on to college, Jerry began to hang around with what several teachers described as a "rough crowd"—the gang that was heir apparent to the Roughnecks. At the end of his second senior year, when he did graduate from high school, Jerry took a job as a used-car salesman, got married and quickly had a child. Although he made several abortive attempts to go to college by attending night school, when I last saw him (ten years after high school) Jerry was unemployed and had been living on unemployment for almost a year. His wife worked as a waitress.

Some of the Roughnecks have lived up to community expectations. A number of them were headed for trouble. A few were not.

Jack and Herb were the athletes among the Roughnecks and their athletic prowess paid off handsomely. Both boys received unsolicited athletic scholarships to college. After Herb received his scholarship (near the end of his senior year), he apparently did an about-face. His demeanor became very similar to that of the Saints. Although he remained a member in good standing of the Roughnecks, he stopped participating in most activities and did not hang on the corner as often.

Jack did not change. If anything, he became more prone to fighting. He even made excuses for accepting the scholarship. He told the other gang members that the school had guaranteed him a "C" average if he would come to play football —an idea that seems far-fetched, even in this day of highly competitive recruiting.

During the summer after graduation from high school, Jack attempted suicide by jumping from a tall building. The jump would certainly have killed most people trying it, but Jack survived. He entered college in the fall and played four years of football. He and Herb graduated in four years, and both are teaching and coaching in high schools. They are married and have stable families. If anything, Jack appears to have a more prestigious position in the community than does Herb, though both are well respected and secure in their positions.

Two of the boys never finished high school. Tommy left at the end of his junior year and went to another state. That summer he was arrested and placed on probation on a manslaughter charge. Three years later he was arrested for murder; he pleaded guilty to second-degree murder and is serving a 30-year sentence in the state penitentiary.

Al, the other boy who did not finish high school, also left the state in his senior year. He is serving a life sentence in a state penitentiary for first-degree murder.

Wes is a small-time gambler. He finished high school and "bummed around." After several years he made contact with a bookmaker who employed him as a runner. Later he acquired his own area and has been working it ever since. His position among the bookmakers is almost identical to the position he had in the gang; he is always around but no one is really aware of him. He makes no trouble and he does not get into any. Steady, reliable, capable of keeping his mouth closed, he plays the game by the rules, even though the game is an illegal one.

That leaves only Ron. Some of his former friends reported that they had heard he was "driving a truck up north," but no one could provide any concrete information.

REINFORCEMENT

The community responded to the Roughnecks as boys in trouble, and the boys agreed with that perception. Their pattern of deviancy was reinforced, and breaking away from it became increasingly unlikely. Once the boys acquired an image of themselves as deviants, they selected new friends who affirmed that self-image. As that self-conception became more firmly entrenched, they also became willing to try new and more extreme deviances. With their growing alienation came freer expression of disrespect and hostility for representatives of the legitimate society. This disrespect increased the community's negativism, perpetuating the entire process of commitment to deviance. Lack of a commitment to deviance works the same way. In either case, the process will perpetuate itself unless some event (like a scholarship to college or a sudden failure) external to the established relationship intervenes. For two of the Roughnecks (Herb and Jack), receiving college athletic scholarships created new relations and culminated in a break with the established pattern of deviance. In the case of one of the Saints (Jerry), his parents' divorce and his failing to graduate from high school changed some of his other relations. Being held back in school for a year and losing his place among the Saints had sufficient impact on Jerry to alter his self-image and virtually to assure that he would not go on to college as his peers did. Although the experiments of life can rarely be reversed, it seems likely in view of the behavior of the other boys who did not enjoy this special treatment by the school that Jerry, too, would have "become something" had he graduated as anticipated. For Herb and Jack outside intervention worked to their advantage; for Jerry it was his undoing.

Selective perception and labeling—finding, processing and punishing some kinds of criminality and not others—means that visible, poor, nonmobile, outspoken, undiplomatic "tough" kids will be noticed, whether their actions are seriously delinquent or not. Other kids, who have established a reputation for being bright (even though underachieving), disciplined and involved in respectable activities, who are mobile and monied, will be invisible when they deviate from sanctioned activities. They'll sow their wild oats—perhaps even wider and thicker than their lower-class cohorts—but they won't be noticed. When it's time to leave adolescence most will follow the expected path, settling into the ways of the middle class, remembering fondly the delinquent but unnoticed fling of their youth. The Roughnecks and others like them may turn around, too. It is more likely that their noticeable deviance will have been so reinforced by police and community that their lives will be effectively channeled into careers consistent with their adolescent background.

It is important, however, to be sensitive to some facets of this inquiry which could easily be misinterpreted. Because of the popularity of the "labeling theory" among criminologists it might easily be assumed that it was the difference in having the label "delinquent" or "bad" attached to them that led the Roughnecks to be more criminalistic in their adult years. This assumption raises two important issues: had the labeling been reversed would the outcome of their lives been reversed as well? And were the Saints less criminal as adults?

To answer the last question first, I can only say I do not know. As the next study shows, there is a great deal of criminality among business, political and law enforcement elites which is systematic, persistent and hidden. Just as the delinquency of the Saints as teenagers was hidden, so it is quite possible that they are today engaged in as much criminality as the adults who were Roughnecks. The same processes which led the law enforcement agencies to find the delinquency of the Roughnecks and not that of the Saints may still be working so that the adult criminality of the Roughnecks is visible but the adult criminality of the Saints is not.

Had the labeling process been reversed, what would have happened? It strikes me as inadequate and somewhat naive to suppose that the criminality of the Roughnecks as adults was solely created by their being labeled delinquent as youth. The delinquency of the Saints as well as the delinquency of the Roughnecks reflected the life conditions created by their social class and experiences growing up in the America they knew. As adults their criminality would reflect the same thing. Labeling may be important in pushing some people into the permanent category of "criminal" but it cannot account for the fact that criminality exists as it does or for the fact that so many people engage in criminal acts throughout their lives, some being labeled as criminals for it, others being praised as successful businessmen, politicians or "public servants."

The point that must be stressed is simply that the process by which law enforcement agencies arrest, prosecute and punish suspected "delinquents" or "criminals" is one that reflects the political organization of law enforcement and the social class power distribution of the economic system. Roughnecks get arrested because theirs is the kind of activity for which the police are established; Saints are ignored because their acts are the kind of things police are supposed to ignore—not according to community values, but according to the realities of politics, economics and bureaucratic demands. That this is as true of the treatment of crime among adults as it is of delinquency among juveniles is demonstrated in the next paper: a study of the political economy of vice and corruption.

VICE, CORRUPTION,
BUREAUCRACY, AND POWER*

William J. Chambliss

At the turn of the century Lincoln Steffens made a career and helped elect a
president by exposing corruption in American cities.[1] In more recent years the task
of exposure has fallen into the generally less daring hands of social scientists who,
unlike their journalistic predecessors, have gathered their information from police
departments, attorney generals' offices, and grand jury records.[2] Unfortunately, this
difference in source of information has probably distorted the descriptions of
organized crime and may well have led to premature acceptance of the Justice
Department's long-espoused view regarding the existence of a national criminal
organization.[3] It almost certainly has led to an overemphasis on the *criminal* in
organized crime and a corresponding deemphasis on *corruption* as an institutionalized component of America's legal-political system.[4] Concomitantly, it has
obscured perception of the degree to which the structure of America's law and
politics creates and perpetuates syndicates that supply the vices in our major cities.

Getting into the bowels of the city, rather than just the records and IBM cards of
the bureaucracies, brings the role of corruption into sharp relief. Organized crime
becomes not something that exists outside law and government but is instead a
creation of them, or perhaps more accurately, a hidden but nonetheless integral
part of the governmental structure. The people most likely to be exposed by public
inquiries (whether conducted by the FBI, a grand jury, or the Internal Revenue
Service) may officially be outside of government, but the cabal of which they are a
part is organized around, run by, and created in the interests of economic, legal,
and political elites.

Study of Rainfall West (a pseudonym), the focus of this analysis of the relationship between vice and the political and economic system, dramatically illustrates

* I am grateful to W. G. O. Carson, Terence Morris, Paul Rock, Charles Michener, Patrick Douglas,
Donald Cressey, and Robert Seidman for helpful comments on earlier versions of this paper.

Source: "Vice, Corruption, Bureaucracy, and Power," *Wisconsin Law Review*, Vol. 1971, No. 4, pp.
1130–1155. By permission of the author and publisher.

the interdependency. The cabal that manages the vices is composed of important businessmen, law enforcement officers, political leaders, and a member of a major trade union. Working for, and with, this cabal of respectable community members is a staff which coordinates the daily activities of prostitution, gambling, bookmaking, the sale and distribution of drugs, and other vices. Representatives from each of these groups, comprising the political and economic power centers of the community, meet regularly to distribute profits, discuss problems, and make the necessary organizational and policy decisions essential to the maintenance of a profitable, trouble-free business.

DATA COLLECTION

The data reported in this paper were gathered over a period of seven years, from 1962 to 1969. Most came from interviews with persons who were members of either the vice syndicate, law enforcement agencies, or both. The interviews ranged in intensity from casual conversations to extended interviewing, complete with tape recording, at frequent intervals over the full seven years of the study. In addition, I participated in many, though not all, of the vices that comprise the cornerstone upon which corruption of the law enforcement agencies is laid.

There is, of course, considerable latitude for discretion on my part as to what I believe ultimately characterizes the situation. Obviously not everyone told the same story, nor did I give equal credibility to all information acquired. The story that does emerge, however, most closely coincides with my own observations and with otherwise inexplicable facts. I am confident that the data are accurate, valid, and reliable; but this cannot be demonstrated by pointing to unbiased sampling, objective measures, and the like for, alas, in this type of research such procedures are impossible.

THE SETTING: RAINFALL WEST

Rainfall West is practically indistinguishable from any other city of a million population. The conspicuous bulk of the population—the middle class—shares with its contemporaries everywhere a smug complacency and a firm belief in the intrinsic worth of the area and the city. Their particular smugness may be exaggerated due to relative freedom from the urban blight that is so often the fate of larger cities and to the fact that Rainfall West's natural surroundings attract tourists, thereby providing the citizenry with confirmation of their faith that this is, indeed, a "chosen land!"[5]

However, an invisible, although fairly large, minority of the population do not believe they live in the promised land. These are the inhabitants of the slums and ghettos that make up the center of the city. Camouflaging the discontent of the center are urban renewal programs which ring the slums with brick buildings and skyscrapers. But satisfaction is illusory; it requires only a slight effort to get past this brick and mortar and into the not-so-enthusiastic city center—a marked contrast to the wildly bubbling civic center located less than a mile away. Despite the ease of access, few of those living in the suburbs and working in the area surrounding the slums take the time to go where the action is. Those who do go for specific reasons: to bet on a football game, to find a prostitute, to see a dirty movie, or to obtain a personal loan that would be unavailable from conventional financial institutions.

BUREAUCRATIC CORRUPTION AND ORGANIZED CRIME: A STUDY IN SYMBIOSIS

Laws prohibiting gambling, prostitution, pornography, drug use, and high interest rates on personal loans are laws about which there is a conspicuous lack of consensus. Even persons who agree that such behavior is improper and should be controlled by law disagree on the proper legal response. Should persons found guilty of committing such acts be imprisoned, or counseled? Reflecting this dissension, large groups of people, some with considerable political power, insist on their right to enjoy the pleasures of vice without interference from the law.

In Rainfall West, those involved in providing gambling and other vices enjoy pointing out that their services are profitable because of the demand for them by members of the respectable community. Prostitutes work in apartments which are on the fringes of the lower-class area of the city, rather than in the heart of the slums, precisely because they must maintain an appearance of ecological respectability so that their clients will not feel contaminated by poverty. While professional pride may stimulate exaggeration on the part of the prostitutes, their verbal reports are always to the effect that "all" of their clients are "very important people." My own observations of the comings and goings in several apartment houses where prostitutes work generally verified the girls' claims. Of some 50 persons seen going to prostitutes' rooms in apartment houses, only one was dressed in anything less casual than a business suit.

Observations of panorama—pornographic films shown in the back rooms of restaurants and game rooms—also confirmed the impression that the principal users of vice are middle- and upper-class clientele. During several weeks of observations, over 70 percent of the consumers of these pornographic vignettes were well-dressed, single-minded visitors to the slums, who came for 15 or 20 minutes of viewing and left as inconspicuously as possible. The remaining 30 percent were poorly dressed, older men who lived in the area.

Information on gambling and bookmaking in the permanently established or floating games is less readily available. Bookmakers report that the bulk of their "real business" comes from "doctors, lawyers and dentists" in the city:

It's the big boys—your professionals—who do the betting down here. Of course, they don't come down themselves; they either send someone or they call up. Most of them call up, 'cause I know them or they know Mr. _____ [one of the key figures in the gambling operation].

Q. How 'bout the guys who walk off the street and bet?

A. Yeh; well, they're important. They do place bets and they sit around here and wait for the results. But that's mostly small stuff. I'd be out of business if I had to depend on them guys.

The poker and card games held throughout the city are of two types: (1) the small, daily game that caters almost exclusively to local residents of the area or working-class men who drop in for a hand or two while they are driving their delivery route or on their lunch hour; (2) and the action game which takes place 24 hours a day, and is located in more obscure places such as a suite in a downtown hotel. Like the prostitutes, these games are located on the edges of the lower-class areas. The action games are the playground of well-dressed men who were by manner, finances, and dress clearly well-to-do businessmen.

Then, of course, there are the games, movies, and gambling nights at private clubs—country clubs, Elks, Lions, and Masons clubs—where gambling is a mainstay. Gambling nights at the different clubs vary in frequency. The largest and most exclusive country club in Rainfall West has a funtime once a month at which one can find every conceivable variety of gambling and a limited, but fairly sophisticated, selection of pornography. Although admission is presumably limited to members of the club, it is relatively easy to gain entrance simply by joining with a temporary membership, paying a two-dollar fee at the door. Other clubs, such as the local fraternal organizations, have pinball machines present at all times; some also provide slot machines. Many of these clubs have ongoing poker and other gambling card games, run by people who work for the crime cabal. In all of these cases, the vices cater exclusively to middle- and upper-class clients.

Not all the business and professional men in Rainfall West partake of the vices. Indeed, some of the leading citizens sincerely oppose the presence of vice in their city. Even larger members of the middle and working classes are adamant in their opposition to vice of all kinds. On occasion, they make their views forcefully known to the politicians and law enforcement officers, thus requiring these public officials to express their own opposition and appear to be snuffing out vice by enforcing the law.

The law enforcement system is thus placed squarely in the middle of two essentially conflicting demands. On the one hand, their job obligates them to enforce the law, albeit with discretion; at the same time, considerable disagreement rages over whether or not some acts should be subject to legal sanction. This conflict is heightened by the fact that some influential persons in the community insist that all laws be rigorously enforced while others demand that some laws not be enforced, at least not against themselves.

Faced with such a dilemma and such an ambivalent situation, the law enforcers do what any well-managed bureaucracy would do under similar circumstances —they follow the line of least resistance. Using the discretion inherent in their positions, they resolve the problem by establishing procedures which minimize organizational strains and which provide the greatest promise of rewards for the organization and the individuals involved. Typically, this means that law enforcers adopt a tolerance policy toward the vices, selectively enforcing these laws only when it is to their advantage to do so. Since the persons demanding enforcement are generally middle-class persons who rarely venture into the less prosperous sections of the city, the enforcers can control visibility and minimize complaints by merely regulating the ecological location of the vices. Limiting the visibility of such activity as sexual deviance, gambling, and prostitution appeases those persons who demand the enforcement of applicable laws. At the same time, since controlling visibility does not eliminate access for persons sufficiently interested to ferret out the tolerated vice areas, those demanding such services are also satisfied.

This policy is also advantageous because it renders the legal system capable of exercising considerable control over potential sources of real trouble. For example, since gambling and prostitution are profitable, competition among persons desiring to provide these services is likely. Understandably, this competition is prone to become violent. If the legal system cannot control those running these vices, competing groups may well go to war to obtain dominance over the rackets. If, however, the legal system cooperates with one group, there will be a sufficient concentration of power to avoid these uprisings. Similarly, prostitution can be kept clean if the law enforcers cooperate with the prostitutes; the law can thus minimize the chance, for instance, that a prostitute will steal money from a customer. In this and many other ways, the law enforcement system maximizes its visible effectiveness by creating and supporting a shadow government that manages the vices.

Initially this may require bringing in people from other cities to help set up the necessary organizational structure. Or it may mean recruiting and training local talent or simply coopting, coercing, or purchasing the knowledge and skills of entrepreneurs who are at the moment engaged in vice operations. When made, this move often involves considerable strain, since some of those brought in may be uncooperative. Whatever the particulars, the ultimate result is the same: a syndicate emerges—composed of politicians, law enforcers, and citizens—capable of supplying and controlling the vices in the city. The most efficient cabal is invariably one that contains representatives of all the leading centers of power. Businessmen must be involved because of their political influence and their ability to control the mass media. This prerequisite is illustrated by the case of a fledgling magazine which published an article intimating that several leading politicians were corrupt. Immediately major advertisers canceled their advertisements in the magazine. One large chain store refused to sell that issue of the magazine in any of its stores. And when one of the leading cabal members was accused of accepting bribes, a number of the community's most prominent businessmen sponsored a large advertisement declaring their unfailing support for and confidence in the integrity of this "outstanding public servant."

The cabal must also have the cooperation of businessmen in procuring the loans which enable them individually and collectively to purchase legitimate businesses, as well as to expand the vice enterprises. A member of the banking community is therefore a considerable asset. In Rainfall West the vice-president of one of the local banks (who was an investigator for a federal law enforcement agency before he entered banking) is a willing and knowledgeable participant in business relations with cabal members. He not only serves on the board of directors of a loan agency controlled by the cabal, but also advises cabal members on how to keep their earnings a secret. Further he sometimes serves as a go-between, passing investment tips from the cabal onto other businessmen in the community. In this way the cabal serves the economic interests of businessmen indirectly as well as directly.

The political influence of the cabal is more directly obtained. Huge, tax-free profits make it possible for the cabal to generously support political candidates of its choice. Often the cabal assists both candidates in an election, thus assuring itself of influence regardless of who wins. While usually there is a favorite, ultracooperative candidate who receives the greater proportion of the contributions, everyone is likely to receive something.

THE BUREAUCRACY

Contrary to the prevailing myth that universal rules govern bureaucracies, the fact is that in day-to-day operations rules can—and must—be selectively applied. As a consequence, some degree of corruption is not merely a possibility, but rather is a virtual certainty which is built into the very structure of bureaucratic organizations.

The starting point for understanding this structural invitation to corruption is the observation that application of all the rules and procedures comprising the foundation of an organization inevitably admits of a high degree of discretion. Rules can only specify what should be done when the actions being considered fall clearly into unambiguously specifiable categories, about which there can be no reasonable grounds of disagreement or conflicting interpretation. But such categories are a virtual impossibility, given the inherently ambiguous nature of language. Instead, most events fall within the penumbra of the bureaucratic rules where the discretion of officeholders must hold sway.

Since discretionary decisionmaking is recognized as inevitable in effect, all bureaucratic decisions become subject to the discretionary will of the officeholder. Moreover, if one has a reason to look, vagueness and ambiguity can be found in any rule, no matter how carefully stipulated. And if ambiguity and vagueness are not sufficient to justify particularistic criteria being applied, contradictory rules or implications of rules can be readily located which have the same effect of justifying the decisions which, for whatever reason the officeholder wishes, can be used to enforce his position. Finally, since organizations characteristically develop their own set of common practices which take on the status of rules (whether written or unwritten), the entire process of applying rules becomes totally dependent on the discretion of the officeholder. The bureaucracy thus has its own set of precedents which can be invoked in cases where the articulated rules do not provide precisely the decision desired by the officeholder.

Ultimately, the officeholder has license to apply rules derived from a practically bottomless set of choices. Individual self-interest then depends on one's ability to ingratiate himself to officeholders at all levels in order to ensure that the rules most useful to him are applied. The bureaucracy therefore is not a rational institution with universal standards, but is instead irrational and particularistic. It is a type of organization in which the organization's reason for being is displaced by a set of goals that often conflict with the organization's presumed purposes. This is precisely the consequence of the organizational response to the dilemma created by laws prohibiting the vices. Hence, the bureaucratic nature of law enforcement and political organization makes possible the corruption of the legal-political bureaucracy.

In the case of Rainfall West the goal of maintaining a smooth functioning organization takes precedence over all other institutional goals. Where conflict arises between the long-range goals of the law and the short-range goal of sustaining the organization, the former lose out, even at the expense of undermining the socially agreed-upon purposes for which the organization presumably exists.

Yet, the law enforcement agency's tendency to follow the line of least resistance of maintaining organizational goals in the face of conflicting demands necessarily embodies a choice as to whose demands will be followed. For bureaucracies are not equally susceptible to all interests in the society. They do not fear the castigation, interference, and disruptive potential of the alcoholics on skid row or the cafe-owners in the slums. In fact, some residents of the black ghetto in Rainfall West and of other lower-class areas of the city have been campaigning for years to rid their communities of the gambling casinos, whore houses, pornography stalls, and bookmaking operations. But these pleas fall on deaf ears. The letters they write and the committees they form receive no publicity and create no stir in the smoothly functioning organizations that occupy the political and legal offices of the city. On the other hand, when the president of a large corporation in the city objected to the "slanderous lies" being spread about one of the leading members of the crime cabal in Rainfall West, the magazine carrying the "lies" was removed from newsstand sale, and the editors lost many of their most profitable advertisers. Similarly, when any question of the honesty or integrity of policemen, prosecuting attorneys, or judges involved in the cabal is raised publicly, it is either squelched before aired (the editor of the leading daily newspaper in Rainfall West is a long-time friend of one of the cabal's leading members) or it arouses the denial of influential members of the banking community (especially those bankers whose institutions loan money to cabal members), as well as leading politicians, law enforcement officers, and the like.

In short, bureaucracies are susceptible to differential influence, according to the economic and political power of the groups attempting to exert influence. Since every facet of politics and the mass media is subject to reprisals by cabal members and friends, exposition of the ongoing relationship between the cabal and the most powerful economic groups in the city is practically impossible.

The fact that the bureaucrats must listen to the economic elites of the city and not the have-nots is then one important element that stimulates the growth and maintenance of a crime cabal. But the links between the elites and the cabal are more than merely spiritual. The economic elite of the city does not simply play golf with the political and legal elite. There are in fact significant economic ties between the two groups.

The most obvious nexus is manifested by the campaign contributions from the economic elite to the political and legal elites. We need not dwell on this observation here; it has been well documented in innumerable other studies.[6] However, what is not well recognized is that the crime cabal is itself an important source of economic revenue for the economic elite. In at least one instance, the leading bankers and industrialists of the city were part of a multi-million-dollar stock swindle engineered and manipulated by the crime cabal with the assistance of confidence-men from another state. This entire case was shrouded in such secrecy that eastern newspapers were calling people at the University of Rainfall West to find out why news about the scandal was not forthcoming from local wire services. When the scandal was finally exposed the fact that industrialists and cabal members heavily financed the operation (and correspondingly reaped the profits) was conveniently ignored in the newspapers and the courts; the evil-doers were limited to the outsiders who were in reality the front men for the entire confidence operation.

In a broader sense, key members of the economic elite in the community are also members of the cabal. While the day-to-day, week-to-week operations of the cabal are determined by the criminal-political-legal elite, the economic elite benefits mightily from the cabal. Not surprisingly, any threat to the cabal is quickly squelched by the economic elite under the name of "concerned citizens," which indeed they are.

The crime cabal is thus an inevitable outgrowth of the political economy of American cities. The ruling elites from every sphere benefit economically and socially from the presence of a smoothly running cabal. Law enforcement and government bureaucracies function best when a cabal is part of the governmental structure. And the general public is satisfied when control of the vices gives an appearance of respectability, but a reality of availability.

VICE IN RAINFALL WEST

The vices available in Rainfall West are varied and tantalizing. Gambling ranges from bookmaking (at practically every street corner in the center of the city) to open poker games, bingo parlors, off-track betting, casinos, roulette and dice games (concentrated in a few locations and also floating out into the suburban country clubs and fraternal organizations), and innumerable two- and five-dollar stud-poker games scattered liberally throughout the city.

The most conspicuous card games take place from about ten in the morning —varying slightly from one fun house to the next—until midnight. A number of other 24-hour games run constantly. In the more public games, the limit ranges

WILLIAM J. CHAMBLISS

from one to five dollars for each bet; in the more select 24-hours-a-day games, there is a pot limit or no limit rule. These games are reported to have betting as high as $20,000 and $30,000. I saw a bet made and called for $1000 in one of these games. During this game, the highest stakes game I witnessed in the six years of the study, the police lieutenant in charge of the vice squad was called in to supervise the game—not, need I add, to break up the game or make any arrests, but only to insure against violence.

Prostitution covers the usual range of ethnic group, age, shape, and size of female. It is found in houses with madams *a la* the New Orleans stereotype, on the street through pimps, or in suburban apartment buildings and hotels. Prices range from $5 for a short time with a street walker to $200 for a night with a lady who has her own apartment (which she usually shares with her boyfriend who is discreetly gone during business operations).

High-interest loans are easy to arrange through stores that advertise, "your signature is worth $5,000." It is really worth considerably more; it may in fact be worth your life. The interest rates vary from a low of 20 percent for three months to as high as 100 percent for varying periods. Repayment is demanded not through the courts, but through the help of "The Gaspipe Gang," who call on recalcitrant debtors and use physical force to bring about payment. "Interest only" repayment is the most popular alternative practiced by borrowers and is preferred by the loan sharks as well. The longer repayment can be prolonged, the more advantageous the loan is to the agent.

Pinball machines are readily available throughout the city, most of them paying off in cash.

The gambling, prostitution, drug distribution, pornography, and usury which flourish in the lower-class center of the city do so with the compliance, encouragement, and cooperation of the major political and law enforcement officials in the city. There is in fact a symbiotic relationship between the law enforcement-political organizations of the city and a group of *local*, as distinct from national, men who control the distribution of vices.

CORRUPTION IN RAINFALL WEST

In the spring of 19— a businessman whom I shall call Mr. Van Meter sold his restaurant and began looking for a new investment when he noticed an advertisement in the paper which read:

Excellent investment opportunity for someone with $30,000 cash to purchase the good will and equipment of a long established restaurant in down town area . . . .

After making the necessary inquiries, inspecting the business, and evaluating its potential, Mr. Van Meter purchased it. In addition to the restaurant, the business consisted of a card room which was legally licensed by the city, operating under a publicly acknowledged tolerance policy which allowed card games, including poker, to be played. These games were limited by the tolerance policy to a maximum one-dollar limit for each bet.

Thus, Mr. Van Meter had purchased a restaurant with a built-in criminal enterprise. It was never clear whether he was, at the time of purchasing the business, fully aware of the criminal nature of the card room. Certainly the official tolerance policy was bound to create confusion over the illegality of gambling in the licensed card rooms. The full extent to which this purchase involved Mr. Van Meter in illegal activities crystallized immediately upon purchase of the property.[7]

> [W]e had just completed taking the inventory of [the restaurant]. I was then handed the $60,000 keys of the premises by Mr. Bataglia, and he approached me and said, "Up until now, I have never discussed with you the fact that we run a bookmaking operation here, and that we did not sell this to you; however if you wish to have this operation continue here, you must place another $5,000 to us, and we will count you in. Now, if you do not buy it, we will put out this bookmaking operation, and you will go broke." "In other words," Mr. Bataglia continued, "we will use you, and you need us." I told Mr. Bataglia that I did not come to this town to bookmake or to operate any form of rackets, and I assumed that I had purchased a legitimate business. Mr. Bataglia said, "You have purchased a legitimate business; however, you must have the bookmaking operation in order to survive." I promptly kicked him out of the place.

The question of how "legitimate" the business Mr. Van Meter had purchased was is not so simple as he thought. It was, to be sure, a licensed operation; there was a license to operate the restaurant, a license to operate the card room attached to the restaurant, and a license to operate the cigar stand (where much of the bookmaking operation had taken place before Mr. Van Meter purchased the place). These licenses, although providing a "legitimate business," also had the effect of making the owner of the business constantly in violation of the law, for the laws were so constructed that no one could possibly operate a "legitimate" business "legally." Thus, anyone operating the business was vulnerable to constant harassment and even closure by the authorities if he failed to cooperate with law enforcement personnel.

The card room attached to the business was the most flagrant example of a legitimate enterprise that was necessarily run illegally. The city of Rainfall West had adopted by ordinance a tolerance policy toward gambling. This tolerance policy consisted of permitting card rooms, which were then licensed by the city, pinball machines that paid off money to winners, and panorama shows. The city ordinance allowed a maximum one-dollar bet at the card table in rooms such as those in Mr. Van Meter's restaurant.

This ordinance was in clear and open violation of state law. The State Attorney General had publicly stated that the tolerance policy of the city was illegal and that the only policy for the state was that all gambling was illegal. Despite these rulings from higher state officials, the tolerance policy continued and flourished in the city although it did so illegally.

This general illegality of the card room was not, however, easily enforceable against any one person running a card room without enforcement against all persons running card rooms. There were, however, wrinkles in the tolerance policy ordinance which made it possible discriminately to close down one card room without being forced to take action against all of them. This was accomplished in part by the limit of one dollar on a bet. The card room was allowed to take a certain percentage of the pot from each game, but the number of people playing and the amount of percentage permitted did not allow one to make a profit if the table limit remained at one dollar. Furthermore, since most people gambling wanted to bet more, they would not patronize a card room that insisted on the one-dollar limit. Mr. Van Meter, like all other card room operators, allowed a two- to five-dollar limit. The ordinance was written in such a way that, in reality, everyone would be in violation of it. It was therefore possible for the police to harass or close down whatever card rooms they chose at their own discretion.

The health and fire regulations of the city were also written in such a way that no one could comply with all the ordinances. It was impossible to serve meals and still avoid violation of the health standards required. Thus, when the health or fire department chose to enforce the rules, they could do so selectively against whatever business they chose.

The same set of circumstances governed the cabaret licenses in the city. The city ordinances required that every cabaret have a restaurant attached; the restaurant, the ordinance stated, had to comprise at least 75 percent of the total floor space of the cabaret and restaurant combined. Since there was a much higher demand for cabarets than restaurants in the central section of the city, this meant that cabaret owners were bound by law to have restaurants attached, some of which would necessarily lose money. Moreover, these restaurants had to be extremely large in order to constitute 75 percent of the total floor space. For a 100-square-foot cabaret, an attached 300-square-foot restaurant was required. The cabaret owners' burden was further increased by an ordinance governing the use of entertainers in the cabaret, requiring that any entertainer be at least 25 feet from the nearest customer during her act. Plainly, the cabaret had to be absolutely gigantic to accommodate any customers after a 25-foot buffer zone encircled the entertainer. Combined with the requirement that this now very large cabaret had to have attached to it a restaurant three times as large, the regulatory scheme simply made it impossible to run a cabaret legally.

The effect of such ordinances was to give the police and the prosecuting attorney complete discretion in choosing who should operate gambling rooms, cabarets, and restaurants. This discretion was used to force payoffs to the police and cooperation with the criminal syndicate.

Mr. Van Meter discovered the payoff system fairly early in his venture:

I found shortages that were occurring in the bar, and asked an employee to explain them, which he did, in this manner: "The money is saved to pay the 'juice' of the place." I asked him what was the "juice." He said in this city you must "pay to stay." Mr. Davis said, "You pay for the beat-man [from the police department] $250.00 per month. That takes care of the various shifts, and you must pay the upper brass, also $200.00 each month. A beat-man collects around the first of each month, and another man collects for the upper brass. You get the privilege to stay in business." That is true; however, you must remember that it is not what they will do for you, but what they will do *to* you, if you don't make these payoffs as are ordered. "If I refuse, what then?" I asked. "The *least* that could happen to you is you will lose your business."

During the next three months, Mr. Van Meter made the payoffs required. He refused, however, to allow the bookmaking operation back into the building or to hire persons to run the card room and bar whom members of the organized crime syndicate and the police recommended to him for the job. He also fired one employee whom he found was taking bets while tending bar.

In August of the same year, a man whom Mr. Van Meter had known prior to buying the restaurant met him in his office:

Mr. Danielski met with me in my office and he came prepared to offer me $500 per month—in cash deductions—of my remaining balance of the contract owing against (the restaurant) if I would give him the bookmaking operation, and he would guarantee me another $800 a month more business. He warned that if he wanted to give my establishment trouble, he would go to a certain faction of the police department; if he wanted me open, he would go to another faction. "So do some thinking on the subject, and I will be in on Monday for your answer." Monday, I gave Mr. Danielski his answer. The answer was no.

In June of 19—, a man by the name of Joe Link, who I found later was a second-string gang member of Mr. Bataglia's, made application to me to operate my card room. I did give him the opportunity to operate the card room because I had known him some 20 years ago when he was attending the same high school that I was. After I had refused the offer of Mr. Danielski, Mr. Joe Link had received orders from Mr. Danielski and Mr. Bataglia to run my customers out and in any way he could, cripple my operation to bring me to terms. I terminated Mr. Link on November 6, 19—, and shortly after, after I had removed Mr. Link, Police Officer Herb C. conferred with me in my office, and Officer Herb C. said that I had better reappoint Mr. Link in my card room; that his superiors were not happy with me. If I did not return Mr. Link to his former position, then it would be necessary to clear anyone that I wanted to replace Mr. Link with. Officer C. felt that no one else would be acceptable. He further stated I had better make a decision soon, because he would not allow the card room to run without an approved boss. I informed Officer C. that I would employ anyone I chose in my card room or in any other department. Officer C. said, "Mr. Van Meter, you, I think, do not realize how powerful a force you will be fighting or how deep in City Hall this reaches. Even I am not let know all the bosses or where the money goes." I did not return Mr. Link, as I was ordered by Officer C., and I did select my own card room bosses.

On November 7, 19—, I received a phone call stating that I soon would have a visitor who was going to shoot me between the eyes if I did not comply with the demands to return Mr. Link to his former position.

The crime cabal in Rainfall West (including police officers, politicians and members of the organized criminal syndicate), like the criminal law which under-pins it, relies on the threat of coercion to maintain order. That threat, however, is not an empty one. Although Mr. Van Meter was not "shot between the eyes" as threatened, others who defied the cabal were less fortunate. Although it has never been established that any of the suspicious deaths that have taken place involving members of the crime cabal were murder, the evidence, nonetheless, points rather strongly in that direction. Eric Tandlin, former county auditor for Rainfall West, is but one of 13 similar cases which occurred from 1955–1969.

Tandlin had been county auditor for 17 years. He kept his nose clean, did the bidding of the right politicians, and received a special gift every Christmas for his cooperation. In the course of doing business with the politicians and criminals, he also developed extensive knowledge of the operations. Suddenly, without warning or expectation on his part, Eric was not supported by his party for reelection as auditor, losing the nomination to the brother-in-law of the chief of police. It was a shock from which Eric did not soon recover. He began drinking heavily and frequenting the gambling houses; he also began talking a great deal. One Friday evening, he made friends with a reporter who promised to put him in touch with someone from the attorney general's office. Saturday night at 6:30, just as the card rooms were being prepared for the evening, word spread through the grapevine along First Street that Eric had been done in: "Danielski took Eric for a walk down by the bay."

The Sunday morning paper carried a small front-page story:

Eric Tandlin aged forty seven was found drowned in back bay yesterday at around 5:00 p.m. The Coroner's office listed the cause of death as possible suicide. Friends said Mr. Tandlin who had been county auditor for many years until his defeat in the primaries last fall had been despondent over his failure to be re-elected.

The coroner, who was the brother-in-law of the chief of police, described the probable cause of death as "suicide." The people of Miriam Street knew better. They also knew that this was a warning not to talk to reporters, sociologists, or anyone else "nosing around." In the last few years the cabal has been responsible for the deaths of several of its members. Drowning is a favorite method of eliminating troublemakers, because it is difficult to ascertain whether or not the person fell from a boat by accident, was held under water by someone else, or committed suicide.[8] L. S., who was in charge of a portion of the pinball operations, but who came into disfavor with the cabal, was found drowned at the edge of a lake near his home. J.B., an assistant police chief who had been a minor member of the cabal for years, drowned while on a fishing trip aboard one of the yachts owned by a leading member of the cabal. In both instances the coroner, who was the brother-in-law of one of the leading cabal members, diagnosed the deaths as "accidental drownings." Over the years, he has often made that diagnosis when cabal members or workers in the organization have met with misfortune.

Other deaths have been arranged in more traditional ways. At least one man, for example, was shot in an argument in a bar. The offender was tried before a judge who has consistently shown great compassion for any crimes committed by members of the cabal (although he has compensated for this leniency with cabal members by being unusually harsh in cases against blacks who appear before him), and the case was dismissed for lack of evidence.

However, murder is not the preferred method of handling uncooperative people. Far better, in the strategy of the crime cabal, is the time-honored technique of blackmail and cooptation. The easiest and safest tactic is to purchase the individual for a reasonable amount, as was attempted with Mr. Van Meter. If this fails, then some form of blackmail or relatively minor coercion may be in order.

For instance, Sheriff McCallister was strongly supported by the cabal in his bid for office. Campaign contributions were generously provided since McCallister was running against a local lawyer who was familiar with the goings-on of the cabal and had vowed to attack its operations. McCallister won the election—cabal candidates almost never lose local elections—but underwent a dramatic change of heart shortly thereafter. He announced in no uncertain terms that he would not permit the operation of gambling houses in the country, although he did not intend to do anything about the operations within the city limits since that was not his jurisdiction. Nevertheless the country, he insisted, would be kept clean.

The cabal was as annoyed as it was surprised. The country operations were only a small portion of the total enterprise, but they were nonetheless important, and no one wanted to give up the territory. Further, the prospect of closing down the layoff center operating in the country was no small matter. The center is crucial to the entire enterprise, because it is here that the results of horse races and other sports events come directly to the bookmakers. The center also enables the cabal to protect itself against potential bankruptcy. When the betting is particularly heavy in one direction, bets are laid off by wiring Las Vegas where the national betting pattern always takes care of local variations. Clearly, something had to be done about McCallister.

No man is entirely pure, and McCallister was less pure than many. He had two major weaknesses: gambling and young girls. One weekend shortly after he took office a good friend of his asked if he would like to go to Las Vegas for the weekend.

He jumped at the opportunity. While the weekend went well in some respects, McCallister was unlucky at cards. When he flew back to Rainfall West Sunday night, he left $14,000 worth of IOUs in Las Vegas.

Monday morning one of the cabal chiefs visited McCallister in his office. The conversation went like this:

> Say, Mac, I understand you was down in Vegas over the weekend.
>
> Yeah.
>
> Hear you lost a little bit at the tables, Mac.
>
> Uuh-huh.
>
> Well the boys wanted me to tell you not to worry about those pieces of paper you left. We got them back for you.
>
> I don't . . . .
>
> Also, Mac, we thought you might like to have a memento of your trip; so we brought you these pictures . . . .

The "mementos" were pictures of McCallister in a hotel room with several young girls. Thereafter things in the country returned to normal.

Lest one think the cabal exploitative, it should be noted that McCallister was not kept in line by the threat of exposure alone. He was, in fact, subsequently placed on the payroll in the amount of $1000 a month. When his term as sheriff was over, an appointment was arranged for him to the state parole board. He was thus able to continue serving the cabal in a variety of ways for the rest of his life. Cooperation paid off much better than would have exposure.

Threats from outside the organization are more rare than are threats from within. Nevertheless, they occur and must be dealt with in the best possible way. Since no set strategy exists, each incident is handled in its own way. During Robert Kennedy's days as attorney general, the federal attorney for the state began a campaign to rid the state of the members of the cabal. People who held political office were generally immune, but some of the higher-ups in the operational section of the cabal were indicted. Ultimately five members of the cabal, including a high-ranking member of the local Teamsters' Union, were sentenced to prison. The entire affair was scandalous; politicians whose lives depended on the cabal fought the nasty business with all their power. They were able to protect the major leaders of the cabal and to avert exposure of the cabal politicians. However, some blood ran, and it was a sad day for the five sentenced to prison terms. Yet the organization remained intact and, indeed, the five men who went to prison continued to receive their full share of profits from the cabal enterprises. Corruption continued unabated, and the net effect on organized crime in the state was nil.

One reason that Mr. Van Meter was not "shot between the eyes" was that, although not fully cooperative, he was nonetheless paying into the cabal $450 a month in "juice." Eventually he cut down on these payments. When this happened Mr. Van Meter became a serious problem for the cabal, and something more than mere threats was necessary:

No extortion was paid by me directly to them, but it involved a third party. Some time shortly after the first of each month, the sum of $250 was paid to (the above-mentioned) Officer C., which he presumably divided up with other patrolmen on the beat. Two hundred dollars each month was given to (another bagman) for what the boys termed as "It was going to the upper braid." The $200 per month was paid each month from June 19—with payment of $200 being made in January 19—. Afrer that I refused to make further payments. . . . After some wrangling back and forth, I just told them that I would not pay any more. They said, "Well, we will take $100 per month on a temporary basis." I paid $100 per month for the next 12 months. Early the next year I had planned to cut off all payments to the patrolmen. . . . About the 8th of July the explosion occurred. Police officers Merrill and Lynch conducted a scare program; jerked patrons off stools, ran others out of my establishment; Patrolman Lynch ordered my card room floorman into the rest room; and ordered my card room closed. When my floorman came out of the rest room, he left white and shaking and never to be seen in the city again.

Following this incident, Mr. Van Meter met with his attorney, the chief of police, and a former mayor. Although the meeting was cordial, he was told they could do nothing unless he could produce affidavits substantiating his claims. He did so, but quickly became enmeshed in requests and demands for more affidavits, while the prosecuting attorney's office resisted cooperating.

The refusal of cooperation from the prosecuting attorney was not surprising. What Mr. Van Meter did not realize was that the prosecuting attorney was the key political figure behind the corruption of the legal and political machinery. He was also the political boss of the county and had great influence on state politics, coming as he did from the most populous area of the state. Over the years his influence had been used to place men in key positions throughout the various government bureaucracies, including the police department, the judiciary, the city council, and relevant governmental agencies such as the tax office and the licensing bureau.

There was, however, a shift in emphasis for a short time in the cabal's dealings with Mr. Van Meter. They offered to buy his business at the price he had paid for it. But when he refused, the pace of harassment increased. Longshoremen came into his restaurant and started fights. Police stood around the card room day and night observing. City health officials would come to inspect the cooking area during mealtimes, thereby delaying the food being served to customers; the fire department made frequent visits to inspect fire precautions. On several occasions, Mr. Van Meter was cited for violating health and safety standards.

Finally, he was called to the city council to answer an adverse police report stating that he allowed drunks and brawling in his establishment. At the hearing, he was warned that he would lose all of his licenses if a drunk were ever again found in his restaurant.

During the next six months, the pressure on Mr. Van Meter continued at an ever-increasing rate. Longshoremen came into the restaurant and card room and picked fights with customers, employees, and Mr. Van Meter himself. The health department chose five o'clock in the evening several days running to inspect the health facilities of the establishment. The fire inspector came at the lunch hour to inspect the fire equipment, writing up every minor defect detectable. Toward the end of Mr. Van Meter's attempt to fight the combine of the government, the police force, and the criminal syndicate, he received innumerable threats to his life. Bricks and stones were thrown through the windows of his building. Ultimately, he sold his business back to the man from whom he had purchased it at a loss of $30,000 and left the city.

The affair caused considerable consternation among the legal-political-criminal cabal which controlled and profited from the rackets in Rainfall West. In the "good old days" the problem would have been quickly solved, one informant remarked, "by a bullet through the fat slob's head." But ready resort to murder as a solution to problems was clearly frowned upon by the powers that operated organized crime in Rainfall West. Although the syndicate had been responsible for many murders over the past ten years, these murders were limited to troublesome persons *within* the syndicate. As nearly as could be determined, no outsider had been murdered for a number of years.

Overall the gambling, bookmaking, pinball, and usury operations grossed at least $25 million a year in the city alone. It was literally the case that drunks were arrested on the street for public intoxication while gamblers made thousands of dollars and policemen accepted bribes five feet away.

Payoffs, bribes, and associated corruption were not limited solely to illegal activities. To obtain a license for tow-truck operations one had to pay $10,000 to the licensing bureau; a license for a taxi franchise cost $15,000. In addition, taxi drivers who sold bootleg liquor (standard brand liquors sold after hours or on Sunday) or who would steer customers to prostitutes or gambling places paid the beat policeman and the sergeant of the vice squad. Tow-truck operators also paid the policeman who called the company when an accident occurred.

As one informant commented:

> When I would go out on a call from a policeman I would always carry matchbooks with three dollars tucked behind the covers. I would hand this to the cops when I came to the scene of the accident.
>
> Q. Did every policeman accept these bribes?
>
> A. No. Once in a while you would run into a cop who would say he wasn't interested. But that was rare. Almost all of them would take it.

Most of the cabarets, topless bars, and taverns were owned either directly or indirectly by members of the organized crime syndicate. Thus, the syndicate not only controlled the gambling enterprises, but also "legitimate" businesses associated with night life as well. In addition, several of the hotels and restaurants were also owned by the syndicate. Ownership of these establishments was disguised in several ways, such as placing them formally in the name of a corporation with a board of directors who were really front-men for the syndicate or placing them in the names of relatives of syndicate members. It should further be underlined that the official ownership by the syndicate must be interpreted to mean by all of the members who were in the political and legal bureaucracies and simultaneously members of the syndicate, as well as those who were solely involved in the day-to-day operations of the vice syndicate.

The governing board of the syndicate consisted of seven men, four of whom held high positions in the government and three of whom were responsible for the operation of the various enterprises. The profits were split among these seven men. We are *not* then talking about a syndicate that paid off officials, but about a syndicate that was part and parcel of the government, although not subject to election.

CONCLUSION

There is abundant data indicating that what is true in Rainfall West is true in virtually every city in the United States and has been true since at least the early 1900s. Writing at the turn of the century, Lincoln Steffens observed that "the spirit of graft and of lawlessness is the American spirit." He went on to describe the results of his inquiries:

> in the very first study—St. Louis—the startling truth lay bare that corruption was not merely political; it was financial, commercial, social; the ramifications of boodle were so complex, various and far-reaching, that our mind could hardly grasp them. . . . St. Louis exemplified boodle; Minneapolis Police graft; Pittsburgh a political and Industrial machine; Philadelphia general civil corruption. . . .[9]

In 1931, after completing an inquiry into the police, the National Commission on Law Observance and Enforcement concluded:

> Nearly all of the large cities suffer from an alliance between politicians and criminals. For example, Los Angeles was controlled by a few gamblers for a number of years. San Francisco suffered similarly some years ago and at one period in its history was so completely dominated by the gamblers that three prominent gamblers who were in control of the politics of the city and who quarrelled about the appointment of the police chief settled their quarrel by shaking dice to determine who would name the chief for the first two years, who for the second two years, and who for the third.
>
> Recently the gamblers were driven out of Detroit by the commissioner. These gamblers were strong enough politically to oust this commissioner from office despite the fact that he was recognized by police chiefs as one of the

strongest and ablest police executives in America. For a number of years Kansas City, Mo., was controlled by a vice ring and no interference with their enterprises was tolerated. Chicago, *despite its unenviable reputation*, is but one of numerous cities where the people have frequently been betrayed by their elected officials. [10]

Frank Tannenbaum once noted:

It is clear from the evidence at hand—that a considerable measure of the crime in the community is made possible and perhaps inevitable by the peculiar connection that exists between the political organizations of our large cities and the criminal activities of various gangs that are permitted and even encouraged to operate. [11]

Similarly, the Kefauver Commission summarized the results of its extensive investigation into organized crime in 1951:

(1) There is a nationwide crime syndicate known as the Mafia, whose tentacles are found in many large cities. It has international ramifications which appear most clearly in connection with the narcotics traffic.

(2) Its leaders are usually found in control of the most lucrative rackets in their cities.

(3) There are indications of centralized direction and control of these rackets, but leadership appears to be in a group rather than in a single individual. [12]

And in 1969, Donald R. Cressey, using data gathered from the attorney general of the United States and the Local Crime Commission, capsulized the state of organized crime in the U.S.:

In the United States, criminals have managed to put together an organization which is at once a nationwide illicit cartel and a nationwide confederation. This organization is dedicated to amassing millions of dollars by means of extortion, and from usury, the illicit sale of lottery tickets, chances on the outcome of horse races and athletic events, narcotics and untaxed liquor. [13]

The frequency of major scandals linking organized criminals with leading political and legal figures suggests the same general conclusion. Detroit, Chicago, Denver, Reading, Pennsylvania; Columbus and Cleveland, Ohio; Miami, New York, Boston, and a hoard of other cities have been scandalized and cleansed innumerable times. [14] Yet organized crime persists and, in fact, thrives. Despite periodic forays, exposures, and reform movements prompted by journalists, sociologists, and politicians, organized crime has become an institution in the United States and in many other parts of the world as well. [15]

Once established, the effect of a syndicate on the entire legal and political system is profound. Maintenance of order in such an organization requires the use of extralegal procedures since, obviously, the law cannot always be relied on to serve the interests of the crime cabal. The law can harass uncooperative people; it can even be used to send persons to prison on real or faked charges. But to make discipline and obedience certain, it is often necessary to enforce the rules of the syndicate in extralegal ways. To avoid detection of these procedures, the police, prosecuting attorney's office, and judiciary must be organized in ways that make them incapable of discovering events that the cabal does not want disclosed. In actual practice, policemen, prosecutors, and judges who are *not* members of the cabal must not be in a position to investigate those things that the syndicate does not want investigated. The military chain of command of the police is, of course, well-suited to such a purpose. So, in fact, is the availability of such subtle but nonetheless important sanctions as relegating uncooperative policemen to undesirable positions in the department. Conversely, cooperative policemen are rewarded with promotions, prestigious positions on the force, and of course a piece of the action.

Another consequence is widespread acceptance of petty graft. The matchbox fee for accident officers is but one illustration. Free meals and cigarettes, bottles of whiskey at Christmas, and the like are practically universal in the police department. Television sets, cases of expensive whiskey, and on occasion new automobiles or inside information on investments are commonplace in the prosecuting attorney's office.

Significantly, the symbiotic relationship between organized crime and the legal system not only negates the law enforcement function of the law vis-à-vis these types of crimes but actually increases crime in a number of ways. Perhaps most important, gradual commitment to maintaining the secrecy of the relationship in turn necessitates the commission of crimes other than those involved in the vices per se. At times, it becomes necessary to intimidate through physical punishment and even to murder recalcitrant members of the syndicate. Calculating the extent of such activities is risky business. From 1955 to 1969 in Rainfall West, a conservative estimate of the number of persons killed by the syndicate is 15. However, estimates range as high as "hundreds." Although such information is impossible to verify in a manner that creates confidence, it is virtually certain that some murders have been perpetrated by the syndicate in order to protect the secrecy of their operations. It is also certain that the local law enforcement officials, politicians and businessmen involved with the syndicate have cooperated in these murders.

The location of the vices in the ghettos and slums of the city may well contribute to a host of other types of criminality as well. The disdain which ghetto residents have for the law and law enforcers is likely derived from more than simply their own experiences with injustice and police harassment. Their day-to-day observations that criminal syndicates operate openly and freely in their areas with complete immunity from punishment, while persons standing on a corner or playing cards in an apartment are subject to arrest, can not help but affect their perception of the legal system. We do not know that such observations undermine respect for and willingness to comply with the law, but that conclusion would not seem unreasonable.

It is no accident that whenever the presence of vice and organizations that provide the vices is exposed to public view by politicians, exposure is always couched in terms of organized crime. The question of corruption is conveniently left in the shadows. Similarly, it is no accident that organized crime is inevitably seen as consisting of an organization of criminals with names like Valachi, Genovesse and Joe Bonana. Yet the data from the study of Rainfall West, as well as that of earlier studies of vice, makes it abundantly clear that this analysis is fundamentally misleading.

I have argued, and I think the data demonstrate quite convincingly, that the people who run the organizations which supply the vices in American cities are members of the business, political, and law enforcement communities—not simply members of a criminal society. Furthermore, it is also clear from this study that corruption of political-legal organizations is a critical part of the lifeblood of the crime cabal. The study of organized crime is thus a misnomer; the study should consider corruption, bureaucracy, and power. By relying on governmental agencies for their information on vice and the rackets, social scientists and lawyers have inadvertently contributed to the miscasting of the issue in terms that are descriptively biased and theoretically sterile. Further, they have been diverted from sociologically interesting and important issues raised by the persistence of crime cabals. As a consequence, the real significance of the existence of syndicates has been overlooked; for instead of seeing these social entities as intimately tied to, and in symbiosis with, the legal and political bureaucracies of the state, they have emphasized the criminality of only a portion of those involved. Such a view contributes little to our knowledge of crime and even less to attempts at crime control.

NOTES

[1] Joseph Lincoln Steffens, *The Shame of the Cities* (New York: McClure, Phillips and Company, 1904). See Joseph Lincoln Steffens, *The Autobiography of Lincoln Steffens* (New York: Harcourt, Brace & Co., 1931).

[2] Donald Cressey, *Theft of the Nation* (New York: Harper and Row, 1969); John A. Gardiner, "Wincanton: The Politics of Corruption," in The President's Commission on Law Enforcement and Administration of Justice, *Task Force on Organized Crime* (Washington: Government Printing Office, 1967), reprinted in William Chambliss, *Crime and the Legal Process* (New York: McGraw-Hill, 1969), pp. 103–135.

[3] The view of organized crime as controlled by a national syndicate appears in Cressey, *Theft of the Nation*. For a criticism of this view see Norval Morris and Gordon Hawkins, *The Honest Politician's Guide to Crime Control* (Chicago: University of Chicago Press, 1970).

[4] Most recent examples of this are Cressey, *Theft of the Nation*; Morris and Hawkins, *Honest Politician's Guide*; Rufus King, "Wild Shots in the War on Crime," *Journal of Public Law* 20, no. 1 (1971), pp. 85–115; William S. Lynch and James W. Phillips, "Organized Crime: Violence and Corruption," *Journal of Public Law* 20, no. 1 (1971), pp. 59–70; Thomas J. McKeon, "The Incursion by Organized Crime into Legitimate Business," *Journal of Public Law* 20, no. 1 (1971), pp. 117–141;

Thomas C. Schelling, "What is the Business of Organized Crime?" *Journal of Public Law* 20, no. 1 (1971), pp. 71–84; Randolph W. Thrower, "Symposium: Organized Crime, Introduction," *Journal of Public Law* 20, no. 1 (1971), pp. 33–40; Gus Tyler, "Sociodynamics of Organized Crime," *Journal of Public Law* 20, no. 1 (1971), pp. 41–58. For a discussion of the importance of studying corruption see Chambliss, *Crime and the Legal Process*, p. 89, William Chambliss and Robert Seidman, *Law, Order and Power* (Reading, Mass.: Addison-Wesley, 1971); Eric L. McKitrick, "The Study of Corruption," *Political Science Quarterly* 72 (December 1957), pp. 502–514.

[5] Thinking of one's own residence as a "chosen land" need not of course be connected with any objectively verifiable evidence. A small Indian farm town where the standard of living is scarcely ever above the poverty level has painted signs on sidewalks which read "Isn't God good to Indians?" Any outside observer knowing something of the hardships and disadvantages that derive from living in this town might well answer an unequivocal "no." Most members of this community nevertheless answer affirmatively.

[6] See generally G. William Domhoff, *Who Rules America?* (Englewood Cliffs, N. J.: Prentice-Hall, 1967); Louise Overacker, *Presidential Campaign Funds* (Boston: Boston University Press, 1946); Jasper B. Shannon, *Money and Politics* (New York: Random House, 1959); Louise Overacker, *Money in Elections* (New York: Macmillan, 1932); Victor Bernstein, "Private Wealth and Public Office: The High Cost of Campaigning," *The Nation* 202, June 27, 1966, pp. 770–775.

[7] All quotations are from taped interviews. The names of persons and places are fictitious.

[8] According to one informant: "Murder is the easiest crime of all to get away with. There are 101 ways to commit murder that are guaranteed to let you get away with it." He might have added that this was especially true when the coroner, the prosecuting attorney and key policy officials were cooperating with the murderers.

[9] See Steffens, *The Shame of the Cities*, p. 151.

[10] Garrett and Monroe, "Police Conditions in the United States," *National Commission on Law Observance and Enforcement Report on Police* 14 (1931), p. 45.

[11] Frank Tannenbaum, *Crime and the Community* (New York: Columbia University Press, 1938).

[12] President's Commission on Law Enforcement and Administration of Justice, *Challenge of Crime*, p. 7.

[13] Cressey, *Theft of the Nation*. For a discussion of similar phenomena in Great Britain see Norman Lucas, *Britain's Gangland* (London: W. H. Allen, 1969). See also Daniel Bell, *The End of Ideology* (Glencoe, Ill.: Free Press, 1960).

[14] James Q. Wilson, "The Police and Their Problems," *Public Policy* 12 (1963), pp. 189–216.

[15] See M. McMullan, "A Theory of Corruption," *Sociological Review* 9 (July 1961), pp. 181–201.

PART THREE

PERSPECTIVES
ON THE PROBLEM OF CRIME

INTRODUCTION

Milton Mankoff

Although the earlier sections of this volume have strongly implied that "crime rates" largely reflect the routine practices of economic, political, and bureaucratic elites in conjunction with law enforcement officers, it is still true that people in all parts of the world have been victimized by acts which do violence to them or threaten their private possessions. Elites may indeed be selective in determining which behaviors should be designated as crimes and which classes of people should be permitted to go relatively unpunished for law violations, but the suffering experienced by the victims of bodily assault and robbery cannot simply be dismissed as irrelevant to the study of crime, as too many liberals and radicals have been prone to do in the past. In the United States, where violent acts against persons and theft of their private possessions (excluding overtly political violence and theft) are apparently far greater than in any other advanced industrial nation, the cry for "law and order" has long been the exclusive province of conservatives. The time has come for a radical analysis of the crime problem, one that tran-

scends the call for bigger police budgets and meager economic and social reforms advocated by conservatives and liberals.[1]

The articles in this concluding section of the book argue that the fear that grips Americans as they walk the streets is the consequence of patterns of victimization which originate in the institutional foundations of the society. It is the same institutional structure that produces great wealth and comfort and choice of life style for some and that drives others to kill, mug, and rape. Moreover, identical impulses often propel people to succeed in accumulating wealth and power and in victimizing others. An obvious example of this process can be seen in the problem of "organized crime." The distinction between the Mafia, for example, and "legitimate business" is difficult to determine. It was, after all, the illegal practices of the robber barons, the patriarchs of the modern American business elite, which made their vast fortunes possible.[2] In addition, contemporary corporate violation of the law is rampant.[3] The rational division of the market for many goods and services (frequently by monopolization) has contributed to a reduction of corporate violence against domestic competitors and employees not yet possible for those "firms" operating in the unregulated laissez-faire capitalism of the rackets. Outside the United States, American-owned corporations such as ITT have shown little reluctance to use their economic and political power and influence to try to overthrow governments whose policies threatened American corporate profits. When people fret about the possibility that the Mafia is infiltrating "legitimate business" it is difficult to comprehend what they are worried about. Unless one assumes that the racketeers are primarily motivated to do violence to others rather than to acquire wealth, it is impossible to imagine what depredations will be heaped upon the consuming public by ex-gangster entrepreneurs that have not already occurred at the hands of General Foods, ITT, General Motors, Reynolds Tobacco Company, and a host of other companies which have poisoned our foods, corrupted our political system, destroyed public transportation, and encouraged the spread of habits injurious to our health.

But what about murder and assault? Are people who commit these crimes impelled by the same forces that move the rest of us? Let us take murder as a case in point. Despite the great fear of being murdered in cold blood by a perfect stranger on a dimly lit street or as a by-product of a robbery in one's home, the vast majority of murders involve perpetrators known to the victim.[4] About two-thirds of the victims of homicide are relatives, friends, or acquaintances of their assailant. It is rare when a stranger can arouse the intense emotions needed to make a person want to take someone's life. Armed forces everywhere exert great efforts to train people to kill and meet with only mild success in transforming ordinary citizens into killers.[5] Regardless of the claims of the ethologists human beings do not walk around with deep urges to harm others. Rather routine arguments over money and fidelity between friends, lovers, husbands and wives—arguments that large numbers of Americans participate in during the course of a lifetime—seem to precipitate homicidal rage in a few persons under certain circumstances (e. g., after heavy drinking). If murderers are beset by the same concerns as others it follows that they have generally had arguments over similar matters at other points in their lives and have not resorted to assault. The fact that murderers are very unlikely to repeat their offense when and if they are released from custody supports the generalization that they do not differ greatly from the non-murdering population.[6] Finally, substantial numbers of "law-abiding" citizens engage in violent acts against others (typically spouses or children)[7] during their lives.

To reduce the number of violent acts, some of which culminate in murder, requires a restructuring of social relationships as they exist in this country: the reduction of economic, social, and sexual competition, a changing consciousness about what "success" in these areas is, and the construction of political institutions that genuinely strive to create a fair and decent place for people to live in. No small order, to be sure; and one probably impossible without a total transformation of the political, economic, and cultural life of Americans. The point, however, is that more police on hand will not help solve the problem of violent crimes unless the powers given to the police include sitting in people's homes, where a large proportion of such acts occur. A policeman on every doorstep and in every living room would doubtless reduce the amount of violent crime, but the price paid would be far worse for everyone than a restructuring of the institutions to eliminate the forces that lead to the violence in the first place.

All this is not to deny, however, that in recent years there has been a marked increase in *impersonal* murder (i.e., where the victim does not know the assailant) and street muggings. It is possible to attribute some of the rise to an increasing victimization of *middle-class* persons who confuse their own difficulties with the very existence of social problems. Regardless, the acts are occurring and must be accounted for.

David Gordon's article, "Class and the Economics of Crime," skillfully argues that street crime is highly rational for disadvantaged members of society who do not have access either to legitimate sources or less violent illegitimate opportunities for economic security (e.g., embezzlement, price-fixing). Moreover, he shows how the differential penalty structure for the crimes committed by the upper and lower classes contributes to the violent nature of many street crimes. In addition, Gordon maintains that street crime as a rational enterprise is directly related to the nature of a capitalist economic system with its stress on competition, and the production and reproduction of inequalities. Finally, the author claims that crime and punishment help to stabilize the existing American social order. Crime serves to deflect criticism away from social institu-

tions and onto individuals; imprisonment, by removing large numbers of people who cannot find decent jobs from the labor market and segregating these dehumanized and despairing citizens from others, preserves the image of a smoothly functioning society which benefits all Americans. It also serves as a smokescreen behind which the daily routine of upper-class crime and political and economic corruption can take place unnoticed.

Andrew Hacker's witty and informed essay, "Getting Used to Mugging," supplements Gordon's analysis in a detailed study of muggings in New York City. Hacker dispels several commonplace theories of street crime (e.g., that it is simply a response to poverty or narcotic addicts' needs for large amounts of money to maintain their supply of drugs) as well as beliefs in the deterrent potential of the police. Essentially, he feels that street crime has become less a matter of economics *per se* than a response to powerlessness and alienation on the part of a certain proportion of predominantly lower-class young males. As long as the rhetoric of equal opportunity encourages young people to succeed in the world and then fails to provide genuine chances for achieving economic and social advancement for the offspring of the poor, street crime will abound. It is a primitive means of striking out at symbols of authority, defying the dominant culture (while acquiescing to its subterranean ethic of Darwinian struggle, accumulation, and the belief that the ends justify the means), and engaging in exciting "work" for one's livelihood.

Just as murder may well be an extreme form of personal violence that is commonplace in American families (as well as being legitimized in sports, films, novels, and warfare), rape, according to Susan Griffin in her provocative essay, "Rape: The All-American Crime," may also be a mere extension of normal sexual politics. In societies where women are viewed as property and sexual conquest is considered a male prerogative and a substitute for or component of economic and political power, rape can be expected to flourish. If Griffin's analysis is correct, rape cannot be greatly reduced unless the economic, political, racial, and sexual inequalities that characterize American society are eliminated. Rape is a symbolic form of political struggle, one that would have little meaning if power itself did not afford great status and privilege.

If conservative "law and order" rhetoric is incapable, short of totalitarianism, of being translated into an effective policy to curb violent crime, what of the approach of liberal social analysts? Within the social sciences an influential analysis of crime and other forms of deviance has developed in the past two decades which has rejected punishment as a sound remedy for reducing socially unacceptable behavior. Its proponents, known as labeling or societal reaction theorists, have suggested that societal labeling of deviants, by stigmatizing them, makes it difficult for them to reintegrate within their community. As noted in the introduction to Part Two, socially labeled criminals often have great problems in acquiring jobs and finding social acceptance in their communities. Frequently they resort to criminal acts to survive and perhaps also to "reject the rejectors." The effects of stigmatization are no

doubt profound and liberal social scientists are clearly correct in advocating practices that make it easier for criminals to anonymously return to the outside world after receiving whatever punishment is meted out to them.

Despite the valuable insights of the labeling theorists, one should not presume that the crime problem depends solely upon the existence of a repressive and unforgiving society. As Milton Mankoff points out in "Societal Reaction and Career Deviance: A Critical Analysis," rule-breakers who repeat their deviant acts may not be responding to the harmful consequences of labeling so much as to the same conditions which drove them to violate rules in the first place (e.g., powerlessness, alienation, poverty). Liberal analysts and even some radical scholars such as Gordon also assume that all criminality flows from the thwarting of conventional aspirations for success. While such concerns may indeed account for most rule-breaking, it is also true that rule-breakers may become attached to certain forms of deviation for their own sake. This is particularly the case in regard to drug users, homosexuals (who are still persecuted in many parts of the United States and the rest of the world), and political criminals (e.g., Weathermen, Symbionese Liberation Army). These rule-breakers find positive values in their acts and do not wish a chance to "make it" in the existing social world.

The crucial point to remember is that deviant patterns of behavior grow out of the imbalances, flaws, and contradictions in the social order and the needs and desires of people in societies. These needs and desires are typically conventional, but sometimes they transcend the commonplace. Both the common and the uncommon aspirations of people may be thwarted, thus leading some to engage in extreme acts which are injurious to others. A repressive societal reaction to rule-breaking may not noticeably increase or decrease the crime rate, which is a reflection of more basic institutional patterns.

To some extent liberal social analysts are aware of the relationship between societal flaws and violent criminality. Their policy recommendations do involve both economic and social reform as well as a less repressive penal system. Yet, having what is essentially a naive economic theory of crime, liberals often ignore the fact that men and women do not live by bread alone. If very poor people may steal to survive, the offspring of the well-to-do occasionally see the limits of materialism and strive to realize other goals which lead them into conflict with the existing social order. Most participants in the student movement in the United States in the 1960s came from affluent social backgrounds, where the radical ideological impulse is most strongly felt. Moreover, crimes are committed throughout all social classes in America, as we have seen in the previous sections of this book.

One of the themes that emerges in the articles in this section is that street crime is a natural outgrowth of capitalist society. While the lack of adequate statistical data makes it difficult to determine whether street crime in socialist societies is considerably less than in the United States, it seems true that advanced Western European capitalist societies exhibit less of this social pathology than can be found in America. New York City, for example, has more murders in a few months than occur in England in a year. A possible solution to the problem posed by comparative criminal rates is to accept the notion that all societies today frustrate their citizens in varying degrees. Capitalist societies may increase this sense of frustration because of their ideological emphasis on material accumulation, competition, and individual achievement despite their having gross inequalities in wealth, power, and the opportunity for changing one's social position. However, there are countervailing forces which may reduce the expression of frustration in violent behavior. Thus, even within the capitalist world violent crime rates differ depending upon the specific economic, political, social and cultural characteristics of the society under examination.

If Western European capitalist societies have less street crime than the United States, it may be because of several countervailing factors. First, they have more fully developed welfare policies than in America where laissez-faire ideology, puritan individualism, and ethnic and racial pluralism have inhibited the growth of community responsibility for the disadvantaged.[8] The fact that the poor in Western European capitalist countries have better unemployment benefits (and lower unemployment), medical care and other welfare amenities means that people do not reach the level of dehumanization possible in the United States. With a greater sense of dignity there is less likelihood of striking out violently against innocent fellow citizens to vent one's grievances.

A second factor, and one which has

received virtually no attention in the criminological literature, builds on the insight of Andrew Hacker and others that street crime represents a primitive pre-political form of protest against power-lessness, alienation, and class society. It can be argued that the growth of a mass radical political movement in the United States could provide a constructive alternative to misdirected, individualistic, and unjustified attacks on persons who are often equally oppressed by the social order. A lower incidence of violent crime in Western European capitalist societies might possibly reflect the fact that the working classes there generally have a much higher degree of class conscious-ness, a greater involvement in trade unions (most likely with Socialist or Communist leadership), and a greater allegiance to Socialist or Communist political parties than their American counterparts. The United States is virtu-ally the only advanced capitalist society in the world which does not have a powerful Labor, Socialist, or Commu-nist party representing the working class.

Finally, some capitalist societies such as England do not have radical working-class traditions, as exist in France, Italy, and to a lesser extent in Germany. England appears, on the con-trary, to have a political culture which includes a high degree of class con-sciousness but also an acceptance of class hierarchy and deference toward societal elites. Under these circumstances crimi-nal violence is minimized since the feel-ings of *unjustified* powerlessness are relatively absent compared to those found among the working classes of societies which have long-standing radical traditions.

The United States, having a minimal welfare system, rampant individualism, and weak radical and deferential tradi-tions within the working class, exhibits few countervailing forces which might channel frustrations away from street crime and into more constructive or harmless paths.

NOTES

[1] Richard Quinney, *Critique of Legal Order: Crime Control in Capitalist Society* (Boston: Little, Brown, 1974).

[2] Matthew Josephson, *The Robber Barons: The Great American Capitalists: 1861–1901* (New York: Harcourt, Brace and World, 1962).

[3] Edwin H. Sutherland, *White Collar Crime* (New York: Dryden Press, 1949); Gilbert Geis, "Avo-cational Crime" in *Handbook of Criminology*, ed. by Daniel Glaser (Chicago: Rand McNally, 1974), pp. 273–298; Richard Quinney, "Occu-pational Structure and Criminal Behavior: Pre-scription Violations by Retail Pharmacists," *Social Problems* 11 (Fall 1963), pp. 179–185; William J. Chambliss and David Keown, "The Crime Cabal," mimeographed (Santa Barbara, 1974).

[4] Marvin Wolfgang, *Patterns in Criminal Homicide* (Philadelphia: University of Pennsyl-vania Press, 1958); Marvin Wolfgang, *Studies in Homicide* (New York: Harper and Row, 1967); J. C. M. Matheson, "Infanticide," *Medical Le-gal Review* 9 (1941), pp. 135–152; President's Commission on Law Enforcement and Ad-ministration of Justice, *The Challenge of Crime in a Free Society* (New York: Dutton, 1970), pp. 138–139.

[5] Studies of combat behavior during the Korean War indicated that a great majority of foot soldiers refused to fire their weapons. Air war-fare, being more impersonal, results in a greater willingness to perform combat roles.

[6] Daniel Glaser, *The Effectiveness of a Prison and Parole System* (Indianapolis: Bobbs-Merrill, 1964), pp. 41–49.

[7] Suzanne K. Steinmetz and Murray A. Strauss, "The Family as Cradle of Violence," *Society* 10 (September–October 1973), pp. 50–56.

[8] Dorothy Wedderburn, "Facts and Theories of the Welfare State," in *The Poverty of Progress: The Political Economy of American Social Prob-lems*, ed. by Milton Mankoff (New York: Holt, Rinehart & Winston, 1972), pp. 190–206.

CLASS AND THE
ECONOMICS OF CRIME

David M. Gordon

Then in his second semester at Eastern District High School, he gave up working in school altogether. "I don't really know why, and I don't want to rationalize about it, but it may have been that I had been systematically de-educated. With all the emphasis on discipline, all the fire gets damped down. I knew I had a given role in society, and you wonder what do you need to know about Plato to fix the engine of an automobile. Anyhow, I flew apart, I began cutting classes, gambling in the bathroom, the whole bit . . . I picked pockets. I was a little crook.

(Nine months in a reformatory intervened.) When he came out, Franklin K. Lane High School never jelled, and eventually he began to hustle. "I took a bunch of nothing jobs—they lasted a month on the average, and then I'd go to the movies instead. I bounced around, I'd hustle when it was necessary —gambling, numbers, a little petty larceny. And when I was 19 I committed a burglary and that was the end of the ball game."

. . . From the story of a 30-year-old black ex-con[1]

Crime in the United States has become another domestic "crisis." Crime rates have been soaring. Central city residents hide in their homes at night, frightened by the ubiquitous muggers. Public efforts to prevent crime have mushroomed into a veritable military campaign; like our other recent war adventures, the campaign seems essentially to have failed. Compounding the sense of crisis, inmates have been rebelling in the prisons, forging what one observer recently called a "low-visibility revolution."[2]

Although sociologists and criminologists have been studying the problem of crime for years, economists have largely ignored it. Suddenly, at the end of the 1960s, they strode confidently into the breach. Applying the standard tools of

Source: "Class and the Economics of Crime," *The Review of Radical Political Economics*, Vol. 3, No. 3, Summer, 1971, pp. 51–72. By permission of the author and publisher.

DAVID M. GORDON

neoclassical economics, they promised to guide us toward "optimal" crime prevention and control. In his pioneering essay, Gary Becker explains how easily the problem can be understood (3, p. 170): ". . . a useful theory of criminal behavior can dispense with special theories of anomic, psychological inadequacies, or inheritance of special traits and simply extend the economist's usual analysis of choice."

The orthodox analysis seems to me to offer neither a valid framework within which to understand the problem of crime nor a useful guide toward its solution. In this essay, I have tried to articulate an alternative radical economic analysis of crime in the United States. The essay applies some of the basic tools of radical theory to try to illuminate the causes of crime in this country and to explain our failures to curb its growth. The paper has three sections. The first section provides a brief descriptive summary of the nature and extent of crime in America. The second section very briefly surveys some of the conventional public perspectives motivating our efforts to control crime and outlines recent orthodox economic analyses of the problem. The third section suggests a radical economic analysis of crime, arguing that we cannot realistically expect to "solve" the problem of crime in the United States without first effecting a fundamental redistribution of power in our society.

CRIME IN AMERICA

Several useful summaries of the nature and extent of American crime are easily available.[3] Based on those sources, the following paragraphs outline the most important questions about the problem of crime which any economic analysis must try to resolve.

It seems important to emphasize, first of all, that crime is ubiquitous in the United States. Our laws are so pervasive that one must virtually retire to a hermitage in order to avoid committing a crime. According to a national survey conducted in 1965 by the President's Crime Commission (32, p. v), 91 percent of all adult Americans "admitted that they had committed acts for which they might have received jail or prison sentences." The Crime Commission also found that in 1965 "more than two million Americans were received in prisons or juvenile training schools, or placed on probation"—well over 2 percent of the labor force. Criminal behavior, it appears, is clearly a norm and not an aberration.

Given that ubiquity, one should also emphasize the extraordinary selectivity of our attention to the problem of crime. We focus all our paranoia about "law'n'order" and "safe streets" on a limited number of crimes while we totally ignore many other kinds of crime, equally serious and of much greater economic importance.

The crimes on which the public *does* concentrate its fears and canons are often lumped together as "urban" or "violent" crimes. These crimes can be usefully summarized by those for which the FBI accumulates a general statistical Index. Seven "Index Crimes" are traced in the Bureau's periodic Crime Report: willful

194

homicide, forcible rape, aggravated assault, robbery, larceny (of more than $50), and motor vehicle theft.

Some basic facts about these seven fearsome crimes are well known. The measured incidence of the Index Crimes has been increasing rapidly in the United States in the past 10 to 15 years.[4] The Index Crimes occur twice as frequently in large cities as they do on average throughout the country. Within large cities, they occur most frequently in ghetto areas. The threat and tragedy of violent crime notwithstanding, almost all of these crimes are economically motivated; Clark concludes quite simply (8, p. 38) that "their main purpose is to obtain money or property." Fully seven-eighths of Index Crimes are crimes against property and only one-eighth are crimes against person. Moreover, many of the relatively few "violent" crimes against person occur inadvertently in the process of committing crimes against property.

A large part of the crime against property is committed by youth. Clark concludes from the scattered statistics (8, p. 54) that half of all property crime is committed by people under 21.[5] Certainly more important in considering the evolution of public attitudes, Blacks commit disproportionate numbers of these seven Index Crimes (and are also disproportionately the victims of the same crimes). Although arrest rates bear an obviously spurious relationship to the actual incidence of crime, some of the figures seem astonishing.[6] In 1968, for instance, official statistics indicate that 61 percent of those arrested for robbery were Black and nearly half of those arrested for aggravated assault were Black, despite the fact that Blacks represented only 12 percent of the population. And the public exaggerates these figures even further; public attitudes often appear to presume that *all* of the Index Crimes are committed by Blacks and that every Black male is on the verge of committing a crime.[7]

The crimes our society chooses consistently to *ignore* seem just as obvious. Many kinds of relatively hidden crimes, most of them called "white-collar" crimes, occur both frequently and profitably. Tax evasion, price fixing, embezzlement, swindling and consumer fraud capture billions of dollars every year. Clark provides some simple examples of the magnitudes of these kinds of crime:

> Illicit gains from white-collar crime far exceed those of all other crime combined . . . One corporate price-fixing conspiracy criminally converted more money each year it continued than all of the hundreds of thousands of burglaries, larcenies, or thefts in the entire nation during those same years. Reported bank embezzlements cost ten times more than bank robberies each year (8, p. 38).

As Clark also notes, the public and the media choose to pay almost no attention to either the existence or the causes of those kinds of crime.

The selectivity of public opinion is matched by the biases of our governmental system of law enforcement and the administration of justice. The system prosecutes and punishes some crimes and criminals heavily while leaving others alone. Some defenders of the system occasionally argue that it concentrates most heavily on those crimes of the greatest magnitude and importance, but the data do not support this view: the Index Crimes on which the system focuses account for small proportions of the total personal harm and property loss resulting from crime in the United States. For example, deaths resulting from "willful homicide" are one-fifth as frequent as deaths from motor vehicle accidents; although many experts ascribe nearly half of motor vehicle accidents to mechanical failure, the system rarely pays attention to those liable for that failure. The economic loss attributable to Index Crimes against property—robbery, burglary, and so on—are one-fifth the losses attributable to embezzlement, fraud and unreported commercial theft, and yet the system concentrates almost exclusively, on the former.

One can much more reasonably argue that the selectivity of our police, courts and prisons corresponds to the relative *class status* of those who perpetrate different kinds of crimes. We seem to have a dual system of justice in this country, as both the Crime Commission (32) and Goldfarb (13) have most clearly shown. The public system concentrates on crimes committed by the poor, while crimes by the more affluent are left to private auspices. Our prisons function, as Goldfarb notes, like a "national poorhouse," swallowing the poor, chewing them up and occasionally spitting them back at the larger society. When the more affluent get in trouble, in contrast, private psychiatric and counseling assistance supplant prosecution. Goldfarb concludes (13, p. 312; Goldfarb's emphasis): ". . . in the classes of offenses committed by rich and poor *equally*, it is rarely the rich who end up behind bars."[8]

None of the systems' selectivity seems to work, finally, as we claim that we intend it to work. The public seems to think that concentration on a few crimes will at least improve the effectiveness of the system in controlling those few crimes —leading to greater prevention and deterrence and perhaps equally to greater rehabilitation. Buoyed by that hope, the various governments in the United States spent roughly $4.2 billion on police, prisons and the courts in 1965, while private individuals and corporations spent an additional $1.9 billion on prevention and insurance. And yet, despite those billions, our system of law enforcement and the administration of justice appears not only to be failing to curb the growth of crime but actually to be *exacerbating* the criminality it seeks selectively to control. The prisons themselves are veritable factories of crime; Clark notes (8, p. 212): "Jails and prisons in the United States today are more often than not manufacturers of crime. Of those who come to jail undecided, capable either of criminal conduct or of lives free of crime, most are turned to crime." More generally, very few of those who get started in crime ever actually leave it as a result of the system's deterrent or rehabilitative effects. According to Clark's statistical summaries (8, p. 55), roughly half of those released from prison eventually return, and fully 80 percent of serious crime is committed by "repeaters"—by those who have been convicted of crime before.

These very brief descriptive observations clearly suggest the questions an economic analysis must seek to answer about the problem of crime: *why* is there so much crime? Why do the public and the government concentrate so selectively on such a small part of the criminal activity in this country? And why do all our billions of dollars fail so miserably in curbing even that small part of the total problem?

CONVENTIONAL ANALYSIS

Conventional public analyses of crime divide roughly into two views—"conservative" and "liberal"—which tend to agree on basic assumptions and to diverge as they debate the specifics of crime prevention and control.

The conservative perspective on crime has an appealing simplicity.[9] Since conservatives believe that the social "order" is ultimately rational and is adequately reflected in the laws of our governments, they also believe that those who violate it can be regarded as "irrational" citizens and social misfits. The more violent the crimes, the more seriously we must regard their consequences. And since criminals (and especially violent ones) act irrationally, we can deter and prevent their actions only by responding to them with comparably irrational actions—principally by the threat or application of raw force. Toward that end, conservatives engage in two kinds of policy calculations. First, they discuss the potential deterrence of a variety of crime-prevention techniques. If only enough deterrent force could be mustered, they assume, crime could be stopped. Typically, they urge more police and more equipment to prevent crime. Second, they tend to favor preventive detention as a necessary means of protecting the social order from the threat of probable criminality; they make their argument, normally, on relatively pragmatic grounds.[10]

Liberals tend to regard the problem of criminal activity as a more complicated dilemma.[11] They agree that those who violate the "social order" can indeed be regarded as "irrational." At the same time, however, liberals regard the interactions of individuals with society as extremely complex processes, fraught with imperfections, and they are likely to argue that some individuals are much more likely than others to be *pushed* toward the irrationality of criminal behavior; we should therefore try to avoid *blaming* some criminals for their irrational acts. And since different individuals are pushed in very different ways by different social circumstances, there is a wide variety of behavior among criminals. The Crime Commission concludes (32, p. 5), "No single formula, no single theory, no single generalization can explain the vast range of behavior called crime."

Some of these heterogeneous crimes are more serious than others, liberals continue, because they are more violent and therefore more threatening. Liberals tend to agree with conservatives and the FBI that the FBI Crime Index adequately encompasses the potentially most violent crimes. But liberals tend to disagree with conservatives in arguing that these kinds of relatively violent crimes cannot simply be prevented by force, that they cannot ultimately be curbed until the social imperfections which underlie them are eliminated. The prevalence of "violent" crime among youth, Blacks and ghetto residents derives from the diseases of poverty and racism in American society; given those basic social imperfections, as the Crime Commission argues (35, p. 5), ". . . it is probable that crime will continue to increase . . . unless there are drastic changes in general social and economic conditions."

Can we do nothing about crime until we eliminate the sores of poverty and racism? Liberals respond ambivalently, but they often argue that we can marginally improve our prevention of crime and our treatment of criminals if we can at least marginally rationalize our system of law enforcement and administration of justice. We need more research, more analysis, more technology, more money, better administration, and more numerous and professional personnel.[12]

In the past few years, redressing an historic neglect, several orthodox economists have tried to clarify our analysis of criminal behavior and our evaluation of alternative public policies to combat it.[13] Although a few nineteenth-century classical economists like Jeremy Bentham had originally applied economics to the analysis of the problem of crime, as Becker (3) and Tullock (49) note, economists since then have generally ignored the problem. Recent advances in neoclassical microeconomic theory permit us, we are now told, to "extend the economist's usual analysis of choice" to an analysis of criminal behavior and its "optimal" prevention and punishment. Since each of the recent applications of orthodox economics outlines the mode of analysis rather clearly and the approach so directly reflects the more general predispositions of orthodox microeconomics, a few very brief observations about the orthodox analysis are sufficient to clarify its differences with both the "public" perspectives outlined above and the radical analysis developed below.

The central and most important thrust of the orthodox analysis is that criminal behavior, like any other economic activity, is eminently rational; in this important respect, the economists differ fundamentally with the conventional liberal and conservative public views. Becker formulates this central contention quite simply:

> . . . a person commits an offense if the expected utility to him exceeds the utility he could get by using his time and other resources at other activities. Some persons become "criminals," therefore, not because their basic motivation differs from that of other persons, but because their benefits and costs differ (3, p. 176).

More specifically, individuals are assumed to calculate the returns to and the risks of "legitimate" employment and "criminal" activity and base their choices between those two modes of activity on their cost/benefit calculations. Stigler adds (42, p. 530), "The details of occupational choice in illegal activity are not different from those encountered in the legitimate occupations."

Given those assumptions of rationality, orthodox economists argue that we can construct some "optimal" social policies to combat crime. They assume, first of all, that there is a social welfare function through which the costs and benefits of criminal offenses to each member of society can be translated into a common metric. Society (through its several governments) should then try to minimize the "social loss" from criminal offenses as measured by the social welfare function. In their formulation of the parameters of these calculations, they hypothesize that criminals respond quite sensitively in their own decision making to variations in the level and probability of punishment. They also assume, as Becker puts it (3, p. 174), that "the more that is spent on policemen, court personnel, and specialized equipment, the easier it is to discover offenses and convict offenders." They then proceed to the final argument: we can choose (through our governments) some combination of punishment levels and social expenditures—with expenditures determining the probability of capture and conviction—which will minimize our social losses from crime subject to the revenue constraints in our public and private budgets.

Behind the orthodox economic analysis lie two obvious and fundamental assumptions. First, although the assumption is rarely made explicit, the analysis assumes that governments behave in democratic societies in such a way that everyone's preferences have an equal chance of influencing the final outcome, that public policy formulations can adequately reflect the costs and benefits of criminal offenses to all individuals in society.[14]

Second, orthodox economists assume some simple and identifiable relationships between the amount of money we actually spend on prevention and enforcement, the amount of prevention and enforcement we would *like to achieve*, and the amount of prevention and enforcement we can *actually achieve*. This involves the assumption, noted above, that larger expenditures monotonically increase the probability of apprehension and conviction. It also involves another, related assumption—that the level of government expenditures on prevention and punishment accurately reflects society's desired level of prevention and enforcement instead of, for example, the influence of vested interests in maximizing expenditures; if a state or locality spends more on its police, courts and prisons, *ceteris paribus*, orthodox economists assume that they do so because they seek to deter crime more effectively through the (expected) increase in the probability of arrest and punishment, and not for any other reason.

A RADICAL ANALYSIS OF CRIME

This section outlines the structure of a radical economic analysis of crime in the United States. Many points in the argument will seem quite obvious, simple elaborations of common sense. Other points will bear some important similarities to one or another of the views described in the preceding section. Taken together, however, the arguments in the following analysis seem to me to provide a more useful, coherent, and realistic interpretation of the problem than the more conventional models. In the analysis, I have tried as simply as possible to apply some general hypotheses of radical economic analysis to a discussion of the specific problem of crime in this country.[15]

The analysis has five separate parts. The first tries to explain a basic behavioral *similarity* among all the major kinds of crime in the United States. Given that fundamental similarity, the second part seeks to explain the most important dimensions of *difference* among various crimes in this country. Given a delineation of the sources of difference among crimes, the third part attempts an historical explanation of the sources of those sources of difference—analysis, as it were, of the underlying causes of some immediate causes of difference. The fourth part argues that we cannot easily reverse history, that we cannot easily alter the fundamental social structures and trends which have produced the problem of crime today. A final section provides a brief review of the central hypotheses of the argument and some comments on its implications.

COMPETITIVE CAPITALISM AND RATIONAL CRIME

Capitalist societies depend, as radicals often argue, on basically competitive forms of social and economic interaction and upon substantial inequalities in the allocation of social resources. Without inequalities, it would be much more difficult to induce workers to work in alienating environments. Without competition and a competitive ideology, workers might not be inclined to struggle to improve their relative income and status in society by working harder. Finally, although rights of property are protected, capitalist societies do not guarantee economic security to most of their individual members. Individuals must fend for themselves, finding the best available opportunities to provide for themselves and their families. At the same time, history bequeaths a corpus of laws and statutes to any social epoch which may or may not correspond to the social morality of that epoch. Inevitably, at any point in time, many of the "best" opportunities for economic survival open to different citizens will violate some of these historically determined laws. Driven by the fear of economic insecurity and by a competitive desire to gain some of the goods unequally distributed throughout the society, many individuals will eventually become "criminals." As Adam Smith himself admitted in *The Wealth of Nations* (41, p. 670), "Where there is no property . . . civil government is not so necessary."

In that respect, therefore, radicals would argue that nearly all crimes in capitalist societies represent perfectly *rational* responses to the structure of institutions upon which capitalist societies are based. Crimes of many different varieties constitute functionally similar responses to the organization of capitalist institutions, for those crimes help provide a means of survival in a society within which survival is never assured. Three different kinds of crime in the United States provide the most important examples of this functionally similar rationality among different kinds of crime: ghetto crime, organized crime, and corporate (or "white-collar") crime.[16]

It seems especially clear, first of all, that ghetto crime is committed by people responding quite reasonably to the structure of economic opportunities available to them. Only rarely, it appears, can ghetto criminals be regarded as raving, irrational, antisocial lunatics.[17] The "legitimate" jobs open to many ghetto residents, especially to young black males, typically pay low wages, offer relatively demanding assignments and carry the constant risk of layoff. In contrast, many kinds of crime "available" in the ghetto often bring higher monetary return, even higher social status, and—at least in some cases like numbers running—sometimes carry relatively low risk of arrest and punishment.[18] Given those alternative opportunities, the choice between "legitimate" and "illegitimate" activities is often quite simple. As Arthur Dunmeyer, a black hustler from Harlem, has put it:

> In some cases this is the way you get your drug dealers and prostitutes and your numbers runners . . . They see that these things are the only way that they can compete in the society, to get some sort of status. They realize that there aren't any real doors open to them, and so, to commit crime was the only thing to do, they can't go back (5, p. 292).

The fact that these activities are often "illegal" sometimes doesn't really matter; since life out of jail often seems as bad as life inside prison, the deterrent effect of punishment is negligible. Dunmeyer expresses this point clearly as well:

> It is not a matter of a guy saying, "I want to go to jail (or) I am afraid of jail." Jail is on the street just like it is on the inside. The same as, like when you are in jail, they tell you, "Look, if you do something wrong you are going to be put in the hole." You are still in jail, in the hole or out of the hole. You are in jail in the street or behind bars. It is the same thing . . . (5, p. 293).

In much the same way, organized crime represents a perfectly rational kind of economic activity.[19] Activities like gambling and prostitution are illegal for varieties of historical reasons, but there is a demand for those activities nonetheless. As Donald Cressey writes (10, p. 294), "The American confederation of criminals thrives because a large minority of citizens demands the illicit goods and services it has for sale." Clark makes the same point (8, p. 68), arguing that organized crimes are essentially "consensual crimes . . . , desired by the consuming public." The simple fact that they are both illegal and in such demand provides a simple explanation for the secrecy, relative efficiency and occasional violence of those who provide them. In nearly every sense, for example, the organization of the heroin industry bears as rational and reasonable a relationship to the nature of the product as the structures of the tobacco and alcoholic beverages industries bear to the nature of their own products.[20]

Finally, briefly to amplify the third example, corporate crime also represents a quite rational response to life in capitalist societies. Corporations exist to protect and augment the capital of their owners. If it becomes difficult to perform that function one way, corporate officials will quite inevitably try to do it another. When Westinghouse and General Electric conspired to fix prices, for instance, they were resorting to one of many possible devices for limiting the potential threat of competition to their price structures. Similarly, when Ford and General Motors proliferate new car model after new car model, each differing only slightly from its siblings, they are choosing to protect their price structures by product differentiation. In one case, the corporations were using oligopolistic power quite directly. In the other, they rely on the power of advertising to generate demand for the differentiated products. In the context of the perpetual and highly competitive race among corporations for profits and capital accumulation, each response seems quite reasonable. In his pioneering studies of corporate crime, Sutherland made the same points about corporate criminals and linked their behavior to lower-class criminality:

> I have attempted to demonstrate that businessmen violate the law with great frequency . . . If these conclusions are correct, it is very clear that the criminal behavior of businessmen cannot be explained by poverty, in the usual sense, or by bad housing or lack of recreational facilities or feeblemindedness or emotional instability. Business leaders are capable, emotionally-balanced and in no sense pathological . . . The assumption that an offender must have some such pathological distortion of the intellect or the emotions seems to me absurd, and if it is absurd regarding the crimes of businessmen, it is equally absurd regarding the crimes of persons in the lower economic class (44, p. 310).

CLASS INSTITUTIONS AND DIFFERENCES AMONG CRIMES

If most crime in the United States in one way or another reflects the same kind of rational response to the insecurity and inequality of capitalist institutions, what explains the manifold differences among different kinds of crime? Some crimes are much more violent than others, some are much more heavily prosecuted, and some are much more profitable. Why?

As a first step in explaining differences among crimes, I would apply the general perspective in a relatively straightforward manner, arguing quite simply that many of the most important differences among different kinds of crime in this country are determined by the *structure of class institutions* in our society and by the *class biases* of the State. That argument has two separate components.

First, I would argue that many of the important differences among crimes in this society derive quite directly from the different socioeconomic classes to which individuals belong. Relatively affluent citizens have access to jobs in large corporations, to institutions involved in complicated paper transactions involving lots of money, and to avenues of relatively unobtrusive communication. Members of these classes who decide to break the law, as Clark puts it (8, p. 38), have "an easier, less offensive, less visible way of doing wrong." Those raised in poverty, on the other hand, do not have such easy access to money. If they are to obtain it criminally, they must impinge on those who already have it or direct its flow. As Robert Morgenthau has written (25, p. 20), those growing up in the ghetto "will probably never have the opportunity to embezzle funds from a bank or to promote a multimillion dollar stock fraud scheme. The criminal ways which we encourage (them) to choose will be those closest at hand—from vandalism to mugging to armed robbery."

Second, I would argue that the biases of our police, courts and prisons *explain* the relative violence of many crimes—that many of the differences in the degree of violence among different kinds of crime do not cause the selectivity of public concern about those crimes but *are in fact caused by* that selectivity. For a variety of historical reasons, as I noted above, we have a dual system of justice in this country; the police, courts and prisons pay careful attention to only a few crimes. It is only natural, as a result, that those who run the highest risks of arrest and conviction may have to rely on the threat or commission of violence in order to protect themselves. Many kinds of ghetto crimes generate violence, for instance, because the participants are severely prosecuted for their crimes and must try to protect themselves however they can. Other kinds of ghetto crimes are openly tolerated by the police, like the numbers racket, and those crimes rarely involve violence. It may be true, as Clark argues (8, p. 39), that "violent crime springs from a violent environment," but violent environments like the ghetto do not always produce violent crimes. Those crimes to which the police pay attention usually involve violence, while those which the police tend to ignore quite normally do not. In similar ways, organized crime has become violent historically, as Cressey especially argues (10), principally because its participants are often prosecuted. As long as that remains true, the suppliers of illegal goods require secrecy, organization and a bit of violence to protect their livelihood. Completely in contrast, corporate crime does not require violence because it is ignored by the police; corporate criminals can safely assume they do not face the threat of jail and do not therefore have to cover their tracks with the threat of harming those who betray them. When Lockheed Aircraft accountants and executives falsified their public reports in order to disguise cost over-runs on the C-5A airplane in 1967 and 1968, for instance, they did not have to force Defense Department officials at knife-point to play along with their falsifications. As Robert Sherrill reports in his investigation of the Lockheed affair (40, p. 43), the Defense Department officials were entirely willing to cooperate. "This sympathy," Sherrill writes, "was reflected in orders from top Air Force officials to withhold information regarding Lockheed's dilemma from all reports that would be widely circulated." If only local police were equally sympathetic to the "dilemmas" of street-corner junkies, the violent patterns of drug-related crimes might be considerably transformed.[21]

In short, it seems important to view some of the most important differences among crimes—differences in their violence, their style and their impact—as fundamental outgrowths of the class structure of society and the class biases of our major institutions, including the State and its system of enforcement and administration of justice. Given that argument, it places a special burden on attempts to explain the historical sources of the duality of the public system of justice in this country, for that duality, coupled with the class biases of other institutions, plays such an important role in determining the patterns of American crime.

THE SOURCES OF DUALITY

One can explain the duality of our public system of justice quite easily, it seems to me, if one is willing to view the State through the radical perspective. The analysis involves answers to two separate questions. First, one must ask why the State *ignores* certain kinds of crimes, especially white-collar crimes and corporate crimes. Second, given that most crimes among the poor claim the poor as their victims, one must ask why the State bothers to worry so incessantly about those crimes.

The answer to the first question draws directly from the radical theory of the State. According to the radical theory, the government in a capitalist society like the United States exists primarily to preserve the stability of the system which provides, preserves and protects returns to the owners of capital. As long as crimes among the corporate class tend in general to harm members of other classes, like those in the "consuming" class, the State will not spontaneously move to prevent those crimes from taking place. On the other hand, as Paul Sweezy has especially argued (45), the State may be pressured either nominally or effectively to prosecute the wealthy if their criminal practices become so egregiously offensive that their victims may move to overthrow the system itself. In those cases, the State may punish individual members of the class in order to protect the interests of the entire class. Latent opposition to the practices of corporations may be forestalled, to pick several examples, by token public efforts to enact and enforce antitrust, truth-in-lending, antipollution, industrial safety, and auto safety legislation. As James Ridgeway has most clearly shown in the case of pollution (37), however, the gap between the enactment of the statutes and their effective enforcement seems quite cavernous.[22]

The answer to the second question seems slightly more complicated historically. Public responses to crime among the poor have changed periodically through-out American history, responding both to changes in the patterns of the crimes themselves and to changes in public morality. The subtlety of that historical process would be difficult to trace in this kind of discussion, but some patterns do seem clear.

Earlier in American history, as Clark has pointed out (8, pp. 55–56), we tended to ignore many crimes among the poor because those crimes rarely impinged upon the lives of the more affluent. Gambling, prostitution, dope and robbery seemed to flourish in the slums of the early twentieth century, and the police rarely moved to intervene. More recently, however, some of the traditional patterns of crime have changed. Two dimensions of change seem most important. On the one hand, much of the crime has moved out of the ghettos. As Clark explains (8, p. 55), "Our concern arose when social dynamics and population movements brought crime and addiction out of the slums and inflicted it on or threatened the powerful and well-to-do." On the other hand, the styles in which ghetto criminals have fulfilled their criminal intent may have grown more hostile since World War II, flowing through what I have elsewhere called the "promised land effect" (in 15), after the title of the book by Claude Brown (4). As Brown points out, second-generation Northern Blacks—the sons and daughters of Southern migrants born in Northern slums—have relatively little reason to hope that their lives will improve. Their parents migrated in search of better times, but some of those born in the North probably believe that their avenues for escape from poverty have disappeared. Brown puts it well:

> The children of these disillusioned colored pioneers inherited the total lot of their parents—the disappointments, the anger. To add to their misery, they had little hope of deliverance. For where does one run to when he's already in the promised land? (4, p. 8).

Out of frustration, some of the crime among younger ghetto-born Blacks may be more vengeful now, more concerned with sticking it to whitey. Coupled with the spread of ghetto crime into other parts of the city, this symbolic expression of vengefulness undoubtedly heightens the fear that many affluent citizens feel about ghetto crime. Given their influence with the government, they quite naturally have moved toward increasing public attention to the prevention and punishment of crimes among the poor.

Once the patterns of public duality have been established, of course, they acquire a momentum and dynamic all their own. To begin with, vested interests develop, deriving their livelihood and status from the system. The prison system, like the defense industry, becomes a power of its own, with access to public bureaucracies, with workers to support and with power to defend. Eldridge Cleaver has made special note of this feature of our public system:

> The only conclusion one can draw is that the parole system is a procedure devised primarily for the purpose of running people in and out of jail—most of them black—in order to create and maintain a lot of jobs for the white prison system. In California, which I know best—and I'm sure it's the same in other states—there are thousands and thousands of people who draw their living directly or indirectly from the prison system; all the clerks, all the guards, all the bailiffs, all the people who sell goods to the prisons. They regard the inmates as a sort of product from which they all draw their livelihood, and the part of the crop they keep exploiting most are the black inmates (9, p. 185).

In much the same way, the police become an interest and a power of their own.[23] They are used and manipulated by the larger society to enforce the law selectively; as Clark writes (8, p. 137), "We send police to maintain order, to arrest, to jail—and to ignore vital laws also intended to protect life and to prevent death . . ." As agents of selective social control, the police also inevitably become the focus of increasing animosity among those they are asked selectively to control. Manipulated by the larger society, hated by those at the bottom, the police tend to develop the mentality, as Westley (50) has called it, of a "garrison." They eventually seek to serve neither the interests of the larger society nor the interests of the law but the interests of the garrison. One reaches the point, finally, where police interests interject an intermediate membrane screening the priorities of the state and society on the one hand and the interests of their victims on the other. Westley concludes (50): "When enforcement of the law conflicts with the ends of the police, the law is not enforced. When it supports the ends of the police, they are fully behind it. When it bears no relation to the ends of the police, they enforce it as a matter of routine."

THE IMPLAUSIBILITY OF REFORM

One needs to ask, finally, whether these patterns can be changed and the trends reversed. Can we simultaneously eradicate the causes of crime and reform our dual system of justice? At the heart of that question lies the question posed at the beginning of this essay, for it simultaneously raises the necessity of explaining the failures of our present system to prevent the crime it seeks most systematically to control.

I would argue, quite simply, that reform is implausible unless we change the basic institutions upon which capitalism in the United States depends. We cannot legitimately expect to eradicate the initial causes of crime for two reasons. First, capitalism depends quite substantially on the preservation of the conditions of competition and inequality. Those conditions, as I argued above, will tend to lead almost inevitably to relatively pervasive criminal behavior; without those conditions, the capitalist system would scarcely work at all. Second, as many have argued, the general presence of racism in this country, though capitalists may not in fact have created it, tends to support and maintain the power of the capitalists as a class by providing cheap labor and dividing the working class. Given the substantial control of capitalists over the policies and priorities of the State, we cannot easily expect to prod the State to eliminate the fundamental causes of racism in this country. In that respect, it seems likely that the particular inequalities facing Blacks and their consequent attraction to the opportunities available in crime seem likely to continue.

Given expectations that crime will continue, it seems equally unlikely that we shall be able to reform our systems of prosecution and punishment in order to mitigate their harmful effects on criminals and to equalize their treatment of different kinds of crime. First and superficially, as I noted above, several important and powerful vested interests have acquired a stake in the current system and seem likely to resist efforts to change it. Second and more fundamentally, the cumulative effect of the patterns of crime, violence, prosecution and punishment in this country play an important role in helping legitimize and stabilize the capitalist system. Although capitalists as a class may not have created the current patterns of crime and punishment, those patterns currently serve their interests in several different ways. We should expect that the capitalists as a class will hardly be eager to push reform of the system. Given their relative reluctance to reform the system, we should expect to be able to push reform only in the event that we can substantially change the structure of power to which the State responds.

The current patterns of crime and punishment help support the capitalist system in three different ways. First, the pervasive patterns of selective enforcement seem to reinforce a prevalent ideology in this society that individuals, rather than institutions, are to blame for social problems. Individuals are criminally prosecuted for motor accidents because of negligent or drunken driving, for instance, but auto manufacturers are never criminally prosecuted for the negligent construction of unsafe cars or for their roles in increasing the likelihood of death through air pollution. Individual citizens are often prosecuted and punished for violence and for resisting arrest, equally, but those agents of institutions, like police and prison guards, or institutions themselves, like Dow Chemical, are never prosecuted for inflicting unwarranted violence on others. These patterns of selectivity reinforce our pervasive preconceptions of the invulnerability of institutions, leading us to blame ourselves for social failure; this pattern of individual blame, as Edwards and MacEwan have especially argued (11), plays an important role in legitimizing the basic institutions of this kind of capitalist society.

Second, and critically important, the patterns of crime and punishment manage "legitimately" to neutralize the potential opposition to the system of many of our most oppressed citizens. In particular, the system serves ultimately to keep thousands of men out of the job market or trapped in the secondary labor market by perpetuating a set of institutions which serves functionally to feed large numbers of Blacks (and poor whites) through the cycle of crime, imprisonment, parole, and recidivism. The system has this same ultimate effect in many different ways. It locks up many for life, first of all, guaranteeing that those potentially disaffected souls keep "out of trouble." For those whom it occasionally releases, it tends to drive them deeper into criminality, intensifying their criminal and violent behavior, filling their heads with paranoia and hatred, keeping them perpetually on the run and unable, ultimately, to organize with others to change the institutions which pursue them. Finally, it blots their records with the stigma of criminality, effectively precluding the reform of even those who vow to escape the system and go "straight" by denying them many decent employment opportunities.[24]

The importance of this neutralization should not be underestimated. If all young black men in this country do not eventually become criminals, most of them are conscious of the trap into which they might fall. George Jackson has written from prison (20), "Blackmen born in the U.S. and fortunate enough to live past the age of eighteen are conditioned to accept the inevitability of prison. For most of us, it simply looms as the next phase in a sequence of humiliations." And once they are trapped, the cycle continues almost regardless of the will of those involved. Prison, parole and the eventual return to prison become standard points on the itinerary. Cleaver has written:

I noticed that every time I went back to jail, the same guys who were in Juvenile

Hall with me were also there again. They arrived there soon after I got there, or a little bit before I left. They always seemed to make the scene. In the California prison system, they carry you from Juvenile Hall to the old folks' colony, down in San Luis Obispo, and wait for you to die. Then they bury you there . . . I noticed these waves, these generations . . . graduating classes moving up from Juvenile Hall, all the way up (9, pp. 154–155).

And those who succeed finally in understanding the trap and in pulling themselves out of it, like Malcolm X, Claude Brown, Eldridge Cleaver and George Jackson, seem to succeed precisely because they understand how debilitating the cycle becomes, how totally dehumanizing it will remain. Another black ex-con has perfectly expressed the sudden insight which allowed him to pull out of the trap:

It didn't take me any time to decide I wasn't going back to commit crimes. Because it's stupid, it's a trap, it only makes it easier for them to neutralize you. It's hard to explain, because you can't say it's a question of right and wrong, but of being free or (being) trapped (6).

If the system did not effect this neutralization, if so many of the poor were not trapped in the debilitating system of crime and punishment, then they might otherwise gather the strength to oppose the system which reinforces their misery. Like many other institutions in this country, the system of crime and punishment serves an important function for the capitalist class by dividing and weakening those who might potentially seek to overthrow the capitalist system. Although the capitalists have not created the system, in any direct sense, they would doubtless hate to have to do without it. [25]

The third and perhaps most important functionally supportive role of the current patterns of crime and punishment is that those patterns allow us to ignore some basic issues about the relationships in our society between institutions and individuals. By treating criminals as animals and misfits, as enemies of the state, we are permitted to continue avoiding some basic questions about the dehumanizing effects of our social institutions. We keep our criminals out of sight, so we are never forced to recognize and deal with the psychic punishment we inflict on them. Like the schools and the welfare system, the legal system turns out, upon close inspection, to rob most of its "clients" of the last vestiges of their personal dignity. Each one of those institutions, in its own way, helps us forget about the responsibilities we might alternatively assume for providing the best possible environment within which all of us could grow and develop as individuals. Cleaver sees this "role" of the system quite clearly:

Those who are now in prisons could be put through a process of real rehabilitation before their release . . . By rehabilitation I mean they would be trained for jobs that would not be an insult to their dignity, that would give them some sense of security, that would allow them to achieve some brotherly connection with their fellow man. But for this kind of rehabilitation to happen on a large scale would entail the complete reorganization of society, not to mention the prison system. It would call for the teaching of a new set of ethics, based on the principle of cooperation, as opposed to the presently dominating principle of competition. It would require the transformation of the entire moral fabric of this country . . . (9, pp. 179–182).

By keeping its victims so thoroughly hidden and rendering them so apparently inhuman, our system of crime and punishment allows us to forget how sweeping a "transformation" of our social ideology we would require in order to begin solving the problem of crime. The more we forget, the more protected capitalists remain from a thorough reexamination of the ideological basis of the institutions upon which they depend.

SUMMARY AND IMPLICATIONS

It seems useful briefly to summarize the analysis outlined in this section, in order both to emphasize the connections among its arguments and to clarify its differences with other "models" of crime and punishment. Most crimes in this country share a single important similarity—they represent rational responses to the competitiveness and inequality of life in capitalist societies. (In this emphasis on the rationality of crime, the analysis differs with the "conventional public analyses" of crime and resembles the orthodox economic approach.) Many crimes seem very different at the same time, but many of their differences—in character and degree of violence—can usefully be explained by the structure of class institutions in this country and the duality of the public system of the enforcement and administration of justice. (In this central deployment of the radical concepts of class and the class-biased State, the analysis differs fundamentally with both the "public" and the orthodox economic perspectives.) That duality, in turn, can fruitfully be explained by a dynamic view of the class-biased role of public institutions and the vested interests which evolve out of the state's activities. For many reasons, finally, it seems unlikely that we can change the patterns of crime and punishment, for the kinds of changes we would need would appear substantially to threaten the stability of the capitalist system. If we managed somehow to eliminate ghetto crime, for instance, the competitiveness, inequalities and racism of our institutions would tend to reproduce it. And if, by chance, the pattern of ghetto crime was not reproduced, the capitalists might simply have to invent some other way of neutralizing the potential opposition of so many black men, against which they might once again be forced to rebel with "criminal acts." It is in that sense of fundamental causality that we must somehow change the entire structure of institutions in this country in order to eliminate the causes of crime.

Could any of this be any different in any society? Is it not inevitable that criminals must be severely punished and that vast quantities of social resources must be applied to "deter" potential criminality? I don't see why. It seems entirely possible to imagine a radically different kind of society in which social institutions would serve the needs of citizens and foster their development as creative human beings, and, as a natural consequence, in which "criminals" would be treated in the ways that many families deal with those family members who betray the family trust. John Griffiths has projected a society in which legal and penal institutions would be motivated by this "Family Model," where social response to criminal behavior would be motivated by an underlying assumption, as Griffiths writes (18, p. 371), "of reconcilable—even mutually supportive—interest, a state of love.[26] Such a society would "make plain that while the criminal has transgressed, we do not therefore cut him off from us; our concern and dedication to his well-being continue. We have punished him and drawn him back in among us; we have not cast him out to fend for himself against our systematic enmity." In such a society, rather than forcing the criminal to admit his failure and reform himself, we would all admit our mutual failures and seek to reform the total community—in which effort the criminal would play an important, constructive and educative role. The distance of that vision simply indicates how deeply our present treatment of criminals is imbedded in the basic institutional structure of this country.

NOTES

[1] Quoted in B. G. Chevigny (6).
[2] See Ronald L. Goldfarb, "The Horror of Prisons," *The New York Times*, October 28, 1970, p. 47.
[3] For two very brief summaries of data, see the first two reading selections in the chapter on crime in Gordon, ed. (15). For the two most useful general summaries, see Clark (8) and the Report of the President's Commission on Law Enforcement and the Administration of Justice (32). Another useful summary is contained in Wolfgang (55). For more detail, see the appendices to the Crime Commission Report (33), (34), (35). For interesting critical comments on the Crime Commission Report, see Wilson (51).
[4] The statistical increase may be misleading, of course, because many kinds of crime are much more likely to be reported now than comparable crimes of thirty or forty years ago. See Clark (8).
[5] Violent crimes, on the other hand, are more frequently committed by adults; as Clark explains it (8, p. 55), "It takes longer to harden the young to violence."
[6] The reason that the arrest rates may be spurious is that, as the Crime Commission Report (32), Clark (8), and Goldfarb (13) have documented, Blacks are much more likely than whites to be arrested whether they have committed a crime or not. Despite that immeasurable bias in the arrest statistics, it is nonetheless assumed that Blacks commit a much larger percentage of most crimes than their share of urban population.
[7] Fred P. Graham provides a useful analysis of the myths and realities of black crime in a recent article (17).
[8] It is one thing to cite this "duality" as fact, of course, and quite another thing to explain it. I shall cite it now as a phenomenon requiring explanation and try to explain it later.
[9] For the clearest exposition of the conservative view on crime, see Banfield (2).
[10] Banfield has formulated the conservative equation (2, p. 184): "If some people's freedom is not abridged by law-enforcement agencies, that of others will be abridged by lawbreakers. The question, therefore, is not whether abridging the freedom of those who may commit serious crimes is an evil—it is—but whether it is a lesser or a greater one than the alternative." For a description of the Nixon Administration's basically conservative position, see Harris (19). For a superb analysis of the legal aspects of the major Nixon crime legislation, see Packer (31).
[11] The clearest expressions of the liberal view on crime are contained in three reports of Presidential commissions published in the late 1960s: The Presidential Commission on Law Enforcement and the Administration of Justice (32), the National Advisory Commission on Civil Disorders (27), and the National Commission on Violence (28).

[12] See Wolfgang (55, p. 275) and the Commission on Violence Report (28, p. 40) for explicit statements of this inclination.

[13] For the most notable pieces of recent literature, see Becker (3), Stigler (42), Thurow (46), and Tullock (48, 49). Some attempts have been made to apply the orthodox analysis empirically; for one such attempt, see Landes (22).

[14] Becker admits (3, p. 209), that the analysis is hampered by "the absence of a reliable theory of political decision-making." Tullock is the only one who makes the underlying political assumption precise and explicit. He writes (48, p. II-2): "My first general assumption, then, is that the reader is not in a position to assure himself of special treatment in any legal system. That is, if I argue that the reader should favor a law against theft, one of the basic assumptions will be that he does not have a real opportunity to get a law enacted which prohibits theft by everyone else but leaves him free to steal himself." He adds that this assumption ". . . will . . . underlie all of the specific proposals" he makes in his manuscript.

[15] I am relying, essentially, on the general hypotheses outlined and evoked in Edwards and MacEwan (11), Gordon, ed. (15), and other recent radical works. For two useful discussions of the meaning of the radical concept of class, especially as Marx used the term, see Ossowski (29) and Tucker (47). For two summaries of the radical theory of the State, see Sweezy (45) and Milliband (24).

[16] This is not meant to imply, obviously, that there would be no crime in a communist society in which perfectly secure equal support was provided for all. It suggests, quite simply, that one would have to analyze crime in such a society with reference to a different set of ideas and a different set of institutions.

[17] Our knowledge of ghetto crime draws primarily from the testimony of several ex-ghetto criminals, as in Brown (4), Cleaver (9), Jackson (20), and Malcolm X (23). For other more analytic studies, see Shaw and McKay (39), and Wolfgang and Ferracuti (54). For interesting evidence on the different attitudes toward crime of poor and middle-class youth, see Goodwin (14). For a bit of empirical evidence on the critical interaction between job prospects and rates of recidivism, see Evans (12).

[18] For more on the structure of jobs available, see Chapter Two in Gordon, ed. (15). One often finds informal support for such contentions. A Manhattan prostitute once said about her crimes, "What is there to say. We've got a living to earn. There wouldn't be any prostitution if there weren't a demand for it." Quoted in the *New York Times*, May 29, 1970. A black high school graduate discussed the problem at greater length with an interviewer in a recent book (quoted in Goro [16], p. 146): "That's why a lot of brothers are out on the street now, stinging, robbing people, mugging, 'cause when they get a job, man, they be doing their best, and the white man get jealous 'cause he feel this man could do better than he doing. 'I got to get rid of him.' So they fire him, so a man, he lose his pride . . . They give you something, and then they take it away from you . . . There's no reason for you to be stealing. That's a lie! If you're a thief, I'd advise you to be a good thief. 'Cause you working, Jim, you ain't going to succeed unless you got some kind of influence."

[19] For two of the best available analyses of organized crime, see Cressey (10) and Morris and Hawkins (26).

[20] As Cressey points out (10), for instance, it makes a great deal of sense in the heroin industry for the supplier to seek a monopoly on the source of the heroin but to permit many individual sellers of heroin at its final destination, usually without organization backing, because the risks occur primarily at the consumers' end.

[21] Many would argue, along these lines, that heroin addicts would not be prone either to violence or to crime if heroin were legal and free. The fact that it is illegal and that the police go after its consumers means that a cycle of crime and violence is established from which it becomes increasingly difficult to escape.

[22] This argument rests on an assumption, of course, that one learns more about the priorities of the State by looking at its patterns of enforcement than at the nature of its statutes. This seems quite reasonable. The statutory process is often cumbersome, whereas the patterns of enforcement can sometimes be changed quite easily. (Stigler [42] makes the same point.) Furthermore, as many radicals would argue, the State in democratic societies can often support the capitalist class most effectively by selective enforcement of the laws, rather than by selective legislation. For varieties of relatively complicated historical reasons, selective enforcement of the law seems to arouse less fear for the erosion of democratic tradition than selective legislation itself. As long as we have statutes which nominally outlaw racial inequality, for instance, inadequate enforcement of those laws seems to cause relatively little furor; before we had such laws in this country, protests against the selective statutes could ultimately be mounted.

[23] For some useful references on the police, see P. Chevigny (7), Westley (50), and Wilson (52). For a review of that literature, with some very interesting comments about the police, see Kempton (21). For one discussion of the first hints of evidence that there may not, in fact, be any kind of identifiable relationship between the number of police we have and their effectiveness, see Reeves (36).

[24] For the most devastating story I've seen about how the neutralization occurs to even the most innocent of ghetto Blacks, see Asinof (1).

[25] One should not underestimate the importance of this effect for quantitative as well as qualitative reasons. In July 1968, for instance, an estimated 140,000 blacks were serving time in penal institutions at federal, state, and local levels. If the percentage of black males in prison had been as low as the proportions of white men (controlling for age), there would have been only 25,000 blacks in jail. If those extra 115,000 black men were not in prison, they would likely be unemployed or intermittently employed. (See Evans [12].) In addition, official labor force figures radically undercount the number of blacks in the census because many black males are simply missed by the census-taker. In July 1968, almost one million black males were "missed" in that way. On the arbitrary assumption that one-fifth of those "missing males" were in one way or another evading the law, involved in hustling, or otherwise trapped in the legal system, then a total of 315,000 black men who might be unemployed were it not for the effects of the law were not counted in "measured" unemployment statistics. Total "measured" black male unemployment in July 1968 was 317,000, so that the total black unemployment problem might be nearly twice as large as we "think" it is were it not for the selective effects of our police, courts and prisons on black men.

[26] Griffiths' article attempts to offer a reply to an earlier legal article by Packer (30). In his essay, Griffiths contrasts the "Family Model of the Criminal Process" with what he calls the "Battle Model of the Criminal Process"—a model which he argues motivates both the theory and the reality of our social treatment of criminals.

REFERENCES

1. Eliot Asinof, *People vs. Blutcher* (New York: Viking, 1970).
2. Edward C. Banfield, *The Unheavenly City* (Boston: Little, Brown, 1970).
3. Gary Becker, "Crime and Punishment: An Economic Approach," *Journal of Political Economy*, March/April 1968.
4. Claude Brown, *Manchild in the Promised Land* (New York: Macmillan, 1965).
5. Claude Brown and Arthur Dunmeyer, "A Way of Life in the Ghetto," in Gordon, ed. (15).
6. Bell Gale Chevigny, "After the Death of Jail," *The Village Voice*, July 10, 1969. Partially reprinted in Gordon, ed. (15).
7. Paul Chevigny, *Police Power* (New York: Pantheon, 1969).
8. Ramsey Clark, *Crime in America* (New York: Simon and Schuster, 1970).
9. Eldridge Cleaver, *Post-Prison Writings and Speeches* (New York: A Ramparts Book by Random House, 1969).
10. Donald Cressey, *Theft of the Nation: The Structure and Operations of Organized Crime* (New York: Harper & Row, 1969).
11. Richard Edwards, Arthur MacEwan, et al., "A Radical Approach to Economics," *American Economic Review*, May 1970. Reprinted in Gordon, ed. (15).
12. Robert Evans, Jr. "The Labor Market and Parole Success," *Journal of Human Resources*, Spring 1968.
13. Ronald Goldfarb, "Prison: The National Poorhouse," *The New Republic*, November 1969. Reprinted in Gordon, ed. (15).
14. Leonard Goodwin, "Work Orientations of the Underemployed Poor," *Journal of Human Resources*, Fall 1969.

15. David M. Gordon, ed., *Problems in Political Economy: An Urban Perspective* (Lexington, Mass.: D. C. Heath, 1971).
16. Herb Goro, *The Block* (New York: Random House, 1970).
17. Fred P. Graham, "Black Crime: The Lawless Image," *Harper's*, September 1970.
18. John Griffiths, "Ideology in Criminal Procedure, or a Third 'Model' of the Criminal Process," *Yale Law Journal*, January 1970.
19. Richard Harris, *Justice* (New York: Dutton, 1970).
20. George Jackson, *Soledad Brother* (New York: Bantam Books, 1970.
21. Murray Kempton, "Cops," *The New York Review of Books*, November 5, 1970.
22. William Landes, "An Economic Analysis of the Courts," *Journal of Law and Economics*, April 1970.
23. Malcolm X, *Autobiography* (New York: Grove Press, 1964).
24. Ralph Milliband, *The State in Capitalist Society* (New York: Basic Books, 1969).
25. Robert Morgenthau, "Equal Justice and the Problem of White Collar Crime," *The Conference Board Record*, August 1969.
26. Norval Morris and Gordon Hawkins, *The Honest Politician's Guide to Crime Control* (Chicago: University of Chicago Press, 1969).
27. National Advisory Commission on Civil Disorders, *Report* (New York: Bantam Books, 1968).
28. National Commission on the Causes and Prevention of Violence, *To Establish Justice, To Insure Domestic Tranquility* (New York: Bantam Books, 1970).
29. Stanislaw Ossowski, *Class Structure in the Social Consciousness* (New York: Free Press, 1963), trans. by Sheila Patterson.
30. Herbert Packer, "Two Models of the Criminal Process," *University of Pennsylvania Law Review*, 1964.
31. ———, "Nixon's Crime Program and What It Means," *New York Review of Books*, October 22, 1970.
32. President's Commission on Law Enforcement and Administration of Justice, *The Challenge of Crime in a Free Society* (Washington: U.S. Government Printing Office, 1967).
33. ———, *Corrections* (Washington: U.S. Government Printing Office, 1967).
34. ———, *The Courts* (Washington: U.S. Government Printing Office, 1967).
35. ———, *Crime and Its Impact—An Assessment* (Washington: U.S. Government Printing Office, 1967).
36. Richard Reeves, "Police: Maybe They Should Be Doing Something Different," *The New York Times*, January 24, 1971.
37. James Ridgeway, *The Politics of Ecology*, (New York: Dutton, 1970).
38. Arnold Rose, *The Power Structure: Political Process in America* (New York: Oxford University Press, 1968).
39. Clifford Shaw and Henry McKay, *Juvenile Delinquency and Urban Areas* (Chicago: University of Chicago Press, 1969).
40. Robert Sherrill, "The Convenience of Being Lockheed," *Scanlan's Monthly*, August 1970.
41. Adam Smith, *The Wealth of Nations* (New York: Modern Library, 1937).
42. George Stigler, "The Optimum Enforcement of Laws," *Journal of Political Economy*, May/June 1970.
43. Edmund H. Sutherland, *Principles of Criminology*, 6th ed. (Philadelphia: Lippincott, 1960).

44. ———, "The Crime of Corporations," in Gordon, ed. (15).
45. Paul Sweezy, "The State," Chap. XIII of *The Theory of Capitalist Development* (New York: Monthly Review Press, 1968). Partially reprinted in Gordon, ed. (15).
46. Lester C. Thurow, "Equity and Efficiency in Justice," *Public Policy*, Summer 1970.
47. Robert Tucker, *The Marxian Revolutionary Idea* (New York: W. W. Norton, 1969).
48. Gordon Tullock, *General Standards: The Logic of Law and Ethics*, Virginia Polytechnic Institute, 1968, unpublished manuscript.
49. ———, "An Economic Approach to Crime," *Social Science Quarterly*, June 1969.
50. William Westley, *Violence and Police* (Cambridge, Mass.: M.I.T. Press, 1970).
51. James Q. Wilson, "Crime in the Streets," *The Public Interest*, No. 5 (Fall 1966).
52. ———, *Varieties of Police Behavior* (New York: Basic Books, 1969).
53. Robert Paul Wolff, *The Poverty of Liberalism* (Boston: Beacon Press, 1968).
54. Marvin E. Wolfgang and Franco Ferracuti, *The Subculture of Violence* (New York: Barnes and Noble, 1967).
55. Marvin E. Wolfgang, "Urban Crime," in James Q. Wilson, ed., *The Metropolitan Enigma* (Cambridge, Mass.: Harvard University Press, 1968).

GETTING USED TO MUGGING

Andrew Hacker

The most urgent issue in American cities, we are told, is the fear of crime. Yet if this is true, writers and politicians no longer speak confidently on the subject, only reuttering commonplaces we already know. (The age-old recourse to draconian punishments is a case in point.) But perhaps most exasperating is the unwillingness of too many of us to follow through on the implications of our arguments. Let us suppose, for example, that we wish to have crime-free cities, or at least some approximation of that condition. The standard solutions run as follows:

(1) That we change the basic conditions which turn people into criminals: slum housing, bad schools, absent fathers, lack of employment opportunities. But the unpursued implication here is not the cost itself (anyone can conjure up a figure) but rather the extent to which the rest of us would have less money to spend and would lead quite different lives were this aim to be achieved.

(2) That the police be so omnipresent that would-be criminals would forebear from assaulting anyone, in view of the extremely high chances of getting caught. Here the undiscussed issue (over and above the cost) is the impact such expanded policing would have on everyone's private habits and pursuits. We now have about one policeman for every 380 citizens. Do we really want a lower ratio that that?

(3) That all persons who commit crimes be caught, convicted, and imprisoned until the rest of us are assured that, upon release, they will lead law-abiding lives. Here, too, leave to one side the costs of more efficient apprehension, streamlined courts, and additional prisons. What is implied is the assumption that some young toughs had better be kept behind bars until they are at least 70. Some people prefer to suppose that the places we call prisons will remove criminal tendencies, that there *must* be some correctional arrangements which will effect changes in the attitudes of inmates. Suggestions range from more highly paid and psychologically sensitive professionals to community-controlled institutions to no prisons at all. But

Source: "Getting Used to Mugging," *The New York Review of Books*, April 19, 1973. Reprinted with permission from *The New York Review of Books*. Copyright © 1973 Nyrev, Inc.

apart from gouging out a criminal's eyes, no one has any convincing proposals on how to prevent his reversion upon release.

Indeed no politician I have heard has a "plan" for dealing with crime, including the President of the United States, various governors, and former policemen who seek or have gained municipal office. Variations on one or another of the proposals I have just cited do not contain strategies for reducing criminality, for they shy away from specific suggestions. The fear of crime has produced more snake-oil merchants than we have seen in a long time, ranging from the domestic armaments industry to university-based rip-off artists who reroof their summer cottages with research grants. Several thousand criminals have succeeded in terrorizing several tens of millions of their fellow citizens. What are we, the public, to do? People who have had all sorts of bright ideas on everything from curing schizophrenia to bringing peace to Southeast Asia content themselves with reciting the "causes" of crime. Why have we reached this impasse?

Certainly crime tests the limits of liberalism. It is one thing to express compassion for women and children on welfare or underpaid agricultural workers. But it is quite another to regard the man nudging a knife into your ribs as someone to whom society offered no other choice. The tough position on crime is no longer a monopoly of the right. Even while opposing a return to capital punishment or mandatory life sentences, many of us wonder whether we can still afford to treat our street-corner gunslingers as sociological casualties. Writing off any human being certainly seems wrong, but then our New Deal parents never faced Saturday Night Specials.

I will deal here mainly with street crime, and particularly robbery. In fact the phrase "street crime" is a misnomer, at least in New York. Most robberies now occur inside: in hallways, elevators, shops, or subways. You are safer out on the sidewalk. I realize that muggers take much less from us than do corporate, syndicate, and white-collar criminals. I have little doubt that the average executive swindles more on his taxes and expense account than the average addict steals in a typical year. Moreover I am well aware that concentrating on street crime provides yet another opportunity for picking on the poor, a campaign I have no wish to assist. It is a scandal that a bank embezzler gets six months while a holdup man is hit with five years. Yet it is not entirely their disparate backgrounds that produce this discrimination.

A face-to-face threat of bodily harm or possibly violent death is so terrifying to most people that the $20 or so stolen in a typical mugging must be multiplied many times if comparisons with other offenses are to be made. I have a hunch that a majority of city-dwellers would accept a bargain under which if they would not be mugged this year they would be willing to allow white-collar crime to take an extra 10 percent of their incomes. Of course we are annoyed by corporate thievery that drives up prices, but the kind of dread induced by thuggery has no dollar equivalent or, if it does, an extremely high one.[1]

How pervasive is street crime? There are more than enough people prepared to attest that "almost everyone on this block has been held up at least once." Even so, there is only one official statistic. In the case of New York City, citizens reported a total of 78,202 robberies to the police during 1972. The immediate reply, of course, is that some (many? most?) robberies are not reported to the authorities. But do reported crimes represent half or a tenth or a twentieth of the actual offenses? It is a case of pick your expert, and I happen to have picked Sydney Cooper, the former Chief of Inspectional Services in the New York Police Department and an almost-hero in the Frank Serpico story,[2] who has been keeping track of various studies for the Rand Institute's research on cities.

In Cooper's judgment there are at most about three unreported robberies for every one divulged to the police, and in most cases the nonreporting victim will be poor and disillusioned about any increase in his safety. On this speculation—and that is all that it is—300,000 robberies took place in New York throughout 1972. As the city has approximately 6 million residents aged 16 and over, a New Yorker stands a chance of being robbed about once every 20 years. While the odds are clearly greater in the South Bronx, the Lower East Side, and Bedford-Stuyvesant, ironically the most noise about crime comes from Parchester, Bay Ridge, and Staten Island, where the likelihood of being held up in an average lifetime is almost nil.

Even the most confident experts will refuse to hazard a guess about how many people commit most of a city's robberies. I will be arguing that every large city contains a stratum of people I will call its criminal class. But estimating its size depends on a string of suppositions, none of which can be grounded on reliable data. Until recently, police officials have asserted that half of all robberies are committed by addicts. (In fact there is reason to believe that addicts prefer burglary and shoplifting.) In New York, this would mean they are responsible for about 150,000 such crimes each year.

This may sound plausible until we remember that the average addict needs $50 a week to support his habit, and perhaps another $50 for food and other expenses. Suppose that he can obtain this sum, or merchandise that will yield its equivalent, with one robbery a week and a few burglaries on the side. This means that if a typical addict performs about 50 holdups per year, it takes only 3,000 addicts to account for the 150,000 robberies attributed to persons on drugs. This seems a bit odd, since the head of the New York Police Department's narcotics division talks about the city having 200,000 drug addicts; and even the New York Times's specialist on the question writes that "there are 150,000 to 300,000 heroin addicts and users in the city, according to prevailing estimates."

What seems to emerge is that the number of addicts who commit robberies is a very small proportion of the total. Apparently many addicts raise their cash by selling drugs to each other and by noncriminal means.[3] More likely, most so-called "addicts" can actually take it or leave it alone and do not want or need a dose every day. Reducing the incidence of addiction would clearly cut down the level of crime. Still, I am not persuaded that slavery to a drug habit is the major cause of

217

holdups, especially when we look at the number of robberies committed by people who are not addicted. At all events, it does not take many thugs to terrorize a city the size of New York. My guess is that they are fewer than 10,000.

How much better a job the police might be doing, no one knows. Cities have no choice but to work on the assumption that a uniformed policeman, pounding a beat or patroling in a car, deters would-be robbers. Hence the demand that the number of men on patrol, particularly on foot, be substantially increased. Still, no one is willing to predict how many fewer robberies we might have were there a police officer on every corner. (Back in 1969 the New York department estimated that such a deployment would cost $2.5 billion a year.) In theory, the presence of the police makes a potential criminal realize the high odds of getting caught.

John Conklin's informative and unpretentious study of 1,240 robberies committed in Boston in 1964 and 1968 shows that only 62 of these were "discovered by an officer sighting the offense in progress."[4] He also cites an estimate of the President's Commission on Law Enforcement and the Administration of Justice (1967) that the chance of a patrolman happening on a robbery while it was actually taking place is about once in every 14 years. Perhaps some sympathy should be extended to police commanders who have to decide which proportions of their force they will assign to walking beats, riding patrol cars, and staking out likely locations in plainclothes. A good case can be made for putting the entire force in mufti and letting it wander unrecognized throughout the city. But how many of us are willing to give up even an infrequent glimpse of a blue uniform?

If prevention is moot, then the alternative must be apprehension. Catch those who have committed crimes (that is what plainclothesmen do best) and put them where they will not be able to harm the rest of us for some time to come. I won't pursue here the question whether prison terms can ever rehabilitate criminals or even if such punishment can discourage subsequent lawbreaking. Nor can I consider, now, the propensity of courts to suspend sentences, accept reduced pleas, and throw out cases they consider too flimsy for convictions. I will merely note that New York City's criminal courts apparently cannot handle more than about 600 felony trials in a year, and that New York State's prisons have fewer than 22,000 beds in less-than-ideal conditions, where the annual cost of keeping an inmate comes to $6,000. I think it will be more useful to explore how the police go about catching criminals, which after all is one of their jobs, whatever happens further along in the judicial process.

In 1972, New York's police force of about 30,000 men and women made 19,227 robbery arrests. In other words, the average police officer goes a full year without making an arrest. Compared with 78,202 reported robberies, a record of 19,227 arrests is not the worst imaginable. Compared with what some say is a more realistic figure of 300,000 robberies, the arrest ratio looks less auspicious.

However arrest figures are tricky: To begin with, 19,227 robbery arrests signify the number of times that policemen charged citizens. Thus contained within those

19,227 arrests may be only 5,000 or 10,000 people, some of whom were arrested twice or more times during the year. The New York Police Department says it does not have the resources to keep track of how many people are arrested each year. Second, if two or more people are arrested for performing a single robbery, each person is recorded as a separate arrest. Third, and clearly most worrisome, at least some of those citizens arrested for robbery are in fact innocent of any such crime. The police have been known to bring in the wrong man, who may even plead guilty on a reduced charge out of despair of ever establishing his innocence. At the same time, many of the persons represented by the 19,227 arrests may have committed robberies in addition to the one for which they were arrested. According to Conklin, after a man is taken in by the Boston police, he "usually understands that if he confesses to other crimes, he will not be charged with these offenses and may even receive more lenient treatment in court."

Still, it seems strange that a police force the size of New York's can make fewer than 20,000 robbery arrests in a year. To be sure, we are continually told that they are doing their best in an impossible situation. In addition to the reported robberies, the police had to deal with reports of 356,101 other crimes ranging from 1,691 murders to 75,865 auto thefts. One detective lamented to me that on a given weekend, 30 such reports could land in his lap. He claimed that he could solve a lot more robberies if he were able to give a full week to each such incident, particularly in tramping the streets seraching for informants. For example, *modus operandi* files are still kept, a holdover from the days when detectives had the leisure for detecting. If, on being questioned, you recall that the man who held you up used a white-handled revolver, the police can make up a list and then produce mug shots of men who seem attached to such weapons.

But this takes time. In Conklin's Boston study, only 19 of the 304 street robbery victims he interviewed were asked to examine mug shots, although others were asked to come to the station house to look at line-ups of men arrested for other reasons. There seems reason to believe that in large cities only murder cases are treated with a full investigation, with a wide search for witnesses and rounding up of suspects.[5]

But it is better to have no arrests at all than ones based on perfunctory investigations. This is something the police themselves acknowledge. Unlike civilian law-and-order buffs, the police still realize that a person can be arrested only for having committed a particular crime. John Smith cannot be charged simply with "being a criminal." It is not enough to protest that everyone in his neighborhood "knows" that Smith is an addict and that he supports his habit by stealing. The police can only arrest Smith if he can be convincingly connected with a specific holdup. If householders demand of their precinct that something be done about Smith, they will be told that the police cannot act until evidence is adduced linking him with an actual crime. If this seems frightening or frustrating, consider the consequences of not permitting Smith the presumption of innocence. If it is your wish that the police lock up all the "known" muggers in the city, such a street-clearing strategy should also indicate how it will ensure that innocent persons do not fall in the net.

Between 1966 and 1970 a young New York policeman named Frank Serpico discovered that his departmental superiors had no desire whatever to act on his reports of widespread corruption. While a succession of chief inspectors and deputy commissioners grudgingly listened to "his story," as did several of John Lindsay's close aides, none of them made any moves. Hence Serpico's recourse to the Knapp Commission hearings during the winter of 1971–1972, which put his name in the headlines and made a book inevitable. It is a forceful book, not least because of Serpico himself, who emerges as a man of rare stature and courage.

Yet there is more here than the wearisome recital of police corruption and cover-ups in a system as much committed to personal careerism as to public safety. What angered me about Serpico's account was not the payoffs but rather the cheating, corner-cutting, and laziness of his colleagues on the force. Not one of them seemed to give a damn about serving the citizens of New York City. Even before joining the department, Serpico was told the score by a veteran:

> Kid, when you're off duty, you're off duty. Say you're driving home some night late and you see this guy breaking into a place. Well, keep driving.

In his first precinct assignment he was warned about the form-filling that follows an automobile accident:

> If you hear the sound of a crash on your post, the smartest thing you can do is run the other way.

While on radio-car duty in Brooklyn, a man rushed up to report that a house down the block was being broken into. But Serpico's partner said, "Wait a minute. That side of the street isn't our precinct."

Here is Serpico's description of the on-the-job life of plainclothesmen who drew pay and pension rights for protecting the householders of Melrose and Mott Haven in the South Bronx:

> The men would sign in, check their mailboxes for any assignments or communications, then kill an hour or two in the coffee-room, and perhaps take in a movie in the afternoon. A number of them lived in nearby suburban counties; some had swimming pools, and in the spring and summer especially, they would often while away their afternoons at one house or another playing cards between dips. . . . Occasionally, someone would say, "Hey, anybody call the office? Better give them a ring."

Clearly one argument for ending corruption is that the energy expended in arranging payoffs might be directed to preventing crime and catching criminals. Similarly, if marijuana, prostitution, and gambling were "decriminalized" even more police would be free for street patrols and detective work. But all this presupposes that the average policeman is someone who will spontaneously dash to the scene when he thinks he can do some good. The major problem seems to be that all too many policemen truly dislike the cities and citizens whose security they are supposed to ensure. Frank Serpico does not articulate this conclusion, but it comes through on every page of his book. If we want better policing, someone will have to suggest how we go about discovering guardians who will show more dedication. (We should be somewhat hesitant about uttering homilies on "more people from the community." The record of locally recruited school and hospital guards has not been a happy one.)

Earlier I suggested that we should be wary of attributing too many robberies to drug addicts. The suspicion arises that even if most addicts shook off their habits, many of them would steal for a living. Suppose that through methadone or some other treatment, an addict manages to kick his craving for drugs; even suppose he can get heroin legally and cheaply, as in England. He may then join the ranks of those who engage in robbery to get money for their food, rent, clothing, and other amenities. Certainly many former addicts have found jobs and stopped performing criminal acts. Drug programs justify themselves even if they lead only a handful of their participants out of the nether world of stalking their fellow citizens. Even so, the options for the young man who has gone off heroin are not much different from what they were before he got hooked. The jobs available to him still mostly involve washing other people's dirty dishes, parking cars, mopping floors, or pushing handtrucks for a take-home wage of about $80 per week. In short, wearying and dead-end jobs. Most poor people take such positions. Crime results from those who prefer theft.

When I say that each American city now contains a criminal class, I refer to its citizens who have few misgivings, perhaps none at all, about stealing from other people. Their thefts differ from those of other dishonest persons in that they are prepared to scare the daylights out of their victims in face-to-face confrontations. (They can also be distinguished from organized killers, whose homicides are largely intramural.) The "crime problem," as every city defines it, centers on the existence and exactions of this class, which consists chiefly of young men who are unwilling to work at the kinds of jobs our economy offers them. (Of course they are not the only ones unwilling to work at the minimum wage. But their middle-class counterparts have college as an option; and even in a tight market a B.A. can get you a selling job at Gimbels.) Above all else this is a violent class, its members ready to traumatize anyone from old women to people of their own background and economic standing.

London, Paris, and America's large cities have all contained such a class in the past. We have heard of the men who would as soon slit your throat for a shilling, of neighborhoods where policemen walked only in pairs or not at all. But that was supposed to be the history, now past, of slums and stews which reduced men to little better than beasts. Indeed by 1900 that period had passed in most cities. For the first five or six decades of this century America's cities were remarkably orderly, with little violent crime and safe streets in most lower-class neighborhoods. These were the generations in which most adult Americans were raised, and their memory is one of relative tranquility. In fact that half-century or so now emerges as exceptional in urban history. Its placidity depended chiefly on the modest ambitions and self-estimates of the poorer citizens. European immigrants and arrivals from our own rural areas displayed the duty and deference of an urban peasantry. Those were the good old days.

When I speak of a criminal class they need not be lifetime criminals. I have had good students who, in earlier incarnations, held up shopkeepers and taxicab drivers. And there is a continual supply of recruits. Has anyone ever wondered from what source 15-year-olds in the slums are supposed to obtain their spending money? If their fathers are poorly paid or their mothers are on welfare, they must raise their own cash for clothing, records, and other entertainments. Not all do so by delivering groceries. Despite all the research into delinquency, no one can say why one brother turns to mugging and the other labors in a laundry. All we know is that more choose the first today than in the recent past, and there are enough of them to terrorize whole cities.

Certainly upswings and downswings of the economy no longer show a significant relation to crime rates. For this reason some skepticism should be directed at those asserting that we must create more "job opportunities" if we are to deal with crime in a serious way. It would be well to wonder what kinds of jobs might induce the average hoodlum to abandon his current occupation. If he rejects a stupefying job at $80 a week, will the offer of $125 move him to give up robbery? Or will it take closer to $175, which raises the question of the kind of work he could do that would merit such a stipend. None of these questions is meant invidiously, but only to suggest that robbery is one way some Americans assert that they deserve better than the economy has offered them.

Nowadays members of the criminal class blend into the general population. (They probably always did. Bill Sikes must have looked much like an average London laborer.) It is likely that some of the young men we pass on the street or see in the subway held up someone the night before. But which ones should we fear? Without knowing for sure, many of us fear them all. A student of mine told me that when he is on an elevator others about to enter often draw back on seeing him there. Some finally enter and, according to his account, he can almost hear their hearts pounding until they alight. Interestingly, one police method operates on the premise that the city contains a quota of persons who can be counted on to commit crimes. To discover who they are, plainclothes policemen dress up as old men and shamble down slum streets on the expectation that they will eventually be jumped. Fairly soon they usually are, at which point backup men dash in to help with the arrest.

Is this in fact provoking a crime that would not otherwise have occurred? The obvious reply is that had the decoy not been there, his assaulter would have attacked a real old man later that evening; thus the trap saved an actual citizen from a mugging, and also put a criminal behind bars, sparing the rest of us from his depredations for a while. Still, buying this argument shows how desperate we have become for we have blotted from our minds the possibility that dangling a decoy may tempt some teenagers who would not otherwise have considered committing a crime. The case is obviously different from putting a box of dollar bills outside a store and then pouncing on anyone who helps himself. Even so, provocation of any sort is a risky business.

If "law and order" has served as a code phrase for racism, then proposals that we unleash the police have a somewhat more specific result in mind. Both black and white robbery victims would probably settle for protection from the black part of the criminal population. In other words, both would be willing to take their chances on encountering a white criminal. Orde Coombs, a Harlem writer, is saying as much when he agonizes that "we stand menaced by our kith and kin."[6] Crimes by blacks against blacks have become so debilitating that Coombs will support any hard line. ("If the liberals cry about constitutional rights, chase them back to Scarsdale. . . .") Needless to say, many whites join him in this sentiment. So let's get it out in the open.

According to the 1970 census, New York City has 187,146 black men between the ages of 15 and 29. The only way to make a dent in street crime (and by this I simply mean getting the criminals off the streets) is by withdrawing the constitutional presumption of innocence from these 187,146 citizens. Within their number lurk most of the city's criminals. The entire stratum will have to endure harsh and humiliating treatment if the dangerous members are to be ferreted out. That is what is being said, or at least whispered, with increasing stridency.

Take, for example, the matter of weapons. Most robbers carry a gun or at least a knife that seems somewhat sharper than needed to cut string. Every patrolman now has the authority to stop and frisk any citizen he has cause to believe may be carrying a felonious item. However the courts have ruled that the officer must be able to give an explicit reason for conducting that frisking. Simply stating that the individual looked "suspicious" is not enough. Many city-dwellers would like nothing better than for the police to stop various persons, as a matter of routine, and pat them down. Perhaps several times a day. Those who harbor such daydreams do not extend them to businessmen's attaché cases being opened or housewives' handbags being subjected to scrutiny. Rather the target would be those 187,146 young men who are statistically most suspect.

Such a procedure might well round up a major share of the city's illegal weapons and also provide an excuse for putting their bearers behind bars. Still, these roundups would have to be sweeping and indiscriminate. Black muggers and murderers seldom dress in rags. Most of them are quite indistinguishable from black Columbia students and Chase Manhattan trainees, so that those subject to fairly frequent friskings would include people like Percy Sutton and Nigerian UN delegates, along with black ministers, shoe shiners, schoolteachers, and writers. Would Orde Coombs show that added patience and put up with public humiliation so that his criminally inclined brothers might be more readily apprehended?

I doubt it, and for a good reason, the one which makes residents of even the most vulnerable black neighborhoods show little enthusiasm for Governor Rockefeller's plan to jail pushers for life. Middle-aged slum-dwellers may live in terror of local muggers, but they also have sons of their own, who they realize would be subject to roundups were the police truly unleashed. Black wives, mothers, and sisters have no great confidence in the ability of the police to distinguish a string-cutting knife from one intended for throats. Nor are any criminals currently being "coddled." The most one can say is that some of those arrested are given a chance to show that the police caught the wrong man. Certainly, once caught in the criminal justice system not a few innocent persons have pleaded guilty on reduced charges as the only way of ever getting home.

To put it very simply, the tougher the police the closer we get to imposing martial law on those 187,146 citizens. Most of those young men are as law-abiding as the rest of us. But all would be treated as presumptive criminals, and some would end up in detention because they were wrongly identified or someone was suspicious of them. All of this should be obvious and in no need of reiteration. But apparently code-talk about crime needs continual deciphering, particularly when that talk comes from circles that should know better. If people have something in mind other than roundups based on race, they ought to say so.

The "street crime" problem should be understood chiefly as one created by a criminal class of young men, a class that we are going to be living with for a long time. The major cause of street crime is not heroin, as we shall discover once we get every addict either unhooked or onto a substitute. (In fact, someone who is not half-incapacitated by hard drugs should make a more efficient mugger.) My own considered—and by no means capricious—view is that we ought to count ourselves fortunate that so small a part of our population has taken to thievery. That so many Americans remain honest, while being treated so shabbily, has never ceased to amaze me.

NOTES

[1] These anxieties are obviously more evident among the middle-aged or older, who lack the litheness to make a quick turn when they sense danger ahead. In addition, young people seem to shrug off a holdup more easily than their elders. Perhaps as most street criminals are relatively young, many noncriminal young people may see themselves as having more in common with the thieves than with their middle-aged victims. On the whole, crime as a public issue has failed to stir the young.

[2] Peter Maas, *Serpico* (New York: Viking, 1973).

[3] See James Markham's article "Heroin Hunger May Not a Mugger Make," *New York Times Magazine,* March 18, 1973.

[4] John E. Conklin, *Robbery and the Criminal Justice System* (Philadelphia: Lippincott, 1972).

[5] Morton Hunt's *The Mugging* (Atheneum, 1972) tells the story of a Bronx man's murder by some young Puerto Ricans. The full panoply of detective work that Hunt describes clearly resulted from the fact that this was a homicide. His account, excellent in its own right, still tells of an untypical case; police seldom make a real search for perpetrators if the victim escapes alive.

[6] "Fear and Trembling in Black Streets," *New York Magazine,* November 20, 1972.

RAPE: THE ALL-AMERICAN CRIME

Susan Griffin

I have never been free of the fear of rape. From a very early age I, like most women, have thought of rape as part of my natural environment—something to be feared and prayed against like fire or lightning. I never asked why men raped; I simply thought it one of the many mysteries of human nature.

I was, however, curious enough about the violent side of humanity to read every crime magazine I was able to ferret away from my grandfather. Each issue featured at least one "sex crime," with pictures of a victim, usually in a pearl necklace, and of the ditch or the orchard where her body was found. I was never certain why the victims were always women, nor what the motives of the murderer were, but I did guess that the world was not a safe place for women. I observed that my grandmother was meticulous about locks, and quick to draw the shades before anyone removed so much as a shoe. I sensed that danger lurked outside.

At the age of eight, my suspicions were confirmed. My grandmother took me to the back of the house where the men wouldn't hear, and told me that strange men wanted to do harm to little girls. I learned not to walk on dark streets, not to talk to strangers, or get into strange cars, to lock doors, and to be modest. She never explained why a man would want to harm a little girl, and I never asked.

If I thought for a while that my grandmother's fears were imaginary, the illusion was brief. That year, on the way home from school, a schoolmate a few years older than I tried to rape me. Later, in an obscure aisle of the local library (while I was reading *Freddy the Pig*) I turned to discover a man exposing himself. Then, the friendly man around the corner was arrested for child molesting.

My initiation to sexuality was typical. Every woman has similar stories to tell—the first man who attacked her may have been a neighbor, a family friend, an uncle, her doctor, or perhaps her own father. And women who grow up in New York City always have tales about the subway.

Source: "Rape: The All-American Crime," *Ramparts*, Vol. 10, No. 3, September, 1971, pp. 26–35. By permission of the author.

But though rape and the fear of rape are a daily part of every woman's consciousness, the subject is so rarely discussed by that unofficial staff of male intellectuals (who write the books which study seemingly every other form of male activity) that one begins to suspect a conspiracy of silence. And indeed, the obscurity of rape in print exists in marked contrast to the frequency of rape in reality, for *forcible rape is the most frequently committed violent crime in America today*. The Federal Bureau of Investigation classes three crimes as violent: murder, aggravated assault and forcible rape. In 1968, 31,060 rapes were *reported*. According to the FBI and independent criminologists, however, to approach accuracy this figure must be multiplied by at least a factor of ten to compensate for the fact that most rapes are not reported; when these compensatory mathematics are used, there are more rapes committed than aggravated assaults and homicides.

When I asked Berkeley, California's Police Inspector in charge of rape investigation if he knew why men rape women, he replied that he had not spoken with "these people and delved into what really makes them tick, because that really isn't my job. . . ." However, when I asked him how a woman might prevent being raped, he was not so reticent, "I wouldn't advise any female to go walking around alone at night . . . and she should lock her car at all times." The Inspector illustrated his warning with a grisly story about a man who lay in wait for women in the back seats of their cars, while they were shopping in a local supermarket. This man eventually murdered one of his rape victims. "Always lock your car," the Inspector repeated, and then added, without a hint of irony, "Of course, you don't have to be paranoid about this type of thing."

The Inspector wondered why I wanted to write about rape. Like most men he did not understand the urgency of the topic, for, after all, men are not raped. But like most women I had spent considerable time speculating on the true nature of the rapist. When I was very young, my image of the "sexual offender" was a nightmarish amalgamation of the bogey man and Captain Hook: he wore a black cape, and he cackled. As I matured, so did my image of the rapist. Born into the psychoanayltic age, I tried to "understand" the rapist. Rape, I came to believe, was only one of many unfortunate evils produced by sexual repression. Reasoning by tautology, I concluded that any man who would rape a woman must be out of his mind.

Yet, though the theory that rapists are insane is a popular one, this belief has no basis in fact. According to Professor Menachem Amir's study of 646 rape cases in Philadelphia, *Patterns in Forcible Rape*, men who rape are not abnormal. Amir writes, "Studies indicate that sex offenders do not constitute a unique or psychopathological type; nor are they as a group invariably more disturbed than the control groups to which they are compared." Alan Taylor, a parole officer who has worked with rapists in the prison facilities at San Luis Obispo, California, stated the question in plainer language, "Those men were the most normal men there. They had a lot of hang-ups, but they were the same hang-ups as men walking out on the street."

Another canon in the apologetics of rape is that, if it were not for learned social controls, all men would rape. Rape is held to be natural behavior, and not to rape must be learned. But in truth rape is not universal to the human species. Moreover, studies of rape in our culture reveal that, far from being impulsive behavior, most rape is planned. Professor Amir's study reveals that in cases of group rape (the "gangbang" of masculine slang) 90 percent of the rapes were planned; in pair rapes, 83 percent of the rapes were planned; and in single rapes, 58 percent were planned. These figures should significantly discredit the image of the rapist as a man who is suddenly overcome by sexual needs society does not allow him to fulfill.

Far from the social control of rape being learned, comparisons with other cultures lead one to suspect that, in our society, it is rape itself that is learned. (The fact that rape is against the law should not be considered proof that rape is not in fact encouraged as part of our culture.)

This culture's concept of rape as an illegal, but still understandable, form of behavior is not a universal one. In her study *Sex and Temperament*, Margaret Mead describes a society that does not share our views. The Arapesh do not ". . . have any conception of the male nature that might make rape understandable to them." Indeed our interpretation of rape is a product of our conception of the nature of male sexuality. A common retort to the question, why don't women rape men, is the myth that men have greater sexual needs, that their sexuality is more urgent than women's. And it is the nature of human beings to want to live up to what is expected of them.

And this same culture which expects aggression from the male expects passivity from the female. Conveniently, the companion myth about the nature of female sexuality is that all women secretly want to be raped. Lurking beneath her modest female exterior is a subconscious desire to be ravished. The following description of a stag movie, written by Brenda Starr in Los Angeles' underground paper, *Everywoman*, typifies this male fantasy. The movie "showed a woman in her underclothes reading on her bed. She is interrupted by a rapist with a knife. He immediately wins her over with his charm and they get busy sucking and fucking." An advertisement in the *Berkeley Barb* reads, "Now as all women know from their daydreams, rape has a lot of advantages. Best of all it's so simple. No preparation necessary, no planning ahead of time, no wondering if you should or shouldn't; just whang! bang!" Thanks to Masters and Johnson even the scientific canon recognizes that for the female, "whang! bang!" can scarcely be described as pleasurable.

Still, the male psyche persists in believing that, protestations and struggles to the contrary, deep inside her mysterious feminine soul, the female victim has wished for her own fate. A young woman who was raped by the husband of a friend said that days after the incident the man returned to her home, pounded on the door and screamed to her, "Jane, Jane. You loved it. You know you loved it."

The theory that women like being raped extends itself by deduction into the proposition that most or much of rape is provoked by the victim. But this too is only myth. Though provocation, considered a mitigating factor in a court of law, may consist of only "a gesture," according to the Federal Commission on Crimes of Violence, only 4 percent of reported rapes involved any precipitative behavior by the woman.

The notion that rape is enjoyed by the victim is also convenient for the man who, though he would not commit forcible rape, enjoys the idea of its existence, as if rape confirms that enormous sexual potency which he secretly knows to be his own. It is for the pleasure of the armchair rapist that detailed accounts of violent rapes exist in the media. Indeed, many men appear to take sexual pleasure from nearly all forms of violence. Whatever the motivation, male sexuality and violence in our culture seem to be inseparable. James Bond alternately whips out his revolver and his cock, and though there is no known connection between the skills of gunfighting and lovemaking, pacifism seems suspiciously effeminate.

In a recent fictional treatment of the Manson case, Frank Conroy writes of his vicarious titillation when describing the murders to his wife:

"Every single person there was killed." She didn't move.
"It sounds like there was torture," I said. As the words left my mouth I knew there was no need to say them to frighten her into believing that she needed me for protection.

The pleasure he feels as his wife's protector is inextricably mixed with pleasure in the violence itself. Conroy writes, "I was excited by the killings, as one is excited by catastrophe on a grand scale, as one is alert to pre-echoes of unknown changes, hints of unrevealed secrets, rumblings of chaos. . . ."

The attraction of the male in our culture to violence and death is a tradition Manson and his admirers are carrying on with tireless avidity (even presuming Manson's innocence, he dreams of the purification of fire and destruction). It was Malraux in his *Anti-Memoirs* who said that, for the male, facing death was *the* illuminating experience analogous to childbirth for the female. Certainly our culture does glorify war and shroud the agonies of the gunfighter in veils of mystery.

And in the spectrum of male behavior, rape, the perfect combination of sex and violence, is the penultimate act. Erotic pleasure cannot be separated from culture, and in our culture male eroticism is wedded to power. Not only should a man be taller and stronger than a female in the perfect love-match, but he must also demonstrate his superior strength in gestures of dominance which are perceived as amorous. Though the law attempts to make a clear division between rape and sexual intercourse, in fact the courts find it difficult to distinguish between a case where the decision to copulate was mutual and one where a man forced himself upon his partner.

The scenario is even further complicated by the expectation that, not only does a woman mean "yes" when she says "no," but that a really decent woman ought to begin by saying "no," and then be led down the primrose path to acquiescence.

Ovid, the author of Western Civilization's most celebrated sex manual, makes this expectation perfectly clear:

> . . . and when I beg you to say "yes," say "no." Then let me lie outside your bolted door. . . . So Love grows strong. . . .

That the basic elements of rape are involved in all heterosexual relationships may explain why men often identify with the offender in this crime. But to regard the rapist as the victim, a man driven by his inherent sexual needs to take what will not be given him, reveals a basic ignorance of sexual politics. For in our culture heterosexual love finds an erotic expression through male dominance and female submission. A man who derives pleasure from raping a woman clearly must enjoy force and dominance as much or more than the simple pleasures of the flesh. Coitus cannot be experienced in isolation. The weather, the state of the nation, the level of sugar in the blood—all will affect a man's ability to achieve orgasm. If a man can achieve sexual pleasure after terrorizing and humiliating the object of his passion, and in fact while inflicting pain upon her, one must assume he derives pleasure directly from terrorizing, humiliating and harming a woman. According to Amir's study of forcible rape, on a statistical average the man who has been convicted of rape was found to have a normal sexual personality, tending to be different from the normal, well-adjusted male only in having a greater tendency to express violence and rage.

And if the professional rapist is to be separated from the average dominant heterosexual, it may be mainly a quantitative difference. For the existence of rape as an index to masculinity is not entirely metaphorical. Though this measure of masculinity seems to be more publicly exhibited among "bad boys" or aging bikers who practice sexual initiation through group rape, in fact, "good boys" engage in the same rites to prove their manhood. In Stockton, a small town in California which epitomizes silent-majority America, a bachelor party was given last summer for a young man about to be married. A woman was hired to dance "topless" for the amusement of the guests. At the high point of the evening the bridegroom-to-be dragged the woman into a bedroom. No move was made by any of his companions to stop what was clearly going to be an attempted rape. Far from it. As the woman described, "I tried to keep him away—told him of my Herpes Genitalis, et cetera, but he couldn't face the guys if he didn't screw me." After the bridegroom had finished raping the woman and returned with her to the party, far from chastising him, his friends heckled the woman and covered her with wine.

It was fortunate for the dancer that the bridegroom's friends did not follow him into the bedroom for, though one might suppose that in group rape, since the victim is outnumbered, less force would be inflicted on her, in fact, Amir's studies indicate, "the most excessive degrees of violence occurred in group rape." Far from discouraging violence, the presence of other men may in fact encourage sadism, and even cause the behavior. In an unpublished study of group rape by Gilbert Geis and Duncan Chappell, the authors refer to a study by W. H. Blanchard which relates, "The leader of the male group . . . apparently precipitated and maintained the activity, despite misgivings, because of a need to fulfill the role that the other two men had assigned to him. 'I was scared when it began to happen,' he says. 'I wanted to leave but I didn't want to say it to the other guys—you know—that I was scared.' "

Thus it becomes clear that not only does our culture teach men the rudiments of rape, but society, or more specifically other men, encourage the practice of it.

If a male society rewards aggressive, domineering sexual behavior, it contains within itself a sexual schizophrenia. For the masculine man is also expected to prove his mettle as a protector of women. To the naïve eye, this dichotomy implies that men fall into one of two categories: those who rape and those who protect. In fact, life does not prove so simple. In a study euphemistically entitled "Sex Aggression by College Men," it was discovered that men who believe in a double standard of morality for men and women, who in fact believe most fervently in the ultimate value of virginity, are more liable to commit "this aggresive variety of sexual exploitation."

(At this point in our narrative it should come as no surprise that Sir Thomas Malory, creator of that classic tale of chivalry, *The Knights of the Round Table,* was himself arrested and found guilty for repeated incidents of rape.)

In the system of chivalry, men protect women against men. This is not unlike the protection relationship which the Mafia established with small businesses in the early part of this century. Indeed, chivalry is an age-old protection racket which depends for its existence on rape.

According to the male mythology which defines and perpetuates rape, it is an animal instinct inherent in the male. The story goes that sometime in our prehistorical past, the male, more hirsute and burly than today's counterparts, roamed about an uncivilized landscape until he found a desirable female. (Oddly enough, this female is *not* pictured as more muscular than the modern woman.) Her mate does not bother with courtship. He simply grabs her by the hair and drags her to the closest cave. Presumably, one of the major advantages of modern civilization for the female has been the civilizing of the male. We call it chivalry.

But women do not get chivalry for free. According to the logic of sexual politics, we too have to civilize our behavior. (Enter chastity. Enter virginity. Enter monogamy.) For the female, civilized behavior means chastity before marriage and faithfulness within it. Chivalrous behavior in the male is supposed to protect that chastity from involuntary defilement. The fly in the ointment of this otherwise peaceful system is the fallen woman. She does not behave. And therefore she does not deserve protection. Or, to use another argument, a major tenet of the same value system: what has once been defiled cannot again be violated. One begins to suspect that it is the behavior of the fallen woman, and not that of the male, that civilization aims to control.

The assumption that a woman who does not respect the double standard deserves whatever she gets (or at the very least "asks for it") operates in the courts today. While in some states a man's previous rape convictions are not considered admissible evidence, the sexual reputation of the rape victim is considered a crucial element of the facts upon which the court must decide innocence or guilt.

The court's respect for the double standard manifested itself particularly clearly in the case of the *People* v. *Jerry Plotkin*. Mr. Plotkin, a 36-year-old jeweler, was tried for rape last spring in a San Francisco Superior Court. According to the woman who brought the charges, Plotkin, along with three other men, forced her at gunpoint to enter a car one night in October 1970. She was taken to Mr. Plotkin's fashionable apartment where he and the three other men first raped her and then, in the delicate language of the *S. F. Chronicle*, "subjected her to perverted sex acts." She was, she said, set free in the morning with the warning that she would be killed if she spoke to anyone about the event. She did report the incident to the police who then searched Plotkin's apartment and discovered a long list of names of women. Her name was on the list and had been crossed out.

In addition to the woman's account of her abduction and rape, the prosecution submitted four of Plotkin's address books containing the names of hundreds of women. Plotkin claimed he did not know all of the women since some of the names had been given to him by friends and he had not yet called on them. Several women, however, did testify in court that Plotkin had, to cite the *Chronicle*, "lured them up to his apartment under one pretext or another, and forced his sexual attentions on them."

Plotkin's defense rested on two premises. First, through his own testimony Plotkin established a reputation for himself as a sexual libertine who frequently picked up girls in bars and took them to his house where sexual relations often took place. He was the Playboy. He claimed that the accusation of rape, therefore, was false—this incident had simply been one of many casual sexual relationships, the victim one of many playmates. The second premise of the defense was that his accuser was also a sexual libertine. However, the picture created of the young woman (fully 13 years younger than Plotkin) was not akin to the light-hearted, gay-bachelor image projected by the defendant. On the contrary, the day after the defense cross-examined the woman, the *Chronicle* printed a story headlined, "Grueling Day For Rape Case Victim." (A leaflet passed out by women in front of the courtroom was more succinct, "Rape was committed by four men in a private apartment in October; on Thursday, it was done by a judge and a lawyer in a public courtroom.")

Through skillful questioning fraught with innuendo, Plotkin's defense attorney, James Martin MacInnis, portrayed the young woman as a licentious opportunist and unfit mother. MacInnis began by asking the young woman (then employed as a secretary) whether or not it was true that she was "familiar with liquor" and had worked as a "cocktail waitress." The young woman replied (the *Chronicle* wrote "admitted") that she had worked once or twice as a cocktail waitress. The attorney then asked if she had worked as a secretary in the financial district but had "left that

SUSAN GRIFFIN

employment after it was discovered that you had sexual intercourse on a couch in the office." The woman replied, "That is a lie. I left because I didn't like working in a one-girl office. It was too lonely." Then the defense asked if, while working as an attendant at a health club, "you were accused of having a sexual affair with a man?" Again the woman denied the story, "I was never accused of that."

Plotkin's attorney then sought to establish that his client's accuser was living with a married man. She responded that the man was separated from his wife. Finally he told the court that she had "spent the night" with another man who lived in the same building.

At this point in the testimony the woman asked Plotkin's defense attorney, "Am I on trial? . . . It is embarrassing and personal to admit these things to all these people. . . . I did not commit a crime. I am a human being." The lawyer, true to the chivalry of his class, apologized and immediately resumed questioning her, turning his attention to her children. (She is divorced, and the children at the time of the trial were in a foster home.) "Isn't it true that your two children have a sex game in which one gets on top of another and they—" "That is a lie!" the young woman interrupted him. She ended her testimony by explaining, "They are wonderful children. They are not perverted."

The jury, divided in favor of acquittal ten to two, asked the court stenographer to read the woman's testimony back to them. After this reading, the Superior Court acquitted the defendant of both the charges of rape and kidnapping.

According to the double standard a woman who has had sexual intercourse out of wedlock cannot be raped. Rape is not only a crime of aggression against the body; it is a transgression against chastity as defined by men. When a woman is forced into a sexual relationship, she has, according to the male ethos, been violated. But she is also defiled if she does not behave according to the double standard, by maintaining her chastity, or confining her sexual activities to a monogamous relationship.

One should not assume, however, that a woman can avoid the possibility of rape simply by behaving. Though myth would have it that mainly "bad girls" are raped, this theory has no basis in fact. Available statistics would lead one to believe that a safer course is promiscuity. In a study of rape done in the District of Columbia, it was found that 82 percent of the rape victims had a "good reputation." Even the Police Inspector's advice to stay off the streets is rather useless, for almost half of reported rapes occur in the home of the victim and are committed by a man she has never before seen. Like indiscriminate terrorism, rape can happen to any woman, and few women are ever without this knowledge.

But the courts and the police, both dominated by white males, continue to suspect the rape victim, *sui generis*, of provoking or asking for her own assault. According to Amir's study, the police tend to believe that a woman without a good reputation cannot be raped. The rape victim is usually submitted to countless questions about her own sexual mores and behavior by the police investigator. This preoccupation is partially justified by the legal requirements for prosecution in a rape case. The rape victim must have been penetrated, and she must have made it clear to her assailant that she did not want penetration (unless of course she is unconscious). A refusal to accompany a man to some isolated place to allow him to touch her does not, in the eyes of the court, constitute rape. She must have said "no" at the crucial genital moment. And the rape victim, to qualify as such, must also have put up a physical struggle—unless she can prove that to do so would have been to endanger her life.

But the zealous interest the police frequently exhibit in the physical details of a rape case is only partially explained by the requirements of the court. A woman who was raped in Berkeley was asked to tell the story of her rape four different times "right out in the street," while her assailant was escaping. She was then required to submit to a pelvic examination to prove that penetration had taken place. Later, she was taken to the police station where she was asked the same questions again: "Were you forced?" "Did he penetrate?" "Are you sure your life was in danger and you had no other choice?" This woman had been pulled off the street by a man who held a 10-inch knife at her throat and forcibly raped her. She was raped at midnight and was not able to return to her home until five in the morning. Police contacted her twice again in the next week, once by telephone at two in the morning and once at four in the morning. In her words, "The rape was probably the least traumatic incident of the whole evening. If I'm ever raped again, . . . I wouldn't report it to the police because of all the degradation. . . ."

If white women are subjected to unnecessary and often hostile questioning after having been raped, third world women are often not believed at all. According to the white male ethos (which is not only sexist but racist), third world women are defined from birth as "impure." Thus the white male is provided with a pool of women who are fair game for sexual imperialism. Third world women frequently do not report rape and for good reason. When blues singer Billie Holliday was 10 years old, she was taken off to a local house by a neighbor and raped. Her mother brought the police to rescue her, and she was taken to the local police station crying and bleeding:

> When we got there, instead of treating me and Mom like somebody who called the cops for help, they treated me like I'd killed somebody. . . . I guess they had me figured for having enticed this old goat into the whorehouse. . . . All I know for sure is they threw me into a cell . . . a fat white matron . . . saw I was still bleeding, she felt sorry for me and gave me a couple glasses of milk. But nobody else did anything for me except give me filthy looks and snicker to themselves.
>
> After a couple of days in a cell they dragged me into a court. Mr. Dick got sentenced to five years. They sentenced me to a Catholic institution.

Clearly the white man's chivalry is aimed only to protect the chastity of "his" women.

As a final irony, that same system of sexual values from which chivalry is derived has also provided womankind with an unwritten code of behavior, called femininity, which makes a feminine woman the perfect victim of sexual aggression. If being chaste does not ward off the possibility of assault, being feminine certainly increases the chances that it will succeed. To be submissive is to defer to masculine strength; is to lack muscular development or any interest in defending oneself; is to let doors be opened, to have one's arm held when crossing the street. To be feminine is to wear shoes which make it difficult to run; skirts which inhibit one's stride; underclothes which inhibit the circulation. Is it not an intriguing observation that those very clothes which are thought to be flattering to the female and attractive to the male are those which make it impossible for a woman to defend herself against aggression?

Each girl as she grows into womanhood is taught fear. Fear is the form in which the female internalizes both chivalry and the double standard. Since, biologically speaking, women in fact have the same if not greater potential for sexual expression as do men, the woman who is taught that she must behave differently from a man must also learn to distrust her own carnality. She must deny her own feelings and learn not to act from them. She fears herself. This is the essence of passivity, and of course, a woman's passivity is not simply sexual but functions to cripple her from self-expression in every area of her life.

Passivity itself prevents a woman from ever considering her own potential for self-defense and forces her to look to men for protection. The woman is taught fear, but this time fear of the other; and yet her only relief from this fear is to seek out the other. Moreover, the passive woman is taught to regard herself as impotent, unable to act, unable even to perceive, in no way self-sufficient, and, finally, as the object and not the subject of human behavior. It is in this sense that a woman is deprived of the status of a human being. She is not free to be.

Since Ibsen's Nora slammed the door on her patriarchal husband, woman's attempt to be free has been more or less fashionable. In this nineteenth-century portrait of a woman leaving her marriage, Nora tells her husband, "Our home has been nothing but a playroom. I have been your doll-wife just as at home I was papa's doll-child." And, at least on the stage, "The Doll's House" crumbled, leaving audiences with hope for the fate of the modern woman. And today, as in the past, womankind has not lacked examples of liberated women to emulate: Emma Goldman, Greta Garbo and Isadora Duncan all denounced marriage and the double standard, and believed their right to freedom included sexual independence; but still their example has not affected the lives of millions of women who continue to marry, divorce and remarry, living out their lives dependent on the status and economic power of men. Patriarchy still holds the average woman prisoner not because she lacks the courage of an Isadora Duncan, but because the material conditions of her life prevent her from being anything but an object.

In the *Elementary Structures of Kinship*, Claude Levi-Strauss gives to marriage this universal description, "It is always a system of exchange that we find at the origin of the rules of marriage." In this system of exchange, a woman is the "most precious possession." Levi-Strauss continues that the custom of including women as booty in the marketplace is still so general that "a whole volume would not be sufficient to enumerate instances of it." Levi-Strauss makes it clear that he does not exclude Western Civilization from his definition of "universal" and cites examples from modern wedding ceremonies. (The marriage ceremony is still one in which the husband and wife become one, and "that one is the husband.")

The legal proscription against rape reflects this possessory view of women. An article in the 1952–53 *Yale Law Journal* describes the legal rationale behind laws against rape: "In our society sexual taboos, often enacted into law, buttress a system of monogamy based upon the law of 'free bargaining' of the potential spouses. Within this process the woman's power to withhold or grant sexual access is an important bargaining weapon." Presumably then, laws against rape are intended to protect the right of a woman, not for physical self-determination, but for physical "bargaining." The article goes on to explain explicitly why the preservation of the bodies of women is important to men:

> The consent standard in our society does more than protect a significant item of social currency for women; it fosters, and is in turn bolstered by, a masculine pride in the exclusive possession of a sexual object. The consent of a woman to sexual intercourse awards the man a privilege of bodily access, a personal "prize" whose value is enhanced by sole ownership. An additional reason for the man's condemnation of rape may be found in the threat to his status from a decrease in the "value" of his sexual possession which would result from forcible violation.

The passage concludes by making clear whose interest the law is designed to protect. "The man responds to this undercutting of his status as *possessor* of the girl with hostility toward the rapist; no other restitution device is available. The law of rape provides an orderly outlet for his vengeance." Presumably the female victim in any case will have been sufficiently socialized so as not to consciously feel any strong need for vengeance. If she does feel this need, society does not speak to it.

The laws against rape exist to protect rights of the male as possessor of the female body, and not the right of the female over her own body. Even without this enlightening passage from the *Yale Law Review*, the laws themselves are clear: in no state can a man be accused of raping his wife. How can any man steal what already belongs to him? It is in the sense of rape as theft of another man's property that Kate Millett writes, "Traditionally rape has been viewed as an offense one male commits against another—a matter of abusing his woman." In raping another man's woman, a man may aggrandize his own manhood and concurrently reduce that of another man. Thus a man's honor is not subject directly to rape, but only indirectly, through "his" woman.

If the basic social unit is the family, in which the woman is a possession of her husband, the superstructure of society is a male hierarchy, in which men dominate other men (or patriarchal families dominate other patriarchal families). And it is no small irony that, while the very social fabric of our male-dominated culture denies women equal access to political, economic and legal power, the literature, myth and humor of our culture depicts women not only as the power behind the throne, but the real source of the oppression of men. The religious version of this fairy tale blames Eve for both carnality and eating of the tree of knowledge, at the same time making her gullible to the obvious devices of a serpent. Adam, of course, is merely the trusting victim of love. Certainly this is a biased story. But no more biased than the one television audiences receive today from the latest slick comedians. Through a media which is owned by men, censored by a State dominated by men, all the evils of this social system which make a man's life unpleasant are blamed upon "the wife." The theory is: were it not for the female who waits and plots to "trap" the male into marriage, modern man would be able to achieve Olympian freedom. She is made the scapegoat for a system which is in fact run by men.

Nowhere is this more clear than in the white racist use of the concept of white womanhood. The white male's open rape of black women, coupled with his overweening concern for the chastity and protection of his wife and daughters, represents an extreme of sexist and racist hypocrisy. While on the one hand she was held up as the standard for purity and virtue, on the other the Southern white woman was never asked if she wanted to be on a pedestal, and in fact any deviance from the male-defined standards for white womanhood was treated severely. (It is a powerful commentary on American racism that the historical role of Blacks as slaves, and thus possessions without power, has robbed black women of legal and economic protection through marriage. Thus black women in Southern society and in the ghettos of the North have long been easy game for white rapists.) The fear that black men would rape white women was, and is, classic paranoia. Quoting from Ann Breen's unpublished study of racism and sexism in the South, *"The New South: White Man's Country,"* Frederick Douglass legitimately points out that, had the black man wished to rape white women, he had ample opportunity to do so during the civil war when white women, the wives, sisters, daughters and mothers of the rebels, were left in the care of Blacks. But yet not a single act of rape was committed during this time. The Ku Klux Klan, who tarred and feathered black men and lynched them in the honor of the purity of white womanhood, also applied tar and feathers to a Southern white woman accused of bigamy, which leads one to suspect that Southern white men were not so much outraged at the violation of the woman as a person, in the few instances where rape was actually committed by black men, but at the violation of his "property rights." In the situation where a black man was found to be having sexual relations with a white woman, the white woman could exercise skin-privilege, and claim that she had been raped, in which case the black man was lynched. But if she did not claim rape, she herself was subject to lynching.

In constructing the myth of white womanhood so as to justify the lynching and oppression of black men and women, the white male has created a convenient symbol of his own power which has resulted in black hostility toward the white "bitch," accompanied by an unreasonable fear on the part of many white women of the black rapist. Moreover, it is not surprising that after being told for two centuries that he wants to rape white women, occasionally a black man does actually commit that act. But it is crucial to note that the frequency of this practice is outrageously exaggerated in the white mythos. Ninety percent of reported rape is intra- not inter-racial.

In *Soul on Ice*, Eldridge Cleaver has described the mixing of a rage against white power with the internalized sexism of a black man raping a white woman. "Somehow I arrived at the conclusion that, as a matter of principle, it was of paramount importance for me to have an antagonistic, ruthless attitude toward white women. . . . Rape was an insurrectionary act. It delighted me that I was defying and trampling upon the white man's law, upon his system of values and that I was defiling his women—and this point, I believe, was the most satisfying to me because I was very resentful over the historical fact of how the white man has used the black woman." Thus a black man uses white women to take out his rage against white men. But in fact, whenever a rape of a white woman by a black man does take place, it is again the white man who benefits. First, the act itself terrorizes the white woman and makes her more dependent on the white male for protection. Then, if the woman prosecutes her attacker, the white man is afforded legal opportunity to exercise overt racism. Of course, the knowledge of the rape helps to perpetuate two myths which are beneficial to white male rule—the bestiality of the black man and the desirability of white women. Finally, the white man surely benefits because he himself is not the object of attack—he has been allowed to stay in power.

Indeed, the existence of rape in any form is beneficial to the ruling class of white males. For rape is a kind of terrorism which severely limits the freedom of women and makes women dependent on men. Moreover, in the act of rape, the rage that one man may harbor toward another higher in the male hierarchy can be deflected toward a female scapegoat. For every man there is always someone lower on the social scale on whom he can take out his aggressions. And that is any woman alive.

This oppressive attitude towards women finds its institutionalization in the traditional family. For it is assumed that a man "wears the pants" in his family—he exercises the option of rule whenever he so chooses. Not that he makes all the decisions—clearly women make most of the important day-to-day decisions in a family. But when a conflict of interest arises, it is the man's interest which will prevail. His word, in itself, is more powerful. He lords it over his wife in the same way his boss lords it over him, so that the very process of exercising his power becomes as important an act as obtaining whatever it is his power can get for him. This notion of power is key to the male ego in this culture, for the two acceptable measures of masculinity are a man's power over women and his power over other men. A man may boast to his friends that "I have 20 men working for me." It is also aggrandizement of his ego if he has the financial power to clothe his wife in furs and jewels. And, if a man lacks the wherewithal to acquire such power, he can always express his rage through equally masculine activities—rape and theft. Since male society defines the female as a possession, it is not surprising that the felony most often committed together with rape is theft. As the following classic tale of rape points out, the elements of theft, violence and forced sexual relations merge into an indistinguishable whole.

The woman who told this story was acquainted with the man who tried to rape her. When the man learned that she was going to be staying alone for the weekend, he began early in the day a polite campaign to get her to go out with him. When she continued to refuse his request, his chivalrous mask dropped away:

> I had locked all the doors because I was afraid, and I don't know how he got in; it was probably through the screen door. When I woke up, he was shaking my leg. His eyes were red, and I knew he had been drinking or smoking. I thought I would try to talk my way out of it. He started by saying that he wanted to sleep with me, and then he got angrier and angrier, until he started to say, "I want pussy," "I want pussy." Then, I got scared and tried to push him away. That's when he started to force himself on me. It was awful. It was the most humiliating, terrible feeling. He was forcing my legs apart and ripping my clothes off. And it was painful. I did fight him—he was slightly drunk and I was able to keep him away. I had taken judo a few years back, but I was afraid to throw a chop for fear that he'd kill me. I could see he was getting more and more violent. I was thinking wildly of some way to get out of this alive, and then I said to him, "Do you want money. I'll give you money." We had money but I was also thinking that if I got to the back room I could telephone the police—as if the police would have even helped. It was a stupid thing to think of because obviously he would follow me. And he did. When he saw me pick up the phone, he tried to tie the cord around my neck. I screamed at him that I did have the money in another room, that I was going to call the police because I was scared, but that I would never tell anybody what happened. It would be an absolute secret. He said, okay, and I went to get the money. But when he got it, all of a sudden he got this crazy look in his eye and he said to me. "Now I'm going to kill you." Then I started saying my prayers. I knew there was nothing I could do. He started to hit me—I still wasn't sure if he wanted to rape me at this point—or just to kill me. He was hurting me, but hadn't yet gotten me into a strangle-hold because he was still drunk and off balance. Somehow we pushed into the kitchen where I kept looking at this big knife. But I didn't pick it up. Somehow, no matter how much I hated him at that moment, I still couldn't imagine putting the knife in his flesh, and then I was afraid he would grab it and stick it into me. Then he was hitting me again and somehow we pushed through the back door of the kitchen and onto the porch steps. We fell down the steps and that's when he started to strangle me. He was on top of me. He just went on and on until finally I lost consciousness. I did scream, though my screams sounded like whispers to me. But what happened was that a cab driver happened by and frightened him away. The cab driver revived me—I was out only a minute at the most. And then I ran across the street and I grabbed the woman who was our neighbor and screamed at her, "Am I alive? Am I still alive?"

Rape is an act of aggression in which the victim is denied her self-determination. It is an act of violence which, if not actually followed by beatings or murder, nevertheless always carries with it the threat of death. And finally, rape is a form of mass terrorism, for the victims of rape are chosen indiscriminately, but the propagandists for male supremacy broadcast that it is women who cause rape by being unchaste or in the wrong place at the wrong time—in essence, by behaving as though they were free.

The threat of rape is used to deny women employment. (In California, the Berkeley Public Library, until pushed by the Federal Employment Practices Commission, refused to hire female shelvers because of perverted men in the stacks.) The fear of rape keeps women off the streets at night. Keeps women at home. Keeps women passive and modest for fear that they be thought provocative.

It is part of human dignity to be able to defend oneself, and women are learning. Some women have learned karate; some to shoot guns. And yet we will not be free until the threat of rape and the atmosphere of violence is ended, and to end that the nature of male behavior must change.

But rape is not an isolated act that can be rooted out from patriarchy without ending patriarchy itself. The same men and power structure who victimize women are engaged in the act of raping Vietnam, raping black people and the very earth we live upon. Rape is a classic act of domination where, in the words of Kate Millett, "the emotions of hatred, contempt, and the desire to break or violate personality," take place. This breaking of the personality characterizes modern life itself. No simple reforms can eliminate rape. As the symbolic expression of the white male hierarchy, rape is the quintessential act of our civilization, one which, Valerie Solanis warns, is in danger of "humping itself to death."

SOCIETAL REACTION AND CAREER DEVIANCE:

A CRITICAL ANALYSIS*

Milton Mankoff

In recent years the societal reaction or labeling perspective of Tannenbaum (1938), as elaborated by Lemert (1951), Erikson (1962), Becker (1963), and Scheff (1966), has become well known and seemingly widely accepted in one form or another by sociologists studying social deviance. Whether Tannenbaum and others *intended* to expound a general theory of deviance (Gibbs, 1966b), particularly career deviance, is not nearly as important as the fact that the work of these sociologists has been perceived by many to form a fairly coherent body of thought on the subject. Accordingly, a great deal of research has been generated by using some central concepts associated with the labeling perspective (i.e., primary and secondary or career deviance and societal reaction) to examine many forms of rule-breaking.

The bulk of the research growing out of this tradition has succeeded in demonstrating that social labeling is not randomly applied throughout the population of rule-breakers (Cicourel, 1968; Piliavin and Briar, 1964). While not wishing to belittle the importance of such documentation and its implications for social theory (and social justice), one must point out that to date there has not been a systematic examination of one of the labeling perspective's most profound derivative "theories"; that is, *rule-breakers become entrenched in deviant roles because they are labeled "deviant" by others and are consequently excluded from resuming normal roles in the community* (Lemert, 1951:75–79; Becker, 1963: 31–36; Scheff, 1966). Much of the documentation of the discriminatory use of labeling is based on the

* This is a revised version of a paper previously delivered at the 1969 meetings of the Pacific Sociological Association in Seattle, Washington. I am deeply indebted for both substantive and editorial assistance to William Chambliss, Marshall Clinard, Irving Horowitz, David Mechanic, Arnold Ross, Thomas Scheff, D. Lawrence Wieder, and several anonymous editorial referees.

Source: "Societal Reaction and Career Deviance: A Critical Analysis," *Sociological Quarterly*, Vol. 12, No. 2, May, 1971, pp. 204–218.

belief that labeling is the primary determinant of career deviance. It is worthwhile, therefore, to examine the validity of this position. Without validation of this central notion, the research on the labeling process loses a great deal of its significance.

Among labeling theorists there are, of course, subtle disagreements concerning whether the labeling process is merely a necessary condition, or approaches a necessary and sufficient condition for the development of secondary or career deviance. Lemert (1967), for example, is extremely sensitive to the indeterminacy of the interaction between rule-breakers and other social actors and is even willing to exclude certain forms of rule-breaking from the general societal reaction model. Yet in focusing on the variety of paths rule-breakers travel he does not develop any explicit formulation of the conditions under which the societal reaction model is most applicable to the phenomena at hand.

The failure of those whose work falls within the boundaries of the labeling tradition to develop typologies that indicate which particular kinds of social deviance can be most fruitfully understood by using the concepts of labeling theory is a serious shortcoming which prevents evaluating the significance of their research. While labeling theorists may think they are only applying the principles of the labeling perspective to one form of deviation, their incidental endorsements of generalizability to other forms of deviant behavior make the critic wary of "straw men" arguments when he attempts to project the implications of specific research for general theory. Those who write about deviance from the labeling perspective, whether they feel they are being general theorists or not, should welcome an attempt to consider the limits of their model for explaining career deviance.

Given the above-mentioned confusion, it is the primary intention of this exploratory paper to examine critically some empirical studies bearing on the validity of labeling theory and to provide some tentative answers to the following queries.

(1) Is societal reaction to rule-breaking a necessary and sufficient condition for career deviance?
(2) Is societal reaction to rule-breaking equally significant in the determination of career deviance for all kinds of rule-breaking phenomena, or is it best applied to a limited number of rule-breaking phenomena?
(3) What are the most serious obstacles to an adequate assessment of the theory?

I shall consider two distinct types of rule-breaking phenomena, ascriptive and achieved, which should illuminate the limitations of the labeling perspective when it addresses itself to the source of career deviance.[1] *Ascribed* rule-breaking occurs if the rule-breaker is characterized in terms of a particular physical or visible "impairment." He does not necessarily have to act in order to be a rule-breaker; he acquires that status regardless of his behavior or wishes. Thus, the very beautiful and the very ugly can be considered ascriptive rule-breakers. By contrast, *achieved* rule-breaking involves activity on the part of the rule-breaker, regardless of his positive attachment to a deviant "way of life." The embezzler who attempts to conceal his rule-breaking act, no less than the regular marijuana user who freely admits his transgression, has had to achieve rule-breaking status, at least to some extent, on the strength of his own actions.[2]

In evaluating the applicability of the labeling perspective on career deviance to both types of rule-breaking phenomena, I shall employ the logic of analytic induction, determining whether invidious societal reaction to primary deviation represents a necessary and/or sufficient condition for career deviance (Denzin, 1970:194–199).

Because the body of the paper shall attempt to demonstrate the severe limitations of labeling theory as a general theory of career deviance and, more significantly, because at least some of the evidence for my argument will come from the empirical research generated by *proponents* of the labeling perspective, I believe it is worthwhile considering the development and wide acceptance of labeling theory among sociologists as a suitable topic for a study in the sociology of knowledge. Thus, in the last section of this paper, I shall present some heuristic remarks on the social sources of labeling theory as an intellectual product and the implications of this analysis for the study of social deviance, the sociological profession, and public policy.

ASCRIPTIVE RULE-BREAKING

Labeling theorists, unlike most sociologists of deviant behavior, have been particularly concerned with the effects of stigmatization on the physically and visibly handicapped. Lemert's (1951: Chapters 5, 6) pioneering text, *Social Pathology*, devoted two entire chapters to the blind and persons with speech defects.

It seems quite evident that societal reaction is probably a *necessary* condition for deviant careers among certain kinds of physically or visibly handicapped persons, that is, those whose rule-breaking would not normally interfere with conventional role playing (e.g., dwarfs, the extremely ugly, women, blacks). One would be hard pressed to think of a group whose members become preoccupied with physical or visible traits they share that are not "labeled" by outsiders.

In considering whether societal reaction represents a sufficient condition for ascriptive career deviance, several problems arise. Labeling theorists have failed to specify which kinds of sanctions lead to career deviance and the degree of severity which is required to produce such an outcome. When considering necessary conditions, the above difficulty is not as severe if one can demonstrate the *absence* of societal reaction . . . it is a qualitative issue. When it comes to the role of labeling as a sufficient condition, however, one is dealing with a question which has a quantitative dimension (Turner, 1953).

Given the lack of clarity in conceptualizing and operationalizing societal reaction, any discussion of sufficient conditions must be exploratory. Gibbs' (1966a) recent attempt to develop a typology of social sanctions is suggestive of the many aspects which must be examined in an adequate treatment of this area.

For the purposes of this paper, I shall treat societal reaction as a qualitative phenomenon exclusively, involving the presence or absence of formal or informal sanctions (e.g., conviction and incarceration, prejudice and discrimination). In the case of ascribed rule-breaking, sanctions are almost always informal, exceptions being Jim Crow laws and physical requirements for certain occupations; achieved rule-breakers face both kinds of sanctions. It is debatable which are more severe, but we can assume that labeling theorists consider the typical sanctions meted out to rule-breakers—ostracism, economic discrimination, and incarceration—as sufficient conditions for career deviance as long as the labeling and punishment of rule-breakers is widely known and practiced by community members. It can always be argued, to be sure, that a more severe societal reaction would succeed in excluding the rule-breaker from normal roles and lead him inexorably to a deviant career. It is impossible to test such an assertion when the requisite degree of severity is left in doubt. Thus, it is possible that the labeling perspective is valid in the abstract, but its use in an historical context may be limited because of the concrete features of sanctions being used in a given society.

In any case, Goffman's (1963) work on stigma testifies to the powerful impact that labeling has on the social behavior of those stigmatized for physical and visible ascriptive rule-breaking. Davis' (1964) study of the attempts at "deviance disavowal" by handicapped persons indicates that deviant self-conceptions develop *even* when one is successful in minimizing stigmatization and discrimination. The "psychological" problems of black people in the United States are, of course, the most obvious examples of the operation of this process (Kardiner and Ovesey, 1951).

On the other hand, even among the severely stigmatized, variations in (a) power, (b) socioeconomic status, (c) the acquisition of compensatory skills, and (d) defense mechanisms may enable some of the victims of labeling to assume a quasi-normal role in the community, while others must accept a deviant career.

Nevertheless, because ascribed rule-breaking is highly visible to community members and often the object of widespread prejudice, labeling may come close to being a sufficient condition for career deviance. Ascribed deviants such as dwarfs, women, the ugly, and blacks are not handicapped because their physical and/or visible traits prevent them from playing any particular roles but rather because of the invidious labeling process and the absence of factors which might tend to mitigate its effects. Ascribed deviance is based upon rule-breaking phenomena that fulfill all the requirements of the labeling paradigm: highly "visible" rule-breaking that is totally *dependent* upon the societal reaction of community members while being totally *independent* of the actions and intentions of rule-breakers.

The normal modes of social reintegration discussed by Parsons (1951:297–325) cannot operate because the interaction between rule-breakers and agents of social control is not based on true reciprocity. The deviant status of the ascriptive rule-breakers can ordinarily be terminated only by drastic cultural, structural, or aesthetic changes in the society in which they are members. Short of such societal transformation, the labeled ascriptive rule-breaker almost inevitably will be caught up in the mechanistic system which the proponents of the labeling perspective have discovered. The so-called black revolution and, on a smaller scale, the "hire the handicapped" campaigns, testify to the inability of ascribed rule-breakers to achieve social reintegration on the basis of individual adaptation as opposed to collective efforts to transform societal values, beliefs, and institutions.

ACHIEVED RULE-BREAKING

While ascribed rule-breaking can perhaps best be understood in terms of the labeling perspective, only a small proportion of the socially sanctioned rule-breaking that has preoccupied sociologists of deviant behavior involves ascribed phenomena. The normal concerns of students in this field, property and violent crime, "crimes without victims" (Schur, 1965), the various exotic subcultures often associated with certain occupational statuses (e.g., dance musicians, taxidancers, strippers), and "residual rule-breaking" (Scheff, 1966), involve the examination of achieved rule-breaking. Although the designation of these phenomena as rule-breaking necessarily involves the violation of normative standards and social labeling as does ascribed rule-breaking, unlike the ascribed case, achieved rule-breaking requires the commission of a norm-violating *act* by the rule-breaker. This act can be engaged in out of regrettable necessity or hedonism, consciously or unconsciously.

Several empirical studies, including, notably, the research of Lemert (1967: 99–134) and Becker (1963:41–78), advocates of the labeling perspective, can be used to question whether societal reaction to achieved rule-breaking is a *necessary* condition for career deviance.

Lemert's (1967:99–134) detailed examination of systematic check forgers, for example, documents the way in which career deviance and deviant self-conceptions can develop prior to societal reaction. The career of the systematic check forger begins with a situation in which "closure" operates, leading to the initial rule-breaking. The naïve forger is involved in "dialectical" behavior, such as heavy gambling or living beyond his means, in which each expenditure forces him deeper in debt without permitting him to abandon his imprudent behavior. At some point he runs out of available cash and the pressures to continue his activities make forgery the only possible step. Among systematic check forgers Lemert finds that there is the thrill and excitement of living beyond one's means, as well as the challenging aspects of forgery itself, which accounts for the systematic nature of the offense. Societal reaction does not appear to be a significant cause of career deviance. In terms of self-conception systematic check forgers at first appear to accept their identity *after* arrest, often seeking capture in order to secure a stable self-image, according to Lemert. Yet, it seems that such offenders may merely feel the need for others to respond to them in the deviant role to which they have already become attached prior to experiencing social sanctions.

Perhaps a stronger case of the adoption of a deviant role without the experience of invidious societal reaction can be found in Cressey's (1953) study of violators of financial trust. Using the method of analytic induction, Cressey shows that a financial trust violation occurs among persons who have a problem that cannot be shared with others, become aware that financial trust violation can solve the problem, and are able to use contacts with criminal values to apply verbalizations to their behavior which act as rationalizations.

Cressey (1953:114–138) suggests that arrest often precedes the recognition of "criminality" on the part of trust violators. However, in other cases the rule-breaker accepts a deviant self-concept prior to any formal sanctions by employers or agents of social control. Chronic peculation is based primarily upon the desire and ability to "borrow" successfully without detection. Often a record of "borrowed" money is kept in the beginning with a clear intention of repayment. After the amount taken becomes too great to return, or perhaps they read about another case of trust violation in the newspaper, trust violators may recognize that they are "in too deep" and accept the fact that they are "criminals," not merely "borrowers." At this point, Cressey reports that trust violators may react in several ways: confess their crime, gamble wildly to restore funds, abscond, commit suicide, or increase defalcations with little discretion and no concern for repayment. In any case, it seems, from Cressey's discussion that career deviance and deviant self-conceptions can arise without the actor experiencing societal reaction to initial rule-breaking.

An examination of Becker's (1963:41–78) classic study of the career development of regular marijuana users casts further doubt on the role of the labeling process in the generation of career deviance. According to Becker marijuana users go through three distinct career stages: (a) beginner, (b) occasional user, and (c) regular user. In terms of the labeling paradigm, the beginner is a primary deviant, and the regular user is a career deviant, with occasional use fitting somewhere in between. Becker was not particularly concerned with the reasons for beginning use of marijuana, but generally he accepted the position that initial use is based on curiosity. How, then, does the initiate go from the beginner stage to the stage of being a "head" or regular user? Becker did not see societal reaction entering into the picture in a traditional sense. Rather, the initiate learns:

(a) to use the proper smoking technique in order to produce the proper subjective state,
(b) to associate marijuana with the feeling state produced, and
(c) to interpret the feeling as pleasurable.

At no point in his narrative does Becker refer to invidious labeling as a factor in bringing about regular marijuana use.[3] At various stages in the career of the user, he is free to discontinue smoking. Regular use of marijuana seems to be dependent upon finding the subjective effects of the drug pleasurable and solving certain problems of supply, discretion, and ethics. Thus, the case of marijuana smoking appears to be an excellent illustration of career deviance based primarily upon finding pleasure in a deviant manner.

Finally, an examination of the literature on homosexuality seems to indicate that a very similar career sequence may be operating as in the case of the marijuana user. Neither forced seduction by older homosexuals nor rejection by peers during childhood or adolescence seems to account for career deviation within this rule-breaking group (Schofield, 1965). Homosexual experimentation seems to be a prevalent feature of so-called normal socialization among adolescents. Some youths find that they enjoy such activity and, depending upon the opportunity structure and the importance of discretion, may choose to continue such activity. Many homosexuals are bisexual and even marry persons of the opposite sex. Career deviation occurs despite lack of visibility and social labeling.

In considering the question of whether societal reaction is a *sufficient* condition for career deviance among achieved rule-breakers, the same difficulties arise as in the earlier consideration of labeling as a sufficient condition for career deviance in the ascriptive case.

Unfortunately, much of the literature focuses on the effects of incarceration, ignoring the importance of informal societal reaction to rule-breaking. It is doubtless true that informal sanctions such as ostracism may be more damaging than legal penalties, but a prison sentence is certainly a severe form of punishment for transgressions.

If incarceration exacerbates attachment to deviant role-playing, one would predict that recidivism rates would be extremely high for ex-convicts. Such persons should be unable to find jobs because of discrimination when their criminal career and prison record become known to employers (Lemert, 1951:331–332). As a result of incarceration we should also expect convicts to harbor a great deal of resentment toward the "free" community and "reject the rejectors," thus facilitating a return to criminal associations and patterns (Lemert, 1951:77).

Data bearing upon the above hypotheses comes from Glaser's (1964) exhaustive research on the effectiveness of the federal prison and parole system. Lengthy reports were obtained from interviews and other modes of data collection pertaining to the experiences of several hundred federal prisoners in a modified panel design.

Using a cohort analysis, Glaser found that approximately one-third of parolees are recidivists between two and five years after parole is granted (Glaser, 1964:13–31).

In the area of post-release occupational adjustment Glaser finds that failure to achieve satisfactory employment is due primarily to unrealistic aspirations in view of the lack of skills held by ex-convicts. Stigma did not seem to play a significant role in occupational adjustment. Only 4 percent of the job terminations of parolees were blamed (by the men themselves) on their previous criminal record. Similarly only 9 percent of the parolees who were unable to obtain a job within one week after parole attributed it to the stigma of their criminal past (Glaser, 1964:358–361).

Glaser's research can be dealt with critically, and it may well be that he underrepresents by far the true recidivism rate and fails to consider the possibility that parolees were "putting on" the interviewers, attributing adjustment failures to their own limitations in order to show a "positive" attitude toward the rehabilitation process.[4] In any case his research suggests that the notion that prisons are criminogenic may require further study.

Cameron's (1964) study of professional and amateur shoplifters offers more evidence that the labeling process does not necessarily lead to career deviance. When amateur shoplifters ("snitches") were apprehended by department store detectives they were unable to accept themselves as "thieves" and ceased pilfering.

Finally, Chambliss (1969:360–378), in summarizing the literature on deterrence, has argued that rule-breakers who have a low commitment to criminal activity as a way of life and whose criminal behavior is instrumental rather than expressive (e.g., snitches, white collar criminals, gangland murders) may be deterred by punishment rather than become career deviants as a consequence of societal reaction.

Thus, the labeling perspective on career deviance does not appear to be very useful in understanding the dynamics of achieved rule-breaking. Societal reaction seems to be neither a necessary nor a sufficient condition for career-achieved deviance. The essential feature of achieved rule-breaking, the necessity for action on the part of the rule-breaker as well as social labeling by community members, makes it possible for rule-breakers to commit themselves to deviant careers without being "forced" by formal or informal agents of social control and to terminate rule-breaking despite the lack of social recognition for "rehabilitation." Moreover, such possibilities have been realized in the empirical world. Achieved rule-breaking permits individual adaptations to social labeling and social structures which are largely precluded in the case of ascribed rule-breaking.

PROBLEMS OF THEORY AND RESEARCH

In the previous section some evidence has been presented to suggest that societal reaction theory is not an adequate general theory of career deviant behavior. As a theoretical model it appears to be most applicable when rule-breaking is ascribed rather than achieved. Even in the ascribed case labeling probably serves only as a necessary rather than a necessary and sufficient condition for career deviance.

In examining some of the evidence pertaining to labeling theory, I have presented perhaps a stronger case for its shortcomings than is warranted. It is conceivable that some of the evidence cited which casts doubt on the "completeness" of labeling theory can be reinterpreted by proponents of the theory in such a manner as to justify its claim to be a general theory of career deviance. Moreover, as Hirschi and Selvin (1967:119–123) point out, it is a false criterion for causality to require "independent" variables to be related to "dependent" variables as necessary and/or sufficient conditions for their existence. Social labeling undoubtedly plays an important role in the generation of career deviation in many cases. Nevertheless, it is probably not as crucial in this process as some of its proponents would claim.

In order to aid in the development of a more complete theory of career deviance, I shall briefly discuss some of the shortcomings which limit the utility of the labeling perspective, particularly in considering achieved rule-breaking.

The most salient theoretical difficulty is in the conception of initial rule-breaking and the nature of the sources which bring it into being. There is a premise in the writings of the labeling theorists that whatever the causes of initial rule-breaking, they assume minimal importance or entirely cease operation after initial rule-breaking (Scheff, 1966:50–54; Lemert, 1967:40). Without such a premise, one might attribute career deviance and its consequences not to societal reaction but to the *continued* effects of social structural strains, psychological stress, or disease states which produced initial rule-breaking.

In this connection, the labeling model fails to seriously consider the possibility that deviant behavior may be persisted in even when the rule-breaker has every opportunity to return to the status of nondeviant (Becker, 1963:37), because of a positive attachment to rule-breaking. Given the fact that theorists within the labeling tradition often see their views as consistent with a conflict interpretation of deviance, as opposed to one involving consensus which attributes deviance to faulty socialization, one can find significant traces of consensual thinking implicit in their theorizing. The societal reaction paradigm implies that labelers really share the same *Weltanschauung* as rule-breakers. The only problem is that rule-breakers are imperfect creatures who stray from the fold on occasion. The logic of the labeling approach to career deviance precludes rule-breakers being credited (or discredited) with freely espousing career deviance as a positive alternative to career conformity. Labeling the rule-breaker will only serve to prevent his rapprochement with the non-rule-breaking elements of the community. Deviant conduct and attachment to a deviant role will strengthen when the community isolates and excludes the transgressor from normal social life. Implicit in the labeling model is the belief that rule-breakers really want to conform, even the most willful ones.

There are some labeling theorists who admit the possibility that initial rule-breaking behavior may be the product of a desire to reorganize the world or a particular segment of it. Scheff (1966:44–45), for example, illustrates this point by a discussion of the Dadaist movement in the arts, but unfortunately his defense of the innovative, willful rule-breaker is obviated by the fact that he traces the growth of the movement in terms of the enormous hostility toward it expressed by orthodox artists and critics. One might argue that it was the severity of the societal reaction which made the Dadaists more self-conscious of their "revolutionary" acts and more tenacious in their defense of those acts. Thus, Scheff (1966:44–45), even when defending the *Weltanschauung* of the rule-breaker, undermines the defense by implying the possibility of involuntary career deviance.

Becker (1963) explicitly considers the possibility of "intended" rule-breaking. Often, in his ethnographic accounts, as in the case of the research on the dance musician (Becker, 1963:79–119) as well as the marijuana user (Becker, 1963: 41–78), he seems to accept the existence of a self-sustaining counterculture based on deviant identities. Nevertheless, a careful reading of Becker's "sequential model" for career deviance makes one conclude that given the chance to resume normal activities, the rule-breaker will invariably do so (Becker, 1963:36–39). His examples range from boys who engage in homosexual behavior without really believing in it to tortured heroin addicts. He talks of deviants forming subcultures which provide them with "rationalizations" for their deviance. The examples used and the terminology employed seem to betray the theorist's doubts about the legitimacy of deviant careers. Such doubts are necessarily linked to the labeling theory of career deviance which sees unfettered rule-breaking coexisting with the maintenance of social order. If rule-breakers truly represented subversive values such a coexistence would be untenable. The discrepancy between empirical research and theory construction is characteristic of labeling theory and shall be discussed shortly.

Another theoretical problem arises in regard to the issue of social sensitivity. After an actor engages in rule-breaking behavior he may feel shame, guilt, or fear of exposure. As Becker (1963:31) realizes, it is possible that this in itself may be sufficient to have the primary deviant label himself as "deviant," and he may then engage in all kinds of behaviors to cover up his initial rule-breaking and unwittingly exacerbate the problem (cf., Matza, 1969:150–152). Such "vicious cycles" apparently occur among stutterers and alcoholics (Lemert, 1967: 56–57). Even granting that cultural standards are ultimately responsible for making the primary deviant self-conscious, simply focusing on labelers while ignoring the qualities of the rule-breaker can lead to a mistaken emphasis in understanding the dynamics of career deviance. It is important to determine the sources and salience of self-labeling in the development of career deviance.

A final theoretical dilemma involves the nature of the societal reaction itself. As mentioned earlier, labeling theorists have not clearly specified what sort of reaction on the part of community members—formal, informal, or both—is necessary and/or sufficient to produce career deviation. Lemert (1967:42) claims that to establish a totally deviant identity, stigmatization must be disseminated throughout the society. This is very unlikely to occur in advanced societies for almost *any* rule-breaking phenomenon. If we ignore Lemert's extreme statement we find that the lack of specification as to the type and severity of societal reaction makes the labeling theory impossible to refute. It can always be maintained that either a mild societal reaction is sufficient or that a different kind of reaction or more severe form of the same one would account for career deviance. In this manner one can explain all findings and predict none. Moreover, it can once again lead to a reductionist position in which it is the extreme sensitivity of the primary deviants (this time, to an *actual* societal reaction) which leads them to permanent entrenchment in deviant roles.

The major theoretical difficulties mentioned above generate related research dilemmas. One problem involves controlling the effects of the sources of initial rule-breaking; another involves controlling for the sensitivity of the rule-breaker to the possibility and actuality of societal reaction. Only by such a procedure can the impact of *actual* societal reaction be weighted.

Unfortunately, natural field settings make it impossible to adequately assess the theory because of the impossibility of controlling for either of the two variables which might confound the effects of actual societal reaction. Comparing experimental and control groups on these variables would require labeling both to see if they are equally "sensitive." To do this would obviously eliminate the usefulness of the control group since it would cease serving that function at the point when its members were influenced by a particular kind (mode and intensity) of societal reaction. An experimental design, as advocated by Scheff (1966:199), on the other hand, is objectionable principally on ethical grounds. Two groups (experimental and control) would have to be chosen from a population of primary deviants unaware that they are rule-breakers. Randomization could be used to control for the sources of primary deviation and social sensitivity. Unfortunately, even if it were possible to locate potential experimental subjects, the necessary invocation of societal reaction with the experimental group would be an obvious violation of professional ethics, particularly if one believed in the validity of labeling theory (since the researcher would suspect that he was possibly dooming his experimental group to career deviance).

LABELING THEORY AND
THE SOCIOLOGY OF KNOWLEDGE

In the previous section I spoke about the seeming incongruity between empirical research and theory construction which characterizes much of the scholarship that falls within the labeling tradition. When "theory" ignores what research uncovers, one often finds a problem that is traceable to "ideology" rather than the competence of professionals. This issue must be squarely addressed if the study of social deviance is to attain scientific respectability and provide a guide to public policy.

Sociologists in general, and those who study deviant behavior in particular, are often beset by ambivalence in carrying out their life's work. On the one hand they are committed to value-neutrality and objectivity as part of their professional training; on the other hand, they frequently side with the perspective of the "underdog" and view themselves as liberal reformers in their role as citizens. Frequently, they try to combine both roles (Tumin, 1965; Becker, 1967).

Because of the operation of unique historical forces, American sociology was based upon the synthesis of liberal reformism and the social theories of European conservatives with their preoccupation with the problem of social order (Parsons, 1937, 1951; Nisbet, 1966; Nicolaus, 1969). As time went by the ideological roots of modern American sociology were forgotten, and the concerns of the field, while still retaining their conservative bias, were rephrased in the seemingly value-neutral language of contemporary sociological discourse (e.g., functions, dysfunctions, social disorganization). The continuing focus of sociological inquiry has, of course, been reinforced by the political context in which American sociologists seek research support (Nicolaus, 1969; Gouldner, 1968, 1970).

Given the intellectual and professional orientation of modern sociologists trained in and practicing their craft in the United States, it is understandable that a conflict should arise between the scientific and citizen roles of the professional sociologist. Thus, most sociologists, who wish "society" to be more tolerant of rule-breaking and solve various "social problems" while still retaining social cohesiveness and institutional continuity, must demonstrate that labeling and repression are inimical to the long-term stability of America's social institutions. Only in this way can they satisfy the requirements of their profession, freely express their political views, and develop cogent arguments acceptable to very conservative public policy decision makers.

Unfortunately, the consequence of such a complex posture is to fail as a competent scientist, lose faith in a liberal political analysis, and meet rejection by "realistic" policy makers, when the "data" fail to conform to expectations. Neither repression nor the lack of it seems to affect the propensity of youth to use psychedelic drugs; student activism grows whether the campuses are administered by "doves" or "hawks." Repression even seems to work better, at least in the short run, but at the expense of increasingly widespread alienation from authority.

The preoccupation with labeling as the source of chronic rule-breaking may blind sociologists to macrosociological analysis which traces social instability and career deviance to the very institutional arrangements—economic, political, cultural—that are supposed to maintain order.[5] Unfortunately, returning to the neglected concerns of an institution- and conflict-oriented macrosociology may upset the symbiotic links between sociology as a profession and the sources of its material sustenance. Moreover, knowledge acquired through such an effort may destroy the strain of optimism that reformers have carefully nurtured despite attacks from the Left and Right. Liberal sociologists may not be able to have their cake and eat it: either certain "subversive" forms of rule-breaking may have to be suppressed via police state methods, or social life may have to be reorganized around values other than profit, productivity, and puritanism. In this regard, Erikson's (1966) macrolabeling perspective, emphasizing the functions of deviance and social control for the maintenance of social order, may demonstrate a willingness to face unpleasant choices not shared by microlabeling theorists who focus on the functions of social control in the generation of deviant careers.

In order not to end on a somber note entirely, it might well be possible to eliminate negative sanctions against ascribed rule-breakers without endangering the social order. However, even this policy would have to be accompanied by a profound alteration in the minds of our citizens as well as the creation of new ways to deal with the economic problems associated with the incorporation of millions of persons into a labor market unable to provide employment, even demeaning employment, for many of its beautiful, healthy, white males.

CONCLUSION

This paper has been concerned with the empirical validation of one of the most significant "theories" derived from the labeling perspective, namely, rule-breakers become entrenched in deviant roles because they are labeled "deviant" by others and are consequently excluded from resuming normal societal roles. By dividing rule-breaking phenomena into two major types, ascribed and achieved rule-breaking distinguished by the necessity of rule-breaking *activity* on the part of the rule-breaker, the paper has attempted to demonstrate that the utility of this theory is severely limited.

Ascribed rule-breaking, because it involves a passive rule-breaker almost totally dependent upon the whims of social labelers, exemplifies the kind of rule-breaking phenomena for which the labeling model is most applicable. Even in this case, however, while social labeling may be a necessary condition for career deviance, it is probably not a sufficient condition for such a development. Variations in power, socioeconomic status, the acquisition of compensatory skills, and defense mechanisms, may permit some labeled ascribed rule-breakers to avoid career deviance. Nevertheless, collective attempts to change social values, beliefs, and institutions are probably necessary to end ascribed deviance in the face of the dependence of ascribed rule-breakers upon prevailing community ideology and behavior.

In the case of achieved rule-breaking, the labeling model is extremely inadequate in providing an explanation for the genesis of career deviance. Labeling theorists ignore the possibility of genuine commitment on the part of the rule-breaker to achieved career deviance. This failure of analysis stems from an underestimation of the importance of social and psychological factors other than labeling in generating deviant careers. Finally, labeling theory underestimates the possibilities for successful social control through labeling. The evidence suggests that while the labeling process may play a significant role in the development of career-achieved deviance it is neither a necessary nor sufficient condition for such an outcome.

Besides considering the particular strengths and weaknesses of the labeling model in regard to the generation of career ascribed and achieved deviance, the paper has also discussed some of the major dilemmas pertaining to theory and research which must be faced by those who may wish to assess labeling theory in the future. Among the theoretical problems are the previously stated failure to consider the *continuing* effects of the social structural and psychological sources of initial rule-breaking in the development of career deviance, the lack of concern with the vulnerability of certain rule-breakers to self-labeling processes which may reduce the significance of *objective* labeling practices in determining deviant careers, and the related omission of any serious analysis of the types and severity of actual social sanction which facilitate "successful" labeling. Ultimately, students of deviance will have to reconsider the mechanistic assumptions of labeling theory when applied to achieved and to a lesser degree ascribed rule-breaking. The implicit notions of human passivity, so characteristic of behaviorism, seem out of place in a sociological tradition that has been founded upon penetrating observations of the creative potential of human beings. Researchers will have to learn to control the effects of the sources of initial rule-breaking and sensitivity to self-labeling and particular types of societal reaction. Only in this way can they demonstrate the power of actual labeling processes by community members in determining career deviance.

Finally, because of the observation that the empirical research of labeling theorists has often provided evidence which contradicts the labeling model of career deviance the paper has briefly explored some of the ideological and social sources of this model. It has suggested that the model arises out of a tension between the reformist ideological orientations of most sociologists of deviance, the conservative bias of American sociology derived from European conservative social theory, and the pressures arising from the sources of political and financial support for the American sociological profession. These three factors have permitted some sociologists to become advocates of a theoretical perspective which resolves the tensions which are rooted in the conflict between ideology, professionalism, and political and financial pressure. Unfortunately, the inadequacy of the labeling perspective leads to ideological, scientific, and political bankruptcy. It is suggested that sociologists of social deviance concern themselves more with macrosociological analysis in the future, focusing primarily on the institutional sources of career deviance. This focus may lead to greater understanding of the nature of career deviance, although it may result in shifting ideological, political and professional orientation for those who undertake this task.

In conclusion, this paper has left many problems unresolved, particularly the difficulties involved in the conceptualization and operationalization of "societal reaction" and the development of a viable research program designed to test the labeling model adequately. Nevertheless, directing attention toward some of the outstanding weaknesses of the model as it currently stands will hopefully lead to more productive attempts to grapple with the problems associated with the phenomenon of career deviance.

NOTES

[1] For discussion of the utility of typological analysis with specific focus on typologies of criminal behavior, see Clinard and Quinney (1967:1–19), cf. McKinney (1966). The particular types under analysis in this paper were drawn from Parsons' (1951) consideration of role relationships. The element of reciprocity and the possibilities for active role-making rather than passive role-accepting implicit in achieved roles, as opposed to ascribed ones, were felt to be in contrast to the lack of autonomy characteristic of the ideal-typical rule-breaker in the labeling perspective. By exploring the implications of Parsons' distinction as it applies to types of rule-breaking, it is possible to see how the labeling perspective is dependent upon a passive actor whose rule-breaking is ascribed.

MILTON MANKOFF

[2] In the case of both ascribed and achieved rule-breaking, it is, of course, possible that persons are falsely accused of rule-breaking (Becker, 1963:20). Nevertheless, the above distinctions hold because the falsely accused ascribed rule-breaker is thought to *be* someone, whereas the falsely accused achieved rule-breaker is felt to have *done* something.

[3] It would not be fair to fault Becker for not looking for a labeling process operating among the marijuana users he studied in the early 1950s. But since he has not revised in any essential manner his original thought on becoming a user and chose to reprint his classic study in a volume which includes his particular version of labeling theory (Becker, 1963:19–39; 41–58) one would imagine that he would have reconsidered either his theoretical perspective on deviance or his marijuana study at the time.

[4] Even if the true recidivism rate is extremely high, it does not follow that societal reaction is a sufficient condition for career criminality. An alternate explanation might be that the causes of initial rule-breaking are still operating after incarceration is over. For example, if a poor man steals and is sent to prison, he may continue to steal after release because he is still poor. Prison may provide temporary protection to the community since the rule-breaker is in no position to engage in certain criminal acts, but it is questionable whether it provides a long-term solution to the problem of "law and order."

As for the issue of "putting on" the interviewer, it is also possible, of course, that the ex-convicts were exhibiting "false consciousness" and were not aware of the operation of discriminatory hiring policies. If this is so it might well prevent recidivism, as ex-convicts may not become embittered and "reject the rejectors." They may simply become career "ritualists" in Merton's (1938) sense of the term.

[5] Merton (1938), in the midst of the Great Depression, did attempt such an analysis of social deviance. The work, while provocative, had numerous flaws (Clinard, 1964) and seems to have gone out of favor in recent years.

REFERENCES

Becker, Howard S.
    1967   "Whose side are we on?" Social Problems 14 (Winter):239–248.
    1963   Outsiders: Studies in the Sociology of Deviance. New York: Free Press.
Cameron, Mary Owen
    1964   The Booster and the Snitch: Department Store Shoplifting. New York: Free Press.
Chambliss, William J.
    1969   Crime and the Legal Process. New York: McGraw-Hill.
Cicourel, Aaron V.
    1968   The Social Organization of Juvenile Justice. New York: Wiley.
Clinard, Marshall
    1964   Anomie and Deviant Behavior: A Discussion and Critique. New York: Free Press.
Clinard, Marshall and Richard Quinney
    1967   Criminal Behavior Systems: A Typology. New York: Holt, Rinehart, & Winston.
Cressey, Donald R.
    1953   Other People's Money. Glencoe, Ill.: Free Press of Glencoe.
Davis, Fred
    1964   "Deviance disavowal: the management of strained interaction by the physically handicapped." Pp. 119–137 in Howard S. Becker (ed.), The Other Side: Perspectives on Deviance. New York: Free Press.
Denzin, Norman K.
    1970   The Research Act: A Theoretical Introduction to Sociological Methods. Chicago: Aldine.
Erikson, Kai
    1966   Wayward Puritans: A Study in the Sociology of Deviance. New York: Wiley.
    1962   "Notes on the sociology of deviance." Social Problems 9 (Spring):307–314.

Gibbs, J.
  1966a "Sanctions." Social Problems 14 (Fall):147–159.
  1966b "Conceptions of deviant behavior: the old and the new." Pacific Sociological
         Review 9 (Spring):9–14.
Glaser, Daniel
  1964 The Effectiveness of a Prison and Parole System. Indianapolis: Bobbs-Merrill.
Goffman, Erving
  1963 Stigma: Notes on the Management of Spoiled Identities. New Jersey: Prentice-Hall.
Gouldner, Alvin
  1970 The Coming Crisis of Western Sociology. New York: Basic Books.
  1968 "The sociologist as partisan: sociology and the welfare state." American Sociologist
         3 (May):103–116.
Hirschi, Travis and Hanan Selvin
  1967 Delinquency Research: An Appraisal of Analytic Methods. New York: Free Press.
Kardiner, Abram and Lionel Ovesey
  1951 The Mark of Oppression: Explorations in the Personality of the American Negro.
         Cleveland: World.
Lemert, Edwin
  1967 Human Deviance, Social Problems, and Social Control. Englewood Cliffs, N.J.:
         Prentice-Hall.
  1951 Social Pathology. New York: McGraw-Hill.
Matza, David
  1969 Becoming Deviant. Englewood Cliffs, N.J.: Prentice-Hall.
McKinney, John C.
  1966 Constructive Typology and Social Theory. New York: Appleton-Century-Crofts.
Merton, R.
  1938 "Social structure and anomie." American Sociological Review 3 (Octo-
         ber):672–682.
Nicolaus, M.
  1969 "The professional organization of sociology: a view from below." Antioch Review
         29 (Fall):375–388.
Nisbet, Robert
  1966 The Sociological Tradition. New York: Basic Books.
Parsons, Talcott
  1951 The Social System. New York: Free Press.
  1937 The Structure of Social Action. New York: McGraw-Hill.
Piliavin, L. and S. Briar
  1964 "Police encounters with juveniles." American Journal of Sociology 69 (September):
         206–214.
Scheff, Thomas
  1966 Being Mentally Ill: A Sociological Theory. Chicago: Aldine.
Schofield, Michael
  1965 Sociological Aspects of Homosexuality. Boston: Little, Brown.
Schur, Edwin
  1965 Crimes Without Victims: Deviant Behavior and Public Policy. Englewood Cliffs,
         N.J.: Prentice-Hall.

MILTON MANKOFF

Tannenbaum, Frank
1938   Crime and the Community. Boston: Ginn and Co.
Tumin, M.
1965   "The functionalist approach to social problems." Social Problems 12 (Spring): 379–388.
Turner, R.
1953   "The quest for universals in sociological research." American Sociological Review 18 (December):604–611.

256